INDIAN COUNCIL OF HISTORICAL RESEARCH

MONOGRAPH SERIES 4

Jallianwala Bagh Massacre

Jallianwala Bagh Massacre

edited by

V. N. DATTA

S. SETTAR

2000

PRAGATI PUBLICATIONS

INDIAN COUNCIL OF HISTORICAL RESEARCH

DELHI

First Published: 2000

Published by

PRAGATI PUBLICATIONS
9926 Library Road,
Azad Market, Delhi 110006

in association with

INDIAN COUNCIL OF HISTORICAL RESEARCH
35 Ferozeshah Road,
New Delhi 110001

ISBN: 81-7307-069-5

Printed in India

Printed and published by Vinod Kapoor for Pragati Publications, 9926 Library Road, Azad Market, Delhi 110006

Contents

Preface

I am most grateful to the Chairman of the Indian Council of Historical Research, Professor S. Settar for asking me to write a Preface to this volume that comprises scholarly articles presented on the seventy-fifth anniversary of the Jallianwala Bagh massacre.

Jawaharlal Nehru was not a professional historian but was deeply interested in history. He remarked in his conversation with Lord Montgomery on 29 January 1961 that the Jallianwala Bagh massacre marked a turning point in Anglo-Indian relations. Surprisingly, the young Nehru had travelled with General Dyer sharing with him the first class railway compartment on his way from Lahore to Delhi towards the end of 1919 when the latter was returning after giving his evidence before the Hunter Committee which was set up to 'investigate the disturbance in Bombay, Delhi and Punjab'. Nehru had proceeded to Lahore in connection with the Congress Enquiry Committee report which was under preparation. In his Autobiography, Nehru comments on how shocked he had felt at Dyer's aggressive and abrasive manner while justifying his action at Jallianwala Bagh to his other fellow-passengers who were military officers.

A number of historical works have appeared on the Jallianwala Bagh massacre, which deal with the various themes connected with it. These studies offer different interpretations of the sombre episode which adds richness to the texture of historiography on the subject. Generally speaking, the British historians have refrained from writing on the Jallianwala Bagh massacre despite the readily available source-material in the British archives. However, only a few British journalists and popular writers have ventured to bring out monographs on the subject.

The Jallianwala Bagh episode provoked much controversy in England and considerable primary literature exists on it there. Besides the contemporary British newspapers and accounts of politicians and army men, J.P. Thompson's

Dairy and Malcolm Darling's papers at the South Asian Centre at Cambridge, and the O'Dwyer vs Nair Case proceedings in the Public Records Office, London provide a wealth of material on the political events in India, 1919, including the Jallianwala Bagh event.

Dyer resorted to firing on the crowd at Jallianwala Bagh without prior warning, and continued to fire even when people were fleeing to save themselves. He was found guilty of infringing the principle of using minimum force and was forced to retire from military service. While forcing Dyer to resign, the British Government regarded his action as an isolated one, quite alien to the British spirit of governance, justice and fair play. But Dyer's supporters, the die-hard conservatives, lauded him as the 'Saviour of the Raj' for saving the Punjab from falling into anarchy.

Dyer's action has to be seen in the context of the functioning of the Punjab mode of governance and the political developments in India since 1919. It is important to note that the Anti-Rowlatt agitation launched by Mahatma Gandhi nowhere gained such tremendous force and popularity as in the Punjab. To explain the character of the popular movement that had stirred the imagination of the people belonging to different segments of society, it is necessary to understand the nature of the Punjab administration and Lieutenant Governor Sir Michael O'Dwyer whose repressive policies caused widespread resentment and violence in the Punjab. It is in the context of O'Dwyer's administration that Dyer's action has to be explained.

The Jallianwala Bagh episode had a profound impact on the growth of the national movement in India. The Rowlatt agitation and the Jallianwala Bagh episode, followed by what came to be called Punjab atrocities, culminated in the Non-cooperation Movement. India produced her distinct and new style of nationalist politics that was to serve as the chief weapon against the British. The country had found a clear object, and a unique leader in Gandhi who could inspire her to her goal to complete independence.

Though much valuable work has been published on the episode, I think there is still scope for further studies in view of the massive source-material on the subject in England which has been insufficiently used. And there are themes which need to be explored like the British reactions to the massacre, the popular base of the movement and the historiography of the episode.

10 August 1999 V. N. Datta

ONE

❖ Perceptions of the Jallianwala Bagh Massacre

V. N. DATTA

THE JALLIANWALA BAGH MASSACRE marked a turning point in India's struggle for freedom.[1] From then onwards political activities increased rapidly and the freedom movement acquired its national character. The sombre episode at Jallianwala Bagh can be viewed from different angles. The starting point for historical interpretations lies in the ideas of people who were living when the event in question was taking place. The simplest way is to trace the causes and circumstances leading up to the massacre and to determine the nature of its impact and consequences. From this perspective, the episode has to be examined within the framework of the British imperial system. The traumatic event can also be seen as a clash between the rising forces of Indian nationalism and British imperialism, an expression of confrontation between ruler and ruled. The historian might feel tempted to provide a social profile of the victims of the brutal massacre who had assembled amidst currents which they could not measure or understand. The Jallianwala Bagh episode could be lifted to a higher altitude and seen how historians and other writers have perceived it. To put it differently, the events could be analysed in historiographical terms and provide some material for the establishment of a critical approach.

The word 'perception' used in the title of this presentation implies taking cognizance of the event and its significance. The perceptions that men have about the events in which they were involved are to be regarded as a dimension of the events themselves. This paper focuses on (1) the historians' perception of the episode and (2) the British perception of it. And finally I have something to offer which calls for elucidation of the episode on 13 April 1919. As there was almost uniformity in the Indian leaders' and their compatriots' condemnation of the massacre, so from this account the Indian perception of the episode has been omitted. Gandhi had viewed the whole event from a larger context. He said, 'We do not wish to punish Dyer. We have no desire for revenge. We want to change the system that produces Dyer.'

THE HISTORIANS' PERCEPTION

I think that B.G. Horniman's *Amritsar and Our Duty to India* (1920), is probably the first account which traces the circumstances leading to the Jallianwala Bagh massacre and Martial Law.[2] Horniman was the chief editor of the *Bombay Chronicle* and a fervent supporter of India's freedom. He was the vice-president of the Home Rule League. He was also elected to the Bombay Corporation. Horniman was the first journalist in the country to give a moving account of the Jallianwala Bagh tragedy in the *Bombay Chronicle* for which the Government deported him to England on 23 April 1919.

Horniman's aim in writing his book was to arouse British public opinion by exposing the atrocities committed by the British bureaucracy in India.[3] According to the author, it was the provocative actions committed by the British bureaucracy in India that triggered the disturbances and led to the massacre. He regards Dyer's action as vindictive, brutality for its own sake, and an exemplification of what he calls 'O Dwyerism and Dyerism'.[4] He holds the Punjab Government, the Government of India and the Secretary of State responsible for unleashing a reign of terror in Punjab. He repudiates the official view that the disturbances constituted a rebellion or war against the King[5] or the Government. The prescription, he offers, is India's right of self-government, which he strongly supports.[6] An eye-witness of the early 1919 political events, using the newspaper versions of the Hunter Committee Evidence, the case that Horniman presents on the Punjab disturbances is a trifle overstated and somewhat on the sensational side. This slender work on Amritsar is tendentious and polemical, reflecting the passion and anger of a news reporter.

The same year (1920) Pearay Mohan, a lawyer from Lahore, brought out a voluminous and hastily-written book entitled *An Imaginary Rebellion*, a collection of disparate material drawn from the Hunter Committee Evidence, Legislative Council Debates, Ordinances and the proceedings of Martial Law trials and other oral testimony.[7] The main idea in this compendium was to challenge O'Dwyer's view that the rebellion was planned and organized. The author asserts that the disturbances were caused by O'Dwyer's brutal regime. He points out that the massacre at Amritsar was a death trap laid by Dyer in collaboration with one Hans Raj, a totally discredited individual (who later turned a government approver) to teach the people of Amritsar a lesson for the murders committed in Amritsar on 10 April. For this the author does not give any evidence and his theory appears only a conjecture! It must be stated that the Amritsar tragedy was not a saga of saints and sinners.

Sir Michael O'Dwyer published his autobiography *India as I Knew It* (1925).[8] A Balliol scholar of classical studies and pupil of the famous Oxford political scientist Benjamin Jowett, he was satanically energetic in whatever he took up. In his autobiography, he emphasizes as he does in his evidence before the Hunter Committee and in the O'Dwyer vs Nair case that there had existed in 1919 a well-planned conspiracy in India to subvert the British rule in which the arch-seditionists, under the leadership of Gandhi, were acting in league with the Afghans and North-Western frontier tribes. O'Dwyer quotes Gandhi as having admitted that there was an 'organized design' to challenge the government.[9] O'Dwyer had approved Dyer's action which he was convinced had saved the situation by crushing the rebellion. He stuck to this view all through which is evident from his testimony in the O'Dwyer vs Nair case in London, in 1924.[10]

Two years after Dyer's death in 1929, Ian Colvin produced a biography on him.[11] It is not a biography but a crusade to vindicate Dyer by insisting that he was a good man imbued with a high sense of duty who was thrown to the wolves owing to political chicanery. He supports O'Dwyer's view that Dyer was made a scapegoat to appease Indian and British politicians. Colvin attempts to reconstruct the entire episode by concentrating only on one side of the personality of his hero and is entirely suspect when he does so with a view to justifying his conduct. This work is blatantly partisan. Colvin concentrates on the early Dyer with his eyes set on the latter one whom he eloquently defends. He takes the position that Dyer acted in self-defence as the crowds were going to rush on him. How could Dyer allow open defiance and a calculated plan to paralyse the government, Colvin asks.

Mark Naidis's *The Punjab Disturbances of 1919 – A Study in Indian Nationalism* apportions responsibility for the disturbances on the corporate shoulders of the official bureaucracy. His thesis is that the bureaucracy stoked the fires of Indian nationalism; hence the disturbances![12]

Rupert Furneaux has presented in *Massacre of Amritsar* (1963) a psychological interpretation of Dyer's conduct at Jallianwala Bagh.[13] According to Furneaux, Dyer's mental state was abnormal. He suffered from arteriosclerosis and his morbid action of firing lacked all sense of proportion. Taking a cue from Edward Thompson's meeting with Miles Irving, Deputy Commissioner Amritsar, after the massacre, Furneaux put forth the view that Dyer was not a bloodthirsty monster but a victim of mental disorder, pitifully suffering from arteriosclerosis. Arteriosclerosis impairs memory, causes exaggerated emotionalism, delirium, morbid fantasies and hallucinations. When Dyer stood before the crowd, the blood flowing to his brain became congested and he imagined that the crowd was massing to attack him. Furneaux thinks that Dyer 'may have misjudged the position because he imagined that the two waves as they surged back were massing to crush him.'[14] Dyer feared that if he did not fire, his men would be attacked from behind. This reasoning provides for Dyer's innocence in that he was unaware of what he was doing.

But Arthur Swinson in *Six Minutes to Sunset* demolishes Furneaux's psychological theory by citing evidence from Dyer's bodyguard, Sergeant W.J. Anderson, and General Inskip, who had met Dyer returning from Jallianwala Bagh.[15] Sergeant Anderson was standing beside Dyer when he ordered firing. According to Anderson, Dyer was perfectly calm, rational and was in full possession of himself.[16] Swinson believed that Dyer's action was influenced by a perceived danger from Afghanistan, a deep concern for the protection of European lives in India, particularly of women, a determination to support his soldiers, and his racial arrogance imbibed in his student days at Bishop Cotton's School, Simla. Swinson does applaud Dyer's action which saved the crisis but thinks that he was sacrificed on grounds of political expediency by the Secretary of State Montagu and his supporters.

To mark the 50th anniversary of the massacre, the Jallianwala Bagh Memorial Committee commissioned the Punjab University to produce a book, and the result was Raja Ram's *The Jallianwala Bagh: A Premeditated Plan* (1969).[17] The author asserts that a premeditated plan carefully devised at Government House Lahore, on 9 April, was executed on the appointed day, and the consequence was the massacre at Jallianwala Bagh.[18] This plan to fire on an assembly on 13 April was hatched on 9 April. This is ridiculous because the murder of Europeans took place on 10 April. There was absolutely no cause for such provocation on the part of the Government. On what this plan was and how it was to be executed, the author says nothing. In fact, this plan is a figment of the author's imagination. Raja Ram twists the Adjutant-General Hudson's note but the file he cites from does not find place in his bibliography.[19] It is further suggested in this work that the people who assembled at the Bagh knew fully well in advance that they would be fired on and thus they made the supreme sacrifice willingly. I do not think the assertion needs any comment. There is no supporting evidence for it either!

Using the British Cabinet papers, Alfred Draper provides a comprehensive study of the Amritsar massacre.[20] He suggests that there may have been a trap laid but he gives no decisive view on it.[21] He states that Dr Saifuddin Kitchlew had strong misgivings about the credibility of his follower, Hans Raj who was probably an *agent provocateur*.[22] The perspective of this work is fuzzy, the author moves backward and forward and fails to account for different aspects of Dyer's action within a single frame of reference.

In the *Imperial Crime and Punishment, The Massacre at Jallianwala Bagh and British Justice, 1919–20* (1977), Helen Fein's exploratory hypothesis is that the colonial rulers exclude the ruled from their own domain of moral obligation.[23] To Fein, Jallianwala Bagh was a prototypical instance of a collective repressive punishment inflicted by the British in black and Asian colonies.

In a meticulosuly researched article based on contemporary British newspapers, Derek Sayer of the University of Alberta, challenges Fein's thesis, and insists that moral obligation was ubiquitous in Dyer's rhetoric.[24] Sayer argues that the British paternalism did not exclude moral obligation it owed to the people of India. That is why Dyer thrashed the naughty boy. Such a course, Sayer emphasizes, was necessary for the governance of the country!

The avenging force of fact is that very little is written on this tragic episode by the British historians, particularly when we contrast it with the substantial literature which exists on the traumatic events of 1857. Helen Fein is an American, Derek Sayer a Canadian, and the four British writers, B.G. Horniman, Rupert Furneaux, Arthur Swinson and Alfred Draper, who produced a comprehensive volume each on this episode, are not professional historians but journalists, novelists and TV script-writers. The Jallianwala Bagh episode has no historian like G.O. Trevelyan of Cawnpore repute. Jawaharlal Nehru's friend and Rabindranath Tagore's biographer, Edward Thompson knew personally some of the leading British officials and Indian political leaders connected with the political events of 1919. He had also some inside information about the episode of Jallianwala Bagh, but he chose to write a book and play on the practice of *suttee.* In a letter published in a collection edited by his son E.P. Thompson before his death, Edward Thompson revealed his stand on the Dyer Debate in London: 'If I were an Indian I should find it impossible to forgive him.'[25] In his textbook, *Rise and Fulfilment of British Rule,* Thompson shows his interest not so much in the massacre as in its significance.[26]

It is rather curious that the School of Oriental Studies, London, which has published a substantial amount of literature on some of the historically sensitive issues relating to Anglo-Indian relations has observed a conspiracy of silence by not producing any monograph on this episode. Why so, particularly when massive material is readily available in British archives? It must be mentioned that the four British writers Horniman, Furneaux, Swinson and Draper do not cite a single source in support of any of their statements.

The Punjabi University, Patiala, brought out in 1997 a volume on the Jallianwala Bagh massacre.[27] The work comprises a number of articles on the episode dealing with a variety of themes connected with it, such as the class and caste analysis of the people participating in the anti-Rowlatt agitation, the legal and constitutional aspects of Dyer's action, the role of political leadership, and the impact of the events of 1919 on the course of the national movement.

THE BRITISH PERCEPTION

Dyer's military superior, Division Commander Major-General Sir William Beynon and the Punjab Lieutenant-Governor O'Dwyer, approved Dyer's action. In approving this, O'Dwyer was merely carrying out instructions issued later that day by the Government of India. These took the form of the resolution in which the Government of India expressed its intention to prevent by all means, however drastic, any recurrences of such excesses, and declared that the Governor-General,

> . . . will not hesitate to employ the ample military resources at his disposal to suppress organized outrage, rioting or concerted opposition to the maintenance of law and order.

The Resolution ended thus:

> To those servants of government who are charged with the onerous responsibility of suppressing excesses against public peace and tranquillity, the Governor-General in Council extends the fullest assurance of countenance and support.[28]

When the prospect of war with the Afghans again became inevitable, Dyer led his brigade to the Frontier where he repulsed the Afghan forces for which the Commander-in-Chief, General Sir Charles Carmichael Munro, who had been a brother officer in the Queen's army for many years, congratulated him at the end of July 1919. Dyer was given permanent command of a brigade in October 1919 and temporary command in January 1920. When his star seemed to be in the ascendant, he was summoned to Delhi on 20 March 1920 and asked to resign his command. This shocked him because both O'Dwyer and Beyon had approved his action before the Hunter Committee. The new Governor of Punjab, Sir S.D. Maclagan had also supported him.[29] Yet within a space of few months, the hero had become the villain of the piece!

Owing to the pressure of strong Indian public opinion, the Disorders Enquiry Committee (known as the Hunter Committee from the name of its Chairman) was appointed on 14 October 1919 to 'inquire into the causes of and measures taken to cope with the recent disturbances in Bombay, Delhi and Punjab'. In paragraph 29 of the Disorders Enquiry Committee Report, Dyer's action was strongly criticized in two respects: first, that he started firing without giving the assembled people a chance to disperse, and secondly, that he continued firing for a substantial period of time even after the crowd had commenced dispersal. The Committee felt that Dyer should have given notice as it would have afforded an opportunity to those 'assembled in ignorance of the proclamation and others to leave the Bagh'. In continuing to fire as he did, the Committee thought that Dyer had committed a grave error of judgement, and had 'demonstrated a mistaken notion of duty'. The Committee submitted its report to the Government of India on 8 March 1920.

The Viceroy's Executive Council reviewed the Hunter Committee proceedings and found Dyer's action indefensible. They did not recommend his impeachment or prosecution but pre-empted his retirement from the service and ruled out any further employment in India. On 23 March 1920 the Adjutant-General Sir Havelock Hudson deprived Dyer of his command, and this action he conveyed to Dyer personally in a very brief interview. Dyer's career came to an end. Broken in health, he sailed for England on 20 April.

The Dyer case was brought before the Army Council on 14 May 1920 in England. Winston Churchill, Secretary of State for War, justified the Cabinet decision to 'throw out Dyer' but the military members resisted it and asked for more time to consider the matter. Churchill stressed that the Cabinet decision was final and that the information given to the Army Council was only as a formality. The military members objected to it. Eventually the deadlock was resolved on 17 May 1920 when Dyer was permitted to submit his statement to the Army Council. After considering his comprehensive report which he submitted on 3 July, the Army Council resolved:

> They consider that in spite of the great difficulties of the position in which this officer (Dyer) found himself on 13 April 1919, and at Jallianwalla Bagh, he cannot be acquitted of an error of judgement. They observe that the Commander-in Chief, India, has removed General Dyer from his employment and that he has been informed that no further employment will be offered to him in India, and that he has, in consequence, reverted to half-way and the selection board in India have passed him over for promotion. These decisions the Army Council accept. They do not consider that further employment should be offered to General Dyer.[30]

On 8 July 1920 the Secretary of State Montagu led the debate on the Dyer case in the House of Commons on behalf of the Government in which Winston Churchill and Bonar Law participated. The debate generated heated controversy. In the House of Commons, 129 votes were cast in favour of Dyer and 230 against him; in the House of Lords, after the debate held on 19 and 20 July, 126 voted in favour, while 86 voted against him. The House of Lords exonerated him and commended his services to the Raj. To many of Dyer's supporters it was the vindication of his action but they were mistaken as a large body of opinion condemned it as misguided and dangerous.

In England there also arose a strong feeling that Dyer had been sacrificed to the clamourings of Indian nationalist politicians. *The Morning Post* set up a fund as a testimonial, on the move initiated by O'Dwyer. The fund reached over £ 26,000, one third having been contributed from India where a majority of Europeans considered that Dyer's action had, indeed, saved the situation.

Five years after the massacre, Justice McCardie, while delivering his judgement in the libel case on O'Dwyer vs Nair in the High Court, London, justified Dyer's action and thought that he was wrongly punished by the Secretary of State. Sir Sankaran Nair had held Sir Michael O'Dwyer responsible for unleashing a reign of terror in Punjab for which the latter had filed a libel suit against the former. Dyer was present in the court when McCardie delivered his judgement. The British public opinion was divided over Dyer's action, and those associated with the governance of India were convinced that Dyer had acted beyond the necessity of the case and harmed the British cause.

The Manual of Military Law prescribed for the Army laid down the general rule that it would be extremely imprudent to use an armed force against a mob before a proclamation had been made and an hour had elapsed. In violating this Dyer had opened the fire the moment he entered the Bagh, without giving any warning to the assembled to disperse. Dyer's firing was used as one of the case studies for a section of the course prescribed for the Army.[31] Broadly, it related to the military action in support by the civil power.

Generally speaking, the British civil and military servants in India lauded Dyer's action. However, Malcolm Darling, a distinguished civil servant, who produced authoritative works on the Punjab peasantry on the rural life in India, was an exception. He felt chagrined by Dyer's action, and thereby incurred the hostility of his colleagues and superiors. His letter to his friend E.M. Forster, dated 11 July 1929, is revealing.[32]

After Eton, Malcolm Darling joined King's College, Cambridge, where Forster resided as Fellow. Both Forster and Darling adopted Gladstonian liberalism as their creed. In what is now known as the *Amritsar Letter*, Darling expressed his anguish over the Jallianwala Bagh massacre. He wrote to Forster:

> We are in a bit of a mess out here. We did not rape and hack to pieces, but one day in Amritsar they shot down hundreds, mostly zamindars. I have seen the place – a death trap. Five or 6,000 there. Enter infuriated General – took thirty seconds to make up his mind, said he to Watkin and then 1,500 rounds. God, it makes me sick to think of it. Yet I was told by my chief ten days later – 'People of the club (Lahore) say you ought to be court-martialled for criticizing. . . .' It is a bad world.

Darling was posted at Gurdaspur and he went out to the countryside to see how things were. His leaving the headquarters was viewed as a dereliction of duty by the Divisional Commissioner, A.J.W. Kitchin, and the matter went up to the Governor Sir E.D. Maclagan who exonerated him. However, things could never be the same for Darling and he found himself a stranger in India. This was a turning point in his life. To Darling, the Jallianwala Bagh massacre revealed British irresponsibility and he tried to get out of India.

The British increasingly began to feel a sense of insecurity which Lord Meston expressed graphically in the House of Lords:

> A lady who knows India very well and who lost her distinguished husband in its service said to me the other day, 'Dyer had done me a great disservice. I used to be quite happy about my son and his young wife in their lovely station in upper India. I am not happy now.'[33]

O'Dwyer had asserted in January 1919 that the British rule rested for its perpetuation on its *iqbal* and *izzat* (honour). I think that Jallianwala Bagh demolished this notion of British *izzat*. In 1951 when this writer asked Pethick-Lawrence, a former Secretary of State, why the British quit India in 1947, he said that it was primarily because of a strong feeling of insecurity which the British civil servants felt in an India seething with unrest and discontent and it had become difficult to find suitable civil servants for India as they were unwilling to go out.[34] Mostly these civil servants were young Oxford and Cambridge scholars.

CONCLUSION

The following account deals with certain aspects of the Jallianwala Bagh massacre which have been neglected.

It is difficult to understand Dyer's motive for his action from his own evidence. He offered three distinct types of versions for the firing in Jallianwala Bagh. He was his own worst enemy and he proved it because he shifted his ground on different occasions – the radical shift in his versions was influenced by strong pressure of public opinion both for and against him. Dyer was either eulogized as a saviour of the Raj or condemned for his brutality on the innocent. He had deceived himself into thinking that he had to face larger issues when in reality his mind was fixed on comparatively a limited part of the situation. The fact remains that he was swayed by passions and showed fundamental lack of candour in dealing with the situation that confronted him. Therefore, his first report of 14 April 1919 to the General Staff Division, his written statement of 25 August 1919 before the Hunter Committee on 19 November 1919 and his defence before the Army Council in June 1920, unless delinked from his wishful thinking and fanciful heroism, would not explain why he resorted to the firing the way he did.

Dyer learnt on 13 April at about 1.30 p.m. from Mr Lewis, the manager of Crown Cinema, that the prohibited meeting was going to be held at Jallianwala Bagh. He had arrived in Amritsar on the 11th evening by 9.00 p.m. Sir William Beynon, the Divisional Commander, had asked him to reach Amritsar. The Divisional Commissioner A.J.W. Kitchen had requested Beynon to render military aid to the civil authority which had broken down. Reaching Amritsar, Dyer held a meeting in the railway compartment with Miles Irving, Deputy Commissioner, the Superintendent and Deputy Superintendent of Police, and other police officers from the *kotwali.* These officers apprised Dyer of the gravity of the situation. Dyer found Irving utterly broken by anxiety and fatigue. Informing Dyer that civil control of the city was over, Irving formally handed over charge of the city to him.[35] On 12 and 13 April, Dyer went round some parts of the town with his military force. Two proclamations were issued prohibiting any meeting or assembly and warning that any violation of the orders would compel immediate firing.

The question is who organized this Jallianwala meeting, and how did it take place? Kitchlew and Satyapal had been arrested on 10 April and their followers Bugga and Ratto faced a similiar fate on 11 and 12 April. Badr-ul-Islam and Dr Hafiz Mohammad Bashir were nowhere to be seen. The moving spirit behind the Jallianwala Bagh meeting was Hans Raj. We find from the police diaries and the Amritsar conspiracy case record that Hans Raj had become politically active as Joint-Secretary of the Satyagraha Sabha from the first week of April.[36] Twenty-three years old and a matriculate, Hans Raj was a man of dubious character. He had been dismissed from service as a travelling ticket collector on the North Western Railway.[37] He served as a clerk in the Municipal Committee, Amritsar. According to Gul Mohammed, who appeared before the Congress Sub-Committee for evidence, Hans Raj lived on the earnings of his mother and sister.[38]

It was Hans Raj who had organized the Hindu Sabha High School meeting in Dhab Khatikan on the 12 April at 4 p.m. He announced there that a meeting on the Baisakhi day would be held in Jallianwala Bagh where two resolutions would be moved; one condemning the firing on 10 April and the other requesting the authorities to release their leaders. Hans Raj said that there was no leader; each one was his own leader.[39] He also announced that Kanehya Lal, a highly respectable citizen of Amritsar, would preside. Kanehya Lal later denied that he had ever been approached by Hans Raj.

Learning about the meeting at Jallianwala Bagh, Dyer, accompanied by Captain F.C. Briggs in one car and with Rehill and Plomer in another, rushed through the gutted buildings of the National Bank and *kotwali* and reached Jallianwala Bagh just a little before 5.00 p.m. The sky was overcast. The dust raised by the crowds in the Bagh hung over the area and added to the gloom. Dyer had two armoured cars with guns fixed on them, which he could not take through due to the narrowness of the lane. All in all he had 90 soldiers, but took only 50 inside the Bagh. J.P. Thompson's *Private Diary* shows that Dyer's force in the garden consisted of only the Gurkhas and Baluchis.[40]

The position in the Bagh was as follows: the third speaker Brij Baikal, a bank clerk, had just finished reciting his poem *Faryad.* An aeroplane circled low, and the people panicked but Hans Raj assured them that there was no cause for alarm. Durga Das Vaid, Editor of the *Waqt,* began to move two resolutions: one, for the repeal of the Rowlatt Act, and the other for the release of their leaders, Kitchlew and Satyapal.

Just at this precise moment Dyer arrived with his troops and people shouted '*aa gaye! aa gaye!*' ('They have come! They have come!'). Instantaneously he placed twenty-five soldiers on one side of the raised platform and twenty-five on the other. Captain Briggs located himself behind him, while Sergeant Anderson stood beside him. When the troops arrived, people jeered at them and shouted, 'They (the bullets) were *phokian* (blanks)'. Dyer ordered firing and 1,650 rounds of 303 marks were fired for ten minutes. J.P. Thompson, Chief Secretary, Punjab (1916–21) notes on 17 July 1919 in his unpublished diary, 'Steward told me that when the troops were firing for some time, Dyer turned to one of them, and said, 'Do you think they have had enough?'. Then he went on and said, 'Let them have four rounds more'.[41]

On 8 August 1919, Thompson further recorded as follows:

> Dyer called on me. He said when he entered Jallianwala Bagh, saw the meeting in progress, his mind made up in three seconds, he thought it his business to suppress the insurrection then and there. The men sometimes collected in knots and he thought they mediated attack. Didn't attend the wounded, his ammunition near exhausted and his men couldn't have defended themselves if attacked. He seemed to regard it his mission, his religious duty, to kill the rebellion.[42]

Thereafter Dyer ordered about turn and returned to the *Baradari.* No Martial Law was imposed on 13 April and it was not formally proclaimed in Amritsar and Lahore till 15 April. The civil authority had not abdicated itself. It was a *de facto* Martial Law, not *de jure.* The question of Martial Law and civil authority generated much discussion in the Hunter Committee. The British officials, O'Dwyer, Beynon, Irving and Dyer made contradictory statements and the issue is still not clear. One might ask then how Dyer could assume the overall authority to do what he did when there was no Martial Law. He was required to assist the civilian authority to restore order. It is extraordinary that to deal with a prohibited meeting an officer of the rank of Brigadier General had to go personally. Dyer could have sent one of his subordinates, either Major Macdonald or Captain Briggs. But he chose to go himself. He did not take the Deputy Commissioner nor was the latter to be seen anywhere. An apprehensive Irving had gone to the fort. In his diary, Thompson notes on 24 March 1920, 'It is unfortunate that Irving was D.C. He was overawed by Dyer'.[43] The Superintendent of Police, J.F. Rehill, did not accompany Dyer either. R. Plomer, the Deputy Superintendent, is said to have arrived at the Bagh after the firing had ceased, but this is also disputed. Dyer took no steps to prevent the holding of the meeting nor did he paste copies of the prohibitory order on the gate of the Bagh. He did not issue any warning to the crowd assembled. He ordered firing immediately. He continued firing even when the people were running for their lives. He fired even at the exits, which is evident from the bullet marks in the Bagh. Some people fell into the well, others died while climbing the wall. He did not attend to the wounded. He proudly declared that it was not his job! Assuming that Dyer was facing an enormous and an agitated mob while his force was small and he was hemmed in and was going to be overwhelmed, he could have made a different choice from the one he did. It is obvious that Dyer's object was not to disperse the assembly; if that had been the object, he could have first issued a warning, then fired a few shots in the air, and finally taken action which was compelling. Instead, he continued to fire even when the crowds were at the exits. Even a riotous assembly could have been dispersed by a volley or two or by a couple of dozen police armed with smooth fire musketry or buckshot.

It was because of Hans Raj's announcement that the meeting took place at Jallianwala Bagh. The British authorities closed the cattle market fair where people from the countryside had poured in on Baisakhi day. Finding the fair closed, quite a number of them went to Jallianwala Bagh to attend the meeting. The number of people estimated at the meeting was approximately 15,000.

The proceedings of the Amritsar Conspiracy case show that after his arrest on 16 April, Hans Raj turned an approver; after extracting evidence against Kitchlew, Satyapal, Bugga, Ratto and others, he was spirited away to Mesopotamia. His house in Amritsar was burnt. Though Irving, the Deputy Commissioner of Amritsar, denied that he was an agent provocateur, there are strong reasons to believe that even before the massacre Hans Raj was acting as a decoy for the British. He was seen talking to two policemen just at about 1 p.m. in the Bagh.[44] Two or three constables left the Bagh just before the meeting. Immediately after the firing, Hans Raj disappeared. Even after the arrival of the troops, Hans Raj was declaring that 'The government will never fire'.[45]

M.R. Jayakar categorically states that the Jallianwala Bagh meeting had been planned by Hans Raj to gather people, but on the question whether the authorities were a party to it, he suspends his judgement.[46] Closely associated with the Congress inquiry, Jayakar had visited Amritsar in this connection and was quite knowledgeable about it. Dr Hafiz Mohammed Ashraf considered Hans Raj as a tool in the hands of the British from the beginning.[47] Madan Mohan Malaviya and C.F. Andrews also condemned him as an informer.[48]

Dewan Niranjan Prasad, Judge of the Patiala High Court, who had assisted Motilal Nehru in the Congress Enquiry, was convinced that Hans Raj had been used by the British authorities for their sinister designs. What could be a more suitable place for Dyer than Jallianwala Bagh! Dyer told his wife that it was necessary to 'get them somehow in the open'.[49] In his letter and a note of 12 September 1968, sent to me, Dewan Niranjan Prasad informed that Principal G.A. Wathen of Khalsa College, Amritsar, knew of the firing in advance. Wathen had warned his pupils including Deva Singh not to go to the town.[50] Deva Singh, however, did go and was crippled for life, and his companion Hazara Singh was killed. In his letter of 10 October 1968, Deva Singh confirmed Dewan Niranjan Prasad's version and blamed Gandhi for the suppression of truth.[51] Lala Hans Raj, a famous advocate at Amritsar and now 91 years old, in his interview for the BBC film on Jallianwala Bagh said that it was the mischievous Hans Raj who had lured people to the Bagh with the connivance of the British.[52]

The question is why did the British embark on this deadly course. The murder of five Europeans and the assault on Miss Sherwood, who was left for dead on the street, had infuriated Dyer. The assault on Miss Sherwood personified for Dyer a symbol of violation, an annihilation of what they regarded as sacred and the contamination of the superior breed by dirty black hands. The British blood boiled with rage over Miss Sherwood's assault. Bertrand Russell touched on the same theme:

> . . . the desire to protect one's family from injury at the hands of an alien race is probably the wildest and most passionate feeling of which a man is capable.[53]

George Orwell has written in a similar vein in his essay *Shooting an Elephant.*[54] Such cruel humiliation arouses the fiercest and the bitterest of impulses. Dyer's Crawling Order, his evidence before the Army Council and his conversation with his wife confirm this violent reaction. When questioned about his Crawling Order, Dyer replied that Miss Sherwood was holy and sacred, so he wanted them (the Indians) to do what they would do in the temple – to crawl and go on all fours! In his report to the Army Council, Dyer emphasizes that it was this that roused his indignation and made him adopt a menacing attitude.

> If any dominant motive can be extracted it was the determination to avert from the European women and children and those of the law-abiding Indian community the fate which I am convinced would be theirs, if I did not meet the challenge and produce the required effect to restore order and security. I am conscious that it was this motive which gave me the strength of will to carry out my duty.[55]

So the inescapable conclusion is that Dyer used Hans Raj as a decoy to inflict a severe punishment on the people of Amritsar for the murder of his five compatriots, and an assault on an English woman so that it might set an example for the governance of the country. Dyer was motivated by revenge. Dyer saved Punjab but well-nigh lost India! That, of course, is another story!

Notes and References

1. For some of the formulations this study is largely based on the following works by the author: *Amritsar, Past and Present*, Amritsar, 1967; *Jallianwala Bagh*, Ludhiana, 1969; *New Light on Punjab Disturbances*, vol. I–II, Simla, 1975; *The Sources of National Movement*, ed., V.N. Datta and S.C. Mittal, New Delhi, 1985; and a dozen articles published in *The Tribune*, Chandigarh. For different historical accounts, see V.N. Datta, *The Tribune*, 13 April 1975, his introduction to *Jallianwala Bagh: Commemoration Volume* (ed., Gursharan Singh), Patiala, 1997; and 'Jallianwala Bagh' in *We Fought Together for Freedom: Chapters from the Indian National Movement* (ed., Ravi Dayal) Oxford University Press, 1995.
2. B.G. Horniman, *Amritsar, Our Duty to India*, London, 1920.
3. *Ibid.*, pp. 9–10.
4. *Ibid.*, pp. 85–95.
5. *Ibid.*, p. 166.
6. *Ibid.*, pp. 192.
7. Pearay Mohan, *An Imaginary Rebellion*, Lahore, 1920.
8. Michael O'Dwyer, *India as I Knew It*, London, 1925.
9. *Ibid.*, p. 128.
10. Public Records Office, Chancery Lane, London, *European Mss. 137/3, Nair vs O'Dwyer, High Court of Justice, King's Bench Division London.* See, O'Dwyer's evidence in my *New Light on Punjab Disturbance*, vol. I, pp. 124, 207, 208, 233.
11. Ian Colvin, *The Life of General Dyer*, India, 1929.
12. Mark Naidis, *The Punjab Disturbance of 1919, A Study in Nationalism.* A dissertation submitted to Stanford University (February 1950), see p. 75.
13. Rupert Furneaux, *Massacre at Amritsar*, London, 1963.
14. *Ibid.*, pp. 170–75. J.P. Thompson, Chief Secretary to the Punjab Government, takes a similar view. In his evidence before the Hunter Committee, Thompson said that Dyer thought that the crowd was going to rush on him. He added, 'I saw Dyer on 16 April – he then told me that the crowd was going to attack him'. See *New Light on Punjab Disturbance*, Vol. I, p. 120. It is curious that at some stage Edward Thompson believed that the Jallianwala Bagh episode was a mistaken, and not calculated, brutality! Miles Irving, informed him that Dyer did not know that there was no way out of the place. See, *The Other Side of the Medal*, ed., Mulk Raj Anand, Delhi, 1989, p. 100.
15. Arthur Swinson, *Six Minutes to Sunset*, London, 1964.
16. *Ibid.*, p. 210.
17. Raja Ram, *The Jallianwala Bagh Massacre: A Premeditated Plan*, Chandigarh, 1969; see Appendix III, p. VII, 75.
18. *Ibid.*, Appendix D. The file in Punjab Government Military – Part B, January 1920, 256, see p. 176.
19. *Ibid.*, p. 146.
20. Alfred Draper, *Amritsar: The Massacre that Ended the Raj*, London, 1981.
21. *Ibid.*, p. 146.
22. *Ibid.*, p. 195.

23. Helen Fein, *Imperial Crime and Punishment: The Massacre at Jallianwala Bagh and British Justice, 1919–20*, Honolulu, 1977.
24. Derek Sayer, 'British Reactions to the Amritsar Massacre, 1919–20,' in *Past and Present*, Winter, May 1991, No. 31, pp. 130–63, 164.
25. *Alien Homage: Edward Thompson, Rabindranath Tagore*, by E.P. Thompson, Delhi, 1993, p. 75.
26. Edward Thompson and G.T. Garratt, *Rise and Fulfilment of British Rule in India*, London, 1934, pp. 607–11.
27. *Jallianwala Bagh: Commemoration Volume* ed., Gursharan Singh, Prem Bakshish Singh, Davendra Kumar Verma and Raj Krishan Ghai, Patiala, 1997.
28. *Op. cit.*, pp. 320–31.
29. *Government of India, House Department, Political*, June 1920, pp. 124–64.
30. *Hansard, Parliamentary Debate (House of Commons)*, 1920, vol. XXX, p. 1442.
31. The Duke of Edinburgh, Prince Philip drew my attention to it in his letter of 2 December 1997 for which I am grateful.
32. *Malcolm Darling Papers* (South Asian Centre, Cambridge, Box No. 11), Darling to E.M. Forster, 11 July 1919.
33. *Hansard (House of Lords), 1920*, vol. XXI, p. 420.
34. Interview with Lord Pethick-Lawrence at Cambridge, 7 December 1951.
35. *Disorders Enquiry Committee*, vol. III, p. 202.
36. *Evidence of the Punjab Sub-Committee of the Indian National Congress*, 1920, p. 59.
37. *Bombay Chronicle*, 17 July 1920; see V.N. Datta, *Jallianwala Bagh*, pp. 162–64. See also *Amritsar Conspiracy Case 1919*, p. 109.
38. *Amritsar Conspiracy Case 1919, Martial Law Commission*, pp. 27, 38.
39. *Ibid.*, pp. 59, 109.
40. *J.P. Thompson's Diary*, 9 August 1919, Mss. Euro. F. 137/13, (Cambridge) South Asian Centre, Cambridge.
41. *Ibid.*, 17 July 1919.
42. *Ibid.*, 8 August 1919.
43. *Ibid.*, 24 May 1920.
44. *Evidence of the Punjab Sub-Committee of the Indian National Congress*, p. 61.
45. *Ibid.*, p. 82.
46. *Jayakar Papers, Inquiry*, vol. III, No. 477, 15 April 1920 to 15 January 1920. See also *Bombay Chronicle*, 17 July 1920.
47. *Bombay Chronicle*, 17 July 1920.
48. *Ibid.*,
49. Colvin, *op. cit.*, p. 168.
50. Dewan Niranjan Prasad's note and his letter to the writer, dated 12 September 1968.
51. Deva Singh's letter to the writer, dated 10 October 1968.
52. Interview with Lala Hans Raj Mittal of Amritsar on 13 June 1990.
53. *The Autobiography of Bertrand Russell*, London, 1968, 1914–44, vol. II, p. 139.
54. George Orwell, *Shooting an Elephant*, London, 1953, p. 10.
55. Comd. Papers (771) statement by Dyer.

TWO

The Jallianwala Bagh Tragedy, the Rowlatt Satyagraha and the Character of the Nationalist Struggle in India: Some Reflections

RAVINDER KUMAR

As part of a worldwide radicalization of social consciousness after the conclusion of World War I, the people of India gave expression to their desire for political liberation, economic dignity and social equality through an epic upsurge in the spring of 1919. This upsurge, popularly known as the Rowlatt Satyagraha, marked a seminal stage in the growth of a nationalist and anti-imperialist movement in India in the twentieth century. Indeed, the Rowlatt Satyagraha was the first truly countrywide nationalist struggle: it heralded the advent of mass action in nationalist politics; it brought to prominence Mahatma Gandhi, who continued to dominate the political arena for the next quarter of a century; it introduced the people to the notion of *ahimsa*, or non-violence, as the basis of social action initiated to secure the realization of specific political objectives; and, finally, it shaped popular politics within India into a communitarian mould which retains its overall character down to our times.

When we embark, today, upon an exploration of the Rowlatt Satyagraha – and of the tragedy enacted at the Jallianwala Bagh in the course of this Satyagraha – it is appropriate for us to ask a series of questions about the larger historical significance of this movement. What was the climate of politics in India in 1919? Can we identify the social classes and religious communities which were drawn into the nationalist discourse? If so, then what were the objectives with which these classes and communities were drawn into the politics of nationalism? Moreover, we can also validly raise questions about Gandhian ideology and the manner in which it reached out to different sections of Indian society. Can the Rowlatt agitation be looked upon as marking a qualitative change in the nationalist movement? If so, what were the distinctive characteristics of the agitation and the attributes they conferred upon popular political consciousness in the country? Finally, did the Satyagraha leave a durable impact upon political mentalities? If so, then how are such mentalities reflected in contemporary politics?

I

It would be appropriate to commence our survey of the Rowlatt Satyagraha and its long-term repercussions with a few observations about the character of political society at this juncture and the quality of social consciousness which informed its constituents. There are two alternative ways in which we can do so. We can examine the manner in which individuals were drawn into social production; and through such activity, grouped into social classes, whose cohesion and consciousness stemmed from their role and location in the processes of wealth generation. Alternatively, we can look upon the issue of social organization from the point of view of the ritual and moral location of the individual, and the communities, large and small, which the individual constituted through such ritual and moral placement. It would, perhaps, be appropriate to keep both these principles of social ordering in view when we examine community and class location within Indian society in the opening decades of our century.

Perhaps the most articulate segment of society consisted of the middle classes, which had largely come into existence under the colonial dispensation in the nineteenth century. The members of such classes were either engaged in the liberal and commercial professions or they lived on rent drawn from holdings in land. The middle classes, in the years under review, were attracted to nationalist ideology and they looked upon the Indian National Congress as their 'natural' party; just as they looked upon constitutional agitation as the only valid means of waging an anti-imperialist struggle. Between the middle classes and the subaltern classes, that is, peasants, artisans, workers and tribals, there stood a great gulf of interest and sentiment, which characterizes society even to the present times. The subaltern classes functioned outside the framework of liberal politics, and before they were drawn into nationalism by Mahatma Gandhi, through a mechanism on which we shall dwell later, they expressed their intense sense of patriotism and anti-imperialism through violent movements against the colonial state. In 1857, the subaltern classes came together in a pan-Indian movement under the old feudal classes and the religious intelligentsia. Alternatively, they staged various local uprisings against the colonial state. Whether the subaltern uprisings were subcontinental, as in 1857, or local, as in 1831 (the Barasat *Vidroha*) and 1855 (the Santhal *Hool*), they had very little to do with the politics of the middle classes which, after 1885, found in the Indian National Congress a singularly appropriate forum for the articulation of their views and the projection of their interests.

No portrayal of political awareness among different social segments in India can be looked upon as valid unless it draws into consideration the varying categories of religious consciousness within society. In the decades under consideration, the Muslim communities of India had distinctive sensibilities of their own. Thus the Muslim landed classes perceived themselves as an aristocratic ruling class and believed that the establishment of British rule had a disastrous effect upon the subcontinent. What was true of the landed classes was also true of the artisans, the merchants, the intelligentsia, and most important of all, the peasantry, which was concentrated in the north-west, the south-west and the south-east of India. This may have been so because the Muslim elite looked upon the British as usurpers, while the poorer Muslim classes had been the victims of colonial exploitation and were, therefore, greatly incensed with the British.

Because of their intense anti-imperialism, the Muslim communities of India – landlords, merchants, the priestly intelligentsia, artisans, workers and peasants – were readily drawn into a great movement led by Pan-Islamic ideologues, prominently Maulana Abul Kalam Azad, the brothers Mohammad and Shaukat Ali, Saifuddin Kitchlew and a host of others, who were also ardent nationalists. At the Lucknow session of the Indian National Congress, sometime earlier, drawing upon the nationalist sentiments abroad in the middle classes, Hindu and Muslim elites had come together in an understanding, which enabled them to present to the British Government a joint proposal for constitutional reforms, seeking for the provinces of the Indian Empire substantial political autonomy as a basis of a post-war constitutional settlement.

Our portrayal of middle class politics in the second decade of the twentieth century deliberately avoids touching upon the social temper of the subaltern classes – of artisans, industrial workers, kisans, and tribals – whatever be the religious system in which they were existentially located. This constraint reflects the great divide between the world of the middle classes, on the one hand, and that of the subalterns, on the other. Yet among the Muslim communities of India, in particular, this divide was not as marked a feature as it may have been among the Hindu communities. The social anger of the Muslim landed gentry and the acute sense of deprivation of Muslim artisans and peasants created the basis of a great coming together among all those located within the world of Islam. Indeed, the *ulema* ensured that Pan-Islamic sentiment and anti-imperialist anger not only reached out to the rich and the poor alike, but they also created among them a restlessness that threatened to express itself in a violent upsurge against the colonial state in the second decade of the twentieth century.

It is highly illuminating to examine the texture and quality of social consciousness among comparable classes within Hindu society. That the Hindu middle classes were actively drawn into constitutional nationalism was a matter of common knowledge in the years under review. What was much more obscure, however, even to the more perceptive nationalist leadership, was the extent to which the sentiment of nationalism had trickled down to social classes located below the educated and the propertied classes. This, at any rate, was what Gandhi discovered in 1916, when acting on the advice of his mentor, Gopal Krishna Gokhale, he travelled around the country for the better part of a year. The temper of the middle classes became obvious to him from the various meetings he held in the cities, large and small, in the course of his journey. Yet nationalist enthusiasm did not end with the literate and the affluent, more or less. At Ahmedabad, where Gandhi had built for himself an Ashram, the textile workers were engaged in a bitter conflict with their employers over a rightful share in the profits earned by the latter. These workers requested Gandhi to take up their cause. Similarly, a kisan from the district of Champaran in Bihar met Gandhi more than once, in a bid to interest him in the fate of his fellows, before Gandhi agreed to lead their struggle. When nearer home, in the rural district of Kheda, the *patidar* community felt aggrieved through an upward revision of their tax obligations to the colonial state and they, too, sought assistance from Gandhi in successfully gaining tax relief from the British Government. From all this, it was clear to the Mahatma, that the sentiment of nationalism had, by 1919, reached not only the educated middle classes, but also the industrial workers, artisans, peasantry and tribal communities within the country.

The Gandhian ideology of non-violence – resting on the twin notions of *ahimsa* and *satya* – has been critiqued so often that it would be difficult to say anything radically new in the present context. It would suffice to mention here that two or three facets of satyagraha, as a mode of political warfare, can with profit be highlighted in our brief review. Firstly, earlier on in faraway South Africa Gandhi was able to cement the bond of unity between Hindus and Muslims as well as between Gujaratis, Tamilians and men and women from the United Provinces. Secondly that Gandhi's reading of Western thinkers was drawn into a strikingly original ideological synthesis that was distinctively Indian in its perception of the social structure, moral values and the place of the poor and the deprived in society. All these facets of Gandhian ideology were brought together into a code of social action of superb tactical and strategic finesse which combined non-violence with political militancy.

Our brief review of the social, religious and economic currents within Indian society provides us with valuable clues to the possibilities of political action open to the nationalist leadership in the aftermath of World War I. When the British realized the extent of nationalist sentiment located within the country, then it was clear to them that a measure of concessions were called for. Hence the Declaration of 1917, which held out the prospect of increasingly significant measures of political autonomy and the visit of the Secretary of State for India, Edwin Montagu, to the subcontinent in 1918, with the objective of hammering out constitutional reforms after interacting with nationalist leaders representing different shades of opinion in the country.

Characteristically, however, the British did not confine themselves to the framing of constitutional reforms in the years under review. For in the so-called revolutionary nationalists, who often took recourse to violence with the belief that such violence could conjure into existence a massive popular uprising, the colonial state faced a very serious problem. It was difficult for the British to secure the conviction of those engaged in acts of violence through regular Courts of Law and normal legal procedures. To remedy the situation, the British Government introduced in the Imperial Legislative Council, in February 1919, two bills – the so-called Rowlatt Bills – which sought to 'facilitate the conviction of nationalist activists accused of political crime. When Gandhi became aware of the proposed Bills, he took the strongest possible exception to the imperial arrogance which motivated the legislation.

He observed, 'To me the Bills are the regulated symptoms of a deep seated disease. They are a striking demonstration of the determination of the Civil Service to retain its grip of our neck. . . . I consider the Bills to be an open challenge to us. If we succumb we are done for. If we may prove our word that the Government will see an agitation such that they have never witnessed before, we shall have proved our capacity for resistance to arbitrary or tyrannical rule. . . .'

To persuade the British Government to withdraw the repressive Rowlatt Bills, Gandhi initiated a satyagraha in the opening days of April 1919. Further, since he had no access to any organized political forum in the country at this juncture, Gandhi set up Satyagraha Sabhas in all the principal cities of India, as the organizational agencies of a massive non-violent movement against the colonial state. All sections of society – Hindus, Muslims and Sikhs; the rich and the poor; industrialists and workers; businessmen and men in the liberal professions; artisans, peasants and tribals – were requested to join this non-violent protest against the action of the British Government. What happened in Amritsar, in the second week of April 1919, provides an insight into the course of the Rowlatt Satyagraha over the country as a whole. Distinguished nationalist leaders within the city, like Satyapal and Saifuddin Kitchlew, who symbolized the magnificent unity achieved in 1919 by Hindus and Muslims, appealed to the British to repeal the ignoble law they had enacted. Their call was taken up by Amritsar as a whole, concerning the colonial state and providing it to reveal the mailed fist behind the velvet glove of British imperialism through a barbarous massacre of peaceful citizens, who had assembled at the Jallianwala Bagh, on 13 April 1919. In the course of this massacre, a senior British army officer ordered his troops to fire into a gathering of 20,000 innocent and peaceful men, women and children, killing 372 and wounding more than 1,000 of them. The brutal killings sent shock waves of horror throughout the civilized world.

It is important to emphasize, with the benefit of hindsight, that what happened in Amritsar on 13 April was, by no means, an isolated occurrence. The Rowlatt Satyagraha affected virtually the whole of India though the social support which flowed to Gandhi varied considerably from one part of the country to another. Broadly speaking, the movement was much stronger in cities and larger towns than in rural areas; though it reached out to involve smaller towns, market centres and even villages in the provinces of Gujarat and Punjab, and to a lesser extent, in the United Provinces and in western Maharashtra. Hindu-Muslim unity was a striking feature of the meetings of protest and popular demonstrations on the occasion. In Bombay, the Satyagraha was observed by the middle classes and the lower middle classes, both Hindu and Muslim. In Ahmedabad, the principal city of Gujarat, both the professional classes and the workers rallied to the Satyagraha in great numbers. The same was true in the cities of north India such as Lahore, Delhi and Amritsar, where the Hindu middle class as well as the lowly Muslim artisans and workers joined in the protest against the Rowlatt Act. Perhaps the most insightful comment on the Rowlatt Satyagraha is an observation made by a scholar who studied the course of the Satyagraha in Gujarat: 'The events of April 1919,' observes this historian, 'mark the transfer of moral authority . . . from the British to the Indian National Congress.'

II

The remarkable success of the Rowlatt Satyagraha highlights certain features of the first countrywide Gandhian movement which need to be recapitulated to enable us to comprehend the manner in which mass politics crystallized within India in the years under consideration. It is our contention that the mode of crystallization of mass politics was inextricably linked to the structure of the Indian society and the quality of social consciousness which informed different classes and communities located within it. To stretch this argument further, it is also our contention that the structure of nationalist politics generated in 1919 provided the basis for collective political behaviour not only for the next three decades, but also for the four decades and more which have lapsed since India became an independent polity.

For a deeper comprehension of the cultural logic of Gandhian nationalism plus the forms of consciousness upon which it rested and in turn reinforced, it is necessary to recapitulate our portrayal of social divisions and political solidarities within Indian society in the second decade of the twentieth century. We have argued, as a general proposition, that it is fruitful to examine the moral ordering of society on the basis of religious ascription, on the one hand, just as it is also fruitful to examine the material ordering of society on the basis of social production and wealth distribution, on the other. Indeed, we need both these frames of reference to understand social structure, political behaviour and moral interplay within Indian society in the 1920s. Perhaps the communities of Islam and the communities of Hinduism constituted the two most important over-arching social constituencies for the political actor at this juncture. The Mahatma certainly acted upon this assumption in the political arena. Indeed, he recognized both the cohesion and the division generated by religion as a dialectical phenomenon. Thus the Hindus were divided into a large number of sectarian movements, denominations and cults which contributed to the remarkably amorphous and differentiated structure of the Hindu social body. As against this, the followers of Islam pursued the revealed truth located within a single text; and in doing so, they could in theory organize themselves into a cohesive macro-community, bound through allegiance to a corpus of common religious values.

Nobody knew better than Gandhi, if only because of the political movements which he had organized among peasants, workers and artisans, that the location of individuals in the cycle of social production generated both solidarities and differences. Precisely because of the marginality of their means of subsistence, industrial workers, artisans and kisans were closely drawn to each other since they had comparable interests and identities to protect in the cycle of social production and the subsequent distribution of the wealth thus generated. Conversely, the gulf between such subalterns and the middle classes was often almost next to impossible to bridge. Nevertheless, so well articulated was the commonality of economic interest in some instances between the subaltern classes, on the one hand, and the propertied classes, on the other, that these interests could link artisans and workers with the middle classes, and even entrepreneurs, across religious boundaries, even as they could generate intense conflict between the propertied and the propertyless within the communities of Islam and Hinduism.

Our brief survey of the dialectical character of solidarity and antagonism within Indian society can help us understand the success achieved by Gandhi when he addressed himself to the question of popular nationalism in the country. Here it is appropriate to recapitulate, very briefly, his trajectory in politics in the second decade of the twentieth century. As already suggested, Gandhi's journey across the length and breadth of India, in 1916, acquainted him fully with the extent to which the middle classes were drawn to nationalism. But in the next few years, the Mahatma also sensed the social anger of the subalterns, whether they were the mill workers of Ahmedabad or the *patidars* of Kheda or the tenants farmers of Champaran. The experience of social life of Ahmedabad, in particular, drove home the point that there were antagonisms within Indian society which it would not profit a political activist to stimulate in the course of the nationalist struggle. As against this, Gandhi felt that the Hindu-Muslim divide – a crucial divide within Indian society – was the most significant challenge facing a nationalist leader seeking to draw a unified country into the fight against British imperialism. As the Mahatma put it:

> There are two things to which I am devoting my life – permanent unity between Hindus and Muslims, and satyagraha. . . . The question that I have to answer this evening is: How can I help in having a Muslim question emerging out of the late war properly solved? . . . It may be asked why I, a Hindu, bother my head about the Muslim question. The answer is that as you are my neighbours and my countrymen, it is my duty to share your sorrow. I cannot talk about Hindu Muslim unity and fail to give effect to the idea when the test has arrived.

Perhaps the success in social mobilization which Gandhi achieved in the course of the Rowlatt Satyagraha of 1919 can be explained on the basis of the possibilities and pitfalls spelt out above. Any attempt to unite India solely on economic issues was unlikely to yield high dividends, for the valid reason that the interests of different classes and communities differed widely; and, indeed, often clashed with each other. Such considerations called for a moral issue as something much more likely to unite India than an economic issue. In the Rowlatt Act, which denied the people the most basic judicial rights, Gandhi located an issue with the far reaching implications which therefore would cement a grand nationalist alliance between Hindus, Muslims and Sikhs, on the one hand, and the rich and the poor, on the other.

Small wonder, then, that the strategy of nationalist politics, as pursued by Gandhi, brought about in the 1920s, 1930s and the 1940s, the most substantial political mobilization known to movements of national liberation in the first half of the twentieth century. At the height of the Gandhian agitations, roughly 10 per cent of the people of India were directly or indirectly drawn into nationalist politics. We can look at the success of Gandhian nationalism in yet another fashion. India consisted at this juncture of approximately half-a-million villages. Virtually every large village in the country – approximately one in the villages can be so described – became a centre of nationalist activity, and housed half-a-dozen substantial peasant households made up of nationalist activists and sympathizers.

When we dwell upon the striking success of the Gandhian agitations, we need also to take account of the mechanisms of political control located within the grand edifice of nationalist politics. At the outset, the political strategy of Gandhi privileged communitarian at the cost of class identities, thus leading to a situation wherein a heightened consciousness of distinctive religious identities became an integral part of the political scene. Over and above this, we need also to examine the mechanisms through which communitarian constituencies were actually drawn into nationalist agitations. As in the case of the Rowlatt Satyagraha, such mobilization was brought about through a minimum of political organization. Instead, the available power and influence of men and women dominantly located within different communities – religious, linguistic, or social – were increasingly utilized to draw the common folk into the ranks of nationalist activists. The political momentum generated through such organization therefore, was controlled by the dominant leadership of different communities, and it sought to sustain middle class interest at the expense of the interest of the poor and the deprived. Not surprisingly, therefore, although the poor and the deprived, whether they be peasants or artisans or workers or tribals, participated in large numbers in the nationalist agitations, effective power rested with well established elites rather than with the humbler folk. Hence August 1947 saw the creation of a truly sovereign India which was designed much more to sustain the middle class interest than to realize the heroic Gandhian vision of 'wiping the tears' of the poorest in the land.

THREE ❖ # The Jallianwala Bagh Tragedy: Its Impact on the Political Awakening and Thinking in India

SATYA M. RAI

THE CESSATION OF WORLD WAR I saw acute discontent among the people of Punjab since they suffered the most from the unsettling effects of the war, like unemployment and rising prices. Sir Michael O'Dwyer, the then Lieutenant Governor of Punjab, had pressed into service his entire administration including the 'judicial process' to collect money and recruit men for the war. By the end of 1916, Punjab had supplied 1,100,000 recruits out of the 1,92,000 fighting men raised in India. The Pathan areas contributed 14,000 and the rest of India (with eleven-twelfth of the population) only 68,000. The valour and heroism that the Punjabis displayed during the fighting won them spontaneous and glowing tributes from the British statesmen. They appreciated the unfaltering spirit of loyalty and sacrifice of the Punjabis.

CAUSES LEADING TO THE TRAGEDY

The year 1918–19, however, was one of several misfortunes in the country. With a stupendous rise in prices and steep increases in taxation, the situation worsened by speculation, blackmarketing and hoarding. Matters were further aggravated by natural calamities such as famine, plague and influenza which took a toll of over 8,000 people in the country. The hardship caused by the dislocation of economic life had a great impact on the political life in India. The Government of India, in general, and the Punjab administration in particular, feared that the return of a large number of soldiers, trained in highly sophisticated weaponry, could create a difficult situation in the existing circumstances. The introduction of the Rowlatt Bills in this situation added fuel to the fire. They were considered an outrage. The people condemned them as the 'Black Acts' designed to suppress the basic rights and stifle political life in India. Mahatma Gandhi described the Act as an 'unmistakable symptom of a deep-rooted disease in the Governing body'. People summed up the Bills in a cryptic phrase *na appeal, na dalil, na vakeel* (no appeal, no argument and no lawyer).

The economic situation, political discontent, Khilafat and the Rowlatt Bills created an explosive environment in the country and when Gandhiji gave a call for satyagraha on 25 February, 1919, it received nationwide support. The people of Punjab, distressed by the turn of events, evinced great enthusiasm for the movement as they were disgusted with the dictatorial rule of Michael O'Dwyer and wanted to break out of the British thraldom. On the call of Mahatma Gandhi, *hartals* were observed in several towns in Punjab under the leadership of Dr Satyapal and Dr Saifuddin Kitchlew. On 8 April, a Hindu-Muslim unity conference was held at Rewari which was considered to be 'the most sinister development of all' by the administrative authorities. The arrest of Gandhiji, who was coming to Punjab to direct the satyagraha movement, sent shock waves throughout the country and further inflamed the people of Punjab. Deportation of Dr Satyapal and Dr Kitchlew exacerbated the situation in the province. Firing on unarmed people who wanted to urge the Deputy Commissioner to release their leaders, infuriated the local people of Amritsar. The sight of the dead and the wounded people who were not allowed to be taken to hospital enraged a crowd who now got completely out of control. The mob entered upon a course of destruction, revenge, murder, arson and it also brutally assaulted any European, man or woman, it came across. They attacked the National and Alliance Banks, killed five to six Englishmen and set fire to the Town Hall, the Post Office, the Mission Hall and Bhagtanwala Railway Station and brutally assaulted Miss Sherwood. The resentment of the people at the deportation of their leaders, thus, took an ugly turn and was condemned by all responsible people. The situation would not have worsened, however, if the authorities had shown some understanding and sympathy for the people who had been provoked by the wanton and unjustifiable firing by the military. The news of the firing and the high-handedness of the military infuriated people in other parts of Punjab. Strikes were observed. The railway station was set on fire at Kasur, European passengers were attacked and government buildings were stoned. Similar reports came from Taran Taran, Gujranwala, Sangla and Lahore. The government panicked and instead of showing some restraint and understanding, Michael O'Dwyer, following instructions from the Centre, transferred control of Amritsar to the army under the command of General Dyer. The situation at Amritsar, according to the authorities, was 'extremely menacing.' The Lieutenant Governor observed that the 'rebel mobs were in complete possession of the city after 10 April and openly defiant' from the 10th to the 12th evening. Simultaneous outbreaks in various parts of the province, according to him, were a proof of a well-planned conspiracy against British rule. The Congress Enquiry Committee, however, described it as a spontaneous uprising of people in distress.

THE GREAT TRAGEDY

General Dyer issued a proclamation prohibiting all gatherings and meetings on the evening of 12 April 1919 but even the Hunter Committee admitted that no steps were taken to ensure that it would be read in all parts of the city. Simultaneously, the Congress volunteers were publicizing the meeting at Jallianwala Bagh. General Dyer took no measures to prevent the meeting which was held as scheduled. This gave him the much sought after opportunity. As Colvin puts it:

> This unexpected gift of fortune, this unhoped for defiance, this concentration of the rebels in an open space – it gave him such an opportunity as he could not have devised. It separated the guilty from the innocent, it placed them where he would have wished them to be, within the reach of his sword, the enemy had committed such another mistake as prompted Cromwell to exclaim at Dunbar, 'The lord hath delivered them into my hands.'

Yet it was not a 'concentration of rebels' as the General himself admitted before the Hunter Commission. People attending the annual fair of Baisakhi had strayed into the Bagh in a joyous mood and some boys came to play there. Swinson, an English journalist, by no means sympathetic to the nationalist opinion, admitted, '. . . hundreds of people were asleep in the sun; others were concentrating on their games of cards . . . a number of them had come with their children – 3 to 12 years old . . .'. Nearly twenty thousand people had gathered at Jallianwala Bagh, surrounded on all sides by houses and high walls with only four very narrow entrances.

When informed about the meeting by Superintendent Rehill at 4 p.m., General Dyer proceeded towards the meeting place with ninety soldiers and two armoured cars (which he had to leave outside on account of the narrow entrance). On arriving there, the troops took their position. By this time seven speakers had already spoken and two resolutions calling upon the government to repeal the Rowlatt Act and condemning the firing on the 10th evening, had been passed. The soldiers loaded their machine guns and Dyer ordered firing within thirty seconds of their arrival. Firing continued, according to various estimates, for 6 to 10 minutes. Altogether 1,650 rounds of ammunition were fired. The General stopped shooting only when ammunition had run out.

The crowds in panic, rushed towards the exits only to face a volley of bullets. Arthur Swinson gives a graphic account of the terrible scene:

> The result was horror: men screamed and went down to be trampled by those coming after. Some were hit again and again. In places the dead and wounded lay in heaps; men would go down wounded to find themselves immediately buried beneath a dozen others.

It is difficult to describe the details of the holocaust and the exact number of those killed in Jallianwala Bagh. But that General Dyer drew sadistic pleasure out of it is certain. According to official figures, 337 men, forty-one boys and a seven-week-old baby died and 1,500 were wounded. The unofficial figures, however, placed the dead between five to six hundred. No arrangements were made for the dead and the wounded because Dyer did not consider it to be 'his job'. 'They could go to hospital' was Dyer's succinct reply. No relief came to them for two days, except whatever could be done by the *Seva Samitis.* On account of the Martial Law which remained in force till 9 June and the curfew, the families and *Seva Samitis* could not do much for their unfortunate brethren after 8 p.m. Children, babes-in-arms, women, boys and elders lay there, soaked in their blood and surrounded by mangled limbs, with the April sun of Amritsar blazing fully on their faces and not a drop of water for the parched lips.

The tragedy of Jallianwala Bagh was followed by the proclamation of Martial Law on 15 April. During this period a number of orders were issued which made the life of the people of Amritsar and other four districts (Lahore, Gujranwala, Gujrat and Lyallpur) difficult. The Congress Enquiry Committee summed up the situation as follows:

(1) The street in which Miss Sherwood was assaulted was set apart for flogging people and for making those who passed through it to crawl on their bellies.

(2) All were made to *salaam,* in theory English officers only, but in practice every Englishman, on pain of being arrested and suffering indignities in case of non-implementation.

(3) Flogging was administrated publicly for trivialities.

(4) All the lawyers of the town were made special constables and some of them were made to work like ordinary coolies.

(5) Indiscriminate arrests were effected of persons irrespective of status and during detention they were subjected to humiliation, discomforts and indiscriminate tortures for the purpose of extorting confession or evidence, or for the purpose of merely humiliating them.

(6) Special tribunals were formed for trying offences, which resulted in

> gross injustice in the name of law, leaving the aggrieved parties without a right to appeal.

Following the Jallianwala Bagh massacre, the government feared widespread resentment among the people. The Government of India, consequently gave approval to enforce Martial Law due to the existence of open rebellion against the authority of government. This fear was, however, misplaced. Even the Hunter Committee strongly disapproved of O'Dwyer's arguments in defence of Martial Law as there was no case of serious disorder, they felt, after 15 April. The Punjab Government itself agreed that the situation had returned to normal in the greater part of the province.

For two months, from 10 April upto the withdrawal of Martial Law, the administration wanted to humiliate the people of Punjab and 'teach them a lesson' for daring to 'revolt' against the British Government. The travails of the people of Punjab during this period need not be narrated but they had a far-reaching impact on the political life of the country and the people of Punjab.

IMPACT OF THE MASSACRE

As the news of the harrowing events at Amritsar and other places in the Punjab reached other parts of India after the withdrawal of the Martial Law and censorship, there was an outcry against the oppressive nature of the British administration. Protest meetings were held all over the country, condemning the 'reign of terror' in Punjab. The Congress condemned the 'cold blooded, calculated massacre of innocent men and children – an act without parallel in modern times . . .'. Resolutions were passed at various meetings condemning every act of tyranny perpetrated on the people of Punjab before and during the Martial Law and authorities were asked to punish the officers responsible for these heinous deeds. Forced by the pressure of public opinion, the British Government appointed an Enquiry Committee under the chairmanship of Lord Hunter to investigate the circumstances of firing in various cities in Punjab during the period of Martial Law. Opposing the composition of the Hunter Committee, the Congress appointed its own Committee under the chairmanship of Pandit Motilal Nehru. The Hunter Committee, in its findings declared its inability to agree on the necessity of the Martial Law, for its continuance for such a long time and on the severity of the Martial Law administration. The people in India, however, found the Hunter Committee's findings totally unsatisfactory and inadequate. They criticized Michael O'Dwyer's attempts to justify the heinous deeds of his administration on the plea that there was an organized rebellion in Punjab – an argument with which the Hunter Committee seemed to agree. Even Lord Montagu admitted that

General Dyer 'was not entitled to select the condign punishment on the unarmed crowd'. The national protest was voiced by one of India's greatest poets, Rabindranath Tagore, through his famous letter renouncing his knighthood:

> The time has come when badges of honour make our shame glaring in their incongruous context by humiliation, and I, for my part, wish to stand shorn of all special distinction by the side of those of my countrymen who for their so-called insignificance, are liable to suffer a degradation not fit for human beings, and these are the reasons which have painfully compelled me to ask Your Excellency, with due deference and regret, to release me of my title of knighthood.

The people in the country, shocked at the barbarous attitude of the Punjab administration, while condemning the 'massacre' in the strongest terms through meetings and resolutions, also tried to assuage the sufferings of the families of the persons who were killed during these 'black days' Men and women contributed generously to the 'Jallianwala Bagh Massacre Fund'. When Dr Satyapal was collecting funds for this purpose, a boy, just nine years old, took a letter to him from his aunt with a gold ornament and a few clothes as a contribution for the fund. Numerous moving instances such as the one as this, can be cited to prove, if any proof is needed, of the sympathy and concern of the people.

While the people of India expressed their disapproval of General Dyer's brutal action, the lead actor of the sordid drama was given a hero's welcome in London as the 'Saviour of India'. The editor of the *Morning Post* collected £ 30,000 which was awarded to Dyer in recognition of the 'services to the Empire'. The Tories of Britain and the majority of the members of the House of Lords rallied round General Dyer to defend him from any adverse government action. They condemned the procedure by which the General had been censured. The Army Council which took up Dyer's case, charged him only with an error of judgement and recommended his retirement on half pay with no prospect of future employment. The British Court of Justice, however, exonerated him later of even this charge. But Winston Churchill, the Secretary of State for War, described the Jallianwala episode as 'an episode which appeared to be without any parallel in the modern history of the British empire.'

There were also sections even in Punjab who failed to react against the massacre of innocent people at Jallianwala Bagh. The Government-appointed manager of the Golden Temple baptised General Dyer as a Sikh and presented him a *saropa* (a robe of honour) after the Amritsar tragedy. Raja Narendra Nath in an address on behalf of 'the Hindu community' expressed his firm belief that a 'benign providence' had brought India under British protection. Speaking in the Legislative House on the occasion of farewell to Michael O'Dwyer, he observed:

> We are very sorry that foolish and mischievous acts of certain misguided men made the last few days of Your Honour's career specially strenuous. We condemn most emphatically all acts of violence and lawlessness and we much deplore the damage done to private and state property.

Umar Hayat Khan regretted that Martial Law had not been imposed earlier. Syed Mehdi Shah, claiming to speak on the occasion on behalf of the Muslims, said:

> Although towards the conclusion of Your Honour's brilliant regime, the enemies of law and order, as a result of organized conspiracy, succeeded in deluding a section of the people into riots and disturbances, yet it is a standing tribute to Your Honour's far-sighted statesmanship and firmness that the situation was soon got well in hand by using the speedy and effective method of Martial Law and peaceful life is once more possible for the law abiding citizens of our chief towns.

Sardar Sunder Singh Majithia, claiming to be the spokesman of the Sikhs, also praised Michael O'Dwyer's repressive administration in these words:

> It is a matter of regret that at the close of Your Honour's successful regime a mischievous attempt has been made by some evilly disposed persons to ruthlessly disturb the peace of the land, and in several places atrocities have been committed which have besmeared the unsullied name of the province, but Your Honour's firm grasp of the situation and the measures adopted have nipped the evil in the bud.

The insulated minds of the Punjab councillors, thus, remained closed to the sufferings of the people of Punjab. These 'worthy' councillors had not uttered a single word of sympathy for their compatriots, nor a word of condemnation for the Jallianwala Bagh massacre or for the atrocities committed during the Martial Law administration. On the contrary, they blamed the nationalist sections for disturbing the law and order situation in the province. Nevertheless, a change occurred among some of the legislators who were re-elected during the 1921 elections when a new electoral process was introduced under the system of Dyarchy.

POLITICAL DEVELOPMENTS IN INDIA FOLLOWING THE MASSACRE

The massacre of innocent people at Jallianwala Bagh, however, evoked unprecedented resentment among the people and proved a turning point in the political history of India. The Indian National Congress held a special session at Amritsar at the end of December in 1919 where it condemned the veritable reign of terror at Amritsar. The happenings in Punjab were responsible to a large extent in changing Mahatma Gandhi's attitude towards the Montagu-Chelmsford Reforms (initially he was in favour of accepting them with some reservations) as well as the technique of the freedom struggle. It was now resolved that the Reforms were 'inadequate, unsatisfactory and disappointing'. As a protest against the Jallianwala Bagh tragedy, he returned his Kaiser-i-Hind title. In a letter to the Viceroy, on 8 June 1919, the Mahatma wrote:

> The awful experience of the past two months and a half have shown me that there is nothing save satyagraha of which civil disobedience is an integral part, that can possibly save India from Bolshevism and even a worse fate. . . .

The atrocities of 1919 had shaken the whole nation. C.F. Andrews in a letter to Mr Haig had written that 'the weapon of the police, like a sharp knife, will turn in the executive hand and cut too deeply for any patchwork remedy.' He wrote of unmentionable things like 'stripping men and women naked and exposing them to unbearable shame' of which he had first hand knowledge in Punjab in 1919. Punjab was burdened by this sense of utter humiliation. The situation was explosive. Some action was imperative. Mahatma Gandhi, recognizing this, announced the Non-cooperation Movement in 1920 which was endorsed by the Congress in September 1920.

The Muslims were also as enthusiastic about the Satyagraha Movement. Though the Khilafat Movement had been started as a protest against the treatment given to the Sultan of Turkey after the end of the World War I, the Khilafat leaders of Punjab Dr Saifuddin Kitchlew, Niaz Hasan and Maulvi Daud exhorted the people to rise against the British in the wake of the Jallianwala Bagh massacre and the atrocities committed during Martial Law. Niaz Hasan, in a speech on 19 June at Ferozepur, said:

> Hindus and Mohammadans had helped the Government with men and money during the war and had been given the Rowlatt Act as a reward for their services. When they questioned the gift, they had been shot down. . . .

The people were, thus, completely disillusioned about the intentions of the British rulers. The Jallianwala Bagh episode had shattered the tradition of loyalty and anyone who was with the government was called a traitor. M.A. Jinnah called the Jallianwala Bagh massacre a 'physical butchery' and to Motilal Nehru it was the 'saddest' incident. The Jallianwala Bagh tragedy also shocked many world leaders. From distant Russia, Lenin sent a message of sympathy to the people of India after reading the dreadful account of the massacre at Amritsar. Condemning the carnage, the Ghadar Party in USA wrote:

> Dyer is not an isolated character in British imperialism. Massacre of unarmed people, outrage on women, use of children as fodders of cannon are not new plans in the British system . . . history bristles with glowing examples of misdeeds, inhuman activities, ruthless repression, oppression and persecution wherever the British have gone.

The working class and the youth were also not unaffected by the Punjab events. There were a number of strikes during the period. There was a rise in terrorist and revolutionary movements all over India and particularly in Punjab such as the Babbar Akali movement and later the Hindustan Republic Association and the Nau Jawan Saba. The Gurdwara Reform Movement also received an impetus from the prevailing anti-British mood of the people. The unity between the members of the three communities unnerved the Punjab administration once again.

Punjab which had not been the nerve-centre of the nationalist movement so far, had now become the centre of the anti-British upsurge. The Congress session attracted 36,000 people. Prominent leaders such as Bal Gangadhar Tilak, Bipin Chandra Pal, Srinivas Sastri, M.A. Jinnah, Pandit Ram Bhaj Datta, Dr Saifuddin Kitchlew, Lala Harkishan Lal, Dr Satyapal, S.R. Bomanjee, Mohammad Ali and Saukat Ali and several others attended the session which was presided over by Lala Lajpat Rai. The focus of discussions at this session was the criticism of the Reforms, wrongs done in Punjab and Khilafat. The resolution on the Jallianwala Bagh massacre, moved in the Subject Committee, condemned the massacre and the mad frenzy of the crowds during the Amritsar riots. The latter part of the resolution, however, had to be initially dropped on account of disapproval by the majority of members. But later on, the resolution was accepted in its original form owing to Gandhi's persuasion.

The Congress adopted fifty resolutions at the Amritsar session. They demanded action against the oppressive regime of Michael O'Dwyer and Lord Chelmsford as well as their recall and asked for exemplary punishment for General Dyer and other officials. They pleaded that fines and indemnities, which had already been recovered by the administration, should be returned. They advocated the release of political prisoners who were still in jails despite the Royal proclamation for their release (during the Martial Law, 108 people were sentenced to death and 7,371 were awarded various periods of imprisonment in Punjab). In their speeches, the speakers emphasized the need for further cementing the relations between the Hindus and the Muslims.

Encouraged by the ferment in the province, the Punjab Congress leaders tried to mobilize the people in the anti-British freedom struggle. The Khilafat and Akali movements had added to the mass unrest in Punjab.

IMPACT ON THE PUNJAB COUNCILLORS

When the province was thus in the grip of one of the severest economic, political and moral crises, the loyalist elements were preparing to contest the new elections and enter the Punjab Legislative Council as 'representatives of the people'. The All India Congress Committee had appealed to the Congress members to boycott elections and the people to desist from voting. The appeal had a profound effect in Punjab when the new Legislative Council met at the beginning of 1921. The memories of the massacre of Jallianwala Bagh and the preceding and following atrocities were too fresh in the minds of the people to accept the working of the Reforms uncritically. The Non-cooperation and the Khilafat Movements and the resultant upsurge made the people conscious of the unworthy role played by the loyalist elements in abetting the foreign rule. Even before the elections the councillors were able to gauge the changing mood and a man like Syed Makhdum Rajan Shah who swore by his loyalty to the King Emperor, had said on 8 March 1920 that the days of *Sat Bachan* and *Ji Hazoor* were over. The resolution moved by Fazl-i-Hussain for the release of political prisoners was supported by all the Indian members. The new Executive Council consisting of Fazl-i-Hussain, Harikishan Lal, Chaudhri Chhotu Ram and Sunder Singh Majitha were, therefore, faced with the difficult task of working according to the Reform Scheme in spite of the political preferences of the country. The elected members of the Council, who were meeting under the shadow of the Jallianwala Bagh massacre, the Martial Law and Non-cooperation Movement, had to take certain immediate steps to save their image from being tarnished as stooges of the British rulers. As they were no longer nominated members, they were acquainted with the mood of the people in the province. The Indian members in the Council were agitated by the question of indemnity realized by the municipal committees of various towns to compensate the victims of riots and for the maintenance of a punitive force. The callousness of the Government of Punjab was made evident when it rendered immediate help to the European riot victims while the Indian victims of the Jallianwala Bagh massacre received no support or sympathy. There was blatant racial discrimination as is clear from the following figures:

Total amount paid to Europeans in Punjab (Amritsar only)	Rs 4,99,905–13–4
Amount paid as compensation to the relations of the Europeans killed at Amritsar	Rs 400,321–26
Amount paid to dependents of Indians killed at Jallianwala Bagh	Rs 11,56,092–4–4

The highest amount in case of Europeans given to Mrs Stewart was Rs 20,000 and in case of Indians it was only Rs 500.

It may be noted that the number of Europeans killed during the riots on 10 April was only six, while the Indians killed was 379, and that too according to official estimates.

Diwan Narendra Nath (Raja) (who had condemned the upsurge in Punjab as 'mischievous' in the previous Legislative Council) questioned the procedure adopted in assessing compensation and the expenditure on maintenance of punitive police. Mian Mohammad Shah Niwaz moved a resolution on 16 March 1921, recommending an amnesty for all those convicted under Martial Law in Punjab. The proposal was, however, not accepted by the Government. Under the Royal Proclamation of general amnesty, many of the political workers had been released, but the terms of persons guilty of isolated acts of murder and arson were not reduced. Shah Niwaz criticized the Government's policy of differentiating between the leaders and the followers who had committed certain crimes under provocation. He, therefore, demanded amnesty for all. Supporting the resolution Atma Ram asked:

> Is the government aware that Martial Law prisoners, notwithstanding their conviction by the Martial Law courts, are still regarded as innocent by a large section of the people of the Punjab? In view of this feeling and in order to allay the public excitement and discontent, will the government be pleased immediately to give amnesty to the rest of the Martial Law prisoners who are still undergoing sentence?

Raja Narendra Nath supporting Shah Niwaz's resolution on the appointment of a committee to recommend the remission or reduction of sentences, wanted it also to consider (a) which official actions during the Martial Law regime should be compensated and (b) what compensation should be paid in each case. He observed that despair and discontent reigned supreme in the province, which was largely responsible for the current ferment in the country. Compelled by the general mood of the people, even men like Narendra Nath were constrained to observe on the floor of the House that 'Swaraj is the only radical remedy' to cure the deep-seated disease from which the body politic was suffering.

Speaking on the resolution, Shah Niwaz Khan said:

> Sir, the wound inflicted during the Martial Law days is too deep. It is still painful . . . Sir we cannot soothe the suffering, humiliation, bereavement and injustice suffered by the inhabitants of this unfortunate province by mere words. Something practical must be done. If the government sincerely desires to heal the old sores, to strengthen the old ties, to remove bitter memories and associations, to create mutual confidence of goodwill, it must compensate the victims of Martial Law.

The resolution was supported by Ganpat Rai, Uttam Chand, Sewa Ram and others, but opposition came from Mohammad Akbar Khan, Daulat Ram Kalia, Fazl Ali, Firoz Khan, and some others. The resolution though passed during the first reading, was lost after John Maynard's reply.

Following the strong protests by the non-official members, an Indemnity Bill was rushed through the Imperial Council under which the officials in India could be dealt with, but only departmentally, for acts of excesses and abuse of authority. The Act made it difficult for the general people of India to sue General Dyer and the Martial Law administrators in Indian courts.

The authorities were, thus, not willing to yield to popular demand. But after the upsurge in Punjab following the Jallianwala Bagh massacre, the Martial Law atrocities and the elections on the basis of the Act of 1919, the members of the Council had developed a new confidence. The members who moved or supported the resolution regarding indemnity or treatment of political prisoners, were neither connected with the Congress nor the Non-cooperation Movement. Many of them were, in fact, critical of the Congress and were known loyalists. They were moderates politically and most of them belonged to the landed aristocracy. But the introduction of the principle of elective majority in the Council and the limited transfer of power to the responsible ministers, brought about a change in the tenor of speeches of certain members. The sufferings of the people of Punjab during the year 1919–20 and the political awakening seen among the people after the Jallianwala Bagh massacre and during the Non-cooperation Movement could not leave even these members completely unaffected. Giving expression to this change, Raja Narendra Nath pointed out:

> We are at the commencement of a new era, and in the words of a high authority, Lord Chelmsford, the time of autocracy has ended and that of democracy has begun. Now the two essential features of democratic government are that it is a government of the people through their representatives.

The Councillors were conscious, of course, about the limitations of the new constitution and their own limited powers and representative capacity. Outside they were being criticized by the nationalist forces as traitors to the cause of the national movement. But it must be noted that these members were, to an extent, responsible for putting pressure on the authorities for the release of political prisoners, provision compensation to the victims of the Jallianwala Bagh massacre and Martial Law as well as the question of 'indemnity'. These issues engaged the attention of the members throughout the Council's first term in addition to the problems of communalism. Thus, even the Councillors, with limited representative capacity, could not remain unaffected by the political upsurge in the province following the Jallianwala Bagh massacre.

The Jallianwala Bagh massacre, one of the most heinous crimes of the British administrators in Punjab, stirred the consciousness of the people of India in general and of the people in Punjab in particular. By Mahatma Gandhi's own admission, it was one of the most crucial events which changed him from a cooperator of the British administration to a non-cooperator. And this change in him was responsible for ushering in an era of mass upsurge and the first ever mass movement in India. It was also on account of these tragic events that Punjab which had, by and large, remained aloof from the mainstream national political unrest, played a notable part in the subsequent Non-cooperation Movement, Khilafat and Akali Lahar.

FOUR ❖

The Imperial Terrorism in Punjab: Its Nature and Implications (1919–25)

GURSHARAN SINGH

TO STUDY AND EVALUATE terrorism in terms of its nature and implication is a task which requires understanding of the divergent forces and urges working at cross purposes. Firstly, the word terrorism may mean different things to different people and secondly, being a purely subjective phenomenon it may prove to be incapable of its evaluation in objective terms. Moreover its quantitative aspect has to be understood within a backdrop of time, space and prevalent environment. The imperial terrorism which Punjab had witnessed right from the days of its annexation down to 1947 has had its variegated dimensions. This imperial strategy, rebellion against which gripped the masses, during the years 1919–25, can be termed as a state-organized system of intimidation with the active use of bullets, bombs, mental agony, physical torture, the denial of personal freedom and the freedom of association. This strategy was aimed at the consolidation of the imperial hold on the people of the region who were a potential threat to their rule. By another definition, terrorism can be defined as 'deliberate and systematic murder, maiming and menacing of the innocent to inspire fear for political ends.'

The freedom struggle in the Punjab presents the spectrum of an increasing participation of the masses in the movement ever since it was annexed in 1849. At the core, its people continued to nurture distrust and resentment towards the foreign rulers who soon after the Revolt of 1857 saw an eruption in northern India in the shape of the Kuka Movement. The Kukas, who claimed to be the protector of the cow, killed some butchers. They were hanged or sentenced to transportation for life. Incensed with rage, the Kuka raided Malodh and Malerkotla with the motive of acquiring weapons. All the raiders were rounded up; seventy-five of them were shot to death by cannons and their chief and some of their *subas* were exiled or banished.

In the years that followed (1900–19), the process of socio-religious transformation released by the reform movement had produced an active and educated middle class. They prepared the people of Punjab for a new phase of national political activity. The members of this class were greatly influenced by the contemporary events in and around India. They had also imbibed the feeling of patriotism.[1] The government in 1901 and 1906 had alienated both the business community and the landholders by passing the Land Alienation Act 1901, by raising the irrigation rates in the Bari Doab Canal Colonies and by tailoring the rights of cultivators with the intention of reducing them to the status of tenants. The result was the beginning of agrarian unrest. The peasant disaffection infiltrated into the ranks of the army. The imminent celebration, in 1901, of the Golden Jubilee of the Revolt of 1857 made the government apprehensive of a popular revolt. Suspecting that Lala Lajpat Rai and Ajit Singh would be the brains behind such a movement, they were whisked away from the scene.

The period from 1909 to 1913 was of comparative silence and tranquillity. However, it proved to be a lull before the storm. The rise of the Ghadar Movement soon after the outbreak of the First World War imparted a new dimension to the freedom movement in Punjab. In 1914 the episode of Komagata Maru occurred in which 18 persons were gunned down and 25 wounded at the Budge Budge Harbour in Calcutta.[2] The incident was followed by the Ghadarites call to the Punjabis settled in USA, Canada and South East Asia to return to India to liberate it from the foreign yoke. To fulfil their mission, the Ghadarites began their journey to India in large numbers. The British Government with the help of its wide net of agents, came to know about the plan. Acting quickly and resorting to repression, it rounded up most of the insurgents, sentenced eighteen of them to death, out of whom twelve were executed. The Government, in order to dispense with the others, passed the Defence of India Act. Summary trials of all suspects of the Lahore Conspiracy Case were instituted. Out of them 46 were sentenced to death, 194 were awarded transportation for life, and 93 were sentenced to varying terms of imprisonment.[3]

It may be recalled that during the years 1914–18 the British Government in its endeavour to secure the maximum number of recruits for war from Punjab, resorted to repressive measures. Recruiting durbars were held in the districts under the chairmanship of local British officials and prominent public men were persuaded to assist them in getting young men from schools, colleges and the peasantry.[4] The Punjab was made to supply nearly 4 lakhs of recruits. According to O'Dwyer, the Punjab was made to strain every nerve in the cause of recruitment and was almost exhausted towards the close of war.[5]

Evidence shows that the oppressiveness of this government was a terror for locals. Men were captured forcibly from villages, they were tortured and stripped naked in the presence of their womenfolk. Prisoners were often released on bail to assist recruitment.[6] People were exhorted to offer recruits and when they did not do so, warrants were issued against them. Persuasion, threats and concealed brutality, were all used to secure the recruits.

The complete victory of Great Britain and the Allies over the Central Powers and Turkey appeared to establish a more secure footing for the empire.

The exceptionally unstable political condition of India increased the severe economic strains under which the country was suffering as a result of the contribution it was compelled to make in the war effort. High prices of the daily necessities was a major cause of general unrest in Punjab. The lower middle class and labouring classes were in serious economic distress. In 1919 indigenous products as a whole registered an increase in prices equal almost to that of imported articles. In 1918, famine swept the Punjab. Food riots broke out in Lyalpur, Karnal, Pathankot and elsewhere in India. The urban population was hit by the imposition of a special income-tax – the increase of which in some cases ranged from 100 to 200 per cent.[7] To cap it all, an epidemic of influenza raged across the entire province taking a heavy toll of life.

India, as stated above, supported the Empire in its war against Germany. Its people had contributed to the war effort in terms of both money and men. For this effort they had endured the hardships of food scarcity, rising prices, increased taxation, the restriction of press freedom and the curtailment of personal liberty. After the war they hoped for freedom and liberty. The Imperial Government had promised Home Rule by phases, but instead it imposed on them the Rowlatt Acts.

"The White Sahib, who had governed India since the days of the Mutiny . . . failed to understand the strength of Indian hopes of self-government or to perceive the depth of Indian detestation of the 'Rowlatt' Acts."[8]

The Acts, aroused a storm of opposition 'unknown before in India' and according to the Congress Sub-Committee, these Acts were an outrage upon society.

An atmosphere of disillusionment and depression came to prevail upon the province. When the people needed succour and reassurance, a balm to soothe their nerves, the government rubbed salt into their wounds.

Restrictive measures introduced during the war were not withdrawn; on the contrary, legislation of a more drastic nature was planned. Sir Michael O'Dwyer, Lieutenant Governor of the Punjab, discounted the notion of self-government for India as a preposterous figment of the mind of the urbanite babu and the wog barrister.[9] He prohibited nationalist leaders from entering the province and took stern measures to repress any form of agitation against the Rowlatt Bills which were intended to combat revolutionary crime. In the Punjab, Rowlatt came to be known as 'raula' (turmoil).

O'Dwyer was a firm believer in strongarm tactics and made no secret of his views on the political reforms beings demanded. He gave severe warnings to the press which were followed by action under the Press Act. He even prevented entry of newspapers like *New India, Amrita Bazar Patrika* and *Independent* into Punjab. These harsh and oppressive measures and the persecution of political leaders kept the resentment not only alive but ready to break into flames. O'Dwyer scented danger in every honest and patriotic speech made by the leaders and detected conspiracy in all gatherings and associations.

When the Rowlatt Report was published, the people felt extremely bitter about it as it was a calculated move designed to curb their aspirations. The British Government projected a distorted image of the Indian national movement as a sum-total of dacoities, robberies, arsons and murders. It argued that the politically conscious middle class was the source of all trouble and danger to society and a threat to the law and order in India. The Rowlatt Report was an index of the imperial mind. The Government by passing this Bill wanted to be armed. It also wanted to create a sense of fear and terror among the masses hoping this would make them disassociate themselves from the nationalists. The nationalists considered this Bill to be an example of an arrogant bureaucracy subjecting Indians to the rod. The Acts were designed to crush and terrorize Indians, so that they would be the slaves of the British for ever.

These circumstances compelled Mahatma Gandhi to launch the Satyagraha Movement on 1 March 1919. In the Satyagraha pledge, Gandhi wrote:

> Being conscientiously of the opinion that the Bills, known as the Indian Criminal Law (Amendment) Bill No. 1 of 1919 and Criminal Law (Emergency Powers) Bill No. 2 of 1919, are unjust, subversive of the principles of liberty and justice, and destructive of the elementary rights of an individual on which the safety of India as a whole and the State itself is based, we solemnly affirm that in the event of these bills becoming law and until they are withdrawn, we shall refuse civility to obey these laws and such other laws as the committee to be hereafter appointed may think fit and we further affirm that in the struggle we will faithfully follow truth and refrain from violence to life, person or property.[10]

Michael O'Dwyer was perhaps the keenest among the British bureaucrats to stage a showdown on the satyagrahis. He wanted to protect himself with the cloak of legal justification for his intended repression. He sought the advice of Legal Remembrance as to whether the Satyagraha Movement was legal. The legal opinion came to suggest that the Satyagraha Movement was a criminal conspiracy according to Section 120-A of the Indian Penal Code. Even *hartals* organized without intimidation or force were illegal, because they created disaffection towards the government.[11]

The above opinion gave the British bureaucracy an excuse for treating even a perfectly peaceful and legal movement as illegal and to use force to crush it.

As the agitation against the Acts intensified, the cry 'No *vakil* (lawyer), no *daleel* (argument), no *appeal*' echoed throughout Punjab. O'Dwyer sniffed the scent of rebellion in the air. He was determined to suppress it before it got out of control. Gandhi's soul force, he said contemptuously, would be met with 'fist force'.[12] A *hartal* took place on 30 March in Amritsar. Meetings at the Jallianwala Bagh were attended by people in their thousands urging the King Emperor to withhold his Royal Assent to the Rowlatt Acts.

Mahatma Gandhi announced his Civil Disobedience Movement to start on 7 April 1919.[13] On 9 April Gandhi was stopped at Palwal and his entry into Punjab was banned. At Amritsar the police opened fire to disperse crowds. On 10 April Dr Satyapal and Dr S.D. Kitchlew were arrested and detained. The people rose in angry protest and were fired upon by the police. Twelve of them were killed. The mob in fury retaliated and killed senior officers of the banks. Miss Sherwood was also beaten up and injured.

In Lahore and in other places also processionists were fired upon. There was a sizeable number of casualties. In Amritsar on 11 April the Deputy Commissioner read the following order to a large crowd:[14]

> The troops have orders to restore order in Amritsar, and to use all the force necessary. No gatherings of persons, no procession of any sort will be allowed. All gatherings will be fired on. Any person leaving the city, or persons gathering in groups of more than four, will be fired on. Respectable persons should keep indoors until order is restored.

On the 11th morning the Deputy Commissioner informed the people that the city was under military occupation.[15] Some officers suggested bombing the city but G.A. Wathen, the Principal of Khalsa College warned them that such an action would result in a general revolt among the Sikh soldiers because of the city's religious character. On the 12th and the 13th April the city remained peaceful till the afternoon.[16] But according to O'Dwyer, Amritsar was in a state of 'tumult and revolt'.[17] Electricity and water connections all over the city were cut off. The Deputy Commissioner thought that the British were confronted with their gravest crisis since the Mutiny of 1857.[18]

On the afternoon of 13 April 1919, Brigadier-General Dyer led his soldiers through the streets of Amritsar to Jallianwala Bagh where the people had gathered in defiance of his proclamation banning such gatherings. Within seconds of his arrival, Dyer ordered his men to open fire. The firing continued for ten minutes. Dyer ordered fire to be focused where the crowd was thickest, including the narrow exits. The firing was stopped only when they ran out of ammunition. According to the official figures, 379 people were gunned down and over 1,200 wounded; Indian estimates are much higher.

Twenty thousand people were caught beneath the hail of bullets all of them frantically trying to escape from the quiet meeting place which had suddenly become a burning hell.[19]

Many of the wounded tried to crawl out of the Bagh and with great difficulty reached the lanes and streets, but unable to move further, they fell all over and a large number of them died in the streets 'in pools of their own blood.'[20]

Reporting to the General Staff Division on 25 August 1919, General Dyer wrote:[21]

> I fired and continued to fire till the crowd dispersed, and I considered that this is the least amount of firing which would produce the necessary moral and widespread effort it was my duty to produce if I was to justify my action. If more troops had been at hand the casualties would have been greater in proportion. It was no longer a question of merely dispersing the crowd, but one of producing a sufficient moral effect, from a military point of view, not only on those who were present, but more specially throughout the Punjab. There could be no question of undue severity.

In a reply to a question by the Hunter Committee, Dyer said,[22] 'I had made up mind that I will do all men to death if they were going to continue the meeting.'

The reply, clearly explains that the main aim of the imperial bureaucracy in indulging in this massacre was to strike terror all over the Punjab.

Even a few days before his death, Dyer told some of his friends that 'if he were to re-act the Amritsar case a million times he would always give the same order to fire'.[23]

Everyone in the administration, it seemed, was pleased with Dyer. He issued a proclamation permitting the burial or the burning of the dead and he made an order drafting the court barristers of the city to act as special constables to maintain order. Dyer visited the city and addressed the citizens:[24]

> You people know well that I am a soldier and a military man. You want war or peace? And if you wish for war, the government is prepared for war. And if you want peace, then obey my orders, and open all your shops, else I will shoot. For me the battlefield of France or Amritsar is the same. . . . You people talk against the government, and persons educated in Germany and Bengal talk sedition. I will uproot them all. Obey orders. I do not wish to hear anything else. I have served in the military for over thirty years. I understand the Indian sepoy and Sikh people very well. You will have to observe peace, otherwise the shops will be opened perforce with rifles. You all must inform me of the *badmashes.* I will shoot them. Obey my orders and open shops and speak up if you want war.

In a speech made by the Deputy Commissioner, he said,[25] 'You have committed a bad act in killing the English. Their revenge will be taken from you and from your children.'

On 15 April 1919, Martial Law was imposed on Amritsar and four other districts of the Punjab. At O'Dwyer's behest, it was backdated to 30 March, in order 'to deal appropriately with the local leaders whose speeches during the preceding fortnight did so much to inflame classes who have joined the disturbances.'[26] Of the 852 accused, 581 were convicted; 108 were sentenced to death, and 264 (including Kitchlew and Satyapal convicted on the testimony of an official approver)[27] to transportation for life. There was no appeal. On protestation, sentences were commuted by the Royal Proclamation in December 1919. But by then eighteen men had been publicly hanged.[28]

In the summary courts flogging was the normal punishment. In about half the cases it was done publicly. European spectators used to urge the wielder of the cane enthusiastically to strike harder. A wedding party was flogged for being an illegal gathering and a group of men were whipped before an audience of prostitutes for visiting brothels during curfew.[29]

Collective punishments were widely imposed. As stated earlier, water and electricity supplies in Amritsar were not restored. Vehicles, including bicycles, were commandeered; so were fans, for the relief of soldiers. The issue of third and intermediate class rail tickets was suspended, effectively barring Indians from the railways. Students were forced to march upto seventeen miles a day in the sun. At places peasants were forbidden to harvest their crops.

Planes were flown to terrorize the people in rural areas. Bombs were dropped on the people in villages in Gujranwala district. Machine guns were fired, killing and injuring many. The Hunter Committee, considering the decision to use aeroplanes at Gujranwala, found the act justified as it was done with the object of saving the lives of Europeans. It did not impute blame on the officer for his decision taken in the air and at that moment, the committee did not feel certain that the machine gunning of villagers was necessary.[30]

'Crawling Order' was imposed on people using the street in which Miss Sherwood had been assaulted. Dyer gave orders for some Indians to be taken into custody for their failing to *salaam* him. They were brought into the street and lashed. A triangle was erected in the lane and the whipping was witnessed by its residents, several of whom told the Congress Sub-Committee what they had seen, corroborating each other with every detail.

Six Indians who were implicated in the assault case were stripped naked, fastened to the triangle and given thirty blows with a heavy cane. All were bleeding profusely when they were dragged away by the soldiers.[31]

Whipping under Martial Law Regulations was carried out in Lahore (80), Kasur (85), Chuharkan (40), Gujranwala (24), Gujrat (3) and Amritsar (38).

Complaints were made of excessive and brutal punishment, wrongful and illegal arrests, 'frame-ups', blackmail to induce false evidence, long internments without charges, intimidation and harsh treatment in prison.[32]

General Campbell's *salaaming* order in Gujranwala – opened with the statement, 'whereas it has come to my notice that certain inhabitants are habitually exhibiting a lack of respect', required all Indians riding in any conveyance to alight and those carrying umbrellas to lower them and to salute all officers with the hand. At Kasur, minor offenders of curfew orders were asked to skip and compose poems in praise of Martial Law and by touching the ground with their foreheads.[33]

O'Dwyer in his bid to explain his conduct during the Martial Law tried to hoodwink world opinion by synchronizing the Jallianwala Bagh massacre with the war on the North West Frontier in May 1919. 'The rebellion', as he described the disorders in the Punjab 'were considered to be the result of an organized conspiracy.'[34]

Leonard Mosley in his book, *The Last Days of the British Raj,* states,[35] 'What is certain is that the Amritsar shootings turned most Indians, including those who had cooperated willingly before, into resentful and mistrustful minors, conscious that the British who ruled them regarded their lives as unimportant and their race as inferior'. He calls the Jallianwala Bagh 'the greatest recruiting poster for Congress ever to be waved before the Indian people.' He says they joined up in their thousands. Jawaharlal Nehru then aged thirty recalls in his autobiography:[36]

> Towards the end of that year (1919) I travelled from Amritsar to Delhi by the night train. . . . In the morning I discovered that all my fellow passengers were military officers. They conversed with each other in loud voices which I could not help overhearing. One of them was holding forth in an aggressive and triumphant tone and soon I discovered that he was Dyer, the hero of Jallianwala Bagh, and he was describing his Amritsar experiences. He pointed out how he had the whole town at his mercy and he felt like reducing the rebellious city to a heap of ashes, but he took pity on it and refrained. He was evidently returning from Lahore after giving his evidence before the Hunter Committee Enquiry. I was greatly shocked to hear his conversation and to observe his callous manner. . .

Despite Gandhi's popular following among the illiterate masses, the Congress following was still small in numbers and confined to the educated English-speaking Indians. What changed this situation was Amritsar. It really was a far greater recruiting slogan than any that Congress could have invented for itself. It provided a focus, a rallying point. It was a word which, once uttered could bring to the boil all Indian feelings of patriotism, political aspiration and hatred.[37]

General Dyer in his endeavour to win over the Sikhs called the manager[38] of the Golden Temple. He and his Brigade Major were made honorary Sikhs at a ceremony in the Golden Temple. The account of the actual ceremony, as given by Colvin, his biographer, provides an impression of affection and respect of the Sikhs. But this episode, by the Sikhs at large, was taken as an insult to the community. As a result of this there was a strong agitation for liberating the Gurdwaras from the government-appointed managers. Though apparently the stir assumed a religious form and had a religious end to achieve, in reality it was a revolt of the community against the system perpetuated by the government. This was duly owned and actively supported by the Congress. The Akalis adopted non-violence and non-cooperation as their creed.

The subsequent events in Punjab bear testimony that the imperialists were not in a mood to give up their policy of terrorizing the people, except that they changed their methods to do so.

To quell the Akali movement, the government, instead of confronting the mass agitation directly, backed their own nominees and encouraged them to make use of bullets and terrorize the masses. In January 1921 two Akalis were killed at Taran Taran. Events of this kind were repeated on a wider scale at Nankana Sahib, the birthplace of Guru Nanak. On 20 February 1921, Bhai Lachman Singh led a *jatha* to put an end to the scandalous state of affairs prevailing under the management of the government-appointee, Mahant Narain Das. Armed Pathans and desperate mercenaries hired by the Mahant with the active support of the government fell upon the peaceful *jatha* and killed more than 200 people. The whole of India was shocked by this outrageous mass murder. A large number of the wounded were also burnt alive. In the face of such inhuman treatment, the Akalis showed a tremendous spirit of tolerance and abidance by not breaking their vow of non-violence. Appreciating their non-violent struggle, Mahatma Gandhi issued an appeal saying,[39] 'The work is not solely of the Sikhs, everybody should share it.'

Condemning the Mahant's cruel deed and commending the Akalis for their passive sufferings, Mahatma Gandhi described the martyrdom of the Akali reformers as an 'act of national bravery'. He also denounced the foreign government whose rule, he said, 'was based on devilish tricks.'[40] Later in a message to the Sikhs, while comparing the tragedy of Nankana to a similar one in April 1919, Gandhi observed,[41] 'Everything I saw and heard points to a second edition of Dyerism, more barbarous, more calculated and more fiendish than the Dyerism of Jallianwala.'

Commenting on the policy of the Government, Dr Mohinder Singh in his book, *The Akali Movement* mentions that on going through the lengthy correspondence and reports of the government, one would conclude that the massacre at Nankana was a well-planned and premeditated conspiracy and the government officials actively backed the Mahant.[42]

On 7 November 1921, the Deputy Commissioner of Amritsar removed the keys of the Golden Temple. Presumably, the motive of the Government was to prevent and obstruct the transfer of control over the management of Gurdwaras to the SGPC. This tended to provoke another agitation. But before the situation took an ugly turn, the Governor of Punjab yielded. He returned the keys and ordered the release of the Akali prisoners. Mahatma Gandhi declared it thus:[43] 'First Battle for India's Freedom Won: Congratulations.'

The history of the Akali struggle at Guru ka Bagh is another instance of imperial terrorism unleashed on the non-violent and passive Akalis. The struggle at Guru ka Bagh acquired national dimensions. The repressive and terrorizing policies of the Government met with firm non-violent resistance by those inspired by Gandhi. The *morcha* was made an issue by the Government whose puppet, Mahant, became a mere tool in the hands of British officials. In August 1922 the police shot down a number of Sikhs. The Working Committee of the Congress, while condemning the ruthless policy of terrorizing the people, appointed a commission to investigate into the events of Guru ka Bagh. Calm and cool courage and the self-restraint displayed by the Akalis fetched them felicitations from Mahatma Gandhi.[44] According to official figures, the total number of arrested Akalis had gone up to 8,000 and 1,300 cases of fractures and dislocations were treated in the hospitals. In the words of C.F. Andrews, 'A great heroism learnt through suffering had risen in the land.'[45] The heartless beating, kicking, dragging, ducking, trampling, strangulation and throwing into the fields of hundreds of Akalis continued for some months. The official action was described as inhuman, brutal, foul, cowardly and incredible to an Englishman and a moral defeat to England. C.F. Andrews during his meeting with the Governor told him that he had seen with his own eyes hundreds of Christs being crucified at Guru ka Bagh.[46]

The imperial terrorism continued even during the days of the Jaito Morcha. Jaito affairs has its history in the forced abdication of Maharaja Ripudaman Singh who was known for his sympathies for the national movement. The Akalis had to launch an agitation for their religious freedom which was snubbed by the British Government with the help of the Nabha State authorities at Jaito. People were arrested and subjected to various kinds of torture. Jawaharlal Nehru, N.K. Gidwani and K. Santhanam visited Jaito. They were arrested by Wilson Johnston, the administrator of Nabha.

When the Jatha was within the reach of Gurdwara Tibbi Sahib in Jaito, the administrator of Nabha, ordered it to stop. But the *jatha* did not do so. A signal to open fire was given by Johnston.[47] The firing lasted for more than five minutes. Many of the Akalis fell dead. Army men prevented the removal of the dead and wounded, thus many of the wounded died for lack of attendance.

Opinions differ regarding the number of casualties. The exact number could not be ascertained as the scene of tragedy was made inaccessible to independent observers. Different newspapers put the number of the dead and wounded at over 500, while the SGPC reported that there were over 300 casualties, including 70 to 150 dead. The press condemned the administrators and British Government for their ruthless barbarity and for enacting another Jallianwala spectacle. *The Onward'* wrote: 'General Dyer is reborn and reincarnated in the person of the administrator of Nabha.' The press also refuted the Government of India's plea that it had no hand in the firing. Bande Mataram asked whether those killed at Jaito were not subjects of British India and whether or not the Indian States were under the Government of India.[48]

As evident from the account, the religio-political struggle of the Akalis – directed against the priests, Mahants and other vested interests in Sikh shrines and consequently against the British imperialism – was one of the most powerful movements of modern India. In a short period of 5 years, no less than 40,000 men went behind the bars, 500 of them died, 2,000 were wounded,[49] while a large number of them suffered dismissal from service, withdrawal of *jagirs* and pensions, and imposition of fines, forfeiture of property and various other forms of punishment.[50] The recruitment of Sikhs into the Army and other services was suspended. A large number of Sikh soldiers were court-martialled for wearing *kirpans* and black turbans. The editors, printers and publishers of some newspapers were fined or imprisoned, their securities forfeited and their publications banned.[51] The SGPC and the Akali Dal were declared unlawful bodies and almost all important Sikh leaders were arrested. Charges of sedition, conspiracy, criminal intimidation and rebellion were levelled.[52]

CONCLUSION

On going through the literature on Jallianwala Bagh, one comes across two divergent views about the responsibility of the tragedy – one of British imperialists, and the other of India nationalists. The imperialists are of the view that Dyer ordered firing because of a 'mistaken conception of his duty' or due to an error of judgement or owing to his excitable disposition because of his mysterious mental disease. On the other hand, the nationalists feel that it was entirely the imperial system which was behind the incident and responsible for this naked barbarity. They also suggest the imperialists did not mind making Dyer a scapegoat in order to whitewash their own sins. Dyer performed his duty, according to the direction of his superiors.

V.N. Datta insists that the Jallianwala Bagh tragedy was not an isolated phenomenon, but 'an expression of a confrontation between the ruler and ruled.' Helen Fein, an American sociologist, likewise concluded that Jallianwala was 'a prototypical instance of a repressive collective punishment practised by the British in black and Asian colonies.'[53]

Sir Michael O'Dwyer, the Lieutenant Governor of the Punjab from 1913–19, had a reputation for 'tough' rule. His allegedly coercive recruiting practices added specific local grievances. He had opposed reforms, ruthlessly crushed dissent – most notably the Ghadar – muzzled the Indian press and prevented Indian activists from entering the Punjab. On 9 April – on the occasion of Ram Naumi – remarkable scenes of 'fraternization between Hindus and Muslims, including the public sharing of water vessels, were witnessed – uneasily by the imperialists.

We must now ask the question: was the massive agitation launched by the Sikhs soon after 1919 related to the Jallianwala Bagh? In my view it was connected and in fact had links in an extraordinary chain of events. There is even a cause for arguing that if the first had not happened, the second would not have occurred too. In other words, it provided the base for germination of the other.

Let us now look at the chain of events – at the risk of over-simplification – we might put it like this: the passing of the Rowlatt Act brought about Gandhi's Satyagraha campaign and non-cooperation non-violent movement; which in turn provoked Dyer's action – which in turn stimulated the Indian movements. Dyer's baptism as an honorary Sikh irked the Sikh masses. They could not bear that their shrine should be used to promote and justify the role of the imperial government. Hence we witness the inception of the Gurdwara Reform Movement. During its span of 5 years the imperialists enacted Jallianwala Baghs at different places while making the Mahants or the administrator play the role of Dyer.

To conclude, it may be stated that the supreme irony of the Jallianwala Bagh story was that the powers under the Rowlatt Act were never used. They had proved to be completely unnecessary.

NOTES AND REFERENCES

1. *The Punjabi*, 21 March 1907. Quoted in Daniel Arjon's *The Moderates and Extremists in the Indian National Movement 1923–24*, Bombay, 1967.
2. Fauja Singh, *Who's Who of Punjab Freedom Fighters*, vol. I, Patiala, 1972, pp. XXI–XXIII.
3. *Ibid.*
4. V.N. Datta, *Jallianwala Bagh*, Ludhiana, 1969, pp. 12–13.
5. *Ibid.*
6. *Ibid.*, pp. 14–15.

7. *Disorder Inquiry Committee Report*, 1919–20, Calcutta, 1920, p. 152.
8. Rupert Furneaux, *Massacre at Amritsar*, London, 1963, pp. 33–34.
9. 'If it is clear that the demands emanate not from the mass of the people, whose interests are at stake but from a small and not quite disinterested miniority . . .' Sir O'Dwyer quoted in *The Congress, Punjab Inquiry Report 1919–20*, p. 14.
10. *Collected Works of Mahatma Gandhi*, vol. XV, pp. 120–22.
11. Evidence taken before *Disorders Inquiry Committee*, vol. VI, Calcutta, 1920, p. 191.
12. Alfred Draper, *Amritsar: The Massacre that Ended The Raj*, London, 1981, pp. 41–42.
13. *Ibid.*, pp. 45–46.
14. Punjab Government, Home-Military – Part B, January 1920, No. 265 quoted by Raja Ram, *The Jallianwala Bagh Massacre*, Chandigarh, 1969, p. 105.
15. V.N. Datta, *op. cit.*, pp. 86–87.
16. *Ibid.*
17. G.O.I., Home Dept. Political B. February 1920, No. 373.
18. *Disorder Inquiry Committee Report*, vol. VI, p. 24.
19. Arthur Swinson, *Six Minutes to Sunset*, London, 1964, p. 48.
20. Raja Ram, *op. cit.*, p. 120.
21. *Ibid.*, and Ian Colvin, *The Life of General Dyer*, London, 1929, p. 160.
22. *Ibid.*, and V.N. Datta, *op. cit.*
23. Alfred Draper, *op. cit.*, p. 265.
24. Rupert Furneaux, *op. cit.*, p. 90.
25. *Ibid.*
26. *Ibid.*, p. 125.
27. Hans Raj, who may have been an agent provocateur, *Ibid.*, pp. 58–62, 79–80, 86–87, 128–36.
28. Derek Sayer, 'British Reaction to the Amritsar Massacre 1919–20,' *Past and Present*, no. 131, 1919, p. 1400.
29. *Ibid.*, p. 141.
30. Rupert Furneaux, *op. cit.*, pp. 85–86.
31. *Ibid.*, p. 94.
32. *Ibid.*, pp. 99–100.
33. *Ibid.*
34. *Ibid.*, p. 105
35. Quoted by Rupert Furneaux, *op. cit.*, p. 107.
36. *Ibid.*, p. 127; and Nehru, *An Autobiography*, London, 1936.
37. Swinson, *Six Minutes to Sunset*, London, 1964, p. 91.
38. Arur Singh was a puppet figure. He was appointed as Manager by the Government.
39. Fauja Singh, *op. cit.*, p. xxxi.
40. Teja Singh, *Gurdwara Reform Movement*, p. 82.
41. *Collected Works of Mahatma Gandhi*, vol. XIX, p. 401.
42. Mohinder Singh, *The Akali Movement*, Delhi, 1978, p. 36.
43. Fauja Singh, *op. cit.*, p. xxxi.
44. *Ibid.*, p. xxxii.
45. Ruchi Ram Sahni, *Struggle for Reform in the Sikh Shrine*, ed., Ganda Singh, Amritsar, 1965, pp. 105–7.
46. Sohan Singh Josh, *Akali Morchian Da Itihas*, Delhi, 1972, pp. 171–72.
47. Mohinder Singh, *op. cit.*, p. 72.
48. *Bande Mataram*, 29 February 1924.

49. Dr Ganda Singh, ed., *Punjab*, vol. II, p. 234.
50. Mohinder Singh, *op. cit.*, p. 137.
51. *Ibid.*, and Sardul Singh Caveeshar, *The Sikh Studies*, Lahore, 1937, p. 199.
52. Sardul Singh Caveeshar, *op. cit.*, p. 206.
53. Fein, *Imperial Crime and Punishment*, pp. xii–xiii quoted by Derek Sayer, 'British Reaction to the Amritsar Massacre 1919–20', *Past and Present*, No. 131, 1991.

FIVE

❖ The Jallianwala Bagh Tragedy: A Catalyst of Indian Consciousness

KAMLESH MOHAN

THE IRON-FISTED PUNJAB administrators had unwillingly performed the bloody baptism of the 'muted groups' in the vocation of politics. Edwin Ardener, the first to propose the theory of 'muted groups', had argued that the dominant groups in society generate and control the dominant modes of expression and if the 'muted groups' wish to express themselves they are forced to do so through the dominant modes of expression whether colonial or indigenous.[1] As far as Ardener is concerned, the problem of muting is a problem of frustrated communication. Until the end of the nineteenth century, the majority of Indians, especially women and the masses, remained 'muted' because their model of reality, their view of the world, could not be realized or expressed in the dominant structures and cultural idiom. Even the English educated Indians, despite their valiant effort to participate in the colonial discourse, were eventually forced to restructure their self-image, world-view and attitudes towards the colonial connection because the racist projections of India and Indians by the West gradually stood exposed in its bias, narrowness, and overblown sense of superiority. The Indians' growing knowledge of the nature of British imperialism and the experiential reality of the colonial social world and politics transformed their consciousness which at the time was predominantly anti-colonial but not strictly nationalist; the latter presupposes a change in perspective from opposition to colonialism to the problems of unity and integration within the country.[2]

The colonial state of India's negative response to the agitation against the Rowlatt Bills, a veiled defence of the Jallianwala Bagh massacre, the subsequent British attempts to whitewash and gloss over the indiscretions of the dictatorial civil authorities and misuse of power by the Martial Law administrators in Punjab altered the mindscape of not only the politically-conscious minority in this region as in the rest of India but also that of the 'muted groups', specifically the poor illiterate masses and women. In the latter case, the dichotomy between domestic and public space was to become increasingly fluid, less restrictive and stifling as the national movement graduated from elitist circles to the nationalist arena.

History-writing from this angle adumbrates an 'inner view' of historical processes and such events alter the perceptions and attitudes of a large number of people (irrespective of their educational and social background or religious affiliation) and mobilize them for joint action. Obviously, the source material for this article is found more in interviews, statements made before non-official bodies, vernacular literature on the Jallianwala Bagh tragedy and biographies as well as autobiographies than in government records and documents.

This paper is divided into five sections:

(*a*) Nature of Colonial State in Punjab;
(*b*) Mindscape of the Colonized;
(*c*) Women in Rowlatt Agitation to Martial Law: An Overview;
(*d*) New Signposts in Indian Consciousness-Ambivalence to Alienation; and
(*e*) Conclusion.

NATURE OF THE COLONIAL STATE IN PUNJAB

The Punjab was a Non-Regulation province and its administrative set-up, dominated and controlled by the colonial state on account of its crucial importance for the solvency and military security of the British Raj, was a curious mix of authoritarian, paternal and democratic elements. The unique character of the state and its policy had influenced the development of the people's attitudes and mental orientation towards the colonial connection as well as the form of political and social movements. The process of the construction of its governmental structure, legal institutions and codes, and revenue system which spread over more than six decades, was characterized by 'masterful attempts' to prolong the atmosphere of military conquest up to the late 1850s.[3] John Lawrence mitigated the harshness of this autocratic phase by his respect for indigenous custom and intimate contact with the people, especially peasantry which may be termed as 'paternal utilitarianism', fired by an evangelical zeal and underpinned by the Platonic conception of being a wise guardian. The long-term authoritarian and domineering mentality was determined by the self-image of the early British conquerors-cum-administrators and functionaries in the Punjab who were faced with a threefold task: (*i*) to convert 'the sullen and bitter resignation of the vanquished into honest, contented and hearty loyalty' (*ii*) infusion of the elements of civilized administration, and (*iii*) to convert the

Punjab into not only ' a secure but also profitable possession'.[4] Such a perception of their role was reinforced by the cataclysm of 1857.

The self-image of the Punjab administrators as saviours of the Raj was moulded by a number of assumptions about the potential threat from the high-spirited and martial local population and the border tribes, and partly by their perception of their role in the newly annexed Punjab and their attitude towards the ruled. Imbued with imperial consciousness, they pursued their mission 'to subdue, administer, convert and improve without halting and without question.'[5] Sense of *'Angrezi dharma'* provided justification and direction to the functionaries of the Raj. Above all, these officers were keen to carve out their image not only as decisive, strong and efficient rulers but as sensitive, fair and as ones accessible to the people.

In other words, legitimacy of their rule was the major concern of the rulers who secured it through various strategies such as the cultivation of goodwill and support of those institutions, social groups, religious elites, landed-aristocracy, *jagirdars,* prominent families and heroic tribes, whose help was regarded vital for social and political control. This major compulsion was highlighted in a document entitled *Social and Political Intercourse with Punjabis* which was distributed amongst young officers.[6]

In the next phase, dominated by Fitz James Stephen (the Law Member 1869–72), the paternal element was replaced by an authoritarian tendency towards utilitarianism, though an evangelical zeal still energized the imperial mission. Believing that the foremost function of government in India was 'to protect peaceable men and to beat down wrong doers, to extort respect and to enforce obedience',[7] he highlighted the positive role of law, backed by power. Following this logic, law constituted the most significant basis of legitimacy to colonial officials. The phase of aggressive legislation during the 1860s and 1870s, which was a direct outcome of this belief, stripped Punjab of its distinction of being a 'Non-Regulation' province and brought it close to the pattern of the other parts of British India. Unlike the Benthamite period, when the movement for modernization had been regarded as a cooperative effort between the English and the Indian middle class, the Punjab school of administrators 'forced reform at sword-point believing that a benighted people had to be compelled towards light.'[8] Now reform was to be carried out in the spirit of racial conquest that characterized the post-Mutiny period coupled with the strong-handedness of the Punjab school but none of the Lawrencian kindliness and harmony between the paternalist and modernizing currents. Despite the increasing advocacy of 'rule of law' through its definition and codification for the modernization of 'despotic and Oriental societies', particularly the Indian, the reactionary and high-handed military mentality remained operative through the regimes of Denzil Ibbetson and Michael O'Dwyer.

Such a perception of the colonial state has been projected by a few scholars who have argued that the colonial state based its power on coercive domination rather than consent or hegemony.[9]

Recent writings have shown that the colonial state cannot be described merely as a coercive institution.[10] Undoubtedly, the power of the colonial state rested on the monopoly over the instruments of force and violence. However, after the conquest of the country, demonstration of coercive power and judicious intervention of repressive measures were regarded essential for creating an awareness of the power of the Raj but not in managing the day-to-day affairs of the state. In the formulation and implementation of policies and laws, the element of forcible imposition was moderated by the desire to secure consent and conciliate opposition. In other words, legitimization of colonial rule remained a major preoccupation of the colonial state. It is in this context that the concepts of consent of the colonial people for legislation or the use of force and collaboration with the potential supporters of the Raj acquired significance.[11] While consent implied a certain degree of willingness on the part of the state to concede space to public opinion and flexibility of approach to the problems of administration in a foreign country, 'collaboration' offered 'a share in the government' in the form of important appointments in the bureaucracy to landed and princely classes at the price of unqualified support to the British rulers and endorsement of their policies. In the imperialist hegemonic discourse, neither 'consent' nor 'collaboration' was entitled to the privileges available to the people in a representative government.

Obviously, the British-Indian-state was semi-hegemonic – an amalgamation of authoritarian and liberal elements. Despite the imperialist content of its policies and essentially exploitative functions and goals, it had replicated many characteristics of the modern state in Western Europe. The nature of democratic freedoms and civil liberties guaranteed in colonial societies certainly differed from those in Europe but while retaining its authoritarian core, the colonial state was obliged to concede 'a semblance of civil liberty in keeping with the democratic practice at home because it had made some constitutional commitments in India'.[12]

The nature of the colonial state was influenced by one major development: transfer of authority and power over the Indian empire from the hands of the Company to the British Parliament under the Government of India Act of 1858. The British approach to the empire, projected as primarily utilitarian by Eric Stokes, is now regarded as a product of the collective application of four doctrines: the Burkean doctrine of imperial trusteeship, the Benthamite theory of state activity as propagated by Mills (James Mill and his son J.S. Mill), the Platonic conception of a ruling elite in the role of wise guardians, and the evangelical zeal to spread the Christian gospel, so as 'to save the souls of a perversely irresponsive people'. Despite the obvious mutual contradictions and affinities in the course of their interaction, the cumulative impact of these doctrines was transmuted into a continuing motive force of the British imperial policy.[13] Its long-term but strange impact on Indian polity was the evolution of colonial constitutionalism without dismantling the autocratic form of imperial government in India.

It may be pointed out that the role of the European ideas, especially these four doctrines, was important in the crystallization of the hard core of the colonial state and its hegemonic discourse but the response of the colonial society in a given situation and its specific needs were crucial to the entire process. Both the top-brass colonial administrators / policy-makers[14] and the nationalist leadership recognized the dependence of the colonial state for ruling India with the consent of the subject people to accept its moral authority and its laws and policies for the regulation of their social and property relations. For example, Gandhi rejected the interpretation of consent as merely passive acquiescence, apathy, submissiveness, and unquestioned obedience to state apparatus. While conceding the fact that the colonial state was militarily too powerful to be dislodged with violence, he proclaimed an active role for and autonomy of an enlightened public opinion in his book *Hind Swaraj:*

> You have great military resources. Your naval power is matchless. If we wanted to fight you on you own ground, we should be unable to do so, but if the above submissions be not acceptable to you, we cease to play the part of the ruled. You may if you like cut us to pieces. You may shatter us at the cannon's mouth. *If you act contrary to our will, we shall not help you and without our help, we know that you cannot move one step forward.*[15] (Emphasis is mine)

However, he acknowledged that the development of such a critical temper and consciousness of the people's strength among the thirty crores of Indians demanded a psychological transformation. It implied the removal of 'slavish and defeatist mentality' underpinned by fear, caused by infliction of brutal physical force and psychological onslaught.

Gandhi's first major countrywide experiment of cultivating critical temper among Indians and mobilizing their armed strength was occasioned by the British imperialist government's decision to curb elementary civil liberties of the people through the legislation of the Rowlatt Act despite nationalist opposition to it. In this context, it is important to analyse the nature of the Indian consciousness with special reference to Punjab which became the centre of display of physical force, coercive power and repression by the new breed of authoritarian functionaries led by its Lieutenant Governor Sir Michael O'Dwyer.

MINDSCAPE OF THE COLONIZED

Despite the time lag in terms of Punjab's encounter with the colonial rule and its legitimizing discourse, its people covered various turns in colonial consciousness in the short span of seven decades, i.e., 1849–19, when the Jallianwala massacre was perpetrated. Whether in Bengal, where the actual process of imperial expansion had been set in motion as early as 1765 with the Battle of Plassey, or in Punjab which became the last but the most valuable outpost of the British empire, the British were constantly haunted by the fear that military conquest had only won them a 'precarious hegemony'. The most enduring and the most profitable conquest was the one over mind. By the mid-nineteenth century, when not plagued by any rivals and threats, the rulers abandoned their majestic aloofness and their compromising and beseeching tone but focused their energies upon forging tools and strategies for legitimizing the presence of the colonial state, its hegemonies, authority and the *raison d'etre* of its economic exploitation.[16]

The colonial state had used two strategies: the first one required the new rulers to adopt the political structure as well as the cultural discourse of the existing Mughal regime which had a practical utility for the Company Government during the period 1765 to 1833 when it did not possess real political authority and lacked the economic power required to enforce social reforms to restructure social relations and manufacture identities. But more relevant to our purpose is the second strategy which stipulated that the structure and discourse of the Indian polity and society be remodelled through a serious missionary effort towards the spread of Western education. Its direct implication was that the British potentates became seriously engaged in increasing colonial consciousness and intensified their drive towards the spread of Western education with a twofold purpose that was both utilitarian and ideological. For its utilitarian purpose, the colonial state was to train an army of English-knowing Indians who would fill in the lower rungs of various administrative departments and that, too, at a meagre cost. Its second purpose, and the main premise underlying the introduction of English education in India, was 'colonization of consciousness'. It was through the dissemination of Western education that the so-called 'moral' mission or 'civilization' mission in India was to be accomplished. It was given utmost importance for moulding India into a replica of England – the best model of social, political and material progress – in order to enable her to serve the needs of industrial England and the British empire. The first generation of Indian intelligentsia in nineteenth century Bengal had eagerly assimilated this ideological perspective. As this theme has been fairly well-researched, I shall probe other related aspects of the transformation of colonial consciousness in the context of the Jallianwala

Bagh tragedy. However, I would like to make one general comment on the above point. The colonial consciousness, which may be called the essence of the Indian response towards the early phase of colonial encounter, reflected an uneasy ambivalence – a knotted combination of an acute awareness of subjection, which was caused by worsening socio-cultural and political decrepitude coupled with a sense of grateful loyalty to the 'intrinsically good' British rule.[17]

Despite regional variations owing to the nature of political consciousness, exposure to English education and consequently new political ideas and institutions, the evolution of colonial consciousness reflected certain common characteristics. One of its major features was the cultural co-optation, which had implied the 'internalization of the colonial role definitions, the language of homology between sexual and political stratarchies' and the imperialist perceptions of Indian history with its 'golden age' in the past and positive projections of the colonial state and its policies by the British rulers and the urban-educated sections of India. Crucial to this exercise was the identification with the aggressor, in the terminology of psychoanalysis.[18] As an end product of the colonization of consciousness, many Indians began to see themselves as crypto-barbarians who ought to civilize themselves and learn to be manly through the agency of the Raj which possessed a vigorous rationalist tradition, superior scientific knowledge and modern political system and theory.[19] It was not surprising that they perceived salvation in becoming more like the British in friendship or enmity. Without fully sharing the British concept of martial races – the hyper-masculine, manifestly courageous, superbly loyal Indian castes – they did resurrect the ideology of the martial races embedded in the traditional Indian concept of statecraft. This explained the new meaning attached to *kshatriya* as a symbol of authentic Indianness in the nineteenth century socio-religious and political reform movements. This new identity made them demand an honourable relationship between the ruler and the ruled.

At this point of time, the colonized while playing the game within the rules set by the colonizer, rejected bisexuality and perceived feminity-in-masculinity as the final negation of man's political identity. It is not surprising that almost all protest movements before 1919 sought to redeem the Indian masculinity by defeating the British in violent conflict. Thus, the vanquished and enslaved Indians legitimized the concepts of manliness in a dominant culture: aggression, achievement, competition and power.[20]

However, the nineteenth century response to the growing Western politico-cultural and economic domination, which had accepted the colonial state as a public authority responsive to popular sentiments and demands while making laws and policies, its self-advertised credentials of being a just and firm ruler as well as the image of India as a supine, sick, prostrate and 'effeminate' polity and civilization, could not remain representative of colonial consciousness from the beginning of the twentieth century onwards. Gandhi's insightful and creative reading of the Western and Indian tradition in the context of the contemporary imperialist scenario produced a 'transcultural protest against the hyper-masculine world-view of colonialism'.[21]

With the induction of women in his experimental satyagraha in South Africa, he had begun to construct his theory that activism and courage were perfectly compatible with womanhood, particularly motherhood. By restating the concept of androgyny, i.e. manliness and womanliness were equal, but the ability to transcend the man-woman dichotomy was superior to both because it was a signifier of godly and saintly qualities. Gandhi had not only rejected the colonial culture's ordering of sexual identities: *Purusatva* (the essence of masculinity), *Naritya* (the essence of femininity) and *Kalibtava* (the essence of hermaphroditism) but also its argument of racial superiority.[22] Even more important was the implication that the colonialism and its culture, which were rooted in violence and aggression, stood negated and discredited. Gandhi seemed clear in his mind that activism and courage could be liberated from aggressiveness and recognized their compatibility with Indian womanhood. Thus began his search for a coherent concept of femininity and empowerment of women for social and political change.

Gandhi's project of the redefinition of 'femininity' and its new role was interlinked with his serious concern (as of other national leaders and social reformers) for retrieving Indian 'masculinity' through the rebuttal of Katherine Mayo's mischievous charge of 'effeminacy' against his countrymen as it was an indirect endorsement of the British imperialist view about their (Indian) unfitness to rule.[23] Obviously, woman's status, which had become a political issue and a point of debate and controversy under the Raj, became a crucial component in the process of transformation of Indian consciousness, especially for liberating it from 'psychological and ethical complexes', also described as 'slavish or defeatist mentality' by the nationalist leadership.

WOMEN IN ROWLATT AGITATION AND MARTIAL LAW

Despite his first encounter with women power as satyagrahis in the course of agitation against the Black Act of 1913 (which declared Hindu, Muslim and Parsi marriages invalid) in South Africa, he made the first explicit connection between women and their role in nation-building in his speeches, campaigning for recruitment of Indians in the army during the First World War.[24] It is only with his emergence as a political leader when he confronted the problem of mass mobilization that he became increasingly aware of women not only in terms of their problems but also as a powerful potential force in society. Refusal of the British Government to concede his request to drop the Rowlatt Bills, which had been consistently opposed in the press and in the Imperial Legislative Council by the non-official members as well as the elected members right from its introduction to its final disposal as an Act,[25] obliged Gandhi to mobilize all Indians for nationwide protest against the 'devilish legislation'.[26] Gandhi issued his famous 'Hartal Manifesto' on 23 March 1919 and fixed 6 April 1919 to be observed as 'All India Hartal Day' and a day of 'humiliation and prayer' entirely based on fasting, prayer and penance for the purification of the soul.[27]

Gandhi made a special appeal to the women of India to join the satyagraha movement in large numbers and cooperate with men in their constitutional struggle which they had launched against the Rowlatt legislation.[28] As he realized that no mass movement could be successful without the participation of the 'muted' sections of society, he thought it fit that the women of India should not be kept ignorant of the prevalent political situation and resentment against injustice in the country. Even if they were not educated, they could cooperate in national constructive work like swadeshi. Instead of reiterating the equation earlier reformers adhered to between education and upliftment of women, Gandhi valued their attitudinal change and contribution as practical thinkers and actors in the nationalist politics. Indian women's consciousness, which had already been awakened by social reformers, particularly the Arya Samajists, to contribute to the process of social reconstruction as enlightened daughters, sisters and mothers, was given a new direction by Gandhi. While urging women to shoulder their new responsibilities as nation builders he said, 'They have to suffer more then men and so long as they do not take equal part with men in the affairs of the world and in religious and political matters, we shall not see India's star rising.'[29] A large number of Indian women such as Rajkumari Amrit Kaur, Sushila Nayar, Bibi Amtus Salaam, Mani Behn Patel, Sucheta Kripalani and Rehana Tayabji acknowledged the powerful impact of Gandhi in moulding their personal lives, attitudes and aspirations.[30] However, it was their own direct participation or of their menfolk in the anti-Rowlatt agitation which transformed their perceptions and attitudes. For the purpose of analysing the role of women in the events from the anti-Rowlatt protest to the Jallianwala Bagh massacre, I have relied on the *The Tribune* reports, personal interviews and official records pertaining to Punjab.

The process of psychological transformation, more specifically raising consciousness among women, was rooted in the experiences during the years of the First World War. Socialized to think in terms of family relationships, the Hindu and Muslim women came to realize that they had sacrificed their sons, grandsons, brothers and husbands for the sake of the empire and yet there was no end to repression.[31] In vain, women of the middle class families, especially those of limited means, had to cope with scarcity of essential commodities and their exorbitant prices on account of famine and wartime constraints. Economic distress of the breadearners of the family, who had been obliged to pay the enhanced taxes and the war contributions,[32] caused such privation and hardship to numerous women that even feeding the children and other members of the family became difficult with the shrinking income in addition to other family expenses. In such a mental state, Punjabi women were vulnerable and sensitive to the rising wave of discontent against the Rowlatt Bills.

At this point, a brief description of the course of the anti-Rowlatt agitation in Punjab, with special reference to Amritsar, is necessary for delineating the process of their disillusionment with the beneficent character of the British rule and of their changing world-view and self-image.

The Rowlatt Act agitation, a spontaneous protest against a pernicious measure, had been conducted along constitutional lines.[32] In Punjab, particularly in Amritsar, it was reinforced by other long-standing local grievances and discontents arising out of the platform ticket agitation, Rate Payer's Tax, high prices, severe income-tax assessment, in addition to the hurt caused by the Khilafat grievances and frustration with the piecemeal reforms. Numerous public meetings, held in Amritsar, Lahore, Jullundur and other towns from 31 January to 12 April 1919, reiterated the issues that had already been publicized through the press. After 18 March, when the Rowlatt Bills became an Act, all other issues paled into insignificance. The growing knowledge about the reactionary and insensitive attitude of the British rulers, as reflected in the course of debates over the Rowlatt Bills, had already made the people ready to be galvanized into action over an issue of national importance.

At this psychological moment, local leaders in Amritsar undertook the task of mobilizing public opinion. In fact, the success of the Rowlatt satyagraha and its nature depended to a great extent on the influence and authority of local leaders among the social groups that took part in the movement. Furthermore, it depended upon the cooperation or provocation offered by the British.[33] It was in proportion to the degree of understanding of Gandhi's teachings by local lieutenants in various parts of India that the satyagraha emerged to be static in Madras, militant in the Punjab and Delhi and dynamic in Bombay. As far as the local leaders in Bengal, Sind and the Punjab were concerned, they had plunged themselves into the Rowlatt satyagraha without having any close association with Gandhi. In fact, Saifuddin Kitchlew and Dr Satyapal had never met Gandhi[34] and their understanding of Gandhi's conception of satyagraha was only partial.

In the course of the Rowlatt agitation in Amritsar, Dr Kitchlew and Dr Satyapal emerged as the primary local leaders.[35] Both played a vital role in mobilizing the public opinion for the redressal of local grievances and for the withdrawal of the Rowlatt Act by the Government of India. While Dr Kitchlew went out to address public meetings at Lahore, Multan, and Jullundur, Dr Satyapal, as the President of the Railway Grievances Committee, concentrated his efforts on launching the Platform Ticket Agitation in Amritsar and concluding it successfully. However, it was their organized propaganda against the Rowlatt Act that magnified their influence and authority among the citizens of Amritsar.

The housewives, too, had been infected by the general awakening and feeling of patriotic excitement that had percolated through their husbands and other male relatives who were either sympathetic witnesses or active participants in the political activities in the various towns of Punjab. Increasing public receptivity to political propaganda through the press and platform and to the strident criticism of the dictatorial functioning of the Punjab Government had created panic in official circles. It furnished the authorities with an excuse to restrict the participation of Dr Satyapal and Dr Kitchlew in public activities and later to deport them to Dharamsala on 10 April 1919.

The Rowlatt Act agitation can be divided into four phases.[36] Its first phase lasted form 23 March to 30 March 1919 when the leaders could guide the course of the agitation. The second phase from 2 to 6 April 1919 reflected the reaction of the local leaders towards the incidents of violence at Delhi during the course of the *hartal* on 30 March 1919. The third phase extended from 6 to 9 April 1919 when the movement had gained such astounding spontaneity and vitality that it took care of itself. Local leaders just watched the course of the agitation, baffled by its overwhelming success. The fourth phase lasted from 10 to 14 April 1919 when the mobs acted according to their own whims or the dictates of their own prudence.

The meeting of 30 March at Amritsar, according to official estimates, is said to have been attended by 30,000 to 40,000 people.[37] This gathering on the National Day consisted of all grades of society. Dr Kitchlew was the prime organiser,[38] while Dr Satyapal was one of its conveners.[39] Pandit Kotu Mal, Dina Nath and Swami Anubhava Nand made speeches, while Lala Girdhari Lal presided over the meeting. Swami Anubhava Nand expressed his indignation and protest against the Rowlatt Act and stressed the importance of Home Rule for India. The *hartal* on 30 March was observed in a thorough manner by the shopkeepers and the trading classes. Participation of the professional classes was automatic since it happened to be Sunday. The *hartal* in the city on 6 April was complete. A large number of women, according to Dr Kitchlew, had also observed a fast on that day and showed great enthusiasm and interest.[40] They held separate protest meetings. One such meeting was held in the Arya Samaj temple in Ludhiana on 31 March 1919. Parbati Devi, daughter of Swami Shraddhanand (earlier known as Munshi Ram), lashed out at the Rowlatt Act.[41]

The *hartal* was again observed on 6 April 1919 over the rest of India according to Gandhi's programme. As a mark of protest and mourning, business was suspended and kitchen-hearths remained closed in thousands of households. In Lahore, politically-conscious men and women, irrespective of colour, caste and creed, took holy baths in the river Ravi before the sunrise and recited prayers for the repeal of the Rowlatt Act. While walking in processions, slogans like 'Rowlatt Act *hai-hai*' were raised.[42]

At other places, too, women and children joined the programme of fasting and prayers in a religious spirit within the four walls of their homes. An unprecedented enthusiasm, interest and earnestness for public activity were evident among the wives, daughters and sisters of Congress men, who attended public meetings and processions. Prominent among them were Mrs Satyawati, wife of Lala Achint Ram (Lahore), Mrs Bhag Devi, wife of Lala Duni Chand (Ambala), Pushpa Gujral, wife of A.N. Gujral (Jhelum), Mrs Gauran Devi, wife of L.C. Dutt (Sialkot).[43] The village women, too, were infected with the religious spirit of protest. For example, in Sanghoi village, several women observed a fast along with the other menfolk and praised Mahatma Gandhi.[44]

In fact, the *hartal* on both the days showed that the common people, the 'muted groups', including women had been stirred so deeply that they lent their unstinted support to it. Their success owed to the ready support of the trading and shopkeeping classes.[45] The professional classes like teachers and pleaders had mobilized the public opinion to such an extent that a mere suggestion from Mahatma Gandhi to observe 6 April as the National Protest Day by observing a *hartal* met with an overwhelming response.[46] There was no pressure or direct organization on the part of local leaders and a complete closure of shops and suspension of traffic, to an appreciable extent, seemed to be spontaneous. Dr Kitchlew, however, had not organized the *hartal*.[47]

Secondary leaders such as Badar-ul-Islam Ali Khan convened a meeting in the evening. The purpose was just to express their appreciation of the unprecedented unity, coordination and self-control exhibited by the people of Amritsar.[48] A resolution was passed requesting the King Emperor to rescind orders against Dr Kitchlew, Dr Satyapal, Pandit Kotu Mal, Dina Nath and Swami Anubhava Nand. Public opinion, as *The Tribune* commented, emphatically condemned the action taken by the Punjab Government under the Defence of India Act against Dr Kitchlew, Dr Satyapal and others.[49]

Obviously, official indifference to public opinion and its failure to appreciate the depth of their emotional attachment for the local leaders unleashed the social anger of the uneducated masses.

Celebration of Ram Naumi (a Hindu religious festival) on 9 April was an ocular demonstration of Hindu-Mulsim unity. In the larger towns it was an occasion for scenes of public fraternization between Hindus and Muslims. Muslims joined in celebrating the festival and the cries of '*Hindu Mussalman ki Jai*' and '*Gandhi ki Jai*' were substituted for the names of Hindu deities. At Amritsar, Muslims and Hindus set up *chabbils* (stalls for serving water) and *jhankis* (pageants). Mahasha Rattan Chand also set up a *chabbil* and showed extraordinary enthusiasm in serving water to various communities. The Hindus drank out of the vessels of Muslims and vice-versa.[50] This was done on a smaller scale on 6 April.

The participants hailed from all walks of life. The Ram Naumi procession presented a cross-section of society, bound by bonds of emotional unity, which was not warped by the considerations of caste or creed or sex. Women, usually not visible in religious processions and other public functions as a matter of social norm, watched its progress from their housetops and balconies on account of its added significance as an occasion of communal harmony. Spontaneity and mass participation formed the chief features of the Ram Naumi celebrations in Amritsar, thus providing a sound basis for the psychological transformation in the Punjab. Michael O'Dwyer found that these spectacular demonstrations of unity, oneness and growing national consciousness were fraught with dangerous potentialities. Bereft of imagination and morose by temperament, O'Dwyer could not but shudder at the possibilities of revolt and its leaders were none other than Kitchlew and Satyapal.[51] On 10 April, Miles Irving, the Deputy Commissioner, whisked them away to Dharamsala unexpectedly. Their deportation on the pretext of violent speeches, as *The Tribune* wrote, was indefensible and it exposed the Punjab Government to the severest criticism for its action against independence of thought and freedom of expression.[52]

The news of their deportation spread like lightning. As the news travelled from one locality to another, the people closed their shops and joined the crowd going to plead with the Deputy Commissioner for release of Kitchlew and Satyapal.[53] Women, too, were emotionally disturbed by this news. Their resentment and strong disapproval of the sly removal of their beloved leader, Dr Kitchlew, was expressed through the recital of songs, composed on the spur of the moment. The refrain of one song ran:

> *Ratin chauran wangar laigaye Dr Kitchlew nun.*[54]
> (The government officials acted like thieves while whisking away Dr Kitchlew under the cover of darkness).

On 10 April 1919, the British Government fuelled the public wrath to a greater intensity by arresting Gandhi at Palwal railway station in order to prevent his entry into the Punjab.[55] Both these developments caused great excitement and ignited the volatile political atmosphere which was tense. Spontaneous public gatherings and processions were organized with the intention of securing the release of their popular leaders. But unprovoked firing on mobs at Amritsar, Lahore and other towns in Punjab led to violence, arson and killing of Europeans. Although Hindu and Muslim women had not participated in these demonstrations, they experienced the agony and torture of losing their male family members at the hands of a tactless, vindictive, unimaginative and racist regime. The victims hailed from all sections of society including those simple-minded people who had gone for a *faryad* to the authorities and not with any rebellious intention.

The Jallianwala Bagh Massacre on 13 April was yet another act of official high-handedness which radically changed the attitude of the politically-conscious men and women towards the colonial rule. General Dyer, who had ordered firing of 1,650 rounds of ammunition, without warning, at a peaceful crowd, regarding it as a great opportunity to show people the might of the British empire for he imagined that 'the Lord hath delivered them into my hands'.[56]

By leaving as many as 379 dead and 1,200 wounded,[57] Dyer brimmed with satisfaction at the discharge of his duty, not realizing that he had created a virtual hell for the surviving women. Imposition of night curfew had obliged a number of women in Amritsar to suffer from mental torture as they could not get any help for locating their husbands, sons and other relatives who lay parched, weltering in their own blood and mangled limbs. The traumatic experience of Rattan Devi, who had ventured to the Bagh despite the curfew order and spent the whole night with her husband's cold head in her lap, was later to draw her out from the security of her *zenana* (women's quarters) to public life.[57] Attar Kaur, whose husband Bhagmal Bhatia was a committed local Congress worker, had been forced to spend a number of frightful hours amidst the dead and the wounded (despite the advanced stage of her pregnancy) until she could bring home the dead body of her husband with the help of her family servant and Udham Singh,[58] who had pledged to avenge the dastardly killing of the innocent people of Punjab.[59] The other women, though not as courageous as these, were obliged to shoulder the responsibilities of looking after their children and families and fend for their survival.

Believing that the inhabitants of Punjab, whom he had earlier lauded for their loyalty, had conspired to wage war against the King Emperor, O'Dwyer had permitted the proclamation of the Seditious Meetings Act, followed by the imposition of Martial Law in Punjab which lasted from mid-April to June 1919. In fact, the very purpose of Michael O'Dwyer's insistence on the promulgation of Martial Law No. IV showed that he was bent upon punishing not only the alleged rioters but also the political agitators. He had always associated political agitation with the educated urban middle classes. Hence, he wanted to spread the net as widely as possible to kill political movement and the imagined rebellion. His paranoid mentality led to the institution of a number of cases of conspiracy and rebellion against prominent members of professional classes and other citizens, including popular leaders, under Martial Law.

In Lahore, the popular leaders, namely Lala Harkishan Lal, Lala Duni Chand, Pandit Rambhuj Dutt and others were arrested on 14 April, tried in camera and sentenced to transportation for life (later released under the King's Proclamation of Amnesty towards the close of 1919) by a special Martial Law Tribunal.[60] Their properties were confiscated and thus exposed their young wives and children to moral and material damage. On the same grounds, Babu Kali Nath Roy, Editor of *The Tribune* and Radha Krishan, Editor of the *Pratap*, were also sentenced to various terms of imprisonment and fines.[61] Similar cases of rebellion and other seditious activities were instituted against Dr Kitchlew, Dr Satyapal, Chauhari Bugga Mal and Mahasha Rattan Chand, the primary and secondary leaders, respectively, of the Rowlatt agitation in Amritsar.[62]

Mahatma Gandhi, while severely criticizing the harsh and disproportionate sentences gives to the accused in the Lahore judgement,[63] also highlighted the hardships of the young wives of other Martial Law victims in the columns of *Young India.*[64] The cases of Mahasha Rattan Chand and Chaudhari Bugga Mal received special notice as the victims' original death sentences were merely changed into transportation for life despite the strong appeals made by Pandit Motilal Nehru, C.R. Das and other leaders.[65]

Besides, the Punjab Government harassed and humiliated lawyers in various ways. By appointing them as Special Constables, they were put to considerable physical discomfort as they had not only to patrol the city throughout the day but also to report to the authorities twice daily. Even a scholarly lawyer like Mr Manohar Lal, the Vice-President of the High Court Bar Association, was disgraced. His family was harassed and locked up on 18 April 1919. His wife and children took shelter in the servant's quarter and they had to borrow bedding from friends. The search took place on 19 April and thereafter the family could return to their house.[66]

In other towns of the Punjab, respectable citizens also had similar experiences. At Wazirabad, the house of Jamiat Singh Bugga was seized in his absence; the women and children of his family were turned out without any alternative arrangements being made for them.[67]

The inhabitants of the Punjab, especially citizens of Amritsar, had to undergo additional suffering and humiliation. For example, the *salaaming* order brought various kinds of punishments to the defaulters in the city of Amritsar of 160,000. Women waited tensely while their husbands, sons and other male relatives were marched through the city by the whimsical police officials. While boys and men were flogged publicly,[68] women watched helplessly. For example, Lachman Kaur articulated the mental agony of many women when she remarked, 'When the people were flogged their cries rent our hearts, we felt helpless. There seemed no remedy against the cruelty and oppression around us.'[69] Owing to panic, men stayed on shops and women huddled alone in homes cowering under fear and tension. They had to stay without food and water and the sick could not get medicine. They complained of the misbehaviour of the soldiers.[70] Ganga Devi's 4-year-old daughter died of fright.[71]

During the Martial Law regime, even the most innocent women of the villages were not spared. They were assaulted by government officials, physically manhandled and even turned out of their homes. The cruelty and barbaric behaviour of Bosworth Smith, Superintendent of Police, is illustrated by the following extract:

> In Manianwali village, on 19 April some soldiers entered the village and shot a few men without any warrant for shooting. Women fled from their houses on hearing the shoot-outs including those who were about to be mothers. . . . Two men, Munshi Nawab Din and Lehna Singh were severely beaten by Mr Boswoth Smith who assaulted their women, unveiled them and used abusive language. He called them 'Flies, bitches, she-asses'! He said to them, 'Your skirts will be examined by the constables. When you were sleeping with your husbands, why did you allow them to get up and go'? He also spat at them.'[72]

Gurdevi, the aged widow of Mangal Jat, recounted similar experience before Mr Labh Singh, an ex-Professor, and a barrister, who was specially deputed by the Congress Committee to investigate the shocking incidents which had occurred in the Punjab.[73]

In Chuharkhana village, a number of women were summoned by the police and warned that their houses would be burnt and land confiscated if they did not produce their husbands. It was not an empty threat. A number of residents later deposed that their wives had borrowed money to pay fines for the release of their husbands.[74]

In Sheikhupura, too, houses were locked and women along with their children turned out.[75] Other forms of harassment were also adopted. The male relatives of those women who could not bribe the police were arrested.[76]

In Hafizabad, Hukma Devi's son was locked up in jail because she was unable to find money to bribe the police.[77]

The Government of Punjab threw a veil of secrecy over the blood-curdling incidents in the province. As the Indian press was completely gagged from 15 April to 9 June, 1919,[78] neither the people nor the political leaders in the Punjab and outside could get any news about the sufferings, emotional trauma, deprivation and economic hardship of the beleaguered inhabitants of the region.

NEW SIGNPOSTS IN THE INDIAN CONSCIOUSNESS: FROM AMBIVALENCE TO ALIENATION

The traumatic experience of the Punjab disturbances right from the anti-Rowlatt agitation, the Jallianwala Bagh tragedy to the Martial Law regime brought an attitudinal change towards the British rule among the politically-conscious as well as the 'muted groups', especially among women. Henceforth, political awakening and disillusionment with the liberal claims of the British rulers grew at a rapid pace. Publication of the *Report of the Commissioners,* which had exposed the inequities of the O'Dwyer regime, eroded faith in the British ideals of justice and fairness. This is evident from the statements and reaction of the citizens of Amritsar. For example, Mian Feroz Din, an Honorary Magistrate since 1898 and a *rais,* remarked:

> I must say, however, that the pride which I myself, and my countrymen, felt in British justice, has received a rude shock. . . . So far as the people of Amritsar are concerned, I pray to God that we may not have to see those Martial Law days again.[79]

The people felt enraged owing to the discriminatory treatment towards Indian passengers including women in spite of holding Martial Law passes.[80]

A comparison between the Reports of the Congress Committee and of the Disorders Inquiry Committee further confirmed the fears and suspicions of Indians regarding the latter's laborious attempts to whitewash and gloss over the indiscretions and misuse of power by the Martial Law administrators in enforcing orders like crawling, flogging and saluting of Europeans in Amritsar, Gujranwala and other towns of Punjab.

As the sufferings and humiliations of the people of the Punjab came to light, the voice of protest also grew louder. The fact that General Dyer, the Commanding Officer at the Jallianwala Bagh Massacre, was lionized on his return to England, had provoked anger and resentment, apart from shaking the Indian faith in the British sense of justice. Gandhi's denunciation of the British rule as 'satanic' expressed his changed views about the Raj.

Writing to C.F. Andrews from England, Rabindranath Tagore underscored his anguish and disillusionment in the following words:

> '... The late events have conclusively proved that our true salvation lies in our own hands, that a nation's greatness can never find its foundation in half-hearted concessions of contemptuous niggardliness'.[81]

Evidently, branding the loyal inhabitants of Punjab as rebels had unwittingly promoted a spirit of defiance and strengthened the desire to overthrow national bondage. In other words, the suspicious and revengeful attitude of the functionaries of the O'Dwyer regime had dispelled illusions in Indians about retaining their self-respect and national pride as British subjects.

Michael O'Dwyer's determined effort to kill ideas and stifle political consciousness invigorated men as well as women. Thus, the virile and action-oriented inhabitants of Punjab became mentally prepared for the resumption of an armed struggle.

The sacrifices of the Kuka women Bibi Attri, Bhagwan Kaur (Sialkot), Jai Kaur (Ludhiana), Bholi and Darmo (Ferozepore), Ratto and Desan (Sirsa)[82] and of the Ghadarite women, particularly Gulab Kaur, were recalled in this context. It also provided an opportunity for a critical look at the heroes and heroic movements. As a result, a search began, tapping the revolutionary potential in local conditions and people. It resulted in a two-pronged experiment with terrorist methods and mass movements. Henceforth, the Indian people set forth on a path of self-discovery, new self-images and a world-view involving the etching of new psychological contours, articulation of alienation and protest.

How was this change in the consciousness articulated by Indian men and women? One concrete expression of alienation and protest against colonial connection found in the surrender of titles as a part of the Non-cooperation Movement having the rectification of Punjab wrongs as its major plank. Mahatma Gandhi returned the *Kaiser-i-Hind* Gold medal, Zulu War Medal and Boer War Medal.[83]

The people of Punjab also followed suit and returned *Kaiser-i-Hind* decorations, certificates, *sanads*, titles of *Rai Sahib, kursinashin*, etc.[84] The women of Punjab were not in possession of such titles or honorary posts. The lone woman was Sarla Debi Chaudharani, who returned her war badge granted for her recruiting services for the formation of the Bengali Regiment[85] during the First World War (1914–18).

An unprecedented increase in the visibility of women in public life was a significant outcome of the Punjab experience. In that moment of personal and national tragedy, the traditional image of women such as: '*Ander baithi lakh di Bahar gayi kakh di*'.[86] (The one who stays indoors is worth a lakh, but one who steps out is worth a straw) was discarded. The 'new' woman, who had developed a heightened awareness of her vulnerability in the course of Dyer's spree of racist revenge from 13 April to mid June (wreaked on the plea of protecting the inviolability of the womanhood of the superior Anglo-Saxon breed, personified by Miss Sherwood, from the dirty black hands),[87] felt emboldened to cross from domestic into public space.

Perceiving Gandhi as a saviour of the bleeding Punjab, especially the womenfolk of one thousand families, who had lost their bread-earners either as a result of police firing or incarceration,[88] Sarla Debi Chaudharni invited Mahatma Gandhi to instil courage and hope into their hearts. The fact that she acted as a hostess to a male leader in the absence of her husband and accompanied him to various towns in the Punjab to organize public meetings, indicated that Sarla Debi was made of different mettle. Already at an advanced stage of political consciousness and intellectual development, she had mobilized Punjabi women to join her struggle against Dyerism. As a result, a fairly large number of women flocked to attend public meetings when Gandhi visited Lahore, Amritsar, Gujranwala, Kasur, Wazirabad, Akalgarh, Ramnagar, Hafizabad, Sangla Hills, Sheikhupura, Lyallpur and Ludhiana.[89] In October 1919, as soon as the ban on his entry into Punjab was lifted,[90] in order to share the grief of the *purdah* women, Gandhi held special meetings for them at Gujranwala, Lyallpur and Hafizabad.[91] The refrain of his message at all these meetings was that they should cast away fear, become autonomous individuals and promote swadeshi.

In the course of his visit, Gandhi came into close contact with the bereaved women of Punjab. At Gujranwala, he comforted the wife of Diwan Mangal Sen (a Martial Law prisoner) and was impressed by her hospitality despite her sorrow.[92] In Amritsar, he met the wives of Dr Satyapal and Dr Kitchlew, whose fortitude in the hour of their mental tension and sorrow elicited his admiration.[93] Wherever he went his heartfelt sympathy helped Punjabi women to abandon their fear and anxiety and devote themselves to constructive work, particularly spinning and propagation of swadeshi.[94] Many Punjabi women adopted *khadi*. Sarla Debi Chaudharani became a trend-setter when she attended parties, marriages and *purdah* club meetings in a *khadi* sari. Increasing use of *khadi* by Punjabi women indicated a change in their self-view.

As a result, a large number of Punjabi women were drawn into national politics. Prominent among them were Sarla Debi Chaudhrani, Phul Kaur (wife of the Martial Law prisoner Chaudhri Bugga Mal), Rattan Devi and Attar Kaur (the widows of the Jallianwala Bagh martyrs Chajju Ram and Bhag Mal Bhatia respectively), Parbati Devi (daughter of Swami Shraddhanand), Radha Devi (wife of Lala Lajpat Rai) and a number of ordinary housewives, with no political background. Chastened by personal suffering and tragedy, these women had learnt to look beyond familial roles and later extended their activities to the broad arena of national work which included anti-imperialist demonstrations, processions, picketting, boycott of foreign cloth, swadeshi, *harijan* work, electoral politics, etc.

A concrete evidence of their new perception of the relationship between individual, family and nation was their enthusiastic response to Gandhi's call for donations towards funds for the support of the families of Martial Law victims, Jallianwala Bagh Memorial Fund and Tilak Swaraj Fund. The Punjabi women showed a touching concern for the support of such families as had been left only with womenfolk and children as a result of Martial Law atrocities, killings and imprisonment. For example, women of Amritsar generously donated their jewellery for this cause. Despite their own economic problems, Mrs Bugga Mal and Mrs Rattan Chand donated their gold bracelets. For the Jallianwala Bagh Memorial Fund, donations came primarily from the relatives of the martyrs. For example, Rattan Devi gave Rs 500; a domestic maid servant, who had lost her son in the Jallianwala Bagh holocaust, donated Rs 50, which amounted to her total annual earnings.[95] Another unidentified woman presented her dead son's clothes and her ornaments to the Jallianwala Bagh Memorial Fund. [96] These examples showed the growing awareness of Punjabi women of the link between their family fortunes and national life.

More remarkable than this was their initiative and involvement in the fund-raising drive. At Ferozepur, on their own initiative women collected funds for the Jallianwala Bagh Memorial during the National Week (6–13 April 1920). Again, at Amritsar, they built up the Tilak Swaraj Fund. At Bhiwani, too, Mrs Desai and other Gujarati women made house to house collections and opened a separate women's section for the National Fund.[97]

After taking the first step in public life in the course of the anti-Rowlatt agitation, the Punjabi women had learnt to articulate their sufferings as a result of the British oppression, symbolized by the Jallianwala Bagh massacre and Martial Law humiliations and deprivations. During his visit to Punjab, Gandhi observed that the songs narrating the story of 'Dyerism', reflecting their new spiritedness and resolve to liberate their motherland from the foreign yoke, were on their lips. One such popular song sung in the course of the Rowlatt agitation was:

Asi nahinaun haarnan,
Bhanve saadi jaan jave,
Taup te bandook kaulon,
Khande walli dhar kaulon,
Agg de sholeyan taun,
Asi nahinaun haarnan.[98]

(We shall not accept defeat even if we lose our lives, we are shot dead or cut into pieces by swords and other sharp-edged weapons or burnt alive. We resolve not to surrender).

This song was composed by Sarla Debi Chaudhrani.

In fact, the Rowlatt agitation, which had roused the spirit of defiance among Punjabi women, had released their creative potential and occasioned the composition of numerous patriotic poems and songs in vernacular languages. I have discussed this aspect in a separate paper, but a brief reference may be relevant here. Kasturi Bai, who was taught the working knowledge of Hindi and Urdu by her nationalist husband Rampat Yadav, was not only active in the Gandhian movements in Rohtak but also a prolific poetess. Published under the title, *Rashtriya Geet aur Bhajan 1930–47,* her compositions in Haryanvi-mixed-Urdu reflected her perception of the British Government – ungrateful, oppressive, exploitative and cunning. This is evident from the following extract from her poem 'Angrezi Raj ka Abhishap' ('Curse of the British Raj'):

Pichle vaade saare bhooli Rowlatt bill inaam diya,
Bus tera yehi sanmaan hai, tu nahin bhoolne paave,
Aisa bura masaan hai, bina jaan liye na jaave.
Rowlatt bill se piche bhai 'phauji' laa ke kari jaan,
Jiski rooh se misle saanp ke Hindi chale pait ke taan,
Gun ke badle avgun kartaa dekho kaisa baimaan, ji.
Duniya bhar mein aisa koi dekha nahin raaj bhai,
Khaali haath praja par goli jisne ho chalvai,
Amritsar mein Jallianwale Dyer ne laash bichai.
Khud taure yehi kanoon hai, praja par dosh lagaave.
Aisa bura masoan hai, bina jaan liye na jaave.[99]

Addressing unsuspecting and innocent Hindi (Indians), Kasturi Bai asked them to beware of the British Raj. It is not a government for the people but a fatal disease which gradually sucks away the life-giving blood. There is no other government like the British one which had ordered firing on the unarmed crowd. Dyer had covered the ground of Jallianwala Bagh with dead bodies. This is a strange *sarkar* which violates the law herself but punishes its subjects for law-breaking.

Kasturi Bai also wrote a number of poems glorifying the *charkha.* She was a bold critic of general passivity and lack of courage among Indian men.[100]

Bhag Devi, (wife of Lala Dunichand, a prominent Congress leader of Ambala) was not formally educated but her anguish over the massacre of innocent men, women and children obliged her to overcome her handicap. Her poems appeared under the caption *Quami Bhajanon ka Guldasta.* She was also the author of *Jagriti* and *Gita Sandesh.*

Highly educated women also expressed their reaction against the Jallianwala

Bagh tragedy and atrocities. Sarla Debi Chaudhrani wrote in Punjabi, Bengali and English. Her writings, *At the Point of the Spindle* and *The Song of Charkha*, which had grown out of her personal experience of the British oppression and cruelty, reflected her strong faith in the efficacy of the *charkha* which symbolized *sudarshan chakra* to her. The nationalists read her compositions with great fervour.[102]

Rameshwari Nehru, though not educated through formal schooling, emerged as one of the pioneering journalists who expressed her anguish over the Jallianwala Bagh tragedy in her articles and editorials in *Stree Darpan* (founded in 1909). Daughter of the orthodox Raja Narender Nath of Lahore, she became a dedicated disciple of Mahatma Gandhi and plunged into the swadeshi and *harijan* movements. She also represented the radical change in the self-view and world-view of Indian women. For example, she flouted *purdah* restrictions and participated in public activities, even against her father's wishes. She had also chosen to differ from her mentor Mahatma Gandhi on the issue of economic empowerment, particularly, employment of women. In fact, Gandhi and Indian women, helped each other to grow and abandon their prejudices.[103]

The Jallianwala Bagh tragedy moved a number of sensitive women not resident in Punjab and it found expression in their writings. Sarojini Naidu's poem 'Punjab in 1919'[104] and Subhadra Kumari Chauhan's long poem 'Jallianwala Bagh Mein Basant' (1929) bear this out.

Obviously, the Jallianwala Bagh tragedy had left an indelible impression on the collective memory of Indians, particularly Punjabis. It continues to be a monument of national resistance against oppression and tyranny even today.

CONCLUSION

My discussion of the anti-Rowlatt agitation, culminating in the Jallianwala Bagh tragedy and followed by the imposition of the Martial Law regime, reveals the indelible and strong impact these events had on the nationalist psyche. This traumatic experience had proved to be a catalyst of the Indian people's consciousness, especially of the 'muted groups' whose projection and involvement were crucial for the success of the Indian freedom struggle.

The colonial state's decision to withdraw this 'devilish legislation' (as done earlier in the case of the Punjab Canal Colonization Bills, 1907) under the overwhelming pressure of public opinion and to issue the Civil and Military Ordinance reflected the shrewd British perception that the perpetuation of their Raj depended more upon the cooperation of the subject people than upon the frequent military interventions. Gandhi was no less conscious of this compulsion of the hegemonic British-Indian state.

However, it was Gandhi's growing awareness of the crucial role of the Indian people in the national struggle for freedom that led to his total involvement in the long-term project of a psychological and moral revolution among his compatriots. It conveyed a positive message to the semi-literate, poor masses and women that hope of some sort was an integral part of the nationalist agenda. It may be pointed out that the 'muted groups' did not form a single category. The problem then is, how to reconcile and relate to the broad process of redefinition of the Indian self-hood with the transformation of the consciousness of the 'muted groups,' especially women (whose deprivation and subordination varied with race, caste and class) in the course of the national struggle against colonialism and capitalism.

Other related issues which demand attention are readjustment or reallocation of physical and communication spaces and reformulation of cultural constructs, self-image and world-view of these 'invisible' and peripheral social groups until Gandhi brought them to the centre of the nationalist arena. Perhaps, the exercise of a detailed investigation into the positioning of the 'muted groups' in the mass movements (from their initiation to their active and large-scale involvement as participants and leaders) requires acceptance of the need to shift theoretical focus away from nations of 'sameness' and uniform and general experience of subordination to regional variations in the social-cultural milieu and economic activity and thus in the nature of oppression and gender politics. However, I would like to emphasize the point that the regional and micro-studies of the national movement and of the role of the 'muted groups' in social movements must be done with a view to contributing to the understanding of the total picture of the process of the transformation of Indian consciousness in the course of the nationalist struggle for liberation from the politico-economic and cultural bondage of the British imperialism.

Having raised these questions, focus must be placed on the real gains from this uncalled for suffering, the material and moral damage occasioned by the Jallianwala Bagh tragedy for the Indian people and their multi-pronged struggle against the foreign yoke. Broadly speaking, the Jallianwala Bagh tragedy sharpened the nationalist perception about the long-term implications of the colonial domination which was bound to affect all classes of society as well as all realms of their existence: social, cultural, political and economic. Perhaps this realization of subjection and their consequent aspiration for freedom led to the convergence of the entire nation's energy, thinking, search and action upon a common target or goal. They chose either the stream of violence or non-violence in concurrence with associated movements on a smaller scale at the regional level.

The 'muted' groups, particularly women (without underrating the psychological leavening among ordinary peasants, workers and other such groups) were perforce brought out of their 'splendid isolation'. Propelled by their personal, albeit, shared experience of the British repressive laws and the brute force of the Martial Law regime, which had assaulted their honour, suppressed the civil rights of their menfolk and effected the well-being and economic security of their kith and kin, they felt obliged to enlarge their working environment from home to nation.

My limited study has shown that the emotional scars of state terrorism, symbolized by the Jallianwala Bagh tragedy, led to positive results in one sense. The general goodwill and ambivalence in the Indian attitude towards what was considered the 'fair, firm and just *Angrezi Raj*' came to be replaced by social anger and alienation, thus facilitating Gandhi's almost impossible task of converting each home into a battle-ground. Once emboldened to articulate their anguish and anger against the public authority in songs and poems, the Indian women, especially Punjabi women (who were purdah-clad and backward in terms of education), were not to be deterred from discovering and harnessing their creative potential for social engineering, nation-building and above all for constructing their own independent identities. Of course, all this was done within the framework of new patriarchy which accommodated mobility without demanding structural changes.

The Indian National Congress (and later the revolutionary groups and the Left party) strengthened its claims as a representative of national aspirations with the induction of women as political workers and leaders. In fact, Gandhi's perceptive action of giving moral and cultural legitimacy to the women's role in Indian public life, especially in reconstruction and the political struggle, paved the way for increasing the visibility of women in the non-violent movements from the 1920s to the 1940s. Thus, one major positive gain from the Jallianwala Bagh tragedy for the Indian national movement can be summed up in one sentence: the 'muted' groups recovered their voice, language, identity and discovered for themselves a dignified presence in the Indian society and polity.

NOTES AND REFERENCES

1. Edwin Ardener, 'The Problem Revisited', in S. Ardener ed., *Perceiving Women* (London, 1975), pp. 21–23.
2. K.N. Panikkar, 'Incomplete Struggle' in *Seminar*, no. 338, October 1987, p.27.
3. Eric Stokes, *The English Utilitarians in India*, (reprinted OUP, Delhi, 1982), p. 268.
4. Charles Gough and Arthur D. Innes, *The Sikhs and the Sikh Wars* (reprinted Delhi, 1984), p. 222. Also Foreign Department, Despatch no. 20, 7 April 1849, Governor-General Lord Dalhousie to Secret Committee.

5. Kenneth W. Jones, *Arya Dharma: Hindu Consciousness in the Nineteenth Century Punjab* (Delhi, 1977), p. 12.
6. Reprinted in N.G. Barrier, 'How to Rule India', *Punjab Past and Present*, no. 5, 1971, pp. 276–96.
7. Eric Stokes, *op. cit.*, p. 299.
8. *Ibid.*, p. 269.
9. For an exposition of this point of view see: Bipan Chandra's 'Colonialism: Stages of Colonialism and the Colonial State, *Journal of Contemporary Asia*, vol. 10, no. 3, 1980. Also Sabyasachi Bhattacharya's 'Notes on the Role of Intelligentsia in Colonial Society: India from Mid-Nineteenth Century,' *Studies in History*, vol. 1, no.1, 1979.
10. Sudipta Kaviraj, *On the Construction of Colonial Power: Structure, Discourse, Hegemony*, Occasional papers on History and Society, Second Series, no. XXXV (Centre for Contemporary Studies, Nehru Memorial Museum and Library, 1991) p. 19, also Shashi Joshi and Bhagwan Josh, *Struggle for Hegemony in India 1920–47* in 2 vols. (New Delhi, 1992), vol. I, pp. 10–42; vol. II, pp. 25–44.
11. For an exposition of the concept of collaboration in terms of patron-client relationship, see Anil Seal, *The Emergence of Indian Nationalism* (London, 1971).
12. Shashi Joshi and Bhagwan Josh, *op. cit.*, vol. I.
13. Raghavan Iyer, *Utilitarianism and All That: The Political Theory of British Imperialism* (London, 1983), pp. 115–23.
14. The policy of establishing hegemonic control was described in various ways such as, possessing moral prestige and retaining 'legal authority' by the colonial state itself. For example, Lord Birkenhead characterized the British Government as a 'government founded completely . . . upon prestige'. Cited in Simon Epstein, District Officers in Decline: The Erosion of British Authority in the Bombay Countryside 1919–47', *Modern Asian Studies*, vol. 16, no. 3. 1982. pp. 483–518.
15. M.K. Gandhi, *Hind Swaraj* (Ahmedabad, 1982), p. 100.
16. Sudipta Kaviraj, *op. cit.*, p. 19.
17. K.N. Pannikar, 'The Intellectual History of Colonial India: Some Historiographic and Conceptual Questions,' in S. Bhattacharya and Romila Thapar, *Situating Indian History* (Delhi, 1986), p. 421.
18. I have borrowed this argument from Ashish Nandy. *The Intimate Enemy: Loss and Recovery of Self under Colonialism* (Delhi, 1983), p. 7.
19. Kamlesh Mohan, 'The Colonial Ethnography: Imperial Pursuit of Knowledge for Hegemony in British India (late nineteenth to early twentieth century) in Roy McLeod and E.L. Ortiz eds., *New Perspectives of Empires and Science* (forthcoming), p.14 (typescript).
20. Ashish Nandy, no.18, pp. 8–9.
21. *Ibid.*, p. 48.
22. *Ibid.*, p. 52.
23. Katherine Mayo, *Mother India* (London, 1917), p.16. Earlier, in his book *History of India*, James Mill had constructed his entire argument for the justification of perpetuating the British rule in India around the issues of the degenerate Indian civilization, abject position of Hindu women and 'effeminacy' of Hindu men who were unfit for self-government.
24. *Collected Works of Mahatma Gandhi* (hereafter *CWMG*), vol.13, 1916, pp. 443, 454, 496. In the course of his tours around India, he exhorted wives, mothers and sisters to involve their men in military service, because voluntary recruitment will lead to swaraj.
25. *The Tribune*, 8 February 1919.

26. *CWMG*, vol. 15, p. 88.
27. *The Indian Annual Register*, 1920, vol. I, p. 36.
28. *CWMG*, vol. 15, p. 189.
29. *Ibid.*, pp. 290–91.
30. Rameshwari Nehru, *Gandhi is My Star* (Patna, 1950), p.29. Rameshwari Nehru, daughter of the renowned Hindu Leader Raja Narendra Nath, was married to Brij Lal Nehru. G. Broker ed., *Selected Speeches and Writings of Raj Kumari Amrit Kaur* (New Delhi, 1961), p. 180. Raj Kumari, the trusted secretary and close confidante of Gandhi for the last thirteen years of his life, was the daughter of Raja Harnam Singh of Kapurthala; Oral transcript of interview with Sucheta Kriplani (New Delhi: Nehru Memorial Museum and Liberary). Sucheta belonged to a Brahmo-Samajist family having links with Keshub Chander Sen. Her father was a medical pratitioner at Ambala. Gandhi gave his permission for Sucheta's marriage with J.B. Kripalani with great reluctance because he was afraid of losing Kripalani – a devoted constructive worker. See Bibi Amtussalaam, 'Bapu ke Pas', in Shadi Ram Joshi ed., *Insaniyat ke Pehredar* in Hindi (New Delhi, 1972), p. 317. Amtussalaam belonged to an orthodox aristocratic family of Patiala. Daughter of Mahammed Abdul Majid Khan, she was not sent to school for formal education owing to the observance of strict *purdah* which she discarded in 1925.
31. *The Tribune*, 7 February 1919.
32. For a detailed discussion of the anti-Rowlatt agitation in Punjab and especially Amritsar, see Kamlesh Mohan, *Militant Nationalism in Punjab* (Delhi, 1985), pp. 13–40.
33. H.F.Owen, 'Organizing Rowlatt Satyagraha of 1919', in R.Kumar ed., *Essays in Gandhian Politics* (Delhi, 1971), p. 82.
34. M.K. Gandhi, *The Story of My Experiments with Truth*, (reprinted Ahmedabad, 1958), p. 340.
35. For biographical details of Dr Satyapal and Dr Kitchlew see Fauja Singh's *Eminent Freedom Fighters of Punjab* (Patiala, 1972), pp. 200–1, 205–6.
36. For the basis of this division, see the chronological record of meetings and *hartals* from 31 January to 13 April 1919 in the Amritsar Conspiracy Case, 1919 (hereafter *ACC* NAI, New Delhi), no. 1, Roll no. I (in one roll).
37. Disorders Inquiry Committee Evidence (hereafter *DICE*), vol. VI, pp. 80, 103-Evidence of Michael O'Dwyer.
38. *ACC*, p. 72- Statement of Dr Satyapal, accused no. 2.
39. *Ibid.*, pp. 74, 105.
40. *Report of the Commissioners*, vol. II, p. 711 – Evidence of Dr Kitchlew.
41. *Disorders Inquiry Report 1919–20*, (hereafter *DICR*), p. 238.
42. *The Tribune*, 8 April 1919.
43. This information is based on my personal interviews with Mrs Satyawati, Mrs Bhag Devi, Mrs Pushpa Gujral and Mrs Guaran Devi on 20 June 1989, 20 January 1984, 20 July 1988, 18 June 1984 respectively.
44. *The Tribune*, 12 April 1919.
45. *Report of the Commissioners*, vol. I, p. 47.
46. *DICE*, vol. VI, p. 100.
47. *ACC*, p. 721 – Statement of Dr Kitchlew. For the official version, see *DICE*, vol. III, p. 19. It was stated that Dr Kitchlew practically ordered the *hartal*. Also see Hans Raj's statement. According to him, Dr Kitchlew, Chaudhri Bugga Mal, Mahasha Rattan Chand, Badr-ul-Islam Ali Khan, Gurdial Singh, Narain Das and Dr Mohammad Bashir planned on 5 April that a *hartal* should be proclaimed on 6 April by the beating of a drum. He further added

that the shopkeepers were to close their shops since they knew that they would be looted otherwise. As his statement was uncorroborated, the theory about the *hartal* being pre-planned and organized peters out.

48. *The Tribune*, 7 April 1919.
49. *The Tribune*, 8 April 1919. The lead article 'Action against Dr Kitchlew and Others' argued that the official action was unjust as none of them had acted in a manner prejudicial to public safety.
50. *DICE*, vol. VI, pp. 30, 165.
51. *Report of the Commissioners*, vol. II, pp. 712–20, statement of Dr Satyapal and Dr Kitchlew.
52. *The Tribune*, 11 April 1919. Editorial 'Blazing Indiscretion'.
53. *Bombay Chronicle*, 12 April 1919.
54. Text of the song – courtesy Professor V.N. Datta, New Delhi.
55. *The Tribune*, 11 April 1919.
56. Cited in Arthur Swinson, *Six Minutes to Sunset* (London, 1964), p. 54.
57. Home Department, Political (Deposit), Proceedings no. 23, September 1919 (NAI, New Delhi).
58. *Ibid.*, pp. 64–65.
59. Sohan Lal Bharati, *Jallianwala Bagh Ki Khooni Dharti aur Mere Mata Pita* (Amritsar n.d). pp. 16–17. Also *The Tribune*, 13 April 1961.
60. K.L. Gauba, *The Rebel Minister: The Story of the Rise and Fall of Lala Harkishan Lal* (Lahore, 1938), p. 87.
61. For the judgements of various Martial Law Commissions, especially Lahore, Amritsar, see Pearay Mohan, *An Imaginary Rebellion: And How It was Suppressed*, with a foreword by Lala Lajpat Rai (Lahore, 1920), pp. 82–121.
62. For a detailed account of the Amritsar Conspiracy Case, see Kamlesh Mohan, *op. cit.*
63. *CWMG*, vol. XVIII, p. 473.
64. M.K. Gandhi, 'A Punjab Victim', in *Young India*, no. 15, October 1919. It also refers to the case of Behari Lal Sachdeva, sentenced to transportation for life.
65. M.K. Gandhi, 'A Hard Case', in *Young India*, 26 May 1920. Chaudhari Bugga Mal and Mahasha Rattan Chand were released in 1936.
66. *Report of the Commissioners*, vol. I, pp. 83–84. Also vol. II, pp. 198–206, Evidence of Mr Manohar Lal, Bar-at-Law.
67. *Ibid.*, pp. 113–14. Also *DICR*, vol. II, p. 210.
68. *DICR*, 1919–20, pp. 208–10.
69. *Report of the Commissioners*, 1919–20, vol. I, pp. 63–64. Also vol. II, Statement no. 125. Also Statement nos. 127, 133.
70. *Ibid.*, vol. II, Statement nos. 125 to 132 – Lachman Kaur, Iswar Kaur (a widow with a sick child), Khem Kaur, Buddhi Devi, Devki and Ganga Devi.
71. *Ibid.*, Statement, no. 132.
72. *Report of the Commissioners*, vol. I, p. 128.
73. *Ibid.*, pp. 128–29.
74. *Ibid.*, p. 139.
75. *CWMG*, vol. 17, p. 275.
76. *Ibid.*, p. 27.
77. *Report of the Commissioners*, vol. I, p. 120.
78. *CWMG*, vol. 15, p. 334. All issues of *The Tribune* from 25 April to 31 July 1919 had been confiscated by the Punjab Government in the case of Kali Nath Roy vs The King

Emperor. These are available in Home Department Proceedings nos. 228–50, October 1919, pp. 77–92.

79. *Report of the Commissioners*, vol. II, Statement no. 2.
80. *Ibid.*, Statement no. 1 – Girdhari Lal, Deputy Chairman, the Punjab Chambers of Commerce and Managing Director, the Amritsar Flour and General Mills Co. Ltd., Amritsar.
81. *Rabindranath Tagore Papers*, Tagore to Andrews, 22 July 1920.
82. For a detailed account about these women, see Home Department Judicial B. Proceedings nos. 192–93, April 1882 (NAI, New Delhi). Also Proceedings nos. 186–89, April 1881, and 188–95.
83. *All India Congress Committee Papers* (hereafter *AICC* papers, Nehru Memorial Museum and Library, New Delhi), File no. 5, 1920.
84. *Ibid.*, Also *The Tribune*, 28 October, 3, 6, 28 November, 1920.
85. *AICC* papers. File no. 5, 1920. *The Tribune*, 4 August 1920, *Adhyudya*, 7 August 1920.
86. *District Gazetteer Multan* 1901–2, p. 28.
87. *Command Papers*. no. 771 – Statement by General Dyer. Also Ian Colvin, *The Life of General Dyer* (London, 1929), p. 172.
88. Home Department, Political (Deposit), Proceedings no. 23, September 1919.
89. *CWMG*, vol. 16, pp. 286, 316, 324, 348.
90. *Ibid.*, p. 261.
91. *CWMG*, vol. 16, pp. 316, 331, 348.
92. *Ibid.*, p. 316.
93. *Ibid.*
94. *Ibid.*, pp. 329–31.
95. The information given in this paragraph is based on *The Tribune*, 15 and 17 April 1920.
96. Home Department, Political A. Proceedings nos. 71–72, August 1920.
97. *The Tribune*, 1 May, 16 February, 2 July 1921.
98. For the text of this song, see Ramesh Vidrohi, *Jab Roya Punjab* in Hindi (New Delhi, 1977).
99. For the text of Kasturi Bai's songs and *bhajans*, see K.C. Yadav ed., *Haryana Swatantrata Andoloan Mein Kaviyon, Shairon, Bhajan Updeshkon aur Loknayakon ka Yogdaan* in Hindi (Delhi, 1988), pp. 184–206. For the text of 'Angrezi Raj Ka Abhishap', see pp. 184–85.
100. *Ibid.*, pp. 203–6.
101. Personal interview with Mrs Bhag Devi on 20 January 1984.
102. The information about Sarla Debi Chaudhrani's role in anti-Rowlatt agitation, popularization of Swadeshi and organization of women on a political basis, is drawn from *CWMG*, vol. 18, p. 20 and her booklets namely, *The Song of Charkah* (Madras, n.d.) and *At the Point of the Spindle* (Madras, n.d.).
103. Kamlesh Mohan, 'Image of Women in *Stree Darpan* 1909–28', in *Indian History Congress Proceedings*, 52nd Session, New Delhi.
104. For the text of Sarojini Naidu's poem (Hindi version) see Ramesh Vidrohi, *op. cit.*
105. For the text of Subhadra Kumari Chauhan's poem see Ramesh Upadhyay ed., *Jallianwala Bagh* (New Delhi, 1969, 1985).

SIX

❖ The Jallianwala Bagh Tragedy: Its Prelude and Aftermath

HARI SINGH

THE YEAR 1919 IS A turning point in the history of the national movement in India. It marked the high watermark in our national movement when the secular values and nationalist feelings were at their peak. The Rowlatt Act, passed in March 1919, marked the culmination of the oppressive policies of the British. So sudden was the reaction that Mahatma Gandhi became the mentor, messiah and protector of human values. Undaunted by British bullets, he gave a call for a nationwide satyagraha and the programme covered unity, self-sacrifice and fighting evil by non-violent means.[1] The movement in the Punjab was so intense that the British administration declared that an Open Rebellion had broken out there.[2]

The aim of this paper is to trace the historical forces which led to the popular reaction, discontent and revolt against the repressive policies of the British leading to the Jallianwala Bagh tragedy. Besides, it seeks to bring to focus the indelible impact it left on the Indian psyche, determining the future course of our national movement.

Some contemporary writings penned as a reaction to the Jallianwala Bagh tragedy and the Punjab administration's atrocities include the works of Kapil Dev Malaviya,[3] Alfred Nundy,[4] Pearay Mohan,[5] Lala Lajpat Rai[6] and B.G. Horniman.[7] These authors represent the popular and nationalist sentiments of the time. During the last three decades, some objective and well researched studies have appeared. These include the studies of V.N. Datta,[8] Ravinder Kumar,[9] Rupert Furneaux,[10] Arthur Swinson,[11] Alfred Draper[12] and Helen Fein.[13] They focus on the war discontents, the Rowlatt satyagraha, the Jallianwala Bagh tragedy and the psychology of General R.E.H. Dyer at the time of shooting.

This paper aims to analyse the Rowlatt satyagraha and the Jallianwala Bagh tragedy on the basis of new sources.[14] The Government and AICC records, contemporary works, English and vernacular newspapers, compositions from folk literature,[15] oral recordings preserved in the Nehru Memorial Museum and Library, New Delhi, and the Motilal Nehru Papers, comprising case files and diaries form the most valuable sources.

Amritsar was the main centre of political activity where violence erupted and led to the Jallianwala Bagh tragedy. The background of mass unrest could be traced back to the years of World War I (1914–18). Economic distress throughout Punjab was the net result of the war. Forced recruitment left few hands to plough the lands. Diseases like influenza and malaria also took a heavy toll in 1918.[16] The crops failed and whatever foodgrains were available were exported for the military. Naturally, the prices of foodgrains rose rapidly. In Amritsar the percentage increase during the war years of wheat was 87.82, jawar 136.35, bajra 127.14 and gram 108.80.[17] In Lahore also the prices of foodgrains rose steeply; even the price of common salt rose by 149.18 per cent.[18] The day-to-day expenditure of a clerk rose by 62 per cent.[19] In Gujranwala, the prices of foodgrains rose from 300 to 400 per cent.[20]

Thus, all over the Punjab, the middle and poor classes suffered greatly due to the price rise. The poor urban labourers with rural backgrounds, owing to habit and custom ate jowar and bajra and the rise in the prices of these coarse grains hit them hardest. The rise in prices of wheat hit the middle classes. Among those affected were artisans, cottage industries workers, masons, builders, coolies and unskilled labourers whose wages were too low to absorb the unprecedented price rise. The traders also felt the impact, as the Government acquired 5,000 tons of wheat from them at a low rate.[21] This also affected the farmer who was forced to sell his produce at a cheaper rate.[22] Chelmsford, realizing the situation, wrote to Montagu stating that the economic position was serious and had reached a boiling point.[23] We find that a sizeable portion of the population was discontented. The Government clerks, workers in railway workshops, students, artisans and tonga-drivers, i.e. the grassroots society, were ready to join a movement against the Raj.[24]

Besides this, Punjab's importance as a border province and a major base for recruitment meant that it was administered with an iron hand by the Lieutenant Governor Sir Michael O' Dwyer, who crushed the liberty of speech, thought and expression of its people.[25] He was always in support of a conservative policy of suppression and Chelmsford had given him *carte blanche* in the Punjab.[26] In such a situation, the Rowlatt Bill created considerable misunderstanding and many rumours were set afloat, which came to be believed by the people of the Punjab.[27]

The Rowlatt satyagraha had a ready response in the Punjab. To start with, the leadership was in the hands of the middle class, mainly the urban lawyers, who waged a constitutional tirade against the Rowlatt Act. They staged demonstrations, led processions and mobilized the masses. Details of the entire movement being beyond the scope of this paper, we may confine the events at Amritsar before analysing its impact on the Jallianwala Bagh tragedy.

About 40,000 people of Amritsar participated in the protest meetings on 30 March 1919. The subject matter of the speeches was clearly anti-British and the speakers brought out the nature of racial hatred which prevailed in their government as Indians were ill-treated at the hill stations, railway stations and in the court room by the Anglo-Indians.[28] An audience of 7,000 persons attended a meeting at the Jallianwala Bagh on 2 April 1919. Swami Satyadev, a follower of Gandhi and a native of Delhi, delivered a speech on 'Soul force' and made a pledge to organize a *satyagraha sabha.*[29] On 6 April, the day of humiliation and prayers the entire business of the city came to a standstill. A procession comprising the youth of the city was taken out and their number swelled to 4,000. This procession converged at the Jallianwala Bagh, where a mass meeting comprising 5,000 people was held and the President of this meeting explained the meaning of the passive resistance. This meeting approved the satyagraha vow, and recommended the organization of the *satyagraha sabha.*[30]

Citizens of Amritsar celebrated the Ram Naumi festival on 9 April as a national festival, in which Hindus, Muslims and Sikhs joined in. The tempo of political activity seemed to have quickened as the processionists now raised slogans like,'*Mahatma Gandhi ki Jai*', '*Satyapal ki Jai*', '*Kitchlew ki Jai*'. However, on 9 April, it was clear that the demonstration of unity did not mean hostility to the British. The procession was led by Dr Hafiz Muhammad Bashir and the bands played 'God Save the King.'[31] The Europeans could move in the procession freely and due respect was paid to the Deputy Commissioner of Amritsar, Miles Irving. Thus the movement was entirely peaceful at Amritsar from 30 March to 9 April, 1919. There was no mob violence till then.

The early phase of the movement provided political education in the methods of protest on the lines of passive resistance. There was no indication of any organized conspiracy to overthrow the British rule or to terrorize the ruling class. However, national sentiment was high and some popular local leaders had emerged. The most popular among them were Saifuddin Kitchlew and Satyapal. They had joined hands in politics; both were secular, worked for Hindu-Muslim unity and organized political meetings during the early months of 1919 .[32]

The citizens of Amritsar were shocked to learn on 10 April that Satyapal and Kitchlew were arrested and lodged in jail at Dharamsala, in the Kangra Valley. It was a miscalculation on the part of O'Dwyer to have ordered their arrest. He was probably influenced by the experience of 1907, when the arrest of Lala Lajpat Rai and Ajit Singh had crushed the peasant movement.[33] With the passage of time people had become better organized and politically more active. The immediate reaction of the Amritsar citizens was to show the strength of their unity to the administration. A mob, possibly numbering 15,000 to 20,000, came together spontaneously. It was initially a mourning procession, with many people appearing bare-headed without sticks or weapons of any kind.[34] People converged from all sides and the mob passed peacefully through the Hall Gate and the destination of their march was the Deputy Commissioner's bungalow where they wanted to press for the release of their leaders.[35]

The Deputy Commissioner of Amritsar, Miles Irving, had a weak personality and lacked tact and confidence. He panicked and was convinced that a rebellion had broken out which ought to be suppressed with force. He thus ordered firing on this unarmed, defenceless, though angry, mob.[36] He testified that the mob threw brickbats, which were returned with bullets. As a result of the police firing, about 20 to 25 persons were either killed or wounded.[37] The mob now armed itself with *lathis.* The police too, started firing with a vengeance, not sparing even a single persons. The dead bodies were taken out in a procession through the bazaar. This added fuel to the fire. More and more people joined this mob as it passed through the streets and lanes; even the hooligan and criminal elements joined it. Now the anti-British feeling was running high. As is natural, in such a situation the mob, in its frenzy, loses its sense of reason and strikes not only those who have harmed but often the most innocent and unsuspecting ones. Now the focus of their anger was directed against the Europeans and their institutions, such as Government property, the telegraph officer, railway station, Christian Book Society and the Normal School.[38]

Leadership of the mob passed on to the rowdy elements and criminals. This was the beginning of the chaos that was to follow later. The lawyers and moderates, who believed in passing resolutions and presenting petitions, seemed to have lost their influence over the mob. As a result, passive resistance or non-violence was relegated to the background. Kotumal, the Congress leader, tried to pacify the mob near the Punjab National Bank; he succeeded for a while but ultimately the desire to take recourse to violent means surfaced. Then he went to Sewan Bazar in an effort to pacify the mob of 2,000 people. They agreed to retreat but within minutes when the news that the English soldiers had fired upon some men and killed them spread, the mob became unruly and rushed to Hall Bazar, the scene of the incident.[39] It appeared Amritsar was engulfed in the throes of violence. First, a mob of about 500 men attacked the Central Telegraph office at 2 p.m., shattering in the process the windows, the switchboard and the telephone communication system. The telegraph master Mr Pinto, was saved from the mob fury by two soldiers. Another mob attacked the railway station and set ablaze the goods shed. At this time Sergeant Rowlands, the electrician, who was on his way to the Municipal Power House from the Fort, was chased, overtaken and clubbed to death.[40]

Another leaderless and disorganized mob moved about in the Hall Bazar, where it attacked the National Bank and clubbed to death, Stewart, the Manager. Scott, the Assistant Manager, too was murdered. Oil was then poured on the bank furniture and in the fire that ensued, dead bodies were burnt.[41] Thereafter the safe was broken and money was looted. The godowns in the rear were plundered, including watches and clothes worth lakhs of rupees.[42] The mob also attacked the Alliance Bank where the manager was killed with *lathis*. The mob looted the bank, the treasuries, safes and set ablaze the building. The looting of the banks continued till late at night.[43]

The murders and looting of banks could not be attributed to the average citizen who had joined the Rowlatt satyagraha. In the confusion that prevailed, a loose mob comprising all sorts of people was formed.[44] New evidence shows that the criminal elements of the city had been active participants.[45] In the National Bank case, two wandering tribes, the Phernas and Sefedas, were also involved.[46] Some prostitutes who belonged to these tribes along with some *Mirasis* and touts were caught in the act of distribution of booty.[47] Another startling fact was reported by the Central Criminal Intelligence Report. It stated that the police also indulged in looting of the banks. However, this report was finally suppressed; O'Dwyer put it in cold storage and as a protest, the Director of Criminal Intelligence resigned.[48] Tilak wrote to Kharparde that if facts became known the Government of India was doomed.[49] But the facts never came out for obvious reasons.

As a result of the mob violence, the killing of Europeans, and the looting of banks, the Civil Administration was completely paralysed.[50] Some Englishmen felt that the 'Revolt of 1857 was being repeated'. The Jallianwala Bagh massacre was the final scene of this sombre tragedy. The peaceful agitation over the Rowlatt Act took the shape of a violent movement, primarily owing to the firing on unarmed mobs. Confusion prevailed in Amritsar after 10 April 1919. The military took over and on 13 April, General R.E.H. Dyer unleashed the greatest and saddest massacre in our history at Jallianwala Bagh.[51]

Dyer's statement before the Hunter Commission sent a shiver of horror throughout India and Great Britain. The public opinion in India and abroad condemned the shooting of innocent defenceless citizens who were holding a peaceful assembly. The progressive section of the press in England was very vocal in its condemnation of Dyer's action at Jallianwala Bagh. So was a section of the Indian press. *The Daily News* described it as 'Imperial atrocities and an act of frightfulness'. The *Manchester Guardian* stated the shooting at Amritsar was as though a mad man had been let loose to massacre at large. *The Star* said that the action of General Dyer was the darkest stain on the British Rule in India.[52]

It appeared that the fabric of the old system was cracking.[53] Dyer's action led to a commotion which spread to all surrounding districts and the rural areas were also electrified. At Gujranwala, there was an outburst on 14 April. Disturbances took place at Wazirabad on 15 April and at Akalgarh and Hafizabad; a *hartal* was organized on 14 and 15 April at Jallalpur, Jattan and at Malkawal on 15 and 16 April. These incidents testify to the fact that the Jaillianwala Bagh firing instead of quelling disturbances and striking terror in the hearts of the people became itself the cause of widespread disturbances in the districts around Amritsar.[54] Politics was no longer confined to intellectuals, professional groups and the elite. It was extended to wider sections of the society, including shopkeepers, moneylenders, students and peasants.[55]

A lot of emotive literature appeared as a result of the Jallianwala Bagh tragedy. The politicians, poets, journalists and other sections of the Indian society, produced a mass of literature, consisting of pamphlets, poetry and write-ups in the press.

The creative literature – be it poetry, fiction, drama or any other literary form – had a much wider impact than the intellectual writings, the difference being that the former appealed to emotions and sentiments and the latter to the intellectual faculty. Our cognative behaviour is forever more rooted in emotionality, therefore, the creative literature produced as an aftermath of this great human tragedy of Indian history, becomes as relevant as any intellectual analysis thereof can claim to be. Vast literature including folklore was produced in the wake of this tragedy.

The poem titled *Punjab in 1919* in English by Sarojini Naidu is not only moving but also thrilling.

'O mournful queen! O martyred Draupadi
The sacred rivers of thy stricken blood
shall prove the five-fold streams of
Freedom's flood
And guard the watch towers of our liberty.'

Another Hindi poem titled 'Jallianwala Bagh Mein Basant' by Subhadra Kumari Chauhan needs a special mention. Written in 1929, this poem represents the injured psyche of the sensitive minds who truly represent the popular feeling. It shows that the wounds of the Jallianwala Bagh massacre were still fresh.

SPRING IN JALLIANWALA BAGH

The sweet notes of the nightingale are no longer heard here.
Instead, cawing of crows renders this place noisy.
The sombrous insects and moths generate an illusion of humming bees.
Buds are semi-bloossomed and engulfed by thorny outgrowth.

The plants and flowers here are either parched or semi-burnt.
The pollen-dust deprived of its usual fragrance had now, turned into an unseemly speck.
Alas! the loveable, beautiful garden is all blood drenched.
Welcome to the king of seasons but come stealthily.

For this being a place of mourning where noise is forbidden.
The wind may blow but she be bade to blow slowly.
Lest she should blow away the sights and sobs of sorrow.
The nightingale may sing and pour out mournful notes.

The humming bees may hum but relate the tale of oppression.
Thou mayest bring flowers but they be not extra decorative.
Their fragrance be mild and they be dew dropped,
Present them not as gifts to one's near and dear;

They be scattered in devotion and in memory of those who are gone.
Children innocent and of tender age fell here to the bullets.
Thou mayest scatter some petals of buds in their name.
Many a heart full of ambitions and longings have been pierced with bullets here

And they by brute force removed from their loving families and country at large.
Some buds semi-blown be offered here in their memory.
And some dew-drops be scattered hither and thither in the form of tears.
The old and elderly died here of bullet wounds writhing in pain.

In their memory too thou mayest scatter some flowers dried up.
O! spring, the king of seasons
Hail to thee
But come stealthily
For it being a place of mourning
Where making a noise is forbidden.[56]

The Jallianwala Bagh tragedy created a stir in England. Its echo was heard in the House of Commons, in the words of Colonel Wedgewood:[57]

> You will have a shrine erected there (Jallianwalla Bagh), and every year there will be processions of Indians visiting the tombs of the martyrs and Englishmen will go there and stand bareheaded.

This prophecy came true. The Jallianwala Bagh today is a symbol of sacrifice of the common people, whose names remain unrecorded in the history of our country.

The conspiracy theory was floated and Michael O'Dwyer maintained that 'Open Rebellion' had broken out in the Punjab.[58] The British administration justified the brutal massacre on the ground that Dyer had averted the Second Mutiny.[59] The press in England also supported Dyer's action.[60] Rabindranath Tagore renounced his Knighthood and wrote to the Viceroy: 'The time has come when badges of honour make our shame glaring in their incongruous context of humiliation and I for my part wish to stand shorn of all special distinctions by the side of my country.'[61] C.F. Andrews called the Jallianwala Bagh massacre a butchery, adding, 'English honour has departed.'[62] Mrs Annie Besant visited Jallianwala Bagh in December 1919. She remained there for half an hour without saying a word, tears flowing from her eyes.[63] Motilal Nehru had visited the Jallianwala Bagh and described it as a most gruesome sight, corpses still decomposing in the big well. Shooting practice on 25,000 natives from a raised platform, walls pierced with bullets.[64]

The national movement took a new turn. Soon the Non-cooperation movement was launched by Gandhi, who turned the Congress into a mass party in 1920, on the strength of the emotive appeal of the Jallianwala Bagh massacre and Martial Law atrocities in the Punjab.[65] The Viceroy never took the trouble of examining the people's case. He expressed a callous indifference to popular feelings and would have carried on the death sentence passed by Martial Law Tribunals but for the pressures of the Secretary of State for India. British officers misbehaved with women.[66]

The Jallianwala Bagh tragedy became an example of the breach of the so-called honoured and sacrosanct rule of law. It was the imperial system which suffered the most. To conclude in the words of Colonel Wedgewood: But this incident you have divided for all times race, that might otherwise have loved another.[67] The racial divide was complete.

NOTES AND REFERENCES

1. H.N. Mitra (ed.), *Punjab Unrest Before and After* (Calcutta, 1921), pp. 34–35.
2. Pearay Mohan, *Imaginary Rebellion and How It Was Suppressed* (Lahore, 1920), p. 60.
3. Malviya, Kapil Dev, *Open Rebellion in the Punjab*, Allahabad, 1919.
4. Alfred Nundy, *Present Situation with Special Reference to Indian Unrest, 1919–20*, Dehradun. ——, *Revolution or Evolution*, Lahore, 1922.

5. Pearay Mohan, *op. cit.*
6. Lala Lajpat Rai, *Agony of Punjab*, Madras, 1920.
7. B.G. Horniman, *Amritsar and Our Duty to India*, London, 1920.
8. V.N. Datta, *Amritsar: Past and Present*, Amritsar, 1967.
   ——-, *Jallianwalla Bagh*, Ludhiana, 1969.
   ——(ed.), *New Light on Punjab Disturbances*, 2 vols., Shimla, 1974–76.
9. Ravinder Kumar (ed.), *Essays in Gandhian Politics: Rowlatt Satyagraha in 1919*, 1971.
10. Rupert Furneaux, *Massacre at Amritsar*, London, 1963.
11. Arthur Swinson, *Six Minutes to Sunset: The Story of General Dyer and the Amritsar Affair*, London, 1964.
12. Alfred Draper, *Amritsar, The Massacre that Ended the Raj*, London, 1981.
13. Helen Fein, *Imperial Crime and Punishment: The Massacre at Jallianwalla Bagh and British Judgment*, Honolulu, 1977.
14. Hari Singh, *Mass Movement in Amritsar*, in *Gandhi, Rowlatt Satyagraha and British Imperialism*, New Delhi, 1990, pp.144–81.
15. Suraj Bhan Verma, *Sangeet – O'Dwyer Shahi-urf-Mazlum Punjab*, Bhiwani (n.d.) See also K.C. Yadav, *Haryana-Swatantrata Mein Kaviyon, Shayron, Bhajan Updeshkon Aur Lok Gayakon Ke Yog Dan*, Delhi, 1988, pp. 215–56.
16. Home Political Deposit, November, 1917, No. 29. National Archives of India, hereafter NAI.
17. *Prices and Wages in India, 1919*, Department of Statistics, Government of India, Calcutta, 1919, p. 151.
18. *Ibid.*
19. C.A.H. Townsend, Director Civil Supplies, Punjab (Evidence), *Disorders Inquiry Committee*, vol. V, Calcutta, 1920, p. 182. (Hereafter, DIC).
20. *Prices and Wages in India*, p. 151. *op. cit.*, DIC, V, p. 10.
21. Statement of J.P. Thompson, Chief Secretary, Punjab DIC, Vol.VI.
22. Some idea about the economic status of the agriculturists can be had from M.L. Darling: *Punjab Peasant in Prosperity and Debt*, London, 1925.
23. Chelmsford to Montagu, 27 June 1918, *Montagu Papers*.
24. *Ibid.*
25. Home Political Deposit, October, 1918, No. 31. Fortnightly reports, Punjab, ending, 15 September 1918.
26. Chelmsford to King, 25 May 1920, *Chelmsford Papers*, NMML, New Delhi.
27. No evidence is available on the origin of these rumours. Rumours may be a reaction to fear psychosis.
28. *Amritsar Police Diary*, Report for 24 March 1919, appended to Amritsar Conspiracy Case, 1919, Microfilm at NAI.
29. *Ibid.*, Report for 2 April 1919.
30. *Ibid.*, Report for 6 April 1919.
31. Report of the Commissioners appointed by the Congress Sub-Committee of the Indian National Congress, vol. II (Evidence), Lahore, 1920, p. 72. Hereafter cited as Punjab Congress enquiry.
32. *The Independent*, Allahabad, 18 May 1919, p. 7.
33. Home Political A, May 1910, Nos. 108–18, N.A.I.
34. Gurbaksh Rai, local leader Amritsar, oral evidence, 23 August 1975. Recorded by Nehru Memorial Museum and Library, New Delhi.

35. Girdhari Lal, Deputy Chairman, Chamber of Commerce Amritsar (Evidence), Punjab Congress Inquiry, 1919–20, vol. II, pp. 2–3.
36. F.A. Cooner, EAC, (Written evidence), *DIC*, vol. III, p. 190.
37. Maqbool Mahmmod, Pleader High Court Amritsar, Punjab Congress Inquiry (Evidence), vol. II, p. 19.
38. Home Political Deposit, July 1919, No. 71.
39. *Ibid.*, See also Kotu Mal to Hansraj, 10 April 1919, Letter No. 655s, II *Gandhi Papers*, Gandhi National Museum, Raj Ghat, New Delhi.
40. Amritsar Telegraph Office Case, Judgement, *Motilal Nehru Papers*, File No. 18 of 1919/B-Part IV, NMML.
41. *Ibid.*
42. Statement of Punjab Government, *DIC*, 1920 (Evidence), vol. VI, p. 118, MSS, NAI.
43. *Ibid.*
44. Home, Judicial, A, October 1919, Nos. 228–50, NAI.
45. See, Motilal Nehru, *Diary*, Pencil notes, *Motilal Nehru Papers*. See also *Kharparde Papers* at NAI.
46. Home Judicial, A, October 1919, Nos. 228–50, NAI.
47. *Ibid.*
48. Tilak to Kharparde, Poona, 28 January 1920. *Kharparde Papers* No. F-2-52. NAI.
49. *Ibid.*
50. A.J.W. Kitchin, Commissioner, Lahore Division (Oral Evidence) *DIC*, vol. III, p. 163.
51. For details see Hari Singh, *Gandhi, Rowlatt Satyagraha and British Imperialism*, New Delhi, 1990, pp. 161–68.
52. Freedom Movement Papers, NAI, File No. III 12/2, 1919, Ruchi Ram Sahni's note.
53. Montagu to Chelmsford, 20 May 1920, *Montagu Papers*, NAI.
54. Home Poll, A, June 1920, No. 126–64 and K.W.
55. V.N. Datta, Dyer Saved Punjab, Lost India, *The Tribune*, 10 April 1994.
56. *Mukul* (Collection of Poems of Subhadra Kumari Chauhan), (Allahabad 1965, 9th impression).
57. Home Poll, A, 1920, Nos 347–58 and K.W. NAI.
58. Montague to Wellington, Letter dated 4 August 1920, *Montagu Papers*, Reel No. 4, pp. 121–24, Amritsar Debate and O' Dwyer Microfilmat NAI.
59. Home Poll, File No. 23, June 1919, Deposit Official report from Punjab Government on Amritsar riots, see also Kanji Dwarkadas, Indian's Fight for Freedom, pp. 115–16.
60. Home Poll, File No. 347–58 A February 1920, NAI newspaper cuttings on Amritsar Disorders.
61. *The Statesman*, 5 June 1919. See also Tagore, R. *Towards Universal Man*, Delhi 1961.
62. *The Statesman*, 18 June 1919. See also C.F. *Andrews Papers*, File No. 1/D-16, NAI. Andrews stated that Gandhi's visit to Amritsar on 4 November 1919, broke effectively the evil spell of terror in Amritsar. It was a day of universal rejoicing, women with children marched with devotion. *The Tribune*, 7 November 1919.
63. Even Pandit Jawaharlal Nehru, walked around Jallianwala Bagh and counted 67 bullet marks on a part of the well. See S. Gopal, *Selected Works of Jawaharlal Nehru*, 1903–24, vol. I, New Delhi, B. 130.
64. Note Book No. II (Pencil Notes). Motilal Nehru Private Paper, NMML.
65. See Proceedings of the Indian National Congress, 34th Session, Amritsar, 1919.
66. Sarojini Naidu's letter to *Bombay Chronicle*, 14 August, 1920. Bosworth Smith forcibly

uncovered the faces of all women with his stick. He repeatedly called them she asses, flies, bitches and swine.

67. *Debates on Indian Affairs, House of Commons*, 13 February to 23 December 1919. Col. 710–12, HMSO, 1920.

SEVEN

The Impact of the Jallianwala Bagh Tragedy on the National Movement in Kerala

K. K. N. KURUP

As early as the dawn of the nineteenth century, Malabar and Travancore, the territorial divisions of the modern state of Kerala, had initiated a series of armed revolts against the British. The rebels had expressed their strong anti-colonial feelings and desire to liberate their regions from the foreign rule. Though they did not possess the modern sentiments of nationalism, their political consciousness was not inferior in character as it was the result of staunch anti-colonialism.[1] Throughout the century there were sporadic agrarian struggles which had promoted anti-British feelings in the rural areas of Malabar.[2]

THE EARLY PHASE OF THE NATIONAL MOVEMENT

The national movement with its modern trends and characteristics of mass participation appeared in this region only during the 1920s, particularly since the Khilafat and Non-cooperation Movements. The educated Malayalis like C. Sankaran Nair and C. Kunhirama Menon, had already participated in the sessions of the Indian National Congress much earlier and Sankaran Nair had even chaired the Amravati session in 1897.[3] The political consciousness in Travancore in the 1890s developed in submitting memorials to the raja, pleading equality of job opportunity, and the mobility of the depressed castes, particularly in the ladder of the state bureaucracy.[4] A conference of the Congress had been held in Calicut in 1903. In 1910 a District Congress Committee existed in Malabar. Simultaneously there was a Kerala Theosophical Federation in Calicut. A provincial conference of the District Congress was held in Calicut in 1913 with C. Vijayaraghavachariar as President. In 1915 the Home Rule League Committee was organized in Calicut with K.P. Kesava

Menon as Sercetary and Mamcheri Rama Iyyer as President. Therefore, it is believed that the first organized political movement in this region was the Home Rule which had the backing of the theosophists.

The First Malabar District Annual Conference was held at Polakkad in 1916 which was chaired by Annie Besant. The Conference passed a Home Rule resolution at one of its sessions. The Second Annual Conference, held at Calicut in 1917, was presided over by C.P. Ramaswamy Iyyer and attended by Annie Besant. The Third Annual Conference was held at Tellicherry in 1918 and was presided over by Mir Azad Alikhan, a zamindar of Banganappalli. At some of these conferences, the tenancy question was discussed and in some places tenancy committees were separately organized seeking redressal of agrarian grievances. In fact agrarian problems were the dynamic forces which articulated national sentiments and anti-British feelings. However, the movement was restricted to a few educated lawyers and theosophists.

The growth of secular literature and the independent native press played an important role in the promotion of nationalism. Further, political journalism subscribed to its immediate growth. These factors were yet to materialize in Kerala society on a large scale. Although there were periodicals and journals, some of them were staunch supporters of the British.[5] In such cases political journalism did not contribute to the promotion of nationalism. The nationalists lacked a common political programme to rally people behind them. It was in this political background that the Jallianwala Bagh tragedy and the Gandhian leadership had influenced the national movement in Kerala to take an entirely different path of radical extremism and mass agitations.

END OF MODERATISM

Immediately after the Punjab tragedy, the Fourth Political Conference was held at Vatakara on 5 and 6 May 1919. It was presided over by eminent nationalist, K.P. Raman Menon, whose speech contained the following passage:

> The Government has till now been proceeding slowly and cautiously in the matter of administrative reforms. But in granting us that Rowlatt Law the Government was firm and quick and unhesitating. . . . Whenever a small boon is to be granted to us there is great delay, but when we are to be curbed that is done very quickly.[6]

The conference condemned the Montagu-Chelmsford Report and demanded self-government within the empire as per the Congress resolution passed at the thirty-third session held at Delhi. It supported the satyagraha started by Gandhiji for the repeal of the notorious Rowlatt Act. The Congress passed resolutions demanding the repeal of the Rowlatt Act and the Moplah Outrages Act.[7]

As the Punjab news was suppressed by the government, the intensity of the Jallianwala massacre and other atrocities could not be properly felt by the nationalists in Kerala.

The Congress Committee sent a cable to the Secretary of State on contemporary unrest in India. It was reported in the local press as follows:

> The policy of repression adopted by the Government in connection with the Rowlatt Law has also caused agitation among the people. The whipping of poor Indians and cruelly shooting them are acts not becoming to any Government. It is the punishment that was inflicted on Mahatma Gandhi for his efforts on behalf of his native land that caused the disturbances at Ahmedabad and Harmagam. Had Dr Satyapal and others not been arrested, there would have been no riot at all at Amritsar.[8]

It would be interesting to note and analyse some of the press reports from Kerala at this critical political juncture. These reports reflect the changing opinions on the Indian political affairs. A local periodical, *Margadarsi* from Calicut carried the following report on contemporary political issues:

> Our opinion is that the present political struggle in India is purely a caste struggle. Two high castes, one black and the other white, are fighting for power and privilege. The rule of the white Brahmans is in no way an ideal rule. We are only afraid that the rule of Black Brahman will be worse. Whoever wins, the people of India will gain nothing. If any man thinks that either the white Brahman or the Black Brahman will uphold the real interests of the Indian people when their selfish interests are opposed to these, he is deluded. The people must work out their own salvation without much help from either class of Brahmans.[9]

This periodical had projected the struggle as a caste conflict between the black and the white and believed that the rest of the Indian masses had nothing to do with it. The *West Coast Spectator* criticized the Congress programme and stated that:

> The blood is on their own head, and we hold Mr Gandhi and his followers entirely responsible for the bloodshed and the unsettled state of affairs that prevail in certain parts of the country.[10]

The same periodical further wrote:

> . . . Mr Gandhi has acted like a downright fool, we will not say revolutionary . . . England was never frightened by the Irish rising and she is not going to be frightened by the unarmed Indian mob on the warpath. We are sure that the tragedy enacted in the North will but strengthen the hands of our enemies in England; and we shall not in the least, be surprised if the Reform Bill itself is wrecked.[11]

The *Malayalam Manorama,* which now takes so much pride in its contributions to the freedom struggle, had expressed its views on the Punjab situation in these words:

> When anarchism is so alive in the land it is difficult to understand the meaning of the hubbub created by good men like Mr Gandhi about the Rowlatt Bill, the purpose of which is to put down such anarchism.[12]

This daily further expressed its views saying that 'If the powerful sovereignty and control now exercised by England should suddenly disappear from India, India will go several centuries backwards.'[13]

However, there were newspapers and periodicals that were fully sympathetic towards the emerging group of extremist nationalists. The *Malayali* published an article titled 'Mahatma Gandhi' and pointed out that there was nothing surprising in the concerted efforts of the whole of India to preserve her freedom, because it 'characterizes the Rowlatt Law as a measure that deprives Indians of even the freedom which they now enjoy and makes them mere puppets made to dance to the tune of the British, and hopes that the British government will not act rashly so to fulfil the prophecy of the moderates regarding the satyagraha movement'.[14] In an editorial, the *Samadarsi* wrote:

> The Punjab Governor, Michael O'Dwyer, was even before, a heartless administrator, and *The Hindu* atributes all the present unrest and trouble in the Punjab to his heartless administration and policy of repression.[15]

Frequent news items appeared on the Punjab affairs in periodicals like *Samadarsi*. A note revealed the situation that prevailed in the Punjab:

> The State of the Punjab continues to be heartrending. There is no relaxation as yet of the rigour or terribleness of military rule. The bureaucrats are daily cutting the crop of patriotic citizens. It has been impossible to determine how many have been arrested till now . . . the severity of the punishments under the Martial Law is terrifying. . . . All the public leaders of India are against this Martial Rule of the Punjab. And it remains an undoubted fact that the disturbances became so serious on account of the unjustifiable actions of the bureaucracy.[16]

The suppression of news in the Punjab was also noted by a periodical, the *Yogakshemam.* It stated that:

> In the Punjab the Government manages not to let out the real news by stopping all newspapers and that the Punjab Government seem to have arrested and taken to Delhi Mr C.F. Andrews, who was sent by some of the important newspapers in India as their representative to find out the facts.[17]

In fact, such news items reveal that the public was completely kept in the dark regarding the Punjab affairs.

The Punjab tragedy had its impact on the entire Indian society which finally decided to launch an uncompromising struggle against the imperialists.[18] Indian leaders such as Pandit Madan Mohan Malaviya and Muhammad Ali Jinnah resigned their membership to the Imperial Legislative Council immediately after the tragedy respecting the Indian sentiments.[19] In July 1919

C. Sankaran Nair resigned from the Executive Council of the Viceroy to register his protest against the prolongation of Martial Law after the cessation of the disturbances. He was further annoyed that the accused under Martial Law in the Punjab were denied legal assistance. The Indian National Congress had appreciated his 'courageous attitude' and welcomed him with enthusiasm in Madras. The nationalists decried the very constitution of the Hunter Committee. The indemnity granted by the Viceroy to the British officials concerned with the atrocities further strengthened the anti-colonial feelings in India. These developments in India were rightly understood by the nationalists in Kerala and the Fifth Political Conference which was held at Mancheri in April 1920 resolved to support the Gandhian political programme of mass movement.

THE MANCHERI CONFERENCE

This political conference was a landmark in the national movement in Kerala. It was convened particularly at a time when the Indian nationalists rightly understood the true nature of imperialism. The Rowlatt Act, the Jallianwala Bagh massacre, the atrocities perpetrated by the Government in the Punjab, the character of the Montagu-Chelmsford reform proposals, the recommendations of the Hunter Committee, the failure of the Khilafat deputation that went to England and the repressive measures of the Government had all aggravated the political dissatisfaction among the nationalists. The moderates and the advocates of Home Rule still wanted to accept the constitutional proposals of self-government within the empire. Both trends of national politics were in confrontation at Mancheri.

The conference was attended by nearly 1,300 delegates from several parts of Kerala and Madras. The Home Rule activists like Annie Besant and Mancheri Rama Iyyer were ranged on one side and K.P. Kesava Menon, K. Madhavan Nair, A. Rangaswamy Iyengar and N.S. Ramaswamy Iyengar on the other. Hundreds of Muslim tenants also attended this session.

The conference congratulated C. Sankaran Nair on his resignation. It was resolved that the Hindus and Muslims would cooperate in the Khilafat question and withdraw their cooperation from the government, if the Muslim demands were rejected. A resolution was passed to safeguard the interests of the Malabar tenants. The most important resolution was moved by K.P. Kesava Menon on the new reforms, which were 'unsatisfactory' and 'disappointing'. Annie Besant insisted on the deletion of these words and the resolution which was opposed was passed by a thumping majority. Besant and her followers staged a walkout.[20] These developments are evaluated as follows:

> The Mancheri Political Conference revealed the rising tide of nationalism in Kerala. It was the ground on which Dr Besant fought and lost her battle. She had loomed large in the political firmament for a few years but her influence evidently waned. The days of patient waiting and legal cooperation were over. Soon Malabar was going to be plunged into the vortex of an active movement inspired and led by Gandhiji.[21]

The conference declared the end of an era in the national movement of Kerala and extended its support to the Gandhian experiment of non-cooperation and mass activization. The theosophists and Besant had initiated some political activization in the upper stratum of the Kerala society during the First World War. The Punjab atrocities and the oppressive measures of the government opened the eyes of young nationalists in this region and they immediately found themselves allied with the Gandhian programme of noncooperation. This was one reason why the Non-cooperation and the Khilafat Movements were effective in Kerala with larger participation from the middle and lower classes than ever before.

LATER INFLUENCE

The memories of this tragedy had influenced the poets, writers and the nationalists in the later years. The *thullal* or jump-dance is a traditional late medieval theatre in Kerala. It has a visual and narrative technique of story-telling. A nationalist poet of Kerala, Amsi Narayana Pillai, composed a *thullal* song on the tragedy of Jallianwala Bagh to educate the public. Though it is a propaganda poem, the collective memory of Indian society is reflected in this composition. After describing the atrocities committed by Dyer, it depicts Gandhiji as an emancipator and implores people to join the Non-cooperation Movement.[22] Nationalism itself developed from the collective memory of a nation. Therefore the impact of Jallianwala Bagh on Indian society was deep-rooted and that memory as a collective historical force was utilized to spearhead the non-cooperation and later movements in India's struggle for freedom.

T.S. Thirumumb, a nationalist poet from North Kerala, in one of his poems on the Civil Disobedience Movement, recollected the heroic deeds of the punished with martyrs of the Punjab. The poet was awarded rigorous imprisonment for writing that poem.[23]

A survey of these events highlight that the Jallianwala Bagh tragedy was a major political incident in the history of India's struggle for freedom. Like the memory of the 1857 uprising, this tragic event had influenced the national movement in Kerala and promoted anti-colonial and anti-British feelings. The Punjab situation had brought an end to the Home Rule and moderate politics in this region and the young generation of nationalists opted for Gandhian non-cooperation and the Khilafat movements. The Mancheri Conference of 1920 in South Malabar marked a turning point in the history of the freedom struggle in this region. The conference took Annie Besant and her followers by surprise. These developments inaugurated the Gandhian era of the Indian struggle for independence in Kerala as in the rest of India.

NOTES AND REFERENCES

1. Some of these early revolts are traced in P.K.K. Menon, *History of the Freedom Movement in Kerala,* Trivandrum, 1972, I.
2. Such agrarian movements, in nineteenth century Malabar have been analysed by K.N. Panikkar in the *Against Lord and State: Religion and Peasant Uprisings in Malabar: 1836–1921,* Delhi, 1989.
3. G.P. Pillai, P. Rairu Nambiar, Mannath Krishnan Nair, Dr T.M. Nair, S.K. Nayar and C. Karunakara Menon were some among those Kerala members who had participated in the early Congress Sessions.
4. See the Malayali Memorial (1891) and the Ezhava Memorial (1896) forwarded to the Maharaja of Travancore. See Menon, n.1, II, pp. 8–14.
5. The *Mitavadi* edited by C. Krishnan stood by the British and upheld that the Home Rule would end in the upper caste dominance over the lower and depressed castes.
6. *Manorama,* Calicut, 9 May 1919 (See *Vernacular Press Reports 1919*, Tamil Nadu Archives).
7. *Ibid.*, 6 May 1919.
8. *Malayali,* Quilon, 7 May 1919.
9. *Margadarsi,* Calicut, 9 May 1919.
10. *West Coast Spectator,* Calicut, 17 April 1919.
11. *Ibid.*, 22 April 1919.
12. *Malayala Manorama,* Kottayam, 10 April 1919.
13. *Ibid.*, 22 April 1919.
14. *Malayali,* Quilon, 26 April 1919.
15. *Samadarsi,* Trivandrum, 26 April 1919.
16. *Ibid.*, 10 May 1919.
17. *Yogakshemam,* Trichur, 23 May 1919.
18. The impact of the tragedy on Tamil Nadu has been traced by R. Sobhanan, 'Tamil Response to the Amritsar Tragedy of 1919' in *Punjab University Research Bulletin,* XV, No. 1, April 1984, pp. 213–18. A study of this tragedy is available in Raja Ram, *The Jallianwala Bagh Massacre,* Chandigarh, 1969.
19. Rabindranath Tagore and Jagadish Chandra Bose surrendered their British Honours in this context.
20. Dr Besant's position had been precarious in 1919. *The West Coast Spectator* (27 February) wrote that 'Mrs Besant has at last been found out and shunned by the moderates and looked upon with distrust by the extremists. She must necessarily create a party pledged to and obeying her to the end.'
21. Menon, n.1, II, p. 82.
22. Amsi Narayan Pillai, *Jallianwala Bagh,* Malayalam Pamphlet, (n.d.) Amsi papers, kept by T.P. Sankran Kutty Nair, Thiruvananthapuram. See 'Amsi Literature, Nationalism and

Social Change' presented at the ICHR National Seminar on 'Nationalism and Social Changes – the Role of Literature in India', Department of History, Calicut University, February 1994.

23. See the Malayalam poem, 'An Observation of the Past Righteous Struggle', in T.S. Tirumumb, *Smaranakal, Kavithakal* (Collected Reminiscences and Poems), ed, by K.K.N. Kurup, Trichur, 1989, pp. 192–94.

EIGHT

Jallianwala Bagh and Changing Perceptions of the Sikh Past

MOHINDER SINGH

THE JALLIANWALA BAGH TRAGEDY proved a turning point in India's struggle for freedom. It also became a source of inspiration to the popular people's movements in Punjab. A province which had earned the dubious distinction of being the 'sword arm of India' and traditional supporter of the Raj soon turned into an arena of conflict wherein proud Punjabis like Saifuddin Kitchlew, Satyapal and Kharak Singh gave a rare demonstration of unity and sacrifice to give a lie to the British communal stereotypes. Again while at the national level the tragedy prepared the ground for the larger Non-cooperation Movement under the leadership of Mahatma Gandhi, at the regional level it proved to be the proverbial last straw on the camel's back and set the stage for the Akali struggle for Gurdwara reform. It will be relevant to mention that when the country was busy condemning this most brutal action and was engulfed in a wave of shock, horror and consternation, Arur Singh the Government-appointed *Sarbrah* of the Golden Temple, Amritsar, invited the General to the temple and tried to whitewash his bloodstains by honouring him with a *saropa* and by declaring him a 'Sikh'. The dialogue which took place between Arur Singh and other priests of the Golden Temple and the Akal Takht on the one hand, and General Dyer on the other, is worth quoting here:

> 'Sahib', they said you must become a Sikh even as Nikalseyan Sahib became a Sikh.
> The General thanked them for the honour but he objected that he could not as a British Officer let his hair grow long.
> Arur Singh laughed. 'We will let you off the long hair,' he said.
> General Dyer offered another objection. 'But I cannot give up smoking'.
> 'That you must do', said Arur Singh.
> 'No', said the General. 'I am very sorry but I cannot give up smoking.'
> The priest conceded, 'We will let you give it up gradually.'

'That I promise you', said the General, 'at the rate of one cigarette a year.'

According to Ian Colvin, General Dyer's biographer, the priests proceeded with the pseudo-initiation. General Dyer and Captain Briggs were invested with the five *Kakas*, the sacred emblems of that war-like brotherhood and so became Sikhs.[1]

Perusal of the *Khalsa Samachar,* the only Punjabi weekly published from Amritsar, shows that Arur Singh was not the only one to have provided legitimacy to the offical high-handedness but there were other supporters of the Raj among the Sikh community. Sir Sunder Singh Majithia, Rai Bahadur Bhagat Singh, Raghbir Singh Sandhawalia and others connected with the Chief Khalsa Diwan, a pro-British Sikh organization, published an appeal in the *Khalsa Samachar* of 24 April 1919, wherein they mentioned that Punjab's representatives in the Legislative Council had already voiced their concern when Mr Gandhi had launched his Satyagraha Movement.[2] The appeal further mentioned that these honourable members had apprehensions about Gandhi's peaceful satyagraha turning violent and thus providing an excuse to ordinary citizens to take law into their own hands.

These pro-British Sikh Chiefs mentioned that the Sikhs had served the British empire with utmost loyalty, devotion and distinction and brought 'honour' to their community and province. The appeal mentioned the services rendered by the Sikh soldiers in the First World War and advised the community 'not to participate in anti-British demonstrations or indulge in any such activity which creates problems for the law enforcing agencies.'[3] It was further mentioned that the only way to maintain discipline was to impose Martial Law. The appeal reminded the followers of Guru Nanak and Guru Gobind Singh to recall their long tradition of loyalty to the Crown and help the administration to keep alive the Panth's tradition of loyalty and service to the Raj.[4]

In another message to the Sikh Panth also published in the *Khalsa Samachar*, dated 24 April, the Chief Khalsa Diwan tried to justify the official action at Jallianwala Bagh and warned the members of the Sikh community not to be misled by the false rumours. It called upon the members of the Sikh community to cajole those who had gone astray as a result of 'false propaganda' into cooperation and reminded them of the Sikh Panth's tradition of loyalty to the Crown.

Officials of the Chief Khalsa Diwan prevailed upon the Sikh masses that if they wanted the province and the country to progress and get a legitimate share in the administration the only option before them was loyalty and cooperation. In their traditional style of sycophancy, these leaders mentioned that the British rulers had centuries of experience of ruling various parts of the world and they were gradually training some of our 'capable countrymen' in the art of governing. They called upon people not to become hasty and show patience and restraint. The communique further mentioned that the British rulers had done a great favour by including Indians in the Viceroy's Executive Council and the provincial councils. They advised the Sikhs to pray for the long life of the Viceroy and maintain law and order so that some more constitutional concessions, which had been promised, should be given to the Indians.

The communique ended with repeating the story of the blessings of the British rule which had, through canal irrigation, converted the barren land into the 'granary of India'. It further mentioned that the benefits of the post and telegraphs, railways, trade, commerce and industry had been ushered in by the British rule.

In an editorial note, the *Khalsa Samachar* supported the above arguments of the landed interests and called upon the 'Sikh, Hindu and Muslim brethren of Punjab not to be misled by the false propaganda and help the government in maintaining peace in the province'. Subsequent issues of the *Khalsa Samachar* highlighted the 'act of bravery' of those who risked their lives in saving the 'Gora Sahibs' and their families and condemned popular unrest as 'irresponsible acts of misguided individuals'. The paper justified the high handed actions of the army and police in suppressing the unruly elements. It is interesting to note that while *The Tribune* and other newspapers gave a balanced version of the events, the news items published in the *Khalsa Samachar* were either the communiques issued by the Government giving an official version of the events or the appeals to the members of the Sikh community by the pro-British Sikh aristocracy who had been declared by the British authorities as the 'natural leaders' of the community.[5]

It is interesting to study the contrast in the various attitudes of the Sikhs to the unrest, Rowlatt Bills and the Jallianwala Bagh tragedy. While some of the 'Sikh intellectuals' have attempted to highlight the Sikh suffering by mentioning without any solid evidence, that out of 1,302 persons killed in Jallianwala Bagh, 799 were Sikhs, the *Khalsa Samachar* almost ignored the Sikhs association with the agitation and their suffering during the Jallianwala Bagh tragedy. While going through the issues of the *Khalsa Samachar,* one finds that the Sikhs' only weekly paper did not carry any such figures. On the other hand, it mentioned that Miss Sherwood the British missionary who was assaulted by the mob, was saved by the Sikhs. The paper praised the role of a local Sikh medical practitioner who attended to Miss Sherwood and also prominently mentioned the names of various Sikhs who helped the British officers or their families during the disturbances.

These so called leaders of the Sikh community not only condemned the popular rising but also arranged a farewell function in honour of Sir Michael

O'Dwyer, the controversial Lieutenant Governor of Punjab. In his reply, O'Dwyer praised the Sikh leaders for their assistance during the war. In the course of his speech, he said, 'I was fortunate to avail myself of the opportunity of testifying to the loyalty and devotion of the Sikh community'.[6] He further assured the assembled Sikhs that the Government was preparing a record of the Sikhs who risked their lives in saving the lives of the English officers and their families with a view to rewarding them suitably. This promise made by O'Dwyer was duly honoured by his successor Sir Edward Maclagan who honoured Dr Balwant Singh, the medical practitioner who gave first aid to Miss Sherwood, with a cash award of Rs 1,000 on 12 June 1919.[7] Similar cash awards were given to other loyalist Sikhs at the special Durbar held at Amritsar.

However the role of the leaders of the Chief Khalsa Diwan and other loyalists should not be interpreted to mean that the entire Sikh community was giving an expression of their 'loyalty' to the Raj and its functionaries. In fact, this added to the resentment already prevailing amongst the nationalist Sikhs over the controversial role of the pro-British interests among the Sikh community. It would be interesting to mention that while Rabindranath Tagore, who was living far away from the site of the gruesome tragedy returned his knighthood in protest and Mahatma Gandhi returned his Kaisar-i-Hind Medal and other awards received from the British, we do not hear of any word of protest from Bhai Vir Singh, founder and promoter of the *Khalsa Samachar*. Whatever may be the justification offered by Sikh scholars, the fact remains that those who had so far managed to be the leaders of the Sikh community brought dishonour and disgrace to the Sikhs first by criticizing the role of Mahatma Gandhi and other popular leaders and secondly by advertising their services to the Raj and receiving cash for help given to the British officials and their families. The facade of an honour done to General Dyer by the hereditary custodians of the Sikh shrines brought home to the nationalist Sikhs the urgency of coming out in the open against the vested interests by aligning with the forces of Indian nationalism. It was under these circumstances that the Central Sikh League, a political organization of the nationalist Sikhs, the Shiromani Akali Dal and the Shiromani Gurdwara Prabandhak Committee, were established by the Sikhs. In order to give an unbiased picutre of their activities and to correct the distortions created by the *Khalsa Samachar* and the *Khalsa Advocate*, the nationalist Sikhs first started two vernacular dailies, the *Akali* (Urdu) and the *Akali te Pardesi* (Punjabi), in May 1921. It might come as news to some scholars that it was the nationalist Sikhs who started an English daily, *The Hindustan Times* and appointed Sardar K.M. Panikkar as its editor. They also purchased shares in *The Nation* being brought out from Lahore and enlisted active support from *The Tribune*, a popular nationalist daily founded by Sardar Dayal Singh Majithia. While the corruption and mismanagement in the Sikh Shrines had been agitating the Sikh mind for a long time, it was the strong nationalist fervour created by the Rowlatt Bills agitation and the subsequent tragedy of the Jallianwala Bagh which heralded the Akali struggle for Gurdwara reform.

At a time when the country has just paid its ritual homage to Shahid Bhagat Singh and his companions Rajguru and Sukhdev and is observing the 75th anniversary of the tragedy of Jallianwala Bagh, it will be worthwhile to discuss some of the popular movements in Punjab which were inspired by the sacrifices of these martyrs. It is interesting to note that while the right type of leadership in the past succeeded in providing secular dimensions to otherwise purely religious movements like the Khilafat, the Temple Entry and Gurdwara Reform, present leadership and some 'intellectuals' have started reconstructing the recent past with a view to establishing either the Sikh hegemony in Punjab's struggle for freedom by proving that Shahid Bhagat Singh and Udham Singh had re-embraced the Sikh faith before going to the gallows. There are others who have shown their reaction by emphasizing the Sikhs' numerical strength by quoting figures from the Ghadarites, the Jallianwala Bagh and other popular movements. There are others who have shown their reaction by stressing that the Sikhs' role in the freedom struggle was only marginal as is mentioned by Arun Shourie in a series of articles entitled 'Politics of Pandering'.[8] I feel our best homage to the martyrs of Jallianwala Bagh would be to ignore such attempts and popularize our heritage of common suffering during our struggle for freedom. In this paper I would like to discuss the nationalist implications of the Akali struggle with a view to setting an example before the present leadership which is finding it difficult to rise above the narrow communal considerations.

Emergence of the Sikh nationalist politics was the outcome of increasing Akali-Congress cooperation during the Akali struggle for Gurdwara reform. What began as a purely religious agitation soon became a regional manifestation of the larger Non-cooperation Movement launched by Mahatma Gandhi. After ensuring active cooperation of the Indian National Congress the Khilafat and other nationalist forces the Akalis broadened the scope of their initial struggle for Gurdwara reform and launched a two-pronged attack directed towards the hereditary custodians of the historic Sikh shrines on the one hand, and British imperialism in the province on the other. Since the Akali struggle became a regional manifestation of the larger movement for the country's freedom early Akali victory during the keys' affair was described by Gandhiji as 'the first decisive victory of the forces of Indian nationalism.' While the common enemy (the Mahants) and the common cause (Gurdwara reform) kept the Akalis united a split took place as soon as the movement was over in 1925. The moderate group came out of the jail by accepting conditional release and captured the SGPC. The nationalist group which was unconditionally released in 1926, ousted the moderate group soon after. Further splits occurred in the Akali ranks with Mangal Singh and others joining the Indian National Congress and progressive leaders like Sohan Singh Josh launching the Kirti Kisan Party. Master Tara Singh who controlled both the SGPC and the Akali Dal remained the key figure in the Sikh nationalist politics till 1939 when he resigned from the Congress Working Committee over the issue of Sikhs' recruitment to the army. The first part of this paper attempts to discuss the origin and development of the Akali Movement for Gurdwara Reform and deals with the circumstances under which it turned from religious reform to nationalist politics and emerged as a powerful manifestation of popular people's upsurge. In the second part the Akalis' role in the nationalist politics from 1925–47 is discussed with special focus on Akali-Congress cooperation during the crucial phase of the country's struggle for independence.[9]

THE AKALI MOVEMENT (1920–25)

The Akali Movement began as an attempt of the Sikh reformers to purify their religious places from the evil and non-Sikh like practices and their liberation from the hereditary control of the Mahants, priests and government appointed managers and other vested interests. The movement soon took a political turn with the government in the Punjab coming out in open support of the vested interests in the Sikh shrines and the nationalist forces in the country lending active sympathy and support to the Akalis in their struggle against a foreign Government. As a result of the nationalist forces' influence on the Akalis and their alliance with the Sikh League, the Akali leadership was able to broaden the scope of the movement and to launch a two-pronged struggle directed against the Mahants and other vested interests on the one hand, and against their supporter, British imperialism in the Punjab, on the other.

While the reformers were agitating for the termination of indirect official control over the Golden Temple and the authorities were trying to soft-pedal the issue by deferring the question till the implementation of the Reforms Scheme in the Council, the walk-out by the priests of the Akal Takht in protest against the entry of the newly baptised low-caste members of the Khalsa Biradari into the premises of the Golden Temple virtually brought these important shrines under the control of the reformers who appointed a representative committee for their management.

So far the Akalis had gained control over the important Sikh shrines through peaceful means and without shedding much blood. But the tragedy of Nankana in which over 130 peaceful Akali reformers were done to death by Mahant Narain Das and the mercenaries hired by him proved a turning point both in the annals of the Akali struggle for Gurdwara reform as also in the official policy towards the movement. British officials' involvement in the Nankana tragedy, particularly that of Mr C.M. King, Commissioner of Lahore Division, and the support extended to Mahant Narain Das by the officials, convinced the Akali leadership that the bureaucracy was behind the vested interests.

The Government of India's criticism of the Punjab Government's failure to deal with the Akali Movement 'firmly and consistently from the beginning' and the responsibility of the local officials for their having not taken necessary precautions to avert the tragedy seems to have provided the British officials in the province with a good excuse to come out in open support of the Mahants. In consultation with the Viceroy of India and other members of his Council the Government of Punjab now inaugurated a 'stong policy' towards the movement with two-fold objectives of (*i*) suppressing the Akalis by force and (*ii*) weakening the growing Akali agitation with the promise of suitable legislation.' It was the implementation of the new policy which resulted in the subsequent agitation over the keys' affair and later opening of a fresh front at Guru-ka-Bagh

When the Government realized that the strong policy instead of weakening the movement had made it more and more popular and the Akalis had joined the Congress programme of non-cooperation at the provincial level, it thought of solving the problem first by appointing a committee of a few moderate Sikhs to take the keys from the Government and after their failure to do so by announcing unconditional release of the Akali prisoners.

But as the Akalis even after securing unconditional release of all the prisoners including Dina Nath and other Congress workers, were not willing to go to the Deputy Commissioner to collect the keys. A gazetted officer was sent by the Deputy Commissioner to hand over the keys to Baba Kharak Singh, President of the SGPC at the Diwan at the Akal Takht specially arranged for the purpose. Unconditional release of the Akali and Congress volunteers arrested during the agitation over the keys' affair and the return of the keys to the Akali leadership was described by a contemporary European writer in the following words:

> Never was there a more shameful defeat. One thinks irresistibly of the capture of Calais by an English King when the leading citizens had to bring the keys to him clothed only in their shirts and with ropes round their necks. The Punjab Government had humbled itself to the dust before the Gurdwara Prabandhak Committee.[10]

The defeat of the Government was seen by the nationalist leaders in the country, who had been backing the Akalis in their struggle against the bureaucracy, as a decisive victory for the forces of nationalism. Mahatma Gandhi sent the following telegram to Baba Kharak Singh, President of the SGPC: 'First battle for India's freedom won. Congratulations.'[11]

AKALI POLITICS (1925–47)

The Akali Movement though itself a product of the general awakening and growing political consciousness in the country, seems to have greatly strengthened the forces of nationalism in the Punjab by rejecting the Mahants, the landed aristocracy and other pro-British and vested interests in the Sikh community who had been declared the 'natural leaders' of the Sikhs by the official machinery. The movement provided the Sikh community with a new type of middle-class nationalist leadership, consisting of barristers, *vakils*, school and college teachers and retired military officers. This new leadership instead of playing into the hands of the British officials as the previous leadership of the Chief Khalsa Diwan had done, preferred to join the mainstream of nationalism in the country. It was not surprising, therefore, to find a majority of the Akali leaders turning from the original Akali programme of Gurdwara reform and linking it with the Non-cooperation Movement launched by Mahatma Gandhi and the larger programme of the country's struggle for freedom. It was mainly due to the emergence of this new type of leadership that the Akalis could secure the active sympathy and support of the Indian National Congress and other nationalist forces in the country in their own struggle against British imperialism in the Punjab.

It was mainly due to the Akali-Congress association during the Akali Movement that the two leaderships came closer to each other and the Sikhs got involved in Congress activities. Actually the two groups among the Sikhs: (*i*) the Akali advocates of purely religious reform and (*ii*) others who looked upon the Gurdwara reform only as a part of the larger programme of the country's freedom – remained united till 1939, initially under the leadership of Baba Kharak Singh and later that of Master Tara Singh.

In the Akali Movement, the Congress found an opportunity to further its own programme of non-cooperation launched by Mahatma Gandhi and to strengthen its position in Punjab. By winning over the Akali leadership they were able to influence a large section of the Sikh masses who had till then remained aloof from the Congress programme. As Maulana Mohamed Ali remarked in the course of his presidential address at the Cocanada Session of the Indian National Congress on 31 December 1923: 'A better opportunity for civil disobedience at least on a provincial scale never presented itself since the arrest of the Mahatma.'[12]

Apart from passing formal resolutions lending them moral support, the Congress leadership also rendered the Akalis solid practical help by sending Congress volunteers to assist them in their publicity work. An Akali-Sahayik Bureau was set up at Amritsar to coordinate the Akali-Congress activities and to help the Akalis organize their propaganda machinery. Almost all important national leaders, including Mahatma Gandhi, Pandit Madan Mohan Malaviya, Pandit Jawaharlal Nehru, Maulana Mohamed Ali and Hakim Ajmal Khan personally visited Nanakana, Amritsar, Guru-ka-Bagh and other places of Akali activities to obtain first-hand information about the events and to help the Akalis by giving advice and moral support. During the special session of the Congress held at Delhi in September 1923, a resolution was passed supporting the Akali agitation in the Sikh State of Nabha and it was also decided to send Congress observers to get first-hand information about developments there. Jawaharlal Nehru, A.T. Gidwani and K. Santhanam who were sent there for the purpose were arrested as soon as they entered the state territory and put behind the bars for having entered the state without prior permission of the British Administrator of Nabha. During their stay in Nabha Jail and their subsequent trials, the Congress observers not only gained first-hand knowledge about the Akali cause and the genuineness of their sufferings but also got a chance to observe the high-handedness of the bureaucracy and the arbitrary nature of justice in the Sikh State of Nabha, then put under the control of a British Administrator. In a long hand-written statement, choked with emotion and highly appreciative of the Akalis, Nehru attacked the British Administrator of Nabha and the judicial machinery in the State for their 'unscrupulous and crooked ways.' Having gained first-hand impressions about the Akalis, Nehru became their great admirer and wished to prove worthy of their high tradition and fine courage. The last paragraph of his original statement drafted in the Nabha Jail on 23 November 1923 reads:

> I was in jail when the Guru-ka-Bagh struggle was gallantly fought and won by the Sikhs. I marvelled at the courage and sacrifice of the Akalis and wished that I could be given an opportunity of showing my deep admiration of them by some form of service. That opportunity has now been given to me and I earnestly hope that I shall prove worthy of their high tradition and fine courage. Sat Sri Akal.[13]

In return for the help extended to the Akali Movement, the Congress leadership was able to establish a good deal of influence with the Akali leaders and through them the Congress programme was carried to the Sikh masses. It was mainly due to the nationalist influence upon the Akali leadership that the SGPC was able to adopt non-violent, non-cooperation as a weapon with which to fight the powerful bureaucracy in Punjab and to broaden the scope of their earlier programme of gurdwara reform. A formal resolution in favour of non-cooperation and passive resistance was passed by the SGPC on 11 May 1921. Resolutions were also passed at this meeting to boycott liquor and foreign goods and to substitute Panchayats for courts of laws.

Growing nationalist influence on Sikh politics is evident from the fact that the Central Sikh League which was formed to fight for political rights of the Sikhs with Congress help and guidance time and again opposed communal representation in Punjab as well as in the rest of the country. As early as 1923 the Central Sikh League had passed a resolution condemning British attempts to divide various communities in India by introducing a system of representation on communal lines. The resolution called upon the Sikhs and other minorities to give up communal representation in the best interests of the country. Nationalist Sikhs like Baba Gurdit Singh and Sardul Singh Caveeshar were convinced that communal representation had harmed the Sikhs more then it safeguarded their interests. According to Caveeshar, communal representation was at the bottom of all communal riots and was devised by the British authorities to perpetuate their rule by dividing people in India on communal lines.

When the Simon Commission visited India, an All-Parties Sikh Conference was convened at Amritsar on 30 January 1928 to clarify the Sikh attitude towards the Commission. The Conference attended among others by such prominent leaders as Baba Kharak Singh and Sardar Mangal Singh, decided that the Sikhs should boycott the Commission as advised by the Indian National Congress and appealed to the Sikh community to join the *hartal* on 3 February 1928 when the Commission was to land in Bombay. Again when the Indian National Congress decided to call an All Parties Conference at Delhi to draft a swarajya constitution, the Central Sikh League decided to join the conference and help the nationalist leadership find an agreed solution to the problem of communal representation. Knowing fully well that the abolition of communal representation was not in their immediate interest, the Sikh representatives gave evidence of their nationalist feeling by declaring that their community was 'prepared to accept representation on a non-communal basis and this proves that they are particularly prepared to make sacrifices for national welfare and advancement'.[14] Mangal Singh, the Sikh representative on the Nehru Committee signed the Nehru Report knowing fully well that the final recommendations of the Committee were not acceptable to the majority of his compatriots. In his support to the Nehru Report, Mangal Singh was joined by other Sikh nationalists like Sardul Singh Caveeshar, Amar Singh Jhabbal, Baba Gurdit Singh, Giani Hira Singh Dard, Sarmukh Singh Jhabbal and Giani Kartar Singh. Though Master Tara Singh did not agree with Mangal

Singh's stand on the Nehru Report, he did not favour a boycott of the Congress as was being advocated by a section of the Sikh leadership. In the course of his presidential address at the annual session of the Central Sikh League held in October 1929 at Lyallpur, Master Tara Singh said, 'We cannot boycott the Congress permanently, we are born to fight for freedom and we cannot stand aloof from an organization whose sole object is such a fight.'[15] Exhorting the Sikhs to be firm in the fight for freedom, he said:

> I would not mind if you instead of standing with the Congress, boycott it and stand in front of it in the fight for freedom. But if you boycott the Congress and stand in the backlines, it will be a matter of shame for our community. Those who are for boycotting the Congress must devise some positive fighting programme, and I am sure all the people will be with them. But if you simply pass a resolution to boycott the Congress and oppose whatever the Congress does, you will be caught in the trap of bureaucracy. Some, tired of our inactivity, may rejoin the Congress; the rest may die their natural death. I beseech you to be very cautious when considering this question. On the other hand, if we go on working with the Congress as before, our attitude may be misunderstood and we may not be considered earnest in our demands. This is also dangerous, and we have to chalk out a via media. It is not difficult to chart a course if you gentlemen consider unity to be the chief need of the time.[16]

When the Congress launched the Civil Disobedience Movement, the Sikh leadership again joined hands with the nationalist forces in ensuring the success of the Congress call. On 9 March 1930, the Shiromani Akali Dal offered 5,000 volunteers for the movement. It also called upon all Sikhs to do their duty in this critical hour and rally under the leadership of Mahatma Gandhi. The Provincial Congress Committee reciprocated the gesture of the Akali leadership by nominating Master Tara Singh as a member of the 'War Council' to coordinate the Civil Disobedience Movement in the province. On the arrest of Dr Saifuddin Kitchlew, Tara Singh replaced him as 'Dictator' on this body. When in the heat of the Civil Disobedience Movement shooting took place in the North West Frontier Province, it stirred Master Tara Singh to the depth of his soul. He declared:

> The Sikhs, in sympathy with their tyrannized countrymen will shed their blood at the same place where the Pathans have shed it. It is said that the Sikhs and the Pathans are each other's enemies. That is absolutely wrong. The Sikhs and Pathans are sons of the same motherland and if any such impression prevails that they are enemies, the Sikhs will wash if off by mingling their blood with that of the Pathans. The Sikhs must, therefore, go to their rescue and lay down their lives and do their duties honourably as enjoined upon them by their Gurus.[17]

Master Tara Singh made the above declaration at Jallianwala Bagh before a huge gathering. One hundred Akalis volunteered to march to Peshawar, each fully determined to lay down his life for the country. The *jatha* was stopped by the police at Dina, near Jhelum, and mercilessly lathi-charged till every member became unconscious. Master Tara Singh had been arrested while the *jatha* was still in Lahore and imprisoned at Gujrat.

It was the nationalist spirit and friendship with the Indian National Congress which was greatly responsible for Master Tara Singh and his lieutenants persuading the Shiromani Akali Dal and the Central Sikh League to pass a formal resolution for boycott of general elections in response to the Congress call. On various other national issues Master Tara Singh and his lieutenants supported the Indian National Congress. At the time of the partition when M.A. Jinnah and some other British officials were trying to create a rift in the ranks of Akali leaders with vague promises of 'Azad Panjab' and Sikh Homeland, the Akali leaders refused to fall into the trap and decided to cast their lot with India. Akali Congress confrontation in independent India should not blind us to the period of cooperation and friendship.

While the above account should convince men like Arun Shourie that the Sikhs' sacrifices in India's struggle for independence were second to none, it should not be used by communal historians as an argument that they were participating in these movements as Sikhs and not as Indians. I am consciously mentioning this because on going through the writings and speeches of some of the 'Sikh intellectuals'. I find that systematic attempts are being made by the present Akali leadership to reconstruct the history of Punjab to prove without any historical evidence that those Sikhs who participated in the freedom struggle were doing so as Sikhs and the majority community which had captured political power in independent India is denying them their due. To substantiate this point I would like to quote Kapur Singh's attempt to reconstruct the account of Bhagat Singh's last days. On the basis of Bhai Randhir Singh's meeting with Bhagat Singh as quoted in the *Jail Chhithian*[18] (prison letters), Kapur Singh writes that Bhagat Singh discarded his religious symbols because he was convinced that as a Sikh he would not get much recognition from his non-Sikh countrymen. This statement is not only preposterous but is also insulting to this great martyr who made a supreme sacrifice not to gain cheap publicity but because of his strong conviction and idealism. According to Kapur Singh, Bhagat Singh had expressed a desire that before being hanged he should be allowed to receive Sikh baptism from the Panj Piaras under the supervision of Bhai Randhir Singh who was also serving his term in the Lahore Central Jail at that time. Kapur Singh further mentions that while the jail authorities did not concede Bhagat Singh's first demand, they agreed to his second demand of being cremated according to the Sikh rites. Kapur Singh writes that while the Hindu politicians have deliberately distorted his physical appearance and religious ideology to suit their interests, Bhagat Singh was deeply rooted in Sikh religious tradition. According to Kapur Singh all his letters to his relatives began with 'Ek Onkar' and ended with 'Sat Sri Akal'. On the basis of Bhagat Singh's imagined letters to his relatives, Kapur Singh concludes that Bhagat Singh had clearly realized his mistake in discarding his religious symbols and under the influence of Bhai Randhir Singh had expressed his keen desire to embrace his faith and live up to the expectations of his uncle and father.[19]

While going through the prison letters of Bhai Randhi Singh, I do not find any corroboration of Bhagat Singh expressing his desire to be baptised by the five Sikhs. However, Randhir Singh does mention that he had convinced Bhagat Singh to return to the Sikh faith. Bhai Randhir Singh in his account mentions Bhagat Singh expressing his helplessness in reembracing the Sikh faith because by this act firstly, he was bound to lose the sympathy of his companions and secondly, he would not get as much publicity from the world media which he was getting as a non-Sikh. Bahi Randhir Singh further quotes Bhagat Singh as saying that his sacrifice was nothing compared to those of the Ghadarite heroes of 1914–15. Further, Bhagat Singh is quoted as saying that if he was in the Sikh garb with turban and beard, the newspapers would not have written anything about him. Sikh newspapers were too few and too mild to have highlighted Bhagat Singh sacrifice. Bhai Randhir Singh mentions that as a result of his encounter, Bhagat Singh was deeply impressed and after expressing his regret, promised to return to the Sikh faith.

Ordinarily to a historian studying Punjab's role in the freedom struggle it is quite irrelevant to debate whether Bhagat Singh and other martyrs were Sikhs, Hindus or Muslims. What is important for us to know is their ideology and the motivating spirit behind their daring acts and supreme sacrifice. In this case I am compelled to quote Bhagat Singh's own writings just to prove my point that men like Kapur Singh and Bhai Randhir Singh have lowered the status of great martyrs like Bhagat Singh to further their own plans of communalizing the recent Sikh past.

While there are a number of Bhagat Singh's writings and letters that give us an idea of the development of his mind and ideology, his article entitled 'Why I am an Atheist' is worth mentioning in this context. It seems to have been written in reply to Bhai Randhir Singh's remark that Bhagat Singh had developed an ego resulting from the publicity and fame which stood in the way of his recognizing the existence of God. In the article while on the one hand, Bhagat Singh traces the origins and development of his political ideology and transformation from a romantic revolutionary to a thinker, he traces early religious influences and his reaction thereto. Bhagat Singh convincingly describes how during the trying times he remained firm in his conviction without resorting to softening his hardship through belief in God. To quote him, 'I wanted to settle for myself whether it was in the days of peace and enjoyment alone that I could boast of being an atheist or whether during such hard times as well, I could stick to those principles of mine. After great consideration I decided that I could not lead myself to believe in and pray to God. No. I never did. That was the real test and I came out successful. Never for a moment did I desire to save my neck at the cost of certain other things. So I was a staunch disbeliever, and have ever since been.'[20]

What could be better than Bhagat Singh's own writing to give a lie to Kapur Singh and Bhai Randhir Singh's claims of Bhagat Singh returning to the Sikh fold and requesting the jail authorities to arrange for his baptism and his cremation according to the Sikh rites of passage. And whatever may be the grievances against the state perceived by men like Kapur Singh there are a large number of Sikh heroes like Kartar Singh Sarabha, Ajit Singh and Gurdit Singh of Kamagatta Maru fame who made unique sacrifices for the liberation of their motherland. Contrary to whatever may be Kapur Singh's view, men like Kartar Singh Sarabha, Ajit Singh and Gurdit Singh of Kamagatta Maru fame who made sacrifices for the liberation of their motherland all got due recognition and place in the national roll of honour with their religious symbols intact. Baba Kharak Singh with his long flowing beard, *kirpan* and blue turban got love and respect from his compatriots and was popularly described as 'uncrowned king of the Panth' by Gandhi, Nehru, Azad and other national leaders.

At a time when efforts are being made by vested interests to reconstruct Punjab's recent past we need to remain vigilant. Our best tribute to the martyrs of the Jallianwala Bagh tragedy would be to construct the past which will not only be objective but also highlights the ideals for which these great sons and daughters of India lived and died.

NOTES AND REFERENCES

1. Ian Colvin, *Life of General Dyer*, Blackwood and Sons, London, 1931, p. 201.
2. *Khalsa Samachar*, 24 April 1919 at 60, Lawrence Road, Amritsat.
3. *Ibid.*
4. *Ibid.*
5. *Ibid.*
6. *Khalsa Samachar*, 15 May 1919.
7. *Ibid.*, 12 June 1919.
8. *The Indian Express*, 12, 13 and 14 May 1982.
9. For a detailed account, see Mohinder Singh, *The Akali Movement*, pp. 19, 61.
10. Komma, 'The Sikh Situation in the Punjab,' *Fortnightly Review*, September, p. 123.
11. Ganda Singh (ed.) *Confidential Papers of the Akali Movement*, p. 11.

12. Report of the Cocanada session of the Congress quoted in *The Tribune*, 1 January 1924.
13. For the full text of Nehru's Statement, see S. Gopal's (ed.) *Selected Works of Jawaharlal Nehru*, Vol. I, pp. 369–86.
14. The Central Sikh League was formed by the nationalist Sikhs in 1919 to fight for Sikh rights in the growing struggle for constitutional concessions. For a detailed account of the Central Sikh League, see Sukhmani Bal's (ed.) *Politics of the Central Sikh League*. Acme Publishers, Delhi.
15. Kailash Gulati, *Akalis Past and Present*, pp. 32–33.
16. Master Tara Singh's presidential address at the Central Sikh League meeting, quoted in *The Tribune*, 16 October 1929.
17. Kailash Gulati, *The Akalis, Past and Present*, p. 55.
18. Bhai Randhir Singh's *Jail Chithian* (Punjabi), pp. 447–57.
19. Kapur Singh's *Sachi Saakhi*.
20. Shiv Verma (ed.) *Selected Writings of Shahid Bhagat Singh*, p. 153.

NINE

The Jallianwala Bagh Tragedy: The Official Attitude and its Significance

J. S. GREWAL AND INDU BANGA

YOU CANNOT HAVE DISTURBANCES of this magnitude without an inquiry into the causes of and measures taken to cope with these disturbances. This was what the Secretary of State for India, E.S. Montagu, said in his Budget Speech on 22 May 1919 with reference to the events of March and April in different parts of the British Empire in India. On 30 May, Mahatma Gandhi decided to associate himself with the Press in its request for 'an impartial and independent Committee of Inquiry to examine the causes of disturbances in the Punjab and the administration of Martial Law in the Province, including the sentences passed by the Martial Law Tribunal.' The Government of India had to accept the proposal, much against its own inclination and fears. Lord Hunter was appointed the Chairman of the Disorders Inquiry Committee, popularly known as the Hunter Committee. Three of its seven other members were Indians.

The Committee began its hearings on 29 October 1919 and sat for 46 days in Lahore, Delhi, Ahmedabad and Bombay. Its report consisted of seven volumes but only the first five were published. The publication of the last two volumes was not undertaken in deference to the wishes of the Government of India. These two volumes have been edited by Professor V.N. Datta and published by the Indian Institute of Advanced Study. In Professor Datta's view, the sixth volume is 'perhaps the most illuminating' of all the documents on disturbances in the Punjab. The oral evidence of Sir Michael O'Dwyer, in particular, appears to bring his role and the role of the Punjab Government into clear focus. The purpose of this short paper is to review the evidence presented by Sir Michael O'Dwyer to the Committee, especially with reference to his note and his cross-questioning by an Indian member of the Committee, Sir Chimanlal Hiralal Setalvad.

I

Michael O'Dwyer liked to believe that the Punjab Province held a peculiar position in the Indian Empire, not only because of its geographical location but also because of the character of the people who, moreover, were the mainstay of the British Indian Army. Political agitations in the Punjab tended to assume a more dangerous character than elsewhere because they developed more rapidly into open hostility towards the Government. This was why, in his view, every revolutionary organization tended to establish itself in the Punjab, like the Seditious movement of 1907, the Ghadar conspiracy, the South-West Punjab uprisings of 1914–15 and the Silk Letter conspiracy of 1916–17. This was also the reason why drastic measures became essential, particularly during the War. It was also necessary in his view, to keep agitators out. In fact, he looked upon the movement for Home Rule, which began in the autumn of 1916, as an agitation likely to revive the Ghadar movement and, therefore, it was to be discouraged. It was bound to interfere with the recruiting campaign in the Punjab. In any case, Swaraj, or Home Rule, smacked of violence and rebellion. That was why O'Dwyer did not allow Tilak and Bipin Chandra Pal to enter the Punjab in February 1917, making use of the special powers bestowed on the Punjab Government by the Defence of India Act. O'Dwyer did not like the activity of the Punjab Provincial Congress under the leadership of Harkishan Lal, Fazl-i-Husain and Duni Chand. He also thought that the efforts of the *Arya Gazette* to project Swami Dayananda as the real author of the Home Rule were fraught with danger.

Nevertheless, in April 1918, O'Dwyer expressed his satisfaction with the attitudes of the Punjabis during the war years: 'Since the War began, the people of the Province as a whole, so far from doing anything to embarrass the Government, have rallied enthusiastically to its support.' However, the rest of the year was marked by political activity which did not meet with the approval of the Lieutenant Governor. The towns people felt attracted by the political propaganda after the appearance of the Montagu-Chelmsford Scheme and the Rowlatt Report. The Pan-Islamic press begain to advocate the cause of Turkey, and there were signs of an understanding between the extremist Hindus and Muslims. Dr Kitchlew, Dr Satyapal, Duni Chand and Fazl-i Husain expressed their views regarding the Reform Scheme and the Rowlatt Report as well as Home Rule. Their inflammatory speeches projected the Reform Scheme as inadequate and the Rowlatt Report as 'Prussianism'. The advent of Home Rule would enable the Indians to allow or not to allow an Englishman to stay in India. Dr Kitchlew made a violent pro-Turkish speech, and Maulvi Ataullah declared that the time had come for *jihad* against the rulers. The movement for 'self-determination' for India and the Pan-Islamic manifestations after the collapse of Turkey and Germany in November, appeared to present a combination of both the movements against the Government. This was followed by the 'extremist' Congress meeting at Delhi in December 1918, which synchronized with the meeting of the Muslim League. The Congress meeting was dominated by the Punjabi leaders and at the Muslim League meeting, Dr Ansari gave a veiled incitement to rebellion.

O'Dwyer felt that a revival of violent agitation in the Punjab would have serious effects because of the economic and currency difficulties, high prices and demobilization. Therefore, in February 1919, he issued warnings against extreme agitation. At a meeting in Amritsar, he told the people present in his Darbar: 'You have seen that we have surmounted the difficulties and dangers, internal and external, of recent years because of the mutual trust and cooperation between the Government and the people.' He also said that greater things could be accomplished in the future with 'the same mutual trust and cooperation.' In a similar meeting at Jullundur, his warning was more explicit: 'Recent experience in other countries and even in other parts of India shows how rapidly disorders spread and how powerless are those who promote political agitation to check its dangerous manifestations'.

O'Dwyer believed that no heed was paid to his warnings. Meetings were held at Amritsar, Lahore, Multan and Jullundur in which the extremist leaders delivered inflammatory speeches. In the middle of March, O'Dwyer told the Deputy Commissioner of Amritsar to warn Dr Kitchlew and Dr Satyapal, telling them that he was also prepared, if necessary, to pass restriction orders against them or even deport them. Within three weeks they were forbidden to speak in public. The passing of the Rowlatt Act on 18 March gave further impetus to agitations and Mahatma Gandhi started his Passive Resistance Movement. *Hartals* were held at Amritsar, Multan and Panipat on 30 March, and at Lahore, Amritsar, Multan, Gujranwala, Ramnagar, Akalgarh, Hafizabad, Lyallpur and Jullundur on 6 April. Already, on 4 April, O'Dwyer had issued orders 'to exclude Mr Gandhi from the Punjab.' On 7 April, while addressing the Legislative Council, he took the opportunity to deliver another serious warning against the dangers of violent agitation. 'The Government of this Province is, and will remain, determined that public order which was maintained so successfully during the time of war shall not be disturbed in the time of peace.' He went on to say that the British Government 'which has crushed foreign foes and quelled internal rebellion could afford to despise these agitators, but it has the duty of protecting the young and ignorant whom they may incite to mischief and crime while themselves standing aside.' O'Dwyer thought that the agitation about the Rowlatt Act was uncalled for because the Act was to be invoked only against political conspiracies, i.e. 'anarchical and revolutionary movements.'

In his speech of 7 April, O'Dwyer gave facts and figures about the exceptional contribution of the Punjab in terms of both men and money to the war effort and observed, 'I have often been criticized for dwelling on the achievements of Punjab in season and out of season. But my pride in the Province is based on no narrow parochial spirit.' He could meet the Punjabi as man to man without suspicion or mistrust. He found the Punjabi loyal but not subservient, brave but not boastful, enterprising but not visionary, progressive but not pursuing false ideals or mistaking the show for the substance. This praise of the Punjabis was addressed to the rural constituency in general and large landholders in particular.

O'Dwyer also declared that he was not opposed to the reforms scheme. But it was the duty of his Government to advise how that policy should be given effect with regard to 'the local conditions and the interests of the various classes concerned.' Here again, he had the constituency of landholders in mind: 'There are great masses of the people who are not yet in a position to grasp the wider aspect of self-government institutions, and till their political education is more advanced – and we are endeavouring to hasten it by spreading education, extending local self-government and other means – Government cannot, in fairness to them, renounce its role as trustee of their interests till it can transfer the responsibility to those who are their genuine and deliberately chosen representatives.'

O'Dwyer had no sympathy and no affinity with the urban middle class leaders. In fact, he resented that *The Tribune* reacted strongly to his speech of 7 April. The editor of *The Tribune* thought that Sir Michael O'Dwyer had confounded intemperate language as such with criminal activity and the promotion of disorder. He also objected to the spirit and temper which O'Dwyer brought to the discussion in spite of knowing fully well how highly surcharged the atmosphere was and that the public mind was in a state of unusual excitement. 'If there is bitterness, he increases it immensely.' The number of persons who had taken part in the demonstrations of 6 April were to be counted not by tens of thousands, nor even by hundreds of thousands, but by millions. 'His Honour will probably find that there are few left in our own Province to whom his own appellation of 'men of sanity and common sense' is to be applied.'

Meanwhile, O'Dwyer ordered the deportation of Dr Kitchlew and Dr Satyapal. The day on which these orders were executed, 10 April 1919, 'riots and rebellion' started at Amritsar and Lahore. O'Dwyer asserts that these incidents were 'a natural if not inevitable consequence of anti-Government agitation of the preceding six or eight months.' In the firing at Lahore a few persons were killed. Their bodies were not handed over to their relatives so as to prevent demonstrations of the kind witnessed in the case of the Delhi and

Amritsar 'martyrs' on 30 March. On the evening of 10 April, O'Dwyer addressed the representatives of the 'martial classes' speaking of the measures adopted by the Government in his time as the Lieutenant Governor to extend education in the rural areas, to secure a greater share for the rural classes in civil administration, and to establish their footing in the higher ranks of the army so that they could qualify for 'a further advance.' The representatives of the great landholding and martial tribes of the Province had 'the biggest stake in the Province,' according to O'Dwyer.

By contrast, he denounced the middle class urban leadership for spreading anarchy and revolution. The persistent falsehood and misrepresentation by 'a small but noisy class' was a deadly weapon aimed at the people whom the Government wanted to protect. The Lieutenant Governor declared his intention to check the disorder and bloodshed promptly by enforcing the law. On 12 April, disorders broke out at Kasur, with results similar to those witnessed at Amritsar on the 10th. O'Dwyer refused to consider the suggestion given by the leaders of Lahore. At a dinner that night he told some of the pro-Government leaders that Martial Law was inevitable and it would be difficult to restrain the British troops who were most excited by the news of the brutal murders of their comrades and countrymen at Kasur and Amritsar. Before hearing the news of the shooting at Jallianwala Bagh on 13 April, O'Dwyer had sent a wireless message to Shimla proposing Martial Law in Lahore and Amritsar, and decided to arrest and deport the Lahore leaders, Ram Bhaj Dutt, Duni Chand and Harkrishan Lal. On hearing of General Dyer's action at Jallianwala Bagh, O'Dwyer approved of what he did. The reason given by him is not without significance. If Dyer had failed to disperse the crowd the situation in Amritsar would have gone from bad to worse and the rebellion would have spread widely. His action effectively stopped the rebellion not only in Amritsar but also its spread to many other places. Had he hesitated to fire, the rebellion would have spread with alarming rapidity. As to the amount of firing, the officer on the spot was its best judge.

O'Dwyer liked to believe that the situation was brought under complete control, before the Afghan War broke out on 4 May 1919, due to the enforcement of the Martial Law in five districts and rigorous measures taken in others. The rebellion rapidly collapsed when the attempts to bring in the rural classes, the demobilized soldiers and the Indian troops, failed decisively, and the threatened strike on the Railways was abandoned. Finally, on 12 May 1919, O'Dwyer responded to the farewell addresses of the representatives of the Muslim, Sikh and Hindu communities of the Punjab, acknowledging their loyalty and cooperation and assuring them that their interests were being safeguarded in the Constitutional Reforms. However, he could not help telling the representatives of the Hindu community that their brethren had accumulated wealth in commerce, industry and professions under the protection of the British Government, and they stood to lose more than others by internal disorder or external aggression. The right thing for them to do, therefore, was to 'cooperate with the Government in checking the one and repelling the other.' O'Dwyer reiterated at the same time that from political agitation to rebellion there was only a short but inevitable step.

II

Before turning to the oral evidence of Sir Michael O'Dwyer, we may recapitulate the points emerging from his 'note' which has been reviewed in the foregoing pages. It is quite clear that he did not entertain the idea of any large measure of self-government for India in the foreseeable future. He had no sympathy with 'extremist' politics which he tended to equate with revolution and rebellion. He had no sympathy with the political aspirations of the urban middle classes. His anxiety to retain the support of the landed classes for the empire was the obverse of his attitude towards the urban middle classes. He attached great importance to special legislation to deal with revolutionary upsurges, and had no hesitation in advocating or invoking such legislation. Exclusion and deportation of persons regarded as agitators was part of his considered policy and he believed in prompt action. Afraid of mass upsurge, he tended to see conspiracies behind popular movements. He was unwilling to entertain the idea that his own actions could provoke reactions. Prone to treat crises as a question of law and order, he was unwilling to negotiate even minor concessions. For him, to bow before political pressures was below the dignity of an imperial people. It may now be suggested that O'Dwyer's attitudes arose from a political philosophy that was implicit in the colonial culture during the last quarter of the nineteenth and the first quarter of the twentieth century. The measures he adopted were not ad hoc measures; they were the outcome of his basic attitudes.

From the oral evidence of Michael O'Dwyer it can be safely inferred that he attached crucial importance to special measures. The Seditious movement of 1907 subsided essentially owing to the deportation of Ajit Singh and Lajpat Rai. The speedy success of the Punjab Government in dealing with the Ghadarites and the Muslim peasants in the south-west of the Punjab was only partly due to the support of the people, including the urban middle classes; it was made possible essentially by the Ingress into India Ordinance and the Defence of India Act.

O'Dwyer had no evidence to support his assumption that the disturbances were the result of an organized conspiracy and he was hard put to maintain his position. He accepted the suggestion that the revolutionary people in the Punjab could have taken advantage of the situation created by the Rowlatt agitation. Even for this, the evidence he cited was that of 'revolutionary and rebellious' results of the agitation at certain places. O'Dwyer conceded that the leaders at Amritsar and Lahore did not intend to incite the crowds to violence, but they did not dissociate themselves from the crowds when violence broke out. This, obviously, did not apply to the leaders of Amritsar who had been deported. Of the three leaders deported later from Lahore, at least two had not associated themselves with violence. O'Dwyer was not willing to concede that Rambhaj Datt and Duni Chand had actually tried to quell the disturbances. Nor was he willing to concede that they could have been powerless to control the mobs. In fact, when it was suggested that some minor concessions given by the Government might result in successful negotiations, O'Dwyer refused to accept the suggestion. He thought that the leaders were trying to bring the Government to its knees. Eventually, his position was reduced to admitting in so many words that he had no positive proof for his assertion that there was some organization behind the agitation. The President of the Committee intervened at this point to say that this was merely an inference drawn from the events. When O'Dwyer was asked why the mobs were not armed with guns or swords, he replied that rebels do not always act wisely. When he was told that no serious attempt was made to seduce the troops, he replied that one never knows these things till they actually happen. He went on to add that 'each particular instance seems very trivial, but the cumulative effect of all these coming at a time like that was very serious. These trivial things may be a coincidence which is a preliminary to a sepoy rising or mutiny.'

About the purpose of the Rowlatt agitation, O'Dwyer did not commit himself on the point whether or not it was honest, but he asserted that it was certainly dangerous. The opposition to the Bill in his view was 'press-manufactured.' But he had to concede that the vast majority of the 'political classes' was opposed to the Bill. He could not give any argument as to why the consideration of the Bill was not deferred, particularly in view of the proposed constitutional reform and the fact that the Defence of India Act was still operative. All he could say was that the agitation would have died down 'if Mr Gandhi's movement had not fanned the flame'. He stuck to his view that the Rowlatt Act should have been passed when it was.

O'Dwyer also stuck to his view that Mahatma Gandhi should have been excluded from the Punjab in the first week of April. The people of the Punjab in his view were incapable of appreciating the idea of passive resistance; they were likely to translate it into an active resistance movement. Mahatma

Gandhi himself was looked upon as the champion of the people against an alien and hostile government and he could not have played a pacifying role. When O'Dwyer was reminded that the demonstrations on 30 March and 6 April had been peaceful, he repeated that this was because 'we made very complete military preparations'.

O'Dwyer stood exposed even more clearly on the question of the deportation of Dr Kitchlew and Dr Satyapal. He was told that the Deputy Commissioner of Amritsar had not asked for their deportation. O'Dwyer replied that the situation described by the Deputy Commissioner implies that the government should 'act at once'. He asserted, indeed, that everything would have been lost if their deportation had been postponed. He was not prepared to consider that what happened at Amritsar on 10 April could in some way be connected with the deportation. He reiterated his guiding principle that the 'best way' of dealing with a serious situation was 'prompt action'. Not for nothing had he concluded his initial note with a quotation from Mayne's *Indian Criminal Law:* 'The Governor who waits to recognize a rebellion till it looks like a war will probably find that he has waited too long'.

O'Dwyer was prepared to accept support from the political leaders but not advice or suggestions. Raja Narendra Nath, Rai Bahadur Ram Saran Das, Mian Muhammad Shafi and Bakhshi Sohan Lal, among others, suggested to him that the extremist leaders may be called and asked to give up their propaganda. He told them that 'it was the duty of every citizen to rally to the side of Government in such a critical situation and Government would willingly accept help from anyone, but Government would accept dictation from nobody. That was the line I took. I was quite willing to receive their cooperation, but not willing to submit to their dictation.' In the same way he negated the suggestion of the extremist leaders about the withdrawal of troops on certain terms. For the common people, O'Dwyer cared even less. He did not allow the bodies of the few persons killed in the firing at Lahore on 10 April to be sent to their relatives for burial to obviate further excitement. The resentment of the people who wanted to bury the dead according to their own rites did not count with O'Dwyer.

The crowd at Jallianwala Bagh on 13 April was characterized by O'Dwyer as 'a truculent mob which had already committed murder and rebellion'. This was based on the assumption that 'Amritsar city as a whole had committed murder and rebellion' on the 10th. Since the crowd had gathered there in sympathy with 'the people who had committed rebellion and murder', it could be treated as a rebellious crowd. He was told that there was no evidence about the intentions of this crowd. He replied that the fact that they had assembled there was evidence enough: 'They would not have assembled there without good reason at a critical time like that'. He was told that a number of villagers who had come for the Baisakhi fair were present in the crowd. O'Dwyer replied that property stolen from the city earlier had been recovered from certain villages. The implication was that these villagers too had come with the idea of plunder. No innocent person would have gone to Jallianwala Bagh which, in O'Dwyer's mistaken belief, had been the scene of revolutionary meetings earlier.

About the firing at Jallianwala Bagh, O'Dwyer was asked whether it was justified as a general punishment for the rebels or as a specific measure for dispersing the crowd. He replied that it was General Dyer's duty to disperse the crowd. He was informed that Dyer himself had said in his evidence that the crowd could have been dispersed without firing. O'Dwyer did not agree with this assessment of the situation. He was told that Dyer had immediately opened fire when he reached the Bagh, without any warning at all. Could this be approved? It was for Dyer to judge, O'Dwyer responded, and went on to add: 'I do not criticize his action one way or the other, but I say one is entitled to believe that he did his best under the circumstances'. No amount of new information could induce O'Dwyer to change his view that Dyer's action at Jallianwala Bagh was more than justified.

Nevertheless, O'Dwyer informed the Committee that General Dyer was afraid that his retreat might be cut off: 'After he had fired the first volley, the crowd made a rush. He thought that this was intended to intercept his retreat and he went on firing'. To make it more convincing, O'Dwyer went on to add that Dyer had changed the view afterwards on closer examination of the place which revealed that there was only one way of egress to escape. O'Dwyer was told that Dyer himself had said nothing about this in his evidence.'If that was really the correct position, it was a very important circumstance to put forward'. Perhaps Sir Chimanlal Hiralal Setalvad implied that Sir Michael O'Dwyer was interpolating.

Gallows were put up at Kasur for the public hanging of the convicted murderers of British soldiers. O'Dwyer explained that the idea of public execution originated with the military authorities and he saw no reason to differ 'as the people at Kasur were particularly criminal'. However, the gallows were kept on view for some days near the railway station. O'Dwyer admitted that the idea was to impress upon the people that British justice was 'speedy and stern'. Here again, the implication of the questioning was to show that the military authorities were determined to administer with vengeance what they thought was justice.

Finally, we come to the equation of Home Rule with the Ghadar. O'Dwyer explained that this was his view in 1917 and it was based on Dr Kitchlew's statement and the Ghadarite Mathura Singh, and that was why he had excluded Tilak and Pal from the Punjab at that time. He was told that only the recognized leaders of the movement could say what was really meant by Home Rule. It did not mean the immediate transfer of power to the people of India and the ouster of the British, as contended by O'Dwyer. The object of Home Rule was to transfer provincial administration to the representatives of the Indian people. O'Dwyer insisted that the political doctrines of Home Rule might have been clear to the educated people but not to the ordinary villager. His own concern too was not with ideologies but their effects on the common people: 'What we have to consider is not the ideal in the mind of the political philosopher in his arm-chair or the journalist at his desk but the ideal conveyed to the average man, and we have had positive proof based on judicial findings of several experienced tribunals that the thousands of Punjabis to whom the Swaraj or Home Rule doctrine was preached, some hundreds at least, set themselves as early as possible to realize that ideal by the sword, pistol and the bomb. I think that makes my position quite clear.' From this viewpoint, it is amply clear that there was no difference between the Ghadar and Home Rule, or between Home Rule and the passive resistance movement. A new political phenomenon could thus be fitted into the old colonial framework of political perception and administrative action.

III

It was Mahatma Gandhi's intuition that the violence which broke out in the Punjab in April 1919 'would never have broken out were it not for the serious errors of Sir Michael O'Dwyer'. In the actions of Sir Michael O'Dwyer it is certainly possible to discern the errors of judgement. However, the malady appears to lie much deeper in a whole set of interrelated assumptions and attitudes, produced and nurtured by the colonial situation in India and shared by a large number of British bureaucrats in the Punjab. Neither O'Dwyer nor the Punjab Government was alone in subscribing to those assumptions and attitudes. The attitude of the Government of India towards what was happening in the Punjab, and elsewhere in India, was basically no different. Sir C.H. Setalvad was able to ask some searching questions essentially because of his empathy with the national aspirations. The colonial rule and the national movement had come to a parting of ways. It was almost impossible for the colonial rulers to perceive the change. They lived in a world sealed from the surrounding universe. The Jallianwala Bagh symbolized the isolation of their world as well as its invasion by the citizens of a new universe. Perhaps it was not accidental that O'Dwyer was shot dead in his own country by a person whom he would have called 'a revolutionary', and who had seen the devastating effect of General Dyer's firing at the Jallianwala Bagh.

For the people who suffered directly, the Jallianwala Bagh was a 'tragedy' in the ordinary sense of the word. By extension, it was a tragedy for those who sympathized with the sufferers, in the Punjab and elsewhere in the country as a whole. In the classical sense, however, it was a tragedy for the colonial rulers as well: it revealed the fatal flaw in their assumptions and attitudes which eventually led to their departure from the land which they had hoped to rule for centuries.

TEN

❖ Jallianwala Bagh: The Construction of a Nationalist Symbol

SURJIT HANS

THE PAPER IS LARGELY concerned with published statistical data on the Jallianwala Bagh massacre and Punjab Disturbances.[1] A brief background may be given to the events. The Amritsar Congress Committee was formed in 1917. A call for a 24-hour *hartal* on 30 March 1919 against the Rowlatt Acts was given by Mahatma Gandhi. The date was subsequently changed to 6 April as it was considered that sufficient notice had not been given. On 29 March the Punjab Government passed an order forbidding Dr Satyapal from speaking at public meetings and confined him to the city of Amritsar. The *hartal* was observed on 30 March. All the shops were closed and business was brought to a standstill. A meeting, presided over by Dr Kitchlew, was held at Jallianwala Bagh and attended by 45,000 persons.

On 5 April, the Reception Committee of the Amritsar Session of the National Congress decided to stage a *hartal* again on April 6. An *agent provocateur*, Hans Raj, managed to disturb a cricket match at the Aitchison Park. At nine o'clock in the evening about two hundred people went to the streets proclaiming the *hartal.* A 50,000 strong meeting was held at Jallianwala Bagh. A mysterious handbill appeared declaring: 'Prepare yourself to die and kill others.'

On 8 April, Hans Raj was made the Joint Secretary of the Satyagraha Sabha which kept a register of the satyagrahis, who were under a vow.

On 9 April, which was Ram Naumi, there were unusual scenes of Hindu-Muslim solidarity.

A band played 'God Save the King' in the procession. A group of students, wearing Turkish uniforms (symbolic of their support for Khilafat), began to clap in disrespect to the Deputy Commissioner, standing on a balcony. The Civil Surgeon brought orders from the Governor O'Dwyer for the Deputy

Commissioner that Dr Satyapal and Dr Kitchlew be detained and deported to Dharmsala. And the Punjab Government banned the entry of Mahatma Gandhi into the Punjab.

On the morning of 10 April, the doctors were inveigled into the Deputy Commissioner's bungalow and bundled to Dharmsala. Hans Raj had managed to accompany Dr Kitchlew to the bungalow. The two doctors wrote letters to their families explaining the situation and delivered them to Hans Raj. He made out in the city that Dr Kitchlew had asked for revenge, and Dr Bashir Ahmed gathered a crowd and reached the Deputy Commissioner's residence.

At 11.30 a large crowd had gathered at Aitchison Park. The picket at the railway footbridge was strengthened to stop the crowd from crossing over to the European Civil Lines. Soon there were 40,000 men below what is now called Bhandari Bridge. Improvised theatrical gestures, show of bravado and pelting of stones led to firing. Three or four persons were killed and the sight of dead comrades inflamed the crowd.

By 5.00 p.m. the Telegraph Exchange was burnt; Guard Robinson had been done to death; Queen Victoria's statue had a broken finger; the National Bank was burnt and two Englishmen were killed; Zenana Hospital was attacked; Miss Sherwood was assaulted; the Indian Christian Church and CMS Normal Girls' School burnt; an Englishman was murdered on Rego Bridge; Sub-Post Offices in the Golden Temple, Majith Mandi and Dhab Wasti Ram were gutted.

General Dyer reached Amritsar from Jullundur on the evening of 11 April. The civil administration was handed over to the military that night, between 11 and 12 April.

On 12 April, Dyer marched through the city with a force of 125 British and 310 Indian troops, followed by two armoured cars. At Sultanwind Gate the crowd jeered, spat and refused to disperse. Dyer refrained from firing.

There was trouble at Kasur. Two Europeans were killed and a station looted (12 April 1919).

A meeting outside Dr Bashir Ahmed's house attracted 20,000 men. Hans Raj convened another meeting at Hindu Sabha High School. A reading of letters by Dr Satyapal and Dr Kitchlew was promised in the meeting to be held at Jallianwala Bagh on 13 April.

> Sunday, 13 April was Baisakhi and marked the beginning of one of the most important religious festivals in the Punjab. The roads approaching the city were thronged with thousands of pilgrims from outlying districts who descended on the city to bathe in the pool of immortality and worship in the Golden Temple. Equally large numbers came in for the horse and cattle fair which figured prominently at the festival and lasted for several days.

At 10.30 a.m., Dyer went through the city with a formidable show of force. At 19 places the proclamation was read out (Map I): 'No person is permitted to leave the city without a pass, issued by the authorities. None can leave his home after 8.00 p.m. Any person found in the street after 8.00 is liable to be shot. Any procession or gathering of four men will be treated as unlawful assembly and dispersed by a force of arms, if necessary.'

The proclamation was made at six places in the Hall Bazar. Nearby was the residence of Dr Satyapal. Three proclamations were read at Hathi, Lohgarh and Lahori Gates on the periphery of the city. An exception was made in the case of Dhab Khatikan where the proclamation was read in the heart of the locality, not marked by a paved road or crossing. Dr Kitchlew lived there. No proclamation was made in the residential areas to the east of Dhab Khatikan, starting from Bhagtanwala Gate to Gilwali Gate, Chatiwind Gate, Sultanwind Gate and Ghee Manid Gate on the periphery of the city or from Bhagtanwala Gate to Dhab Wasti Ram, Golden Temple, Jallianwala Bagh and Ghee Mandi Gate which would constitute about one-third of the city in area. The omission is all the more remarkable as Bhagtanwala railway station and Sub-Post Offices in Dhab Wasti Ram and the Golden Temple had suffered arson. Dyer was also jeered at Sultanwind Gate the day before. (This may account for the steep fall in the index of Muslim participation to 0.39 in the Jallianwala massacre from 1.4 of April 10 disturbances).

Martial Law as declared on 15 April later backdated to 30 March to cover the beginning of the Rowlatt Act agitation, and finally withdrawn on 9 June.

On 23 December the Royal Proclamation giving amnesty to political offenders was issued.[2]

The disturbances of 10 April at Amritsar led to the Jallianwala massacre, the latter, to the declaration of Martial Law.

The number of outside victims 87 (70+17) out of the 381 victims constitutes 22.8 per cent of the total, i.e. about one person in four. Their presence cannot be a 'coincidence'. They are the people who came for Baisakhi and the cattle fair.

Of the 17 rank outsiders, 1 hailed from Kot Siddiqui (Campbellpur, Pakistan); 2 from Shobhla and Kharota (Rawalpindi); 1 from Gaddi Guru Jwala Singh (Montgomery); 1 from Mangat Bhim (Gujrat); 4 from Narowal, Talwandi Bhindran, Miyali and Rayya (Sialkot).

There were eight persons from Gurdaspur district, one each from Gurdaspur, Batala, Sri Hargobindpur, Tung, Pipli, Jiwan Bhinder, Rayya, Bahlolpur and Kot Karmchand.

Patently, the rank outsider Hindu Sikhs had come for Baisakhi. In those years, the Hindus could be counted as Sikhs and vice versa.[3] This also explains

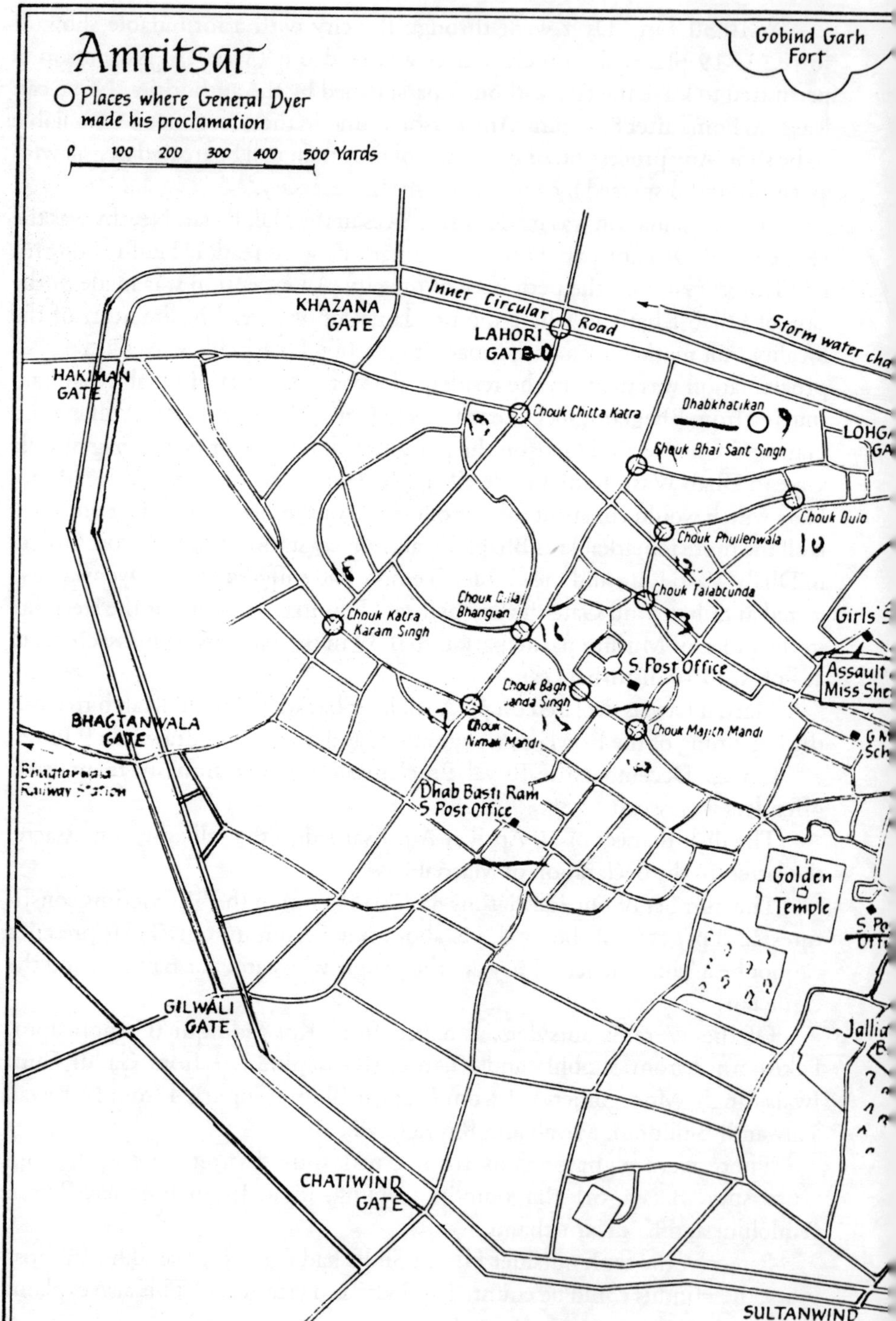
Amritsar
Places where General Dyer made his proclamation
0 100 200 300 400 500 Yards
Gobind Garh Fort
Inner Circular Road
Storm water cha
KHAZANA GATE
LAHORI GATE
HAKIMAN GATE
Chouk Chitta Katra
Dhabkhatikan
Chouk Bhai Sant Singh
Chouk Dulo
Chouk Phullenwala
Chouk Talabtunda
Chouk Gillai Bhangian
Chouk Katra Karam Singh
S. Post Office
Chouk Bagh Janda Singh
Chouk Nimak Mandi
Chouk Majith Mandi
Girls' S
Assault Miss She
BHAGTANWALA GATE
Bhagtanwala Railway Station
Dhab Basti Ram S Post Office
Golden Temple
GILWALI GATE
CHATIWIND GATE
SULTANWIND GATE

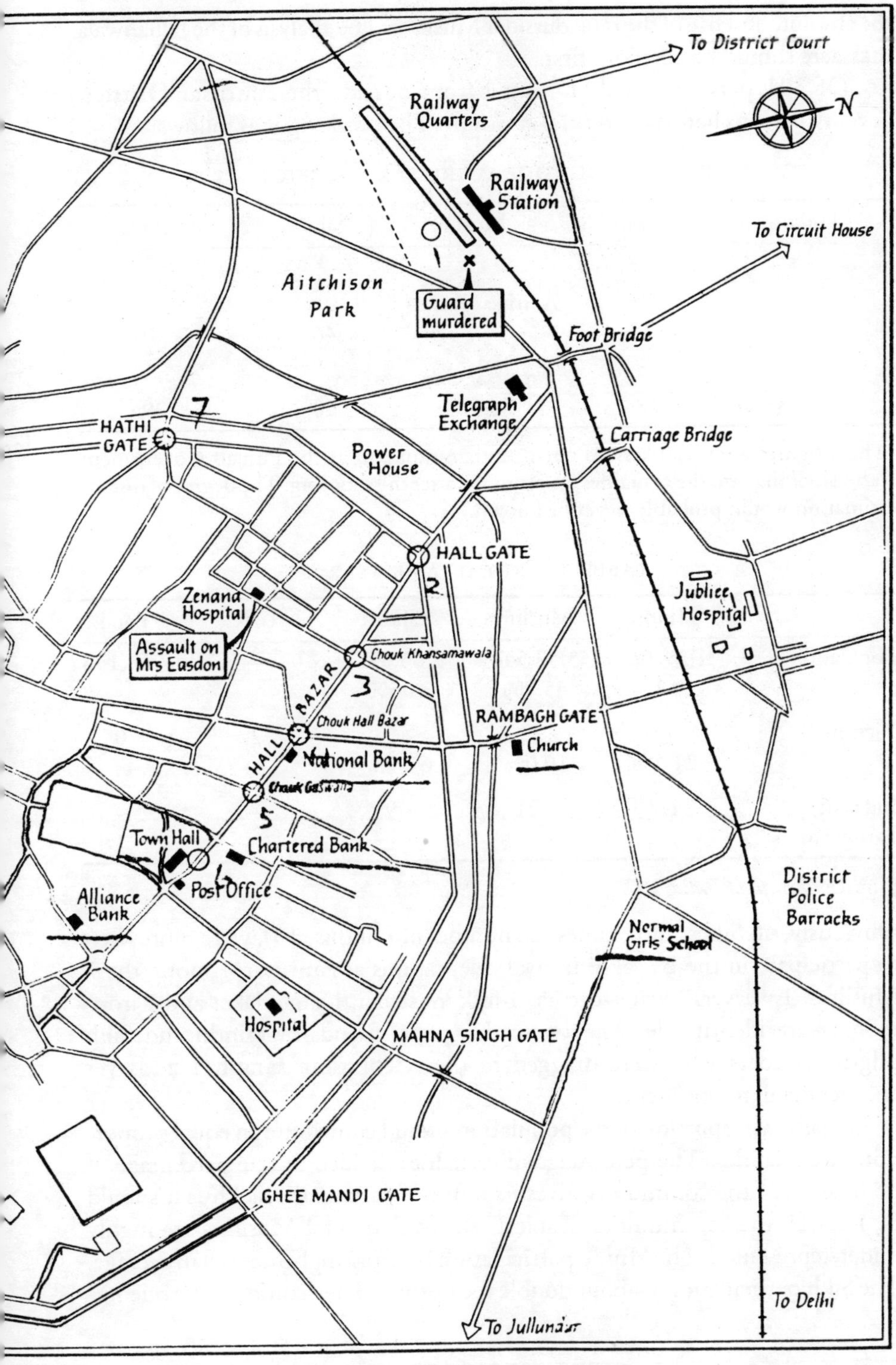
To District Court
Railway Quarters
N
Railway Station
To Circuit House
Aitchison Park
Guard murdered
Foot Bridge
Telegraph Exchange
HATHI GATE
Power House
Carriage Bridge
HALL GATE
Jubliee Hospital
Zenana Hospital
Assault on Mrs Easdon
Chouk Khansamawala
HALL BAZAR
Chouk Hall Bazar
RAMBAGH GATE
Church
National Bank
Town Hall
Chartered Bank
Post Office
Alliance Bank
District Police Barracks
Normal Girls' School
Hospital
MAHNA SINGH GATE
GHEE MANDI GATE
To Delhi
To Jullundur

the absolute absence of the rank outsider Muslims. The analysis of the Jallianwala massacre should be taken up first.

Of 381 persons killed, 17 came from outside the Amritsar District. Seventy persons hailed from rural Amritsar. The break-up is as follows:

TABLE I: OUTSIDE AMRITSAR DISTRICT

Unknown	Hindu	Muslim	Sikh	Total
—	13	—	4	17
		Amritsar Rural		
2	15	7	46	70
		Amritsar City		
18	184	52	40	294

(These figures are very likely to be an underestimation as the Punjab Government started looking into the casualties four months after the shooting. The degree of underestimation would probably never be known.)

TABLE II: RURAL AMRITSAR

	Hindu	Muslim	Sikh	U/K	Total
Population	1,39,122 18.1%	3,52,544 45.8%	2,65,526 34.5%	—	7,69,156
Victims	15 21.4%	7 10.0%	46 65.5%	2 —	70 —
Index of Participation	1.2	0.21	1.9	—	—

(Source: *Census of India,* 1921)

Obviously, 46 Sikhs, three times the number of Hindus (15), were more keen to participate in the Baisakhi festival celebrations at Amritsar. Among the 7 Muslims, 1 weaver, 1 water-carrier, 1 folk musician, 1 shoemaker and 1 ironmonger are identifiable. They were the 'poor' friends of Hindu and Sikh pilgrims/traders who were dragged to the celebration. Graph 1 adds yet another detail to this picture.

Ideally, a proportion of the population should contribute an equal proportion of casualities. The percentage of casualties divided by the percentage of population of the community gives its index of participation. Thus it should be 1 for all the communities. Table II shows that rural Muslims are highly under-represented. The Hindu participation is surprisingly more than average. The Sikh participation is about double the normal. They combine the celebration of a pre-historic festival with a visit to the Golden Temple. (According to Sikh theology, water from the Ganges comes to the pool of immortality in Amritsar).

There are only two female martyrs. Both of them happen to be Jat Sikhs. Out of 46 Sikh victims, 28 are Jats; 2 carpenters; 1 Kamboh; 1 Potter; 1 Sadhs; 9 unknown (in their castes). Jats are clearly a major category.

Of the 15 Hindus, there are 3 Brahmins; 2 Khatris; 2 Aroras; 1 goldsmith; 1 Ahluwalia; 1 petition-writer; 1 *Bairagi*; and 4 unknown (in their castes).

It may be added that the unknown category is filled mostly by low-castes, a fact to be noticed again in Martial Law atrocities. Sathiala village contributed 10 martyrs. Yet no folk memory survives. The reason is that people were afraid of confessing participation for fear of the Martial Law that stalked the province.[4] So is the case of Varpal which registered 4 victims. Contrary to popular belief, no continuity but discontinuity of popular memory is the stuff of history. History is necessarily 'forged' in both senses, by institutions of learning and interested charlatans.

The indices of participation in Amritsar city are shown as under:

TABLE III: AMRITSAR CITY

	Hindu	Muslim	Sikh	U/K	Total
Population	65,313 40.8%	71,180 44.4%	21,478 13.4%	—	—
Victims	184 62.6%	52 17.6%	40 13.6%	18 —	294 —
Index of Participation	15	0.39	1.0	—	—

A steep fall in the index of Muslim participation requires an explanation. It could be that Dyer's proclamations told on their attendance. Dr Kitchlew's stronghold on Dhab Khatikan is in the opposite direction and at a distance from Jallianwala Bagh. The entry of lumpens in the widespread riots of 10 April should be considered. If their ambiguous social ontology be not so there is nothing pejorative about the lumpens.[5] Baisakhi celebrations in the Golden Temple by the Jallianwala Bagh, probably kept Muslims off, like the rank outsiders. An element of exhaustion should be another factor. But complete explanations would never be forthcoming.

Of 184 Hindu casualties from the city, there are 71 Khatris; 57 unknown (in their caste); 27 Aroras; 15 Brahmins; 4 Kambohs; 3 goldsmiths; 3 Rajputs; 2 Banias; 2 *Sadhs*; 2 Bhatias; 1 Ahluwalia; 1 Kaisth; 1 barber; 1 carpenter; 1 petition-writer; 1 clerk; 1 dalal; and 1 pleader. The Khatris register a remarkable presence.

Of the 52 Muslims, there were 13 Kashmiris; 8 unknown; 6 Shaikhs; 4 goldsmiths; 3 carpenters; 3 Rajputs; 2 Arains; 2 ironmongers; 2 oilpressers; 2 *Kharasis;* 1 Faqir; 1 water-carrier; 1 Sayyid; 1 weaver; 1 washerman; 1 bawd; and 1 watchman. The Kashmiris, the compatriots of Dr Kitchlew, were the largest in number. The absence of Sayyids is notable.

Of 40 Sikhs, the unknown come on top. There are 10 carpenters; 10 Aroras; 4 Jats; 1 Saini; 1 Kamboh; 1 tailor; 1 Kashmiri; and 1 Khatri. Khatri is the first category in Hindus, the last in Sikhs. Urban Sikhs are topped by carpenters, which is a reflex of Sikh demography. (After Jats, they constitute the most numerous group of the Sikhs). A lone Kashmiri Sikh stands out.

To have a perceptual idea of the hinterland of rural martyrs of Jallianwala Bagh, individual villages have been bunched with the nearest town. We have the following data available in Table IV:

TABLE IV

Nearest Town in kms. from the village	Distance of the town from Amritsar	Median Distance to the town	No. of Persons
Unknown (1)	—	—	—
Serial no. 173, Kiampur			
Amritsar	—	7	23
Chheharta	8	16	11
Ajnala	21	8.5	3
Mjitha	18	6	9
Jandiala	20	16	14
Tarn Taran	26	15	9

(Source: *Village and Town Directory: Census 1971*, Amrit District, Series 17, Chandigarh).

The constraint of data available has turned Chheharta into a town in 1971. Today it is part of Amritsar city. In 1919 it was a village.

Majitha was not connected then by railway line. Nor is Ajnala today.

Median distance decreases with more backward means of communication available, thus saving on relative discomfort of journey to Amritsar.[6]

If we make the nearest town the centre, and draw an arc of the length of median distance to the town, we get a flower-like pattern of the hinterland of the Jallianwala Bagh massacre. Considering 8 persons from Gurdaspur, the Tarn Taran Batala axis stands out (Map II).

A meagre contribution of 3 from Ajnala stands out in isolation from the hinterland. The *tehsil* suffers from adverse physial features. The Ravi marks

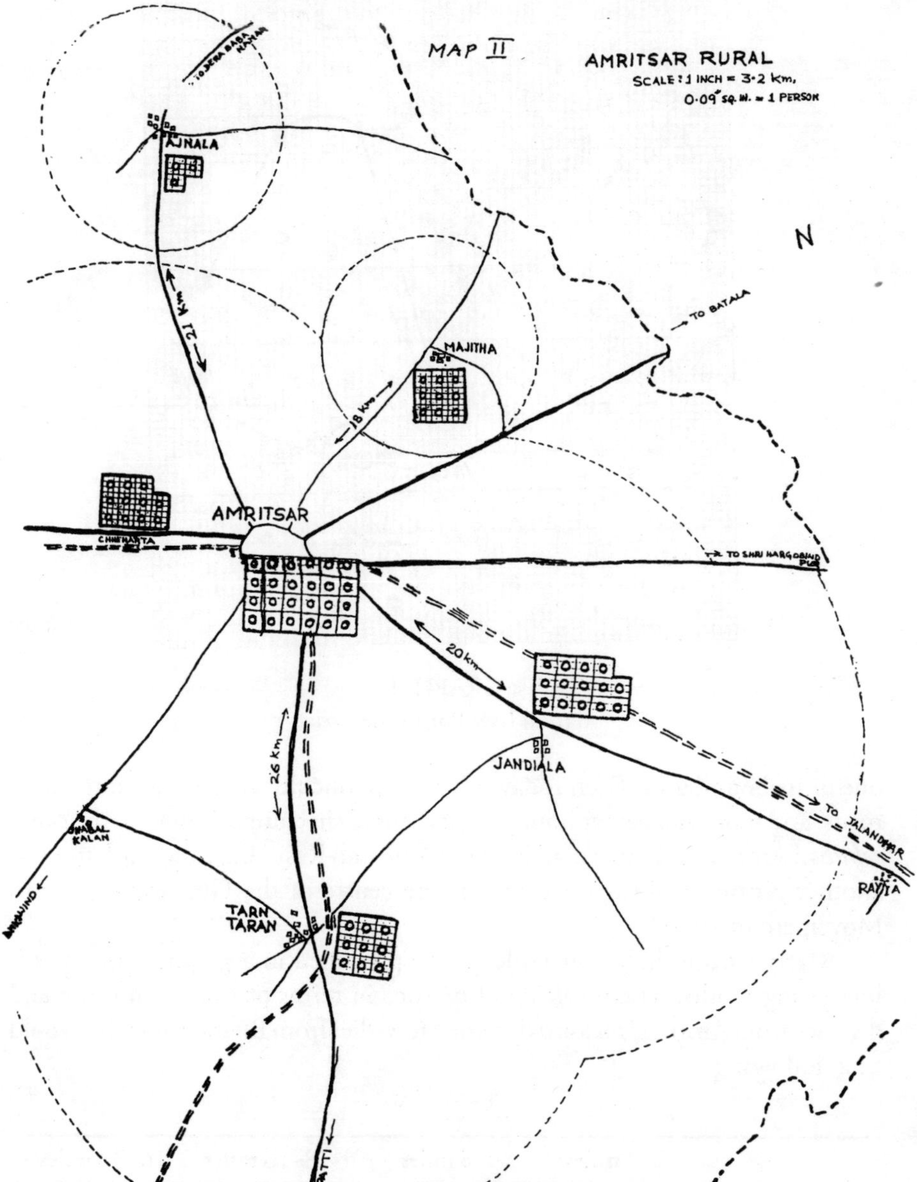

AMRITSAR RURAL MAP
SCALE 1 INCH = 3.2 KM
0.09 SQ. IN. = 1 PERSON

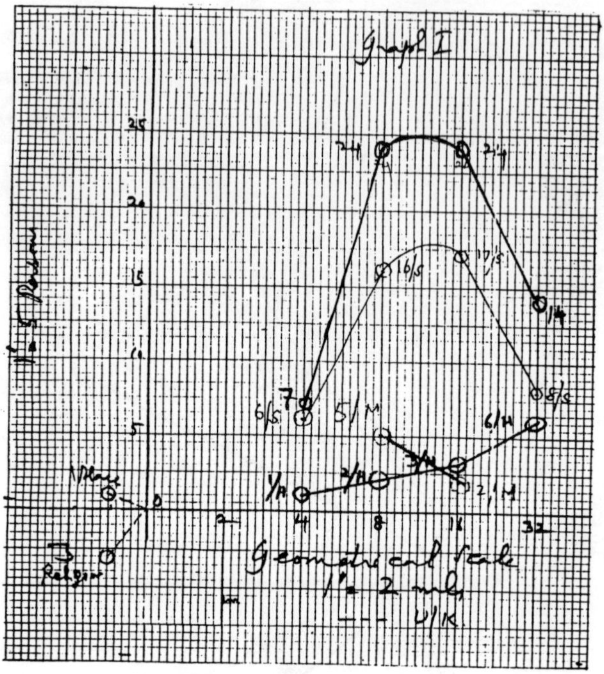

GRAPH–I
Martial Law Punishments/lac

one of its boundaries. Even today it has more uncultivable land, more *kacha* roads, and more villages without primary schools in comparison with the other *tehsils* of Amritsar.[7] Tarn Taran is on the Amritsar-Kasur line, and the latter was another centre of disturbance. It was the centre of the Gurdwara Reforms Movement in 1920.[8]

Martyrs from the countryside can be presented in a graph, which yields interesting results. The break-up of persons in terms of the community and distance from Amritsar measured as-the-crow-flies from Bhandari Bridge would be as follows:

TABLE V

	2–4 miles	4–8 miles	8–16 miles	16–32 miles
Hindu	1	2	3	6
Muslim	—	5	2	—
Sikh	6	16	17	8
Unknown	—	1	2	—
Total	7	24	24	14 = 69

(Kiampur could not be located on the map).

The geometric scale of distance has been adopted keeping in mind the increasing inconvenience of travel.

The graph is shaped like a horse shoe for the total numbers involved. The configure of the graph for the Sikhs is similar. Thus the pattern is largely governed by Sikh participation. It is so because the upward graph of the Hindu representation cancels the downward graph of the Muslims. Expense mattered to Muslims but not to Hindus. They were probably traders coming to the horse/cattle fair. Two Hindus could not reasonably be supposed to have persuaded five Muslims to accompany them at 4 to 8 miles mark, or three, two at 8 to 16 miles point. Fraternal duress on the Muslims has been exercised more by Jat Sikhs than by Brahmin Khatri Hindus. Social anthropology too has its pull.

We may now turn to Martial Law incidents. The break-up of punishments is as follows:

TABLE VII

District	Total	Death Sentence	Transportation	R.I.	Stripes
Amritsar	218	51	44	115	8
Gujranwala	192	36	121	30	5
Lahore	113	26	70	17	—
Gujrat	43	2	29	12	—
Lyallpur	19	—	—	19	—

(See Graph II and Table XI (Part a) line 2 Gujranwala).

Gujranwala suffered the most under the Martial Law. The incidents at Amritsar have received the attention of a number of historians and the Rowlatt Act agitation at Lahore has been eminently covered by Dr Ravinder Kumar. The Gujranwala agitation, however, has yet to find its historian.[9]

TABLE VIII

COMMUNITY-WISE BREAK-UP OF PUNISHMENT

District	Community	Death Sentence	Transportation	R.I.	Stripes
Amritsar	Hindu	12	11	20	2
	Muslim	30	28	59	5
	Sikh	7	5	31	—
Gujranwal	Hindu	11	44	6	—
	Muslim	7	38	22	4
	Sikh	15	32	1	—

Lahore	Hindu	8	26	4	—
	Muslim	15	29	10	—
	Sikh	3	13	—	—
Gujrat	Hindu	1	14	4	—
	Muslim	1	13	6	—
	Sikh	—	1	—	—
Lyallpur	Hindu	—	—	1	—
	Muslim	—	—	1	—
	Sikh	—	—	12	—

(Punishments in Table VIII are fewer than the ones in Table VII because of the 'unknown' elements)

We have the following figures for population:

TABLE IX

Place	Total	Hindu	Muslim	Sikh
Amritsar City	1,60,218	65, 313	71,180	21,478
Amritsar Dist.	9,29,374	2,04,435	4,23,724	2,87,004
Gujranwal Dist.	6,23,581	1,01,566	4,43,147	50,802
Lahore Dist.	11,31,336	2,55,690	6,47,640	1,79,975
Gujrat Dist.	8,24,046	62,529	7,09,684	49,556
Lyallpur Dist.	9,79,463	1,81,488	5,94,917	1,60,821

(Source: *Census 1921*).

Amritsar city is considered individually, as the Martial Law cases largely covered the incidents of 10 April. (Cases 9–18, 20–21, 28–34, 47–49, 51–58, 62, 69; 75, 89–98, 104, 110 of National Bank looting murder; 76 Alliance Bank murder; 80 Chartered Bank; 39–40 Gumanpura derailment; 67 Bhagtanwala Gate; 70 Majith Mandi Post Office; 73 Miss Sherwood; 78 Mrs Easdon's house; 83 Guard Robinson's murder; 86 Jagdeo dacoity; 101 Chheharta's train loot; 103 Normal Girls' School; and 113 Leaders' Case).

Secondly, only Gumanpura, Chheharta and Jagdeo could be included in rural Amritsar. In all other districts, the incidents were scattered in cities, towns and villages. That is why population figures of the districts have been used.

Working on the principle of proportions, we get the following indices of participation for different communities at various places.

TABLE X

INDICES OF PARTICIPATION

Place	Community	Total	Death Sentence	Trans-portation	R.I.
Amritsar City	Hindu	0.6	0.5	0.6	0.7
	Muslim	1.4	1.4	1.5	1.5
	Sikh	0.5	0.9	0.5	0.3
Amritsar Dist.	Hindu	0.9	1.0	1.1	0.7
	Muslim	1.2	1.2	1.4	1.1
	Sikh	0.6	0.4	0.4	0.9
Gujranwala Dist.	Hindu	1.9	1.8	2.2	1.2
	Muslim	0.5	0.2	0.4	0.4
	Sikh	3.0	5.1	3.2	0.4
Lahore Dist.	Hindu	1.4	1.3	1.6	1.0
	Muslim	0.8	1.0	0.7	1.0
	Sikh	0.8	0.7	1.1	—
Gujrat Dist.	Hindu	7.3	6.6	6.4	4.4
	Muslim	0.5	0.58	0.52	0.58
	Sikh	0.3	—	3.56	—
Lyallpur Dist.	Hindu	0.28	—	—	0.28
	Muslim	0.08	—	—	0.28
	Sikh	3.8	—	—	3.8

From the above indices, the following conclusions become self-evident. Muslim participation is most pronounced in Amritsar city. It goes down in Amritsar district. Equating death sentence/transportation with a 'higher' form of political activity and R.I./Stripes with the nuts and bolts of agitation in ordinary men, we can see that all classes of the Muslim population participated in almost equal measure. The indices speak of the political stature of Dr Saifuddin Kitchlew.

Next to Amritsar, the Muslim participation is noticeable in Lahore. In all other places their participation is low.

From the Muslim indices of all the five districts, we see that the Khilafat element is secondary to the resentment towards the Rowlatt Act. Surely, the priorities of the nationalist movement, Khilafat, and Punjab wrongs, were inversely related to the situation on the ground.

It is amazing that the biggest contribution of the Sikhs comes from Gujranwala, then a centre of Sikh educational activities. Next to Gujranwala is Amritsar district. Sikh participation in this city is interesting. The indices of

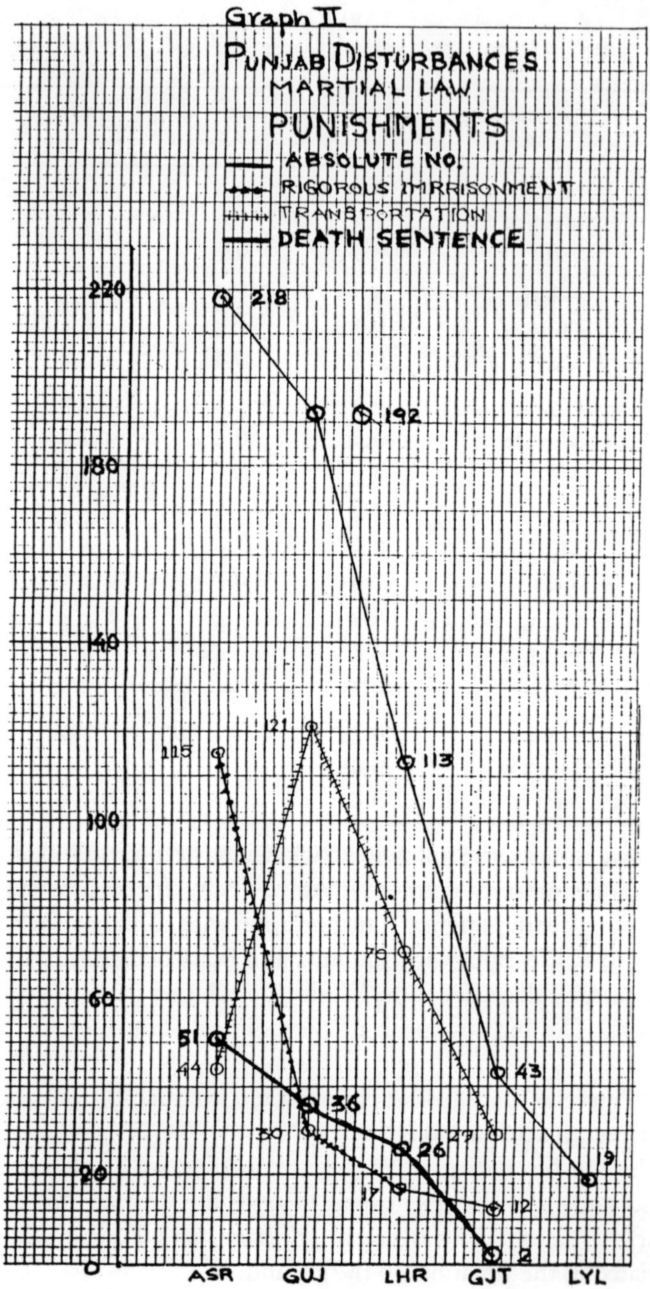

GRAPH–II: PUNJAB DISTURBANCES MARTIAL LAW

death sentence, transportation and rigorous imprisonment are in the descending order. The Sikhs confine themselves to the 'higher' forms of activity.

A still more interesting fact is that only rural Sikhs were agitating in Lyallpur – the future nursery of the Sikh Reform movement. (See fn. 8).

The agitation in Amritsar is by and large that of Muslims. The upsurge in Gujranwala belongs entirely to the Hindus and Sikhs. The Hindus are preponderant in Lahore. The figures speak for Lala Harkishen Lal, Rambhuj Dutt and Duni Chand. The agitation in Gujrat is purely Hindu.

The story of unequal participation continued during the election year in the Punjab.[10]

A statistical analysis of Martial Law punishments, their reduction under amnesty in relation to ratio of mortality of the influenza epidemic preceding the Punjab Disturbance, can tell us a thing or two. Punishments have been calculated per lakh of population. Round figures in lakhs upto a decimal have been used to make the population of Amritsar 9.3 lakhs; of Lyallpur 9.8. Mortality rates are per million. And correlation can be worked as in Table XI (*a*):

TABLE XI (A)

INFLUENZA EPIDEMIC AND MARTIAL LAW PUNISHMENTS

	Influenza Mortal	Punishments			
		Total	Death	Transportation	R.I.
Amritsar	42.2	23.44	5.48	4.73	12.36
Gujranwala	46.4	30.96	5.80	19.51	4.83
Lahore	56.0	10.00	2.30	6.19	1.50
Gujrat	39.8	5.24	0.24	3.53	1.46
Lyallpur	41.2	1.93	—	—	1.93
Correlation	r	+.13	+.2	+.3	–.23

XI (B) AFTER AMNESTY

Amritsar	22.04	1.29	1.72	19.03
Gujranwala	29.35	0.0	.48	28.87
Lahore	9.82	.97	.61	8.23
Gujrat	4.51	0.0	.24	4.26
Lyallpur	1.83	—	—	1.83
Correlation r	+.15	+.41	+.04	+.13

(See Graph III)

					Stripes
Martial Law	586	115	264	193	13
Amnesty	553	23	28	502	—
(Consolidated figures)					

The Amnesty figure is lower. Death sentences and transportations for life were commuted into rigorous imprisonment.

Correlation between the influenza epidemic and Punjab Disturbances (+.13) is very weak (11). But there is no relation (–.23) between epidemic and rigorous imprisonment.

Uniformity in awarding transportation throughout the districts (+.3) is greater than decreeing of the death sentence (+.2). We know from an independent source that a legal technicality attracted mandatory transportation for minor offences, which not only increased the number of transportations but also introduced a mechanical uniformity over the four districts.[12]

The Amnesty correlation for the total number of punishments has slightly improved from +.13 to +.15. The most dramatic change is in rigorous punishments which were earlier entirely unrelated (+.23) to have a semblance of uniformity (+.13). The removal of technicality has changed the uniformity of transportation under the tribunals to an insignificant relation (+.05) in amnesty punishments. The amnesty correlation for death sentences (+.41) is not only the highest but also the most significant in terms of value. The incidence of death sentence has decreased but its correlation has increased – a result of considered judgements and informed policy. Col. Frank Johnson and Bosworth Smith were removed from service. Attitudinal bigotry was being replaced by an intelligent awareness of political realities. This would be a new factor in the future of Anglo-Indian relations.

There is an interesting category of participants who cannot be identified either as Hindus or Muslims. Following Manu, they have been named contemptibly as Mara (weak), Ruldu (rolled in dust) or Buta (plant).[13] They gain strictly limited humanity in the legal proceedings to vanish forever into anonymity.

TABLE XII: THE UNKNOWN

	Total	Death	Transportation	R.I.	Stripes
	585	115	264	193	13
Unknown	33	5	10	16	2
%	5.67	4.34	3.7	8.29	15.38

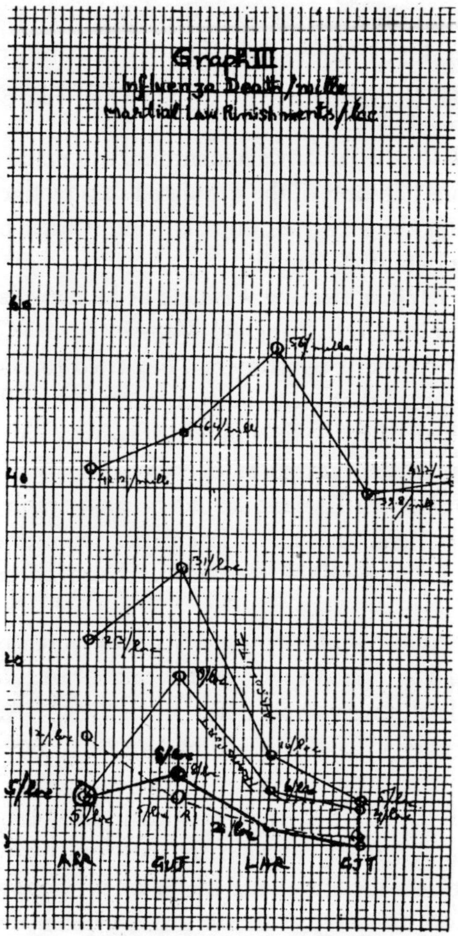

GRAPH–III: Influenza Death/mille
Martial Law Punishments/lac

Firstly, there is a sizeable element of the unknown in the Punjab Disturbances. A five per cent participation by the unknown may conventionally be taken as a norm of popular movement. Secondly, the percentage figures for death sentence, transportation, rigorous imprisonment and stripes are in the ascending order. The poor tend to take to lower forms of political activity.

One may write off contemporary reaction to the Jallianwala Bagh massacre. *The Khalsa Advocate*, the mouthpiece of the natural leaders, wrote that the Sikhs were inveigled into the 13 April meeting by describing it as '*diwan*'. The paper apologetically glosses over the Sikh presence because '*diwan*' to them is 'a religious gathering.[14]

The Akali writes on the anniversary of the Jallianwala Bagh 'On this day, Hindu, Muslim and Sikh blood was spilt. The day can unite the communities. Early in the morning people should go to their respective places of religion and then collect at Jallianwala.'[15]

'Appeal for funds for the Jallianwala memorial was made about six months ago. The contributions fall short of the stipulated sum by five lakh rupees. *The Akali* wonders if this is the way the Punjabis honour their martyrs.'[16] This is indicative of their 'reluctant' nationalism.

On 28 October 1920, a meeting was held at Jallianwala Bagh to sympathize with Zafar Ali for his arrest. Principal Wathen (Khalsa College, Amritsar) was present with a few other Englishmen. They tried to take pictures of the meeting. A rumour spread that machine guns had arrived. People rushed out in panic. The English also left the field in haste fearing an attack.[17]

The Akali mentality is not untypical of the period. 'Lord Chelmsford, the Emperor and the British Parliament would be answerable to God for our suffering' [Jallianwala Bagh massacre]. The paper again draws a parallel between the execution of Haqiqat Rai in the eighteenth century and the Jallianwala tragedy.[18]

The communal divide would soon seek its own sacred places of sacrifice. 'The Sikhs are pained at Jallianwala *but* they keep the Budge Budge Ghat incident (Sikh Ghadarites were shot) before their eyes.'[19] After the Nankana Tragedy on 20 February 1921 the Akalis had an exclusive and proprietorial substitute.

Enamoured with the Amir of Afghanistan and the Moppilla kingdom of Malabar, the Khilafat rhetoric had little use for the Jallianwala Bagh massacre.[20] 'In traditional societies, religion is a mass phenomenon, politics is not. And thus religion can serve as the means by which the masses become politicized.'[21]

NOTES AND REFERENCES

1. Raja Ram, *The Jallianwala Bagh Massacre* Chandigarh, 1969; V.N. Datta, *New Light on the Punjab Disturbances*, Simla, 1975.
   The major offences arising out of the disorder were triable by Commission; breaches of Martial law Regulations were triable by the Area Officers and other officers (including Civil Officers) especially empowered in this behalf. It became necessary to make provision for trial, by some more summary process than that of the ordinary criminal laws, of the large number of minor cases arising out of the disorder which occurred before the proclamation law.
2. Alfred Draper, *Amritsar: The Massacre that Ended the Raj*, Cassell, 1981.
3. Anyone could be a Sikh by declaring oneself so in the court. 'Sikh Community versus Harnami Shah; Deputy Commissioner's Shocking Judgement.' *The Khalsa Advocate*,

21 January 1920. *The Akali*, 1920; *The Punjab Darpan*, 7 July 1920. 'The orthodox Sikhs are more Hindus than the Hindus themselves.' *The Sikh Sipahi*, 28 May 1920. Lala Ganpat Rai claimed in the Punjab Legislative Council that the Sikhs can reform the *gurdwaras* but there should be arrangements for Hindu worship, *The Akali*, 18 March 1921.

4. Gujranwala News, *The Akali*, 17 July 1920.
5. 'As capable of the most heroic deeds and the most exalted sacrifices as of the basest banditry and the foulest corruption', Karl Marx, Frederick Engels *The Class Struggle in France* in *Selected Works* (3 Vols.), vol. I, Moscow, 1976, pp. 219–20.
6. 'If Gujrat had not been situated on the main line, it would probably have escaped entirely the influence of the movement which took place in the Central Punjab.' Punjab Government Report, p. 294.
7.

	Uncultivable land as % of the total	Kacha road per one mile of	% of villages without primary school
	pucca road		
Ajnala	24	.7	50
Amritsar	14	.5	31
Tarn Taran	14	.3	28
Patti	17	.3	31

(Source: *Village and Town Directory*)

At the time Patti was in Lahore District.

'The Amritsar and Tarn Taran *tehsils* are well supplied with roads, but in Ajnala there is but one metalled road running from Amritsar to Ajnala and then to Ramdas. It crosses the Sakki stream by a bridge, which forms the only sure communication between the two parts into which that stream divides the tehsil.' *Amritsar District Gazetteer* (1914), p. 123.

8. The Gurdwara Reform Movement of the next year is vaguely adumbrated in Summary punishments

Kasur	99
Tarn Taran	100
Sheikhupura	444
Lyallpur	141
	784 out of 1435

9. Ravinder Kumar (ed.), *Essays on Gandhian Politics: The Rowlatt Satyagraha*, Calrendon Press, p. 197.
10. *The Akali*, 27 December 1920 gives the break-up of voters in the elections to the Punjab Legislative Council.

Community	Percentage of votes polled
Rural Muslim	33
Rural Hindu	27
Rural Sikh	23
Urban Muslim	7
Urban Hindu	8.5
Zamindar Muslim	67
Zamindar Sikh	50

The Akali, 9 December 1920, gives the break-up of votes of the Provincial and Imperial Assemblies.

	Provincial percentage of electorate	% Polled	Percentage of Electorate	% Polled
Muslim	41	49	40	61
Sikh	35	31	38	49
Hindu	34	28	35	46

The percentage of electorate in both cases exceeds 100 which could be either because of a misprint or because of multiple constituencies.

11. The formula is

$$r = \frac{\int xy - \frac{\int x . \int y}{n}}{\sqrt{\left(\int x^2 - \frac{\left(\int x\right)^2}{n}\right)\left(\int y^2 - \frac{\left(\int y\right)^2}{n}\right)}}$$

12. 'Governor Edward Maclagan at the Gujranwala Darbar.' *The Khalsa Advocate*, 26 August 1919.
13. *Manu Smriti*, Chap. II, 32.
14. *The Khalsa Advocate*, 29 April 1919.
15. *The Akali*, 31 March 1921.
16. *Ibid.*, 2 June 1920
    Within three and a half months of the Nankana tragedy the Sikhs collected Rs 1,50,108, *The Punjab Darpan*, 4 May 1921. A meeting of the Arya Samaj held on 27–28 November at Lahore made a collection of Rs 1,01,180, *The Akali*, 2 December 1920. My impression is that the Jallianwala Bagh memorial was built largely with non-Punjabi money.
    cf. Tilak Swaraj Fund; Bombay 37.5 lakhs: Bengal 25 lakhs; Gujrat 15 lakhs; with the Punjab trailing worth 1 lakh. Gail Minault, *The Khilafat Movement*, OUP, 1982, p. 134.
17. *The Akali*, 4 November 1920.
18. *The Akali*, 10 June and 6 August 1920.
19. *Jallianwala Bagh Da Dukh Hai Par Bujbu Da Wakia Sikh Qaum Dian Nazran De Sahmne Hai.*
20. Gail Minault, p. 148.
21. *Ibid.*, p. 132.

ELEVEN

Demonizing the 'Other' and Mythifying History: Jallianwala Bagh Massacre and Andhra Nationalists

ATLURY MURALI

IN ANDHRA, THE VANDEMATARAM (1905–11) and the post-War Home Rule Movements (1916–19) developed the basic organizational structure for the Congress, described by Mahatma Gandhi as 'principally an institution for developing strength from within.'[1] The extensive nationalist propaganda brought the rural landed elite in touch with the urban Congress politics. The Government of India Act of 1919 could not satisfy the hopes and political expectations of urban and rural elites awakened during the War. It was during this time that the British Government pushed through the controversial Rowlatt Act, ignoring unanimous Indian opposition and sought to make war-time repressive laws into permanent tools of controlling the civil society. Incensed by the Government restrictions on civil rights on the one hand, and responding to the favourable public opinion for agitation on the other, Gandhi proposed an all-India mass protest through non-violent satyagraha, starting with a countrywide *hartal* on 6 April 1919.

The first major public meeting against the Rowlatt Act was organized in Madras by the Provincial Congress on 17 March 1919, one day before Gandhi's visit to the town. From that day onwards a series of public meetings were held in all major towns in Andhra. Mahatma Gandhi's visit to Bezawada, on 31 March, galvanised the peasant masses from the coastal districts into action. On 6 April the entire Andhra was active with mass meetings, protest resolutions and speeches against the Rowlatt Act.[2] Compared to this enthusiasm, the immediate response of Andhra to the Jallianwala Bagh massacre, on 13 April, was conspicuous by its absence and later by its sense of uneasiness. But during the Non-cooperation Movement of 1921–22, the Jallianwala Bagh incident was mythified to highlight the civilizational conflict between the British 'other' and the Indian people. It was this process of mythifying history and 'demonizing' the British by Andhra nationalists/intellectuals which is the central concern of this paper.

Let us first start with the Gandhian idea of satyagraha and contrast it with the popular construct of it in Andhra. On 18 March 1919, in his address to a mammoth public meeting held at Marina beach in Madras, Gandhi laid emphasis on the need for the highest individual resolve to follow satyagraha, once the vow was taken. He assured the people that only after a thorough introspection of truth, did he take a vow to conduct satyagraha against the Rowlatt Act. 'Each struggle, more so the satyagraha movement, should depend on its own internal strength.' One should stick to the truth. He defined truth as 'love' and love as non-violence. By inviting punishment, a satyagrahi will compel the state to act ruthlessly or withdraw the Acts.[3] Once again in Madras, on 23 March, Gandhi issued a statement clarifying his satyagraha programme. On the day of satyagraha, he called on the people to observe a fast for 24 hours and cease work. However, fasting was not a hunger strike; it was training for self-discipline for each satyagrahi. Gandhi also appealed to the people to conduct public meetings all over the country, including villages, and send resolutions to the government for the withdrawal of the Rowlatt Act.[4]

The last public meeting that Gandhi addressed during his tour of the Madras Presidency was at Bezawada on 31 March 1919. Here he repeated the need for non-violence and described the satyagraha as a 'just war', i.e. *dharma yuddhaou* as reported in the Telugu newspapers.[5]

What is important for our analysis is not just what Gandhi said, but the way his message was transformed in the popular imagination. On 6 April, in Guntur town, Pedapalem, Emani, Tenali, Tulluru, Koduru and Duggirala firka in the Guntur district; Berhampur in Ganjam district; Ellore, Subba Reddi Palem and Kovvur in West Godavari district; Rajahmundry and Ramachandrapuram in East Govadari district; Chirivada, Bezawada, Gampalajudem, Ghantasala, Gudivada and Kolavennu in Krishna district; Nellore town and Sangam in Nellore district, and Narayanavaram in Chittoor district were some of the important places where mass congregations were held to protest against the Rowlatt Act.[6] Here the satyagraha was conducted on the lines of Hindu religious festivals.

> Mass processions with Gandhi's photograph, accompanied by music and singing of religious *samkirtanas* (songs) were taken out. People observed fasts; took sacred baths in the Krishna, Godavari and Pinakini rivers; offered prayers both in Hindu temples and masjids; particularly in Hindu temples in the rural areas, the youth conducted *bhajans,* offered *archana, abhisheka* and *sahasranamarchana,* i.e. the traditional forms of Hindu worship; in the evening the devotees / satyagrahis

> conducted mass meetings where, apart from distributing pamphlets, resolutions were passed or petitions were signed and telegraphed to King George for the repeal of the Rowlatt Act.

Let me further illustrate the use of religion in communicating the politics of satyagraha to the rural folk. In Rajahmundry, hundreds of satyagrahis / devotees, after performing worship at the Markandeya Swami temple, went round the town singing nationalist songs and reciting the *Vedas*. In the evening a public meeting was organized, where Barrister Kandula Veeraraghava Swami, addressed a 600-strong crowd: 'We are given this Rowlatt Act as a reward for India's help to the British Government in the First World War. Did you notice this British justice?', he asked.

In Ghantasala village of the Krishna district, a public meeting was held after satyagraha *vratam*. After a speech by Vemuri Rathaiah, a resolution was passed as follows: 'Since the acceptance of the Rowlatt Bills by the British Indian Government takes away the natural freedom (acquired at birth) of the people, this meeting severely condemns those Acts.'

In Gudivada town of the Krishna district, throughout the day specially painted pictures depicting Bharat Mata and Mahatma Gandhi chained to the Rowlatt Act were paraded. At night, a crowd of 1,000 enjoyed the performance of *harikatha* on *Markandeyopakhyanam*. Similarly, in Subbareddy Palem, the youth paraded the streets with *bhajans* praising Lord Hari, throughout the day. One Mr Narasimhulu explained the meaning of the Prahlada story to the people. At a meeting of several villages in Duggirala firka, Mudikonda Kotaiah composed and recited poems on *Matru Devata* (Mother Goddess). The villagers in Koduru in the Guntur district observed the satyagraha *vratam*, on 8 April 1919. After parading Mahatma Gandhi's photograph, they held a meeting at Ankalama temple, where Vedam Venkatakrishna Sarma spoke on the need to repeal the Rowlatt Act.

In Ramachandrapuram town of East Godavari district, it was reported that several prominent people of the area took their sacred bath in the Gowtami river and paraded the streets explaining to the people the meaning of satyagraha. Later they offered prayers at temples, observed fasts and read aloud the *Story of Prahlada*. Like in other places, a mammoth public meeting was held in the evening where resolutions were passed against the Rowlatt Act.

Throughout the above narrative, we have tried to draw the broad contours of the Gandhian satyagraha message, as understood by the common classes in Andhra. The struggle between the British and Indians was basically a conflict of two civilizations and two distinct cultures. Gandhi was recast into various forms of popular mythological figures/heroes who fought against demons (evil) in successive *yugas* / epochs, to uphold Vaishnavism as a *dharma*. Mahatma

Gandhi, as *dharmagnyudu* (righteous one) was fighting, in the form of Vishnu, Sri Krishna, Ram, Christ, Yudistar, etc. to uphold people's freedom, religion and culture from the demonized 'other' British rulers. In this popularly perceived civilizational, cultural, religious satyagraha struggle, there was no scope for violence even against the enemy.

As early as 23 March 1919, the *Hitakarini* wrote in its editorial, with reference to Gandhi's Satyagraha Movement as follows:[7]

> Since words such as satyagraha, passive resistance, etc. are not to be met with in the Hindu scriptures, we should like to use the more familiar expression *Brahma bala* (soul-power). Even ten resolute men will be sufficient for this great sacrifice. The powers of one lakh soul-units are concentrated in Mahatma Gandhi. He alone will be quite enough. The intensity of soul-force in a boy like Prahlada could produce the unknowable Narasimha. Spiritual power has not known failure at any time in any place. Similarly, spiritual power is the only weapon which should be used to curb the strength of arbitrary power when it does not yield to argument and when all other attempts have failed. But its employment on every trivial occasion would be ridiculous and deprives it of its efficacy. . . .

Naturally, the response of the people of Andhra to the police firing, the killing of the English and the burning of the Town Hall and other public buildings by the enraged crowd in Amritsar on 10 April 1919, was very hostile and sensitive. Such a popular and violent response was considered unreligious and against the satyagraha vow. Though the entire Andhra was united in condemning the arrest of Dr Kitchlew and Dr Satyapal in Punjab and Mahatma Gandhi in Bombay,[8] there was no open outrage against the Jallianwala Bagh massacre carried out by General Dyer on 13 April. It was only after the month of May that the nationalists in Andhra (or Presidency?) started demanding a general enquiry into the disturbances in the north and the withdrawal of Army rule. In all these meetings, along with government repression and ordinance rule, the '*prajala dowr janyamulu* (people's atrocities) were also condemned. In its editorial, *Andhra Patrika* of 5 May 1919, went to the extent of arguing that:

> Whatever the troubled / difficult circumstances might be, people leaving their senses and creating disturbances (*allarulu*) is highly condemnable. No government will keep quiet, seeing the disturbances. With the increased disturbances, the country's progress will be harmed rather than benefited. The government took immediate action to stop the disturbances. To this government endeavour, the people have a (*dharmamu*) moral duty to cooperate and this we have explained several times. However, to suppress the disturbances, the use of excess force (army), more than needed, is not proper. Now that the disturbances have subsided all over the country, it is important to lift Army rule. By enquiring into the causes for the disturbances and also by removing them, peace can be established forever . . . (translated from Telugu).

Simultaneously, the nationalist press started arguing in their editorials and lead articles, that the disturbances in Punjab were neither linked with nor the result of Gandhi's satyagraha *vratam.* In May 1919, addressing the 28th Guntur District Conference, held at Dachepally, Choragudi Venkatadri Naidu blamed the government for the Punjab disturbances. His long speech is very interesting but we are not going into the details of it at this juncture.

By 1920, the Andhra nationalists showed a keen interest in the Punjab events, especially the massacre that was carried out by General Dyer on 13 April 1919. This episode was used in several dramas, nationalist songs, novels and other forms of popular arts to demonize the British and undermine the moral and civilizational claims of the colonial masters. This process of adopting the Jallianwala Bagh tragedy to communicate the Gandhian ideology and non-cooperation programme to the masses and mobilize them into the anti-colonial force was very effectively used during the 1920–22 movement.

We start our analysis with some of the precepts in contemporary popular Telugu plays. In 1921 alone around eighteen plays were written and staged to evoke support for nationalism and Gandhi. Among them four were on Gandhi and other nationalists, four on King Krishnadeva Raya of the Vijayanagara Empire, five on Shivaji and five on different mythological and historical personalities.[9] The first popular political play in Telugu, *Navayugarambham* or *Gandhi Mahodayam*, was written by Damaraju Pundarikakhudu of Guntur in 1921. This was followed by *Gandhi Vijayam* or *Navayugam, Panchala Parabhavam* and *Swaraja Ratham.* In all these plays Gandhi was the hero, often personified in various Hindu mythological figures taking on the fight with the unjust British rulers, the demonized 'other', to establish *dharma* or the *Rama Rajya.*

The *Gandhi Vijayam* (Victory of Gandhi), written by Pundarikakhudu, was primarily a political play and its main objective was to communicate contemporary political developments to the common people, using the imagery from the epics and Hindu mythologies.

In the Third Act, the ensuing discussions on Gandhi's proposals, and their subsequent acceptance in the Calcutta Congress are expressed. Here Gandhi says:

> Satyagraha, the path of Prahalad, is the only way suited for the Hindu mentality. . . .
>
> No hope to get freedom by following the old path. . . .
>
> Resolve to non-cooperate for one year; then only Swarajya with all miracles would come.

The play ends with an elaboration by Gandhi of the principles of non-cooperation, constructive programmes and non-violent philosophy. He states that:

> You should not forget that service to the Motherland is the first and foremost act even in dreams . . .
>
> I tell you again and again, do not forget non-violence.

In another popular play by Pundarikashudu, *Panchala Parabhavam,* Gandhi is shown being sent by the 'Lord of the Universe' to avenge the horrible massacres that were perpetrated in Punjab by General Dyer and to restore the freedom taken away by the Rowlatt Bill.[10] In the First Act, Mother India prays:[11]

> Alas! O God, O Protector of the humble,
>
> O Lord of the Universe! Have you no mercy upon me?
>
> Will you not come to protect my sons?

Immediately Gandhi enters the scene and Mother India, addressing Gandhi, says:

> It is my wish that you should devise some means for the emancipation from servitude of the thirty-three crores of your brothers here.

Gandhi then expounds his philosophy of non-violent satyagraha and cites the examples of Prahalad and others. He further adds:[12]

> I am applying the sacred satyagraha vow to the present political conditions of the country. It is such a divine weapon as is calculated to put an end to the arbitrary rule of the Government and as befits our traditions.

In another scene perception of the unjust British rule is put forward through a coolie character. Answering a question as to why the Government prohibited him from working, he observes:

> I do not know, Sir. I only know one thing. Our Government has been doing us injustice and that, while we are dying of famine, all their people drive in motorcars over our heads. A new and strange thing has come.

In the Second Act the success of *hartal* is attributed to Mahatma Gandhi's 'soul force' and the people's confidence in him. Then comes the fascinating Act IV, where in a prison-house, when Dyer insults 'Mother Panchala' by seizing the fringe of her garment, she prays to Sri Krishna, the saviour of Panchala Draupadi's modesty in the epic. Krishna thereafter appears and says to her:

> I have taken a vow to remove your hardships and to put down the pride of the wicked, arrogant, hard-hearted *Kiratas.* I shall appear to people in the form of Gandhi in *Kaliyuga.* You will have salvation by the method shown to you by Mahatma Gandhi, who is sweetly peaceful. . . . Be not grieved. Think of me whenever I am needed to preserve your modesty and I will deliver you from difficulties. Do not lament any longer. Your calamities will soon come to an end.

Sri Krishna disappears and enters again in the form of Gandhi turning the spinning wheel and presents her with a piece of cloth. Dyer, who has been pulling her garment, runs away. The play concludes with a speech by Gandhi:[13]

> The movement of non-cooperation is the only support of our life and a resource based upon self-help. We must give up mendicancy. Be solely devoted to obtain swarajya, your birthright, and behave peacefully. If you do so, Mother India will soon have the pleasures of freedom. There will be democracy benevolently carrying on the administration. Arbitrary authority will meet with destruction and swarajya will be attained.

Since the Hindu religious mythology was reinterpreted for the edification of the then colonial reality, it easily reached the hearts of the popular class. For, 'in religion people make their empirical world into an entity that is only conceived, imagined, that confronts them is something foreign.'[14]

Gandhi's projection into popular psychology as the saviour from above, who came down to remove famines, avenge British deeds and establish swarajya which, of course, was associated with the 'democracy benevolently carrying on the administration', caught the imagination of the masses in the villages. The age-old myths, popular cultural traditions, pantheon of Hindu gods and many historical personalities became vehicles to carry these messianic elements of the Gandhian personality into the perception of the subaltern classes.[15]

What were the implications of the use of religion in politics is another story.

NOTES AND REFERENCES

1. Mahatma Gandhi's 'Presidential Speech' at the Belgaum Congress, 1924, in Sankar Ghose (ed.), *Congress Presidential Speeches,* Calcutta, 1972, p. 165.
2. For details, see Kodali Anjaneyulu (ed.), *Andhra Pradeeshloo Gandhiji* ('Gandhiji in Andhra Pradesh'), Telugu, Hyderabad, 1978, pp. 112–29; *Andhra Patrika,* 1–9 April 1919; *Kistna Patrika and Hithakarini* (Ellore) for April 1919.
3. Kedali Anjaneyulu (ed.), *op. cit.*, pp. 97–99, (translated from the Telugu version of the speech).
4. *Ibid.*, pp. 104–5 (translated from the Telugu version).
5. See *Andhra Patrika,* 1–2 April 1919; also see Ayyadevara Kaleswara Rao's *Naa Jeevitamu Nayandramu,* (Autobiography, Telugu) for his version of Gandhi's tour and speech.
6. The entire story is reconstructed from the material available in Kodali Anjaneyulu (ed.), *op. cit.*, pp. 120–29; *Andhra Patrika,* 7–13 April 1919, and *Kistna Patrika,* for April 1919.
7. *Native Newspaper Reports,* Madras, 1919, p. 551, also reprinted in M. Venkatarangaiya (ed.), *The Freedom Struggle in Andhra Pradesh,* vol. II (1906–20), Hyderabad, 1969, p. 505.
8. Speeches and resolutions at the Madras meeting held on 12 April 1919 and also in Andhra towns, see Kodali Anjaneyulu (ed.), *op. cit.*, pp. 139–41; *Andhra Patrika,* 11 April to 23 May 1919.

9. Modali Nagabhushana Sarma, *Telugu Sahityam: Gandhiji Prabhavam* (Gandhiji's Influence on Telugu Literature), Telugu, Hyderabad, 1970, p. 124.
10. GOM., G.O. No. 792, Pub. Dept. dated 12 November 1921. The text of the English translation is available in this G.O. This play was staged by Tilak Nataka Samajam in many places in spite of the Government restrictions. Madala Veerabhadra Rao, *Desabhakta Jeevitha Charitra,* 'Biography of Desabhakta ', Telugu, Machilipatam, 1966, pp. 68–69; Modali Nagabhushana Sarma, *Telugu Sahityam*, p. 136.
11. G.O. No. 792, *Ibid.*, p. 3.
12. *Ibid.*, p. 4.
13. *Ibid.*, pp. 7–8.
14. Karl Marx and F. Engels, *The German Ideology,* Moscow, 1976, p. 172.
15. In all the plays mentioned, almost all important Hindu gods and kings, popular Muslim leaders and Congress personalities appear on the stage in one scene or the other to strengthen the myth that Gandhi was the incarnation of the Lord of the Universe.

TWELVE ❖ Calcutta in Turmoil: April 1919

SURANJAN DAS

> The recent disturbances in Calcutta . . . definitely point out that sedition and anarchy, which were primarily confined to the young men of the educated community, are finding a large number of recruits from amongst the masses as well.[1]

THAT WAS HOW A contemporary Bengali political detenue assessed the implication of the anti-Rowlatt Act turmoil in Calcutta between 11 and 13 April 1919. Unfortunately, however, in the existing historical literature of the Rowlatt Satyagraha the significance of this unrest has gone unnoticed. This is partly because the disorder in Calcutta was relatively mild in the all-India context. While nine people were killed during the disturbances in Calcutta, the figure for the Punjab was 228, for Delhi 12 and for Ahmedabad 28.[2] Not unnaturally, the British official spokesman was content:

> There were no outrages of the same character in Calcutta, the disorder lasted only a few hours, there was no necessity for the introduction of Martial Law, there were no summary trial.[3]

Similarly, while introducing the best available volume on the Rowlatt Satyagraha, Ravinder Kumar expresses surprise as to how 'Calcutta . . . remained quiet in 1919, despite its great reputation for being the liveliest city in India.'[4] But Calcutta did retort against the Rowlatt Act in its own way and the turbulence connected with it, as the present submission seeks to demonstrate, was an important chapter in the history of agitational politics that continues to be so characteristic of Calcutta.

THE BACKDROP TO THE TURMOIL

The Rowlatt Satyagraha, as Ravinder Kumar aptly remarks, was the 'first countrywide agitation to be launched against the British government and it transformed nationalism in India from a movement representing the classes to a movement representing the masses. . . .'[5] The 'same unmistakable signs of unrest' that had affected the people in Bombay, Delhi, Lahore or the Central Provinces were present in Calcutta. The city shared the general all-India post-war grievance. While the Indian political and educated elite had strained their economic resources to fight for England in the First World War, the Raj retaliated by the repressive Rowlatt Act which resulted in their scepticism about the Montagu-Chelmsford scheme, and convinced them about the need for a 'broader' movement.[6] On the other hand, the Khilafat question had turned the Calcutta Muslims against the British government. Gandhi's call for the Satyagraha in 1919 resulted in a fusion of these various layers of discontent. The potentialities of a major political upsurge were revealed when a Calcutta daily commented that if the Calcuttans had been armed like the Irish 'this unrest would have by this time developed into a rebellion.'[7]

Frequent references are also found in official records to 'scheming revolutionaries' in Calcutta[8] and many contemporary officials ascribed the 'current political crisis' to the influence of Bolshevism.[9] The British were certainly overreacting. The 1917 revolution had such a traumatic effect on the British bureaucracy that any 'violent threat' to the Empire's stability was looked upon as a Bolshevik conspiracy. To quote an official comment:

> The danger of Bolshevism to India lies not in a military victory of Bolshevik arms, but in the insidious effects of Bolshevik propaganda. This propaganda is always directed towards the exploitation of social grievances . . . (which) are so serious . . . (that) . . . the propaganda become(s) formidable.[10]

Micro-level studies have unravelled how 'passions' excited by the Rowlatt Satyagraha 'had little to do with formal organization.'[11] Instead, Gandhi has been shown to 'have relied upon local discontents to draw various classes and communities into a movement of protest against the British Government.'[12] The same was largely true of Calcutta.

The period preceding the April outburst in Calcutta witnessed a rising price-curve of the daily necessities,[13] the situation being further complicated by increasing cases of food adulteration.[14] Certain social developments on the eve of the tumult also made sections of the Calcuttans restive and the Gandhian Satyagraha in Calcutta, as in other cities, drew upon 'local' discontents to unite classes and communities into a movement of protest against the British government.[15] References may, for instance, be made to the distress of a large number of slum dwellers of North Calcutta who had their huts demolished for 'improvement schemes' without being properly rehoused by the Calcutta Improvement Trust.[16] Again, the months preceding the turbulence were exceptionally unhealthy in Calcutta, the mortality rate reaching the highest figure to be recorded since 1907.[17] The Calcutta Corporation's measures to tackle this problem of public health were hopelessly inadequate and widespread public anger was evident. A government report admitted that the victims – most of them Muslims – were found 'talking about their grievances' in shops, masjids and homes.'[18] The Satyagraha provided a means of expressing such popular grievances.

Material discontent alone could not have generated a political climate conducive to a popular outburst. But an ideological disapproval of the Rāj combined with socio-economic discomfort created a strong public distemper in 1919 Calcutta. The nationalist newspapers – English and vernacular – published articles on the 'un-British rule', economic nationalism and heightened racialism which must have touched at least the educated sections of the society.[19] Provocative leaflets in popular language were distributed in different parts of the city immediately before the outbreak.[20] An active propaganda campaign also popularized Gandhi's charisma which made the Mahatma's image a 'rallying point' for popular mobilization. Interestingly, the area most affected by the turmoil experienced the largest circulation of 'provocative leaflets' in Hindi and Bengali.[21]

In tune with the rest of India the Calcuttans had observed 6 April as the protest day against the Rowlatt Act. The northern part of the town wore a deserted look from the morning, and in the afternoon a crowd of 10,000 strong was addressed by C.R. Das at the maidan. But no 'untoward' incident occurred. The news of Gandhi's arrest on 10 April near Delhi, however, had an electrifying effect on the sensitive psychology of the Calcutta crowd. Normal life in the city came to a halt during the next three days.

From the early morning of the 11th (Friday), shops in the entire northern belt of Calcutta encompassing Strand Road, Harrison Road, Chitpur Road, Canning Street and Cornwallis Street remained closed, and crowds collected in street corners persistently interfered with tramcars and other traffic. The same was experienced on the 12th and 13th.[22] Processions, singing national songs and shouting 'Bande Mataram' and 'Hindu-Musalman ki jai' were taken through the main thoroughfares. Often the processionsists ended their March by taking a dip in the Ganges. Any attempt by the police to restore order incited clashes with the crowd. In fact, as soon as patrols appeared they were pelted with bricks, stones and other missiles, causing injuries to the police personnel. By the afternoon of the 12 April the Bengal Governor feared that matters were slipping out of control and called in the army. Order was restored on 14 April, but not without resorting to firings by the police and military.[23]

THE ANATOMY OF THE TURMOIL

Unlike the riots which preceded and followed it – communal and non-communal alike – the April outbreak did not experience any lootings. Instead, its predominant characteristic was the expression of anti-European feelings. Actual cases of assaults on Europeans in 1919 may not have been numerous,[24] but the intense anti-European mentality of the restive crowd was clearly manifest. The Europeans were made to disembark from trams, buses and private vehicles and walk to their destinations.[25] The Sikh drivers boycotted their English employers and the European quarter of the town remained without vehicles for at least two days. At all important crossroads the Europeans were forced to take off their *topees* (hats worn by Europeans) and proceed bareheaded, such actions being invaraibly accompanied with loud cheers and shouts of 'Gandhi ki jai.'[26] European women were chased by the frenzied crowd which often occasioned police intervention.[27] At Chitpur Road in Central Calcutta a man running with a *topee* was readily greeted with appaluse and nationalist slogans.[28] Sometimes when the Europeans tried to force their vehicles through the crowd they faced physical assaults.[29] The hostility faced by Europeans in general becomes evident from what one of them recounted:

> On reaching the Chitpur crossing, I found myself in the midst of a small crowd of about fifty persons. Two or three amongst them ordered me to take off my hat and make my way up to Chitpur. There was loud laughter behind me, so I put my hat on again . . . I was (then) hurled against a shop-window, my hat was snatched off my head, somebody slapped my face, I was struck with a stick on the shoulder, and kicked . . . but suddenly the people moved off, and I saw that a police patrol car had come. . . .[30]

European hotels were another favourite target of the crowd. Particular mention may be made to the ransacking of the Bristol Hotel in Central Calcutta.[31]

Anti-Europeanism went hand in hand with the ventilation of anti-government sentiments. One way of demonstrating this feeling was found by closing the shutters of Indian shops and business establishments.[32] There is hardly any indication of the use of threat or force for keeping the shops closed. Rather, the shopkeepers displayed, as the *Nayak* noted, 'a strong undercurrent of self-restraint and self-sacrifice.'[33] The 1919 agitation, the same paper observed, 'was not the product of ease-loving babus, but of the self-sacrificing people.'

The police, the most visible manifestation of the Raj which the Satyagraha was challenging, became a natural target of the crowd fury. At different points along the Central and Northern parts of Calcutta the police parties were pelted with bricks, stones, pellets of wood and soda water bottles from housetops.[34] The Deputy Commissioner Wilson and Assistant Commissioner Cook were themselves injured while combating a gathering of youths – 'mostly Muslims with a sprinkling of Marwaris' – at Zakaria Street on 12 April.[35] On the same day, a turbulent crowd at Howrah attacked a police picket and set its cars on fire.[36] The extent of popular antagonism against the police is borne out by the following account from a correspondent of the *The Englishman* (14 April 1919):

> On Harrison Road men armed with scaffolding bamboos ran up to the vehicle shouting 'Nai Jane Dega' (we shall not allow you to go). The European sergeant replied, 'Jaye-ga, Hut Jao' (shall go, move away) . . . (Instantly) the crowd closed round us (the police) and stones began to fly rattling on the body and hood of the car. The men with the bamboos thrust them in front of the car . . . there were shouts of 'Mar Sala' and 'Mar dalo' (Beat them). . . .

The police officers in such circumstances were usually saved only by the dexterity of the drivers of their vehicles.

Other incidents can be cited as examples of a general resentment against the police.[37] For example, a crowd greeted a person who was running across the road in North Calcutta carrying a battered white helmet of the 'type worn by the police themselves.' On another occasion, a tall man holding aloft a 12-feet long bamboo stood in the midst of the road, refusing to allow any police patrol to pass. This made the crowd cheer him with shouts of 'Gandhi ki Jai' (Victory to Gandhi). Isolated attacks on the police were also common. For example, two constables escorting a prisoner from Orissa were stopped by a crowd to demand the release of the convict. When the policemen refused, they were beaten up and the prisoner was set at liberty. The two constables had to be hospitalized.[38] The turbulent crowd also obstructed the work of the Fire Brigade.[39]

In combating this crowd fury the police did not hesitate to use all available techniques. In some areas they even dropped 'dacoity wire netting' to prevent the crowd from 'advancing further'.[40] The *Amrita Bazar Patrika* (16 April 1919) reported how Indian public figures like Babu Sarju Prasad Singh, a member of the Executive Committe of the India Home Rule League, were subjected to police high-handedness when they sought to restrain the crowd. Very often, unprovoked firing was resorted to. On the 12th, at the Howrah-Chitpur Road junction, the police discharged volleys of shots towards the upper storeys of the houses of such prominent citizens as Pratap Narayan Roy, resulting at least thirteen to lie 'in a pool of blood.'[41] The *Amrita Bazar Patrika* (16 April 1919) reported on the military's firing of 'bullets . . . on the upper part of the body of the wounded, contrary to the usual humane practice.'

Disruption of the transport system also symbolized the anti-establishment consciousness of the recalcitrant crowd in Calcutta. Trams, buses, taxis, private cars, and hackney carriages were forced off the road to throw the city life out of gear. Initially, persuasive measures were adopted by demonstrators, but when that failed force was applied, vehicles were attacked with missiles and passengers were dragged out of carriages.[42] Cases of the snatching of money bags from tram conductors were also reported.[43]

The Calcutta tumult was characterized by an exceptional Hindu-Muslim fraternity without which the anti-British assertions would not have been as effective as was noticed in those days of April 1919. Muslims and Hindus of all shades – Bengalis, Marwaris, upcountrymen – joined processions in 'tens and thousands'. At a meeting in the Maidan, the Muslims and Marwaris were found embracing one another.[44] The Marwari priests applied vermilion marks on the foreheads of the assembled Muslims; the Hindus cried 'Ali Ali'; national songs were sung in processions and rallies; Muslims lent their voice to 'Bande Mataram'.[45] In large gatherings drinking water was delivered from the same lorries to Hindus and Muslims alike, and cheers of 'Hindu Mussalman ki Jai' filled the air.[46] In an unprecedented move, a joint Hindu-Muslim meeting was also held in the afternoon of the 11th inside the Nakhoda mosque, addressed among others by Hira Lal Gandhi, the Mahatma's son.[47] One Muslim speaker, Syed Ahmed Hossain, reminded the gathering that the closure of shops would 'not go too far' if the government employees continued to join their offices. The meeting ended on a dramatic note with a Marwari priest raising the cry of 'Sultan ki jai.'[48] Of course, such scenes of Hindu-Muslim 'comradeship' were a common feature of the Rowlatt Satyagraha in several other cities also.[49]

THE CROWD

The spread of the agitation was associated with a change in the nature of the political leadership on the ground. The initial rallies adopting the Satyagraha pledge were of a 'composite' nature, comprising lawyers, teachers, students, merchants as well as 'the ordinary men in the streets' whom C.R. Das preferred to address as the 'Daridra Narayan' (the poor is god). Marwaris, Bhatias, Gujaratis, Hindustani *durwans* of Burrabazar and Punjabi and Sikh taxi drivers were particularly prominent.[50] An index to the nature of the Hindu crowd at this stage is provided by the Nakhoda mosque gathering of the 12th, nearly half of which were Bhatias, Marwaris, Jains and upcountry Hindus.[51] Similarly, the Beadon Square rally on the same day reportedly contained 67 per cent upcountry Hindus of various castes.[52]

It is thus not unnatural to find the prominence of young upcountrymen – mostly aged between 18 and 35 – in the list of the wounded and arrested.[53] An official report disdainfully refers to them as 'chokras' (young boys).[54] The upcountry street urchins between 15 and 30 years of age were also active in making the passengers disembark from buses and trams.[55] The following statistics represent a sample indicator of the crowd associated with the violence.[56]

CASUALTIES (KILLED AND WOUNDED) IN CALCUTTA DISTURBANCES ON 12 APRIL

(A) *Persons dead from police/military firing on Harrison Road*

Name	Caste	Age	Address	Remarks
Chandra Pal Singh	Hindu (upcountry)	40	183 Harrison Rd.	
Sagar Mull	Do	35	17 Rup Chand Roy St.	
Ramesh Ch Mukherji	Do	18	12 Patuatola Lane	
Unknown person	Do	27	—	
Nemai Chand	Do	25	68-1 Bartolla St.	
Brijlal Bhatia	Do	30	—	
Puran Mull	Do	30	57 Khengraputty	
Dukharam Ahir	Do	19	—	

B. *Persons who suffered non-fatal injuries from firing on Harrison Road*

Name	Caste	Age	Address
Sewakaram Bias	Upcountry Hindu	24	37 Armenian St.
Peer Bux	Muslim	35	Armenian St.
Ram Dular Tewari	Upcountry Hindu	27	61 Cross St. or 20 Khengraputty
Mali Ram Brahmin	Do	28	1 Goenka Lane
Purusottam Ahir	Do	24	Jagannath Ghat

A contrast between the previous Swadeshi agitators and the 1919 crowd needs to be emphasized here. While the former had a predominance of bhadraloks,[57] that social group was conspicuous by its absence in 1919, except in some stray incidents involving interference with the transport system.[58] The Beadon Square rally of the 11th reportedly contained only 25 per cent Bengali Hindus and there was, as the Chief Secretary to the Bengal government noted, a 'remarkable absence of Bengali (Hindu) students who generally form a large element at a Calcutta mass meeting. . . .'[59] The *Nayak* alleged that none of the Bengali Hindu leaders had signed the Satyagraha vow;[60] the *Dainik Basumati* commented on how the enthusiasm of the upcountry Hindus had 'cast us (the Bengali Hindus) into the shade. . . .'[61] A detailed study needs to be undertaken to explain the poor involvement of Bengali Hindu bhadraloks in the 1919 outburst.

On the other hand, the Marwaris – hitherto renowned for their 'peaceful avocation' – surprised the Bengal government by their participation in the Rowalatt Satyagraha.[62] In his weekly report of 7 July 1919, the Director of Central Intelligence thus remarked on the active Marwari participation in the Calcutta disturbances:

> They (Marwaris) joined the crowds; they wrote and published leaflets and hand bills; asked their *durwans* and other employees to join the sacred cause; helped in organizing volunteer groups and paid for initial expenses.[63]

Some Marwaris even paid the security amount on behalf of the *Amrita Bazar Patrika* which had been prosecuted for 'inflaming popular passions against the Rowlatt Act'. Prominent Marwaris also took the initiative to form a Civil Rights Committee that raised money in aid of the riot victims.

This Marwari involvement in the Calcutta turmoil made the Governor Ronaldshay search for an explanation.[64] A sizeable section among the Marwaris was believed to have been impressed with an idea that a common cause with the Muslims could have a 'restraining influence' on cow-slaughter of which they were the most vociferous Hindu critics. At the same time, noted Ronaldshay, the Mahatma was viewed as a 'supporter of . . . orthodox Hindu aspirations' which made the Marwaris readily respond to the Gandhian call. Moreover, the Marwaris had reacted sharply against the government's new Excise-Profits Tax whose 'searching methods of enquiry' adversely affected their economic pursuits. Ronaldshay refers to 'wildest rumours' of the government's determination to take 'Rs 2-8 out of every Rs 5 that a person possessed' and the anguish against the Raj that followed from it, prompted the Marwari participation in the disturbance. Whatever might have been the 'true reason' for their participation, the presence of the Marwaris and Bhatias among the 1919 turbulent crowd was such that *The Times* spoke of a 'Marwari rebellion' in Calcutta.[65] The Chief Secretary to the Bengal government also characterized the disturbance as an affair of the non-Bengali population of northern Calcutta.[66] The Bengal Governor also accused the Marwaris and Bhatias for the violence.[67]

It is, however, difficult to dissect the components of the Muslim rioting crowd because of the lack of data. It appears that both the Bengali and non-Bengali Muslims, especially of the lower social order, were active. Among the Muslims present at the Nakhoda mosque meeting of the 12 April, the majority were 'illiterates.[68] The Muslim inhabitants of Central and North Calcutta *bustees* (slums), whom the officials disdainfully categorized as 'low class Muhammadans' were singled out by the police as 'notorious' in 'stone throwing incidents.'[69] Butchers were also prominent in the Muslim crowd.[70]

Most contemporary observers referred to a gradual shift in the initiative for action to the 'ordinary people', particularly the upcountrymen – Hindus and Muslims.[71] The government itself acknowledged 'breaking of the monopoly control over political agitation by a handful of educated persons' and admitted that 'the dumb had become voiced.'[72] This popular 'radicalism', however, displayed an 'irresistible tendency' to seek 'shelter behind the Mahatma's banner', a trend which recent studies have shown, manifested itself throughout the period of Gandhian nationalism.[73] The on-the-spot organizers of such 'radical shifts' were by and large the subordinate social groups and established leaders wondered how this could have become possible.[74] The *Calcutta Samachar* observed that the Calcutta event had exploded the myth 'circulated by the Anglo-Indian press that the untouchable and illiterate do not know what political agitation is about. . . .'[75]

THE CROWD-LEADER DICHOTOMY

Increasing participation by members of the lower social strata in the 1919, Calcutta outburst contributed to the spread of the unrest. It, however, alarmed the established leaders – Hindu and Muslim alike – who now issued manifestos condemning the disturbances.[76] The Indian Muslim Association and the Committee of the Central Muhammadan Association even questioned the righteousness of allowing non-Muslims to preach from the pulpit of the Nakhoda mosque.[77] Similarly, the Marwari Association and the Marwari Chambers of Commerce expressed 'deep . . . pain and sorrow at the disturbance' and affirmed 'their loyalty to the government.'[78] Some Marwari leaders disclaimed the responsibility of their community as a whole for the disturbances and 'alleged that those Marwaris who had taken part in them were an insignificant number of men of the lowest class.'[79] The Moderates also disliked 'the degeneration' of the Satyagraha[80] and their leader S.N. Banerjee 'unhesitatingly' approved of the Governor Ronaldshay's plan to censure the *Amrita Bazar Patrika* for 'pouring poison into the mind of the youth of the country. . . .'[81]

All these demonstrate a crowd/leader dichotomy – a contrast between the attitude of the leaders and of the crowd. The two leading contemporary Bengali figures in organized politics – C.R. Das and Byomkesh Chakravarti – were never interested in a calculated 'breach of peace'. In their audience with the Governor on 4 April they promised to exercise 'discretion' so that their speeches remained 'Moderate in tone, short, devoid of provocative language.'[82] Both had confessed to the Governor that they did not even support the 'idea of requesting people to close their shops.'[83] The Governor also drew comfort from the fact that the plan of forming a Committee to frame a list of laws which were to be disobeyed had not materialized in Bengal.[84] But, as has been indicated above, once the subordinate social groups came out on the streets, they could not be made to play the restricted role which the leaders of institutional politics had chalked out for them. Very often the leaders of organized politics were pressurized by the crowd to undertake actions against their own convictions. For example, Byomkesh Chakravarti complained to the Bengal Governor how he was 'compelled' to address the historic joint Hindu-Muslim gathering in the Nakhoda mosque, 'although he had no desire to do so.'[85] This was an apt illustration of the dilemma in which the leaders of organized politics were placed – their resentment at the 'mob' 'going out of hand' but their inability to impose checks at that juncture.

The irony of the situation was exposed when Chakravarti conceded the 'duty of all law-abiding citizens to support (the) Government in putting down (the) disturbance', but added in a sombre vein that 'he must go some way with the organizers of demonstrators (i.e. the subordinate social groups) or they would simply throw him over and any authority or influence he had with them would disappear.' Chakravarti even went to the length of praising the police action which had 'hitherto . . . been all that could be desired and they had sedulously refrained from provocation'. He also agreed to plead with 'the people' for the resumption of normal business since 'Mr Gandhi was not under arrest but was free to move as he wished in the Bombay Presidency.'[86]

Certainly the Moderates such as Chakravarti ultimately had their way and such 'repeated brakes' on 'mass pressures' were experienced throughout the nationalist movement.[87] Yet, short-lived popular initiatives and points of contradictions between organized institutional politics and the world of unorganized and perhaps relatively autonomous popular actions were by themselves noteworthy, whose implications need to be worked out. The outbreak of popular radicalism in Calcutta was particularly important as it came only days after the observers had expressed surprise at the 'lack of excitement' in that city when Bombay and other cities were considerably agitated over the passage of the Rowlatt Act.[88]

CONCLUSION: THE APRIL TURMOIL AND AGITATIONAL POLITICS IN CALCUTTA

The Calcutta outburst, then, demands attention not merely as an episodic event or as a behavourial condition at a given point of time, but as a contributing point in the historical process that converted the once prized city of the Raj into a crucible of the politics of protest which not only fuelled the nationalist struggle but was also directly connected with the evolution of a radical political culture in Calcutta. Throughout the nationalist movement, the colonial government had to confront in Calcutta *hartals*, riots, insurrections, demonstrations and rallies, the incidence of which significantly increased since the second decade of the twentieth century. The 1919 outburst shared the basic features of popular violence with its immediate predecessor – the Swadeshi riot of 1907 – and the long chain of militant outbreaks of subordinate social groups that followed. Expressions of anti-European feelings, attacks on the police as the most palpable instrument of the Raj, the disruption of the communication system to dislocate the normal functioning of the state apparatus and the crowd-leader dichotomy – which characterized the April violence – were replicated in future outbreaks connected with mainstream nationalism, revolutionary terrorism, as well as working class and youth radicalism which reached a climactic point in 1945–46, hailed as 'The Almost Revolution.'[89]

The secular and anti-imperialist trend in popular politics in Calcutta – of which the 1919 outburst forms an important chapter – was not, however, a unilinear development.[90] Instead, it was interspersed with doses of communal rioting which I have tried to delineate in my work on *Communal Riots in Bengal 1905–47*. The communalization of Bengal politics, reaching its climax with the Great Calcutta Killing of August 1946 and the spate of riotings that followed, certainly implied a crucial setback for the secular and anti-imperialist spirit of political Calcutta.

The communal carnage could not, however, destroy the weighty force of secular anti-imperialism in Bengal politics. When we look back from the vantage point of the 1940s into the politics of the earlier decades, we find that until the last moment the political pendulum in Calcutta, or even in Bengal, swung between nationalist and separatist politics. But during the 'prelude to the Partition', as we know, mainstream Congress nationalism lost much of its Muslim political support and a section within it developed a strong Hindu communal identity. Consequently, Calcutta came to suffer from a rather desperate introversion of consciousness, and the Bengali psyche was gripped by an obsessive sense of uncertainty about whether it would go to Pakistan or not. This sense of pain and anguish was compounded by the influx of refugees and its inability to integrate with the national mainstream after the truncated settlement of 1947. Nevertheless, the structural disarticulation between class and politics that was seen during the Partition came to be rapidly bridged in the post-August 1947 days, as is evident from the strength of the organized Left in the political life of West Bengal.

At another level, the 1919 Calcutta turmoil remains a living example of how the regional barriers were transcended to create nationalist linkages. An explication of this trend has become specially important as a possible counterpoise to the thesis that fragmented identities of caste, community or kinship, and not national or class identities, had been the determining factors in Indian history.[91] In a recent fundamental and sophisticated intervention in Indian historiography, Partha Chatterjee[92] has effectively 'reimagined' nationhood in India. The basic presupposition of the treatise is the notion of community, distinct from the 'single determinate, demographically enumerable form of nation'. Chatterjee contends that 'anticolonial nationalism creates its own domain of sovereignty within colonial society well before it begins its political battle with the imperial power'. The emergence of the nation-state in India was contemporaneous with the subjugation, appropriation and marginalization of the fragmented identities which characterized, what Chatterjee calls, the spiritual domain of social institutions and practices. Chatterjee is convinced that these fragments not only resisted the totalizing project of nationalism but represented 'richer ways of imagining a community'.

The 1919 anti-Rowlatt disturbances in Calcutta, however, brought to the fore nationalist assertions across narrow parochial identities. The Intelligence Branch papers record in unequivocal terms the 'general sympathy' of the Calcuttans for the 1919 disturbances.[93] To quote the *Amrita Bazar Patrika* (12 April 1919):

> Another remarkable feature apparent even to the meanest intelligence is the fact that the spirit of nationalism . . . has filtered down to the sub-strata of the society. Hithertofore, the cravings for reforms were confined to the limited intelligentsia of the country and the masses were apathetic to it. But now the whole community, even the neglected 'Daridra Narayan' or the 'proletariat' if we may call them so, have come to realize the situation and have responded to the call of the country . . . .

Perhaps the *Amrita Bazar Patrika* was over enthusiastic. But the fact that *The Englishman* (14 April 1919) – by no means a nationalist organ – cited the remark as an evidence of resurgent nationalism demonstrates that the British administration had been unnerved by the way events were cutting across regional and sectarian barriers to create a more powerful form of anti-colonial agitation.

Due to strict press censorship, the news of the Jallianwala Bagh massacre reached Calcutta somewhat late. But once the story became public, popular indignation ran high, although no violent outburst occurred. Secret 'preachings' in the outlying mill areas urged the Muslim workers to 'lay aside all differences and join the Marwaris' and they was further told 'that if all castes joined it would be impossible for the Government to deal with them.'[94] This propaganda campaign was undertaken by such 'expert' Muslim preachers as

Mohammad Azeem, Mohammad Azimullah and Mohammad Kudratmulla who had originally hailed from the 'upcountry' but had settled down in North Calcutta.[95] Police reports refer to group meetings in Calcutta slums, particularly in the predominantly Muslim ones, to acquaint the people of Dwyer's misdeeds. These gatherings were invariably addressed by, to use police vocabulary, 'unknown characters', obviously implying relatively unimportant mainstream nationalist figures. Rabindranath Tagore renounced his knighthood in protest against the Jallianwala Bagh massacre. The letter that Tagore wrote to the British government on this occasion reflected the anguish of the Bengali intellectual community. It was also in the aftermath of the Jallianwala Bagh tragedy that the Calcutta Punjab Sabha was established. It organized local meetings and distributed leaflets to mobilize public opinion against 'the Punjab wrongs.'[96] One of the organizers of the Sabha – Gopal Das – was a disciple of Lajpat Rai and was known to the police 'for the virulence of his anti-Government and extremist opinion'.

While finalizing this draft, I came across a number of IB files on the *Labour Situation in 1919 Bengal.* Owing to the shortage of time, I could not scrutinize them. But a cursory glance indicated instances of a convergence between labour and nationalist consciousness. The files contain references to a number of labour agitations where slogans demanding economic justice were raised along with condemnation of the Jallianwala Bagh killings. I have cited elsewhere such conjunctures between popular protest and nationalist politics in Bengal around mainstream nationalist stirrings, notably during the Quit India Movement.[97] The 1919 Calcutta disorders perhaps anticipated this trend. The way Calcutta responded to a happening in distant Punjab demonstrated how a sense of national identity could be generated amongst people when pitted against the 'other', and in this case the killers at Jallianwala Bagh represented the 'other'.

Nations can be 'constructs' or 'imagined communities.'[98] But the process of construction of national identity in opposition against the colonial ruler during the liberation movement is not necessarily similar to what is experienced in 'nation-building' under post-colonial regimes. In the course of the anti-colonial struggle when a nation seeks to come into its own, there remain strong possibilities for the merger of narrow identities to fight an alien rule. The subordination of local, regional or ethnic identities by the superimposition of 'unity from the top' in the interest of a national ruling class becomes particularly prominent after the nation-state has been formed.[99] The political turmoil in Calcutta in April 1919 was an event in the continuum of the anti-colonial movement which culminated in the creation of two independent nations in the subcontinent. It was a tragic finale and India after that date was a substantially changed entity. It is in this context that this submission is presented for discussion.

NOTES AND REFERENCES

I am grateful to my colleagues Bhaskar Chakrabarti and Basudeb Chatterjee for going through the preliminary draft of this paper and suggesting necessary changes. All errors are mine.

1. Home (Poll B), August 1919, nos. 315–19, National Archives of India/hereafter NAI/ Weekly Report of the Director, Central Intelligence, 7 July 1919.
2. Home (Poll B), August 1919, nos. 253–54, NAI. The figures for wounded in the Rowlatt violence were 9 in Calcutta, 29 in Delhi, 123 in Ahmedabad and 33 in the Punjab.
3. See the statement of Sir William Vincent, *Proceedings of the Indian Legislative Assembly*, 12 September 1919.
4. *Essays on Gandhian Politics: The Rowlatt Satyagraha of 1919*, ed. R. Kumar, OUP, 1971 (ed.), p. 7.
5. *Ibid.*, p. 4.
6. The *Hitavadi*, Calcutta, 25 April 1919, Report on Native Newspapers (hereafter NNR) no. 18 of 1919, p. 357, para–56, West Bengal State Archives (hereafter WBSA).
7. The *Bengalee*, Calcutta, 16 April 1919, NNR. no. 17 of 1919, p. 355, para–58, WBSA.
8. The *Nayak*, Calcutta, 10 April 1919, NNR. no. 23 of 1919, p. 341, para–81, WBSA.
9. The *Nayak*, Calcutta, 10 April 1919, NNR. no. 23 of 1919, p. 312, WBSA; The *Bengalee* (Calcutta) 26 April 1919, NNR. no.18 of 1919, p. 356, para–65, WBSA.
10. Home (Poll) A, December 1919, nos. 1–7, NAI, p. 11.
11. See D.E.U. Baker, 'The Rowlatt Satyagraha in the Central Provinces and Berar', K.L. Gillion, 'Gujarat in 1919', J. Masselos, 'Some Aspects of Bombay City Politics in 1919', D.W. Ferrell, 'The Rowlatt Satyagraha in Delhi' and R. Kumar, 'The Rowlatt Satyagraha in Lahore' in R. Kumar, *op. cit.*; Also see H. Singh, *Gandhi, the Rowlatt Satyagraha and British Imperialism*, Delhi, 1919.
12. R. Kumar, *op. cit.*, p. 6.
13. *Index Number of Indian Prices 1861–1918*, Department of Statistics, Government of India, Calcutta, p. 1, para–4.
14. The *Dainik Basumati*, Calcutta, 23 April 1919, NNR. no. 35 of 1919, WBSA.
15. R. Kumar, *op. cit.*, see the Introduction.
16. *Report on the Adminstration of Bengal 1918–1919* (Part-II), pp. 48–49, para–226.
17. *Ibid.*, p. 49, para–240. The death rate rose to 35 per thousand, the infant mortality being 200 per registered deaths.
18. Weekly Report of the Director, Central Intelligence, 7 July 1919.
19. For an indication, see *Amrita Bazar Patrika* (hereafter ABP) of the period.
21. File-Home (Poll), 8 May 1919, pp. 514–15, Appendix–A, NAI.
20. *The Englishman*, Calcutta, 14 April 1919.
22. J.H. Kerr, Chief Secretary, Bengal, to the Secretary, Home, India, No. 176–P–D, 29 April 1919, Home (Poll), 8 May 1919, nos. 514–15, NAI.
23. *The Englishman*, Calcutta, 14 April 1919.
24. File-Home (Poll), 8 May 1919, pp. 514–15.

25. *Ibid.*
26. *Ibid.*
27. *Ibid.*
28. *Ibid.*
29. File-Home (Poll), Deposit October 1919, no. 33, NAI.
30. *Ibid.*; See also *The Englishman,* Calcutta, 14 April 1919.
31. *The Statesman* (hereafter ST) 8 April 1919.
32. File-Home (Poll), 8 May 1919, pp. 514–15, *op. cit.*
33. The *Nayak,* Calcutta, 12 April 1919, NNR. no. 16 of 1919, p. 313, para–65.
34. ST. 8 April 1919.
35. File-Home (Poll), 8 May 1919, pp. 514–15, *op. cit.*
36. *Ibid.*
37. *Ibid.*, especially the report of G.D. Pinder, Agent, Bank of Bengal, Burrabazar Branch.
38. ST. 8 April 1919.
39. From Clarke, Police Commissioner, Calcutta, to the Chief Secretary, Bengal, 14 April 1919, *op. cit.*
40. *The Englishman,* Calcutta, 14 April 1919.
41. File-Home (Deposit), October 1919, no. 33, NAI.
42. File-Home (Poll), 8 May 1919, pp. 514–15.
43. File-Home (Poll), Deposit, October 1919, no. 33.
44. The *Bengalee,* Calcutta, 8 April 1919, NNR. no. 14 of 1919, WBSA.
45. *Ibid.*; File-Home (Deposit), October 1919, no. 33.
46. ABP, 7 April 1919.
47. File-Home (Póll), 8 May 1919, pp. 514–15, *op. cit.*
48. *Ibid.*
49. *Essays,* ed., R. Kumar, *op. cit.*; The *Bengalee,* Calcutta, 8 April 1919, NNR. no. 14 of 1919, WBSA.
50. File-Home (Poll), 8 May 1919, pp. 514–15; ST 16 April 1919; File-Home (Poll) Deposit, no. 46, July 1919 NAI.
51. The *Nayak,* Calcutta, 18 April 1919, NNR. no. 16 of 1919, p. 65. The *Bengalee,* Calcutta, 8 April 1919, NNR. no. 15 of 1919, pp. 287–88, WBSA; File-Home (Poll), 8 May 1919, pp. 514–15, *op. cit.*
52. *Ibid.*
53. File-Home (Poll), 8 May 1919, pp. 514–15, *op. cit.*
54. File-Home (Poll) Deposit, October 1919, no. 33, *op. cit.*
55. *Ibid.*
56. *Ibid.*
57. S. Sarkar, *The Swadshi Movement in Bengal,* Calcutta, 1975.
58. File-Home (Poll), Deposit October 1919, no. 33.
59. File-Home (Poll), 8 May 1919, pp. 514–15.
60. The *Nayak,* Calcutta, 8 April 1919, NNR. no. 16 of 1919, para–311.
61. NNR. no. 15 of 1919, p. 288, para–24, WBSA.
62. Mss. Eur. D523/30, India Office Library (hereafter IOL) Ronaldshay to Montagu, 19 May 1919.
63. Weekly Report of Director, Central Intelligence, 7 July 1919, *op. cit.*
64. Mss. Eur. D523/30, IOL, *op. cit.*
65. NNR. No. 20 of 1919, p. 408, para–65.
66. File-Home (conf) 299/1919, serial 3, WBSA.

67. NNR. No. 17 of 1919, WBSA.
68. File-Home (Poll), 8 May 1919, pp. 514–15.
69. *Ibid.*
70. ST 13 April 1919.
71. *Ibid.*
72. File-Home (Poll), 8 May, pp. 514–15.
73. S. Sarkar, *Popular Movements and 'Middle Class' Leadership in Late Colonial India: Perspectives and Problems of a 'History From Below',* Calcutta, 1983; S. Amin, 'Gandhi as Mahatma: Gorakhpur District, Eastern UP 1921–22', *Subaltern Studies-III,* ed,. R. Guha, Delhi, 1984.
74. File-Home (Poll), 8 May 1919, pp. 514–15.
75. *Calcutta Samachar,* 8 April 1919.
76. Kerr, Chief Secy, Bengal, To Secy, Home, India.
77. *Ibid.*
78. *Ibid.*
79. Kerr, Chief Secretary to the Secretary, Home Government of India.
80. *ST,* 18 April 1919.
81. Mss. Eur. D 609/1, IOL, *My Bengal Diary,* vol. I, pp. 224–25.
82. Mss. Eur. D 609/1, IOL, *My Bengal Diary, op. cit.*; Mss. Eur. D 523/30, Ronaldshay to Montagu, 14 April 1919.
83. *My Bengal Diary.*
84. *Ibid.*
85. *Ibid.*, pp. 221–23.
86. From Clarke, Police Commissioner, Calcutta, to Chief Secretary, Bengal, 14 April 1919.
87. S. Sarkar, *Popular Movements.*
88. *My Bengal Diary,* p. 216.
89. G. Chattopadhyay, 'The Almost Revolution' in *Essays in Honour of S. C. Sarkar* eds., B. De, *et. al.*, Delhi, 1976.
90. For an analysis of this trend, see S. Das, 'The Politics of Agitation: Calcutta 1912–47' in S. Chaudhuri ed., *Calcutta: The Living City,* vol. II, OUP, 1990.
91. See *Subaltern Studies.*
92. P. Chatterjee, *The Nation and its Fragments: Colonial and Post Colonial Histories,* Delhi, 1993.
93. IB records, Calcutta, SB Branch, see diary of 10 May1919.
94. *Ibid.*, See diary of 3 May 1919.
95. *Ibid.*, WBSA, see file 221/19.
96. Weekly Report of Director, Central Intelligence, 14 July 1919, Home (Poll) 8 August 1919, nos. 315–19.
97. *Ganasakti,* Calcutta, 10 August 1993.
98. B. Anderson, *Imagined Communities: Reflections on the Origin and Spread of Nationalism,* London, 1983.
99. See S. Das and B. De, 'Ethnic Revivalism: Problems in the Indian Union', *Ethnicity, Caste and People* ed., K.S. Singh, Delhi, 1992.

THIRTEEN ❖ The Jallianwala Bagh Tragedy: Impact on the Indian National Movement

NANDITA HAKSAR

EVALUATION OF THE ROWLATT ACT IN THE CONTEXT OF THE LEGITIMATE RIGHTS OF CITIZENS

I MUST BEGIN BY stating that I am a lawyer and not a historian, but I have used my knowledge of history in the course of my practice and teaching of human rights law. The central concern of a human rights lawyer should be to develop a human rights jurisprudence which will help in the expansion of the meaning and scope of constitutionally guaranteed rights. In my struggle within and outside the court, it has been my constant endeavour to do this in order to set precedents which could become a part of the law of the land. I must confess that I have not been successful in this endeavour and I hope to explain why.

I wish to explore my failure in a historical context. I shall try to show how Mahatma Gandhi, a trained lawyer, did lay a foundation for the development of an Indian human rights jurisprudence, more specifically, a civil disobedience jurisprudence. He gave us a basis for developing creative defences in courts but we failed to make use or develop it. When I say 'we failed, I include all those involved in social, political or cultural movements for justice. These movements have not explored the potential of civil disobedience except perhaps to some extent Chhaktra Yuva Sangharsh Vahini and the Anti-Narmada Dam Movement led by Medha Patkar. Perhaps this is partly a reason for the non-development of a civil disobedience jurisprudence in Gandhi's own country.

Let me begin with an analysis of Gandhi's approach to the Rowlatt Bills.

I

The Congress Punjab Inquiry Committee on the human rights violations during Martial Law which had been largely written by Gandhi was submitted to the All India Congress Committee on 20 February 1920. Chapter 3 of this report is entitled Rowlatt Bills. I need not go into the background of the Bills. Let me straight away enumerate Gandhi's objections to the Anarchical and Revolutionary Crimes Bill, 1919, popularly known as the Rowlatt Bill.

(1) Gandhi's first objection to the Bill is that there was no need for such a law since at that time there was revolutionary crime.

(2) The second objection was that even if there was such a crime the Government had sufficient powers under the Defence of India Act to deal with it.

He does point out that the Defence of India Act itself had been used 'for the purpose of stifling political agitation or hindering the movements of public men; it was used for the purposes of restraining political freedom' like arresting Mrs Annie Besant.

(3) That the 'secret violence is confined to isolated and very small parts of India and to a microscopic body of people.' However, Gandhi feels that the existence of such men is truly a danger to society.'

(4) The fourth objection is that the Rowlatt Bills were designed to serve the interests of the Civil Service and British commercial interests at the cost of Indian interests.

(5) Fifthly, the Bills would intensify hatred and ill-will against the State.

(6) Sixthly, Gandhi asks the Covenanters to 'ascertain whether the disease is sufficiently great to justify the strong remedy, and whether all milder ones have been tried.'

(7) Seventh, Gandhi states that Justice Rowlatt took evidence on criminal conspiracies connected with the revolutionary movement in India in camera.

(8) Gandhi maintained that the British had shown a bankruptcy of statesmanship if they needed repressive legislation to suppress crime of a revolutionary character and it would remain checked only during the continuance of such a legislation. Also, if there were 'yet men at large who are or were suspected to be revolutionaries it betrayed the hopeless inefficiency of the Government.'

(9) Gandhi quotes with approval, Shastri's opposition to the Bills in the Imperial Council that even if there are anarchists, and anarchists have a 'condition of mental derangement' propagating their 'wicked doctrine', what was needed was 'satisfying measures of political emancipation' implying that anarchists were a product of the absence of political emancipation.

(10) A bad law is not always used against the bad.

(11) The Rowlatt Bills would lower public spirit and political tone and thus any talk of responsible government would be only a mockery. Quoting Shastri, he points out 'we are all anxious to punish the wicked. None of us desire that wickedness should go unpunished but even the wicked must be punished in certain ways' not in ways which would shock our sense of justice.

(12) Finally, the point Gandhi emphasized was that the law was a repressive measure which had no public support and it would only scare people from doing political or public work.

Gandhi then goes on to analyse the actual provisions of the 43-clause Bill which had 5 parts. He points out that the Bill gave wide powers to the Executive; even though the Governor-General in Council were to notify, he would base himself on reports of low ranking policemen.

Secondly, the Bill did not allow scope for any appeal, the accused was allowed only one adjournment and the proceedings would be in camera at any place the court chose.

Thirdly, the Criminal Procedure Code and Indian Evidence Act had been given a go by.

Fourthly, Part II of the Bill was in fact punitive. A person who was made to give security could not move out of his residence and the Bill authorized the government to use 'all means reasonably necessary to enforce compliance with its orders.'

Gandhi concludes that: 'Thus upon mere suspicion, the most respectable man may find himself entirely at the mercy of the police,' and it 'is not difficult to picture to oneself a reign not of law and order but of organized terror and disorder, or Martial Law without the name.'

Gandhi once again states that 'we would note, too that the Viceroy has sufficient powers by means of ordinances to deal with extraordinary situations.'

II

The first thing that strikes me after reading Gandhi's critique of the Rowlatt Bill is that Gandhi at no stage tries to define what an 'anarchical and revolutionary' crime is and the Act also defines it nowhere.

In fact he assumes that violence used by nationalists would qualify to be revolutionary crime. In his Satyagraha Pledge, he states that the Rowlatt Bills are unjust, subversive of the principles of liberty and justice, and destructive of the elementary rights of individuals on which the safety of the community, as a whole, and the state itself is based, and therefore, he thinks it is morally justified to disobey the law and also refrain from violence to life, person and property.

Gandhi (and the colonial regime) recognize the concept of political crime and there is no discussion on this. This is a fact which I will return to later but I would like to point out the significance of this fact. In India the law or the state no longer recognizes a category of crime called political crime and also they do not recognize a category of 'political prisoners'. There is a growing trend the world over to look at political activity as criminal activity and thus undermine the movement.

In his *The Dialectics of Legal Repression*, Balbus[1] analyses the structure of legal repression during the Black Ghetto Movements in the 1960s. He argues that formal legal rationality of the kind Max Weber described, requires the judicial authorities to respond only to specific acts, omitting the motivation behind the commission of those crimes. Conflict is therefore limited to the facts of the crime. This 'question of ideological, class, or racial complexion . . . is formally prevented from entering into the meaning of crime.'

Let me emphasize the importance of recognition of a category of crime as 'political crime' by giving one illustration. The European Convention on Suppression of Terrorism was passed on 27 January 1977. It was ratified by 17 of 19 countries, and its purpose was to allow for the extradition of terrorists.

Several European States including the Netherlands have laws which do not permit extradition for offences 'of a political nature, including offences connected with such offences.' The European Convention on transfer of criminal matters also does not allow transfer of political offences.

Article 1 of the European Convention reduces the number of offences for which extradition can be refused on the grounds that they are political offences. The following are the offences which are no longer considered political offences, or offences connected to a political offence or inspired by political motives.

(*a*) an offence within the scope of the Convention for the Suppression of Unlawful Seizure of Aircraft, 1970.

(*b*) an offence within the scope of the Convention for the Suppression of Unlawful Acts against the Safety of Civil Aviation, 1971.

(*c*) a serious offence involving an attack against the life, physical integrity or liberty of internationally protected persons, including diplomatic agents;

(*d*) an offence involving the kidnapping, the taking of a hostage or serious unlawful detention;

(*e*) an offence involving the use of bomb, grenade, rocket, automatic fire arm or parcel bomb which endangers persons;

(*f*) an attempt to commit any of the foregoing offences or participation as an accomplice of a person who commits or attempts to commit such an offence.

Explaining the implications W.H. Nagel[2] states that

(*a*) the privilege of the perpetrator of the 'political crime' must be forfeited;

(*b*) the idea of the 'political crime' is to be extended;

(*c*) 'political crimes' have to be prosecuted and punished more severely instead of being privileged.

All this has been agreed without any indication of what the political crimes are (it assumes) some political offences are found 'very abhorrent' we need the treaty. But the phrase 'very abhorrent' gets us no further forward. The danger here is that we might be preparing to consider 'their' terrorism with our 'terrorism'.

Nagel goes on to point out the dangers of this trend to depoliticize certain offences, which itself is a kind of politicization. He states that the more powerful European States are trying to impose their criminal system on to the smaller powers. In his words: 'The more powerful a state is, the more it will aspire to more power. A State's wish to export its criminal justice system is a part of that aspiration.' Gandhi (and Martin Luther King) insisted that a person protesting through civil disobedience must accept punishment. Herbert Stroring, points out that 'if citizens need not obey the law to show respect for it, why is it necessary for them to accept the law's penalty to show that respect?' Thus Dr King's argument that accepting the penalty is a logical necessary component of civil disobedience seems to be hard to sustain.[3]

The US Courts' response to civil disobedience has been mixed. They have on many occasions held the following kinds of cases to be covered by the First Amendment: breach of peace, symbolic speech, sit-ins, Vietnam war protests, nuclear protest, tax protest and cases concerning political organizations.

This is not the place to discuss in detail strategies and tactics to be used in court but I would like to say that both lawyers and political activists (and many times the lawyers are also a part of the movement) have evolved creative and ingenious ways of defending their acts of civil disobedience in the USA. The judgement in United States vs LaForge and Katt (DC Minn Cr No. 4–84–66) is a reflection of this. The Judge Lord sentenced the defendants to only six months probation and issued the following well-publicized statement:

> As I ponder over the punishment to be meted out to these two people who were

> attempting to unbuild weapons of mass destruction, we must ask ourselves can it be that those of us who build weapons to kill are engaged in a more sanctified endeavour than those who would by their acts attempt to counsel moderation and mediation as an alternative method of settling international disputes? Why are we so fascinated by a power so great that we cannot comprehend its magnitude? What is so sacred about a bomb, so romantic about a missile? Why do we condemn and hang individual killers while extolling the virtues of warmongers? What is that fatal fascination which attracts us to the thought of mass destruction of our brethren in another country? How can we even entertain the thought that all the people on one side of an imaginary line must die or, if we be so ungodly cynical as to countenance that thought, have we given thought to the fact that in executing that decree we will also die? Who draws these lines and who has so decreed?[4]

In this case two people with hammers walked into Speery Univak Plant, found the guidance system of the Trident Submarine and disarmed it. They had walked into a private plant in the State of Minnesota, destroyed property belonging to Speery Corporation and being manufactured for the Donnell-Douglas Corporation which was going to see it to the federal government. They could have got a 10-year prison sentence. This was in 1984.

At that time (between 1984–86) there were over 1,000 civil disobedience arrests of 800–900 individuals at Honeywell Corporation. In 7 jury trials there were acquittals, 13 jury trials when there were convictions and 28 trial groups were dismissed for technical reasons.

There is a great deal of debate in the Civil Disobedience Movement about the morality of getting off on technical grounds. Political implications for people beyond the courtroom are taken into consideration and lawyers and political activists together decide on arguments to be used, including the doctrine of necessity which states that trespass or sit-ins were committed to stop greater harm.

This new jurisprudence had not come about accidentally. Sit-ins by labour unions were brutally suppressed in the USA. As one US criminologist pointed out, 'attempts by workers peaceably to assemble or organize in order to question their share of goods services, or the disproportionate costs of technological change or warfare, have been variously construed as conspiracies to commit crimes, incitement to riot, creating a public disturbance, trespassing. . . . It has been stated that the United States has had the bloodiest or most violent labour history of any industrial nation in the world.'[5]

The growth and development of human rights jurisprudence of which the civil disobedience dimension is so important has been possible because of the long efforts to expand the rights of individuals. As Turk points out, the struggle for democratic means to control polity has been built on the rubrics of civil liberties and human rights. The struggles for individuals' spiritual, intellectual, political, sexual and other personal freedoms have contributed to the expansion of group rights as well. To quote Turk, 'Although the ideology of individual liberty has often run counter to the ideologies of class and racial solidarity, in specific cases the guest for the personal emancipation of human beings has generally coincided with that for their collective emancipation.'

In this struggle the place of civil disobedience has been crucial, as one US attorney, Brian Spears explains. He defines civil disobedience as an 'act of defiance or violation of a prevailing notion or order as a means of political expression. I do not consider an act of civil disobedience to be illegal. I don't accept it as a violation of law since I understand the concept of law as nonstatic, as incorporating some kind of doctrine or norm.' He goes to explain that the significance of civil disobedience has three aspects:

> First CD, as an intermediary strategy to gaining power, is a tactic that gives power to self-conscious political groups. Second, and very important, CD shifts the parameters of resistance towards acceptance of defiance of those in power. CD legitimates all kinds of dissent. Third, CD is a political tactic that begins to offer an ideal of visionary social relations a political struggle. It reflects where the masses of people are right now, and to the extent that it presents a different kind of political act, it is the embodiment of the vision.
>
> Its secondary functions are to strengthen the resolve of the participants to act as moral witnesses or to change the legal doctrine. The primary effects of civil disobedience are outside the courtroom.[6]
>
> I wonder what Gandhi's reaction would be to the new civil disobedience jurisprudence. Perhaps he would not agree with the tendency in the civil liberties movement to demand the legal right to disobey. For instance, Dworkin has argued that if we are to take fundamental human rights seriously, we must be ready to acknowledge that public protest in their defence, even if involving acts contrary to law, such as rioting should be regarded as justifiable and therefore not answerable to legal process.[7]
>
> Another jurist, MacGuigan argues the case for civil disobedience on moral grounds. He states it may be justified if it takes the form of a public non-violent act of illegality performed for a moral purpose, and even violence may justifiable if (like self-defence) it is a proportionate response to serious injustice; though MacGuigan doubts whether a coercive element can ever be an apt reaction to an unjust law within a framework of democratic government.'[8] Why has civil disobedience jurisprudence not developed in Gandhi's own homeland? Historians may be able to give an answer. I would like to only pose a few questions relating to that problem.

IV

The question I have posed, namely, why there is no civil disobedience jurisprudence in our country is not an academic one for me. I am evolving a course on human rights at the National Law School. I have been shocked to see how deeply the students have internalized the social contractual theory of state on that as a basis for political obligation. They have internalized Locke's notion of tacit consent as a foundation for political obligation. One of the exercises, I gave them was to rewrite Gandhi's speech in Court and argue that he was not guilty of sedition. The core of Gandhi's speech is that the law has no consent of the people because 'the administration of the law is thus prostituted consciously or unconsciously for the benefit of the exploiter.' The students do not understand this because they are brought up in the purely utilitarian and positivist school of thought where their concern is only with what the law is and never what the law ought to be.

This is true of the entire legal education. It has been and is being financed by the Ford Foundation. The Indian Law Institute, for instance, began with a grant from that foundation. The Ford Foundation has also given a large grant to the National Law School for its course on Human Rights. This is not enough evidence to explain why the Indian lawyers or judges or jurists have failed to exercise their legal imagination. But it is an important fact to remember while trying to analyse the reasons why civil disobedience jurisprudence has no place in India.

The second reason is of course the nature of social and political movements in India. Whether it is tribal movements for self-determination, or the women's movement, struggles for minimum wages or even the civil liberties movement – none of these have evolved a radical or revolutionary perspective of law and the legal system.

A radical perspective defines crime as a violation of politically-defined human rights: the truly egalitarian rights to decent food or shelter, to human dignity and self-determination, rather the so-called right to compete for an unequal share of wealth or power. A socialist human-rights definition of crime frees us to examine imperialism, racism, capitalism, sexism or other systems of exploitation which contribute to human misery or deprive people of their human potentiality. The state or legal apparatus, rather than directing our investigations, should be the central focus of investigation as a crimogenic institution involved in corruption, deception or crimes of genocide. Under the legal definition of crime, the solutions are primarily aimed at controlling the victims of exploitation (poor, Third World, youth, women) who, as a consequence of their oppression, are channelled through the criminal justice system. Under a radical human rights definition, the solution to 'crime' lies in the revolutionary transformation of society or the elimination of economic or political systems of exploitation.'[9]

Gandhi's critique of the legal system provides a basis for developing not only a civil disobedience jurisprudence, but also for evolving a radical criminology.

Gandhi recognized that the British were perpetuating state violence and he explained this in his famous statement to the court while standing for trial on the charge of sedition. He said, 'I have no doubt whatsoever that both England and the towndwellers of India will have to answer, if there is a God above, for this crime against humanity which is perhaps unequated in history. The law itself in this country has been used to serve the foreign exploiter.'

He adds 'a subtle but effective system of terrorism and an organized display of force on the one hand, and the deprivation of all powers of retaliation or self-defence on the other, have emasculated the people and induced in them the habit of simulation.'

These poignant words of Gandhi are so relevant and they touch the core of our contemporary problems. Yesterday, the world signed the General Agreement on Tariff and Trade (GATT). Even before it was signed, 6,000 people were arrested in a Moroccan town. GATT lays the legal basis for even greater and more systematic exploitation of the Third World by capitalist states of the West.

It is in this context it is important, indeed crucial, to develop Gandhi's ideas on crime, politics and power and his ideas of resistance to foreign domination, because law is the major instrument for neo-colonialism and at the moment, we seem singularly ill-equipped to face the challenge in the absence of a critique of that law.

NOTES AND REFERENCES

1. I. Balbus, *The Dialectics of Legal Repression,* New York, 1973.
2. W.H. Nagel, 'A Socio-Legal View on the Suppression of Terrorists,' *Journal of the Sociology of Law,* 1980, pp. 213–26.
3. Quoted in Narayana Rao Rampilla, 'Civil Disobedience and First Amendment', *Journal of the Indian Law Institute,* vol. 32, no. 4, 1990.
4. Quoted in *National Lawyers Guild Practitioner,* vol. 42, no. 4, Fall, 1985.
5. Austin T. Turk, *Political Criminality 1924 –* reprint, Delhi, 1982
6. NLG, *op. cit.*
7. Llyod's *Jurisprudence,* p. 147.
8. *Op. cit.,* p. 147.
9. Tony Platt, 'Prospects of a Radical Criminology in the USA' *in* Ian Taylor *et al., Critical Criminology,* 1975.

FOURTEEN ❖

British Policy and 'Organized' Crime: Crime Control and Surveillance in Punjab 1848–1911

S. KAVITA

INTRODUCTION

THIS PAPER AIMS TO trace the evolution of British perceptions and policy in Punjab towards certain 'criminal' groups and collectivities. The Punjab officers of the mid-nineteenth century borrowed their understanding of certain 'criminal' associations from the British colonial experience in Central India and the North-Western Provinces. Over this period, groups like Punjab's Mazhabi 'thugs' and certain 'predatory' tribes were identified and considered to be 'professional' criminals who were engaged in 'organized' or 'systematized' crime. Since crime was perceived as their 'calling', they were regarded different and separate from the 'ordinary' criminals.

These groups were identified as possessing certain characteristics such as a hereditary criminal vocation, unsettled lifestyle and habits, wide criminal networks and an out-of-the ordinary mode or operations. Based on this perception, authorities in Punjab and elsewhere felt the need to control and restrain these criminal collectivities. The existing laws were considered inadequate to deal with them, as they had been framed to address 'ordinary' criminals, involving tedious procedures and provisions.

Justified by these arguments, special laws and institutions had already been devised since the early nineteenth century with regard to the thugs in the British provinces. In 1848, when the Mazhabi 'thugs' were uncovered in Punjab, the Punjab Executive pleaded that they be treated by similar methods. Subsequently, as the 'predatory' or 'criminal' tribes came to be perceived as a category of the Mazhabi 'thugs', officers pressed for separate legislation that would treat these groups on the principle of crime deterrence and prevention.

This understanding of 'professional' criminal groups finally resulted in the Criminal Tribes Act of 1871. This legislation initiated a formal process by which a separate set of legal procedures and provisions were instituted with regard to these tribes. Along with powers of surveillance, this legislation also laid down the responsibility of reclamation or reform of these groups, upon the local authorities. During the course of the debate on the Bill in 1870, many officers spoke of the responsibility to 'civilize' these criminal tribes by providing them with a settled and honest means of livelihood.

Apart from those proposals, the administrators were also clarifying and imposing their own norms and definitions that differentiated the 'criminal' from the 'non-criminal', the 'stable' agriculturists from the 'unstable' wandering communities. This legislation as well as the Executive Order of 1856 in Punjab, aimed at making local headmen and landholders accept these definitions, and participate in this control by making them responsible for the local notified tribes.

The reform crusade as enunciated in the Act of 1871 remained largely unimplemented. This could be explained by the perception of the category of 'professional' criminal groups. Administrators who believed in the inherent criminal tendencies of certain groups, could never allow reclamation to be taken to its logical end, by allowing those reformed communities to live unsupervised and as a part of the mainstream. Measures of reform or reclamation as implemented in Punjab therefore remained partial and casual.

Regarding tribes which were considered to be 'less' criminal by reputation, the Punjab authorities failed to establish, even at the time of notification, that they would be providing them with the means to earn an honest livehihood.'

Of the tribes considered to be far more 'predatory' like the Sansis and the Minas of Gurgaon, a process of restricted and controlled reclamation was adopted. They were confined to jail like conditions in reformatory settlements and forced to work on land. This experiment was encouraged since it permitted a close surveillance over these tribes while putting them to work.

These measures were soon found to be deficient, as many of these tribes did not take to agriculture and frequently escaped from the constraint of the reformatories. Yet, little was done to revive the cause of reform even though many Punjab officers had accurately diagnosed the ills of the system.

When an amendment of the Criminal Tribes Act was under consideration in the 1890s, the Punjab Government chose a course that gave precedence to 'suppression', and enhanced deterrent measures. Reform, henceforth, was to be carried out by 'coercion', though some lip service continued to be paid to it by espousing the cause of the children of these registered tribes. Clearly, the

Punjab authorities had little interest in initiating freer and more flexible reclamation measures.

The choices that the Punjab officers had implicitly made in the 1890s were clarified a decade later when the need to tighten control mechanisms became more urgent. At the turn of the century, crime controlling agencies in Punjab were increasingly sensitive to the rise of 'serious crime' in the preceding years as well as to the general climate of lawlessness.

Spurred by the need to rationalize policing agencies and encouraged by the Report of the Police Commission in 1900, the Punjab authorities sought to tighten their control over wandering criminal tribes. As a part of this, they initiated an important change in policy that was to be a decisive break from reform responsibilities and ensure henceforth a course of renewed control and restraint over these 'professional' criminals.

Perhaps the earliest instance that illustrates British understanding and related policy towards 'professional' criminal groups in Punjab, is the 'thagi' campaign of 1848–53.

The first cases of 'thagi' in Punjab were brought to light in 1848, even as the scaffolding of the British administration was being erected. Captain Larkins, Deputy Commissioner of Ludhiana reported to the Board of Administration, that he had uncovered 15 cases of 'thagi' and further suspected that there was an 'extensive system' of 'thagi' in Punjab that needed to be suppressed.[1]

Larkins' discovery came as a surprise to the administration. For many years, a special policing agency named the 'Thagi and Dakaiti Department' had been in operation in Central India and subsequently in the North-Western Provinces. Employing separate methods of operation and jurisdiction, this Department under the energetic leadership of its head Captain Sleeman, had declared the suppression of thagi to be completed by 1839.[2]

Thus, the discovery of these cases of 'thagi', with a suspected network of organized 'thugs' extending 'further north than the Ravi, probably even to Peshawar,'[3] galvanized the nascent Punjab administration to seek the help of the Thagi and Dakaiti Department. With the help of its Najeebs and old approvers, some 'thug' gangs were rounded up, and an Agency was set up in Ludhiana. Soon, an earnest campaign was launched, 'not only with a view to the apprehension[sic] of those who have been committing these outrages, but for the suppression of this crime generally.'[4] In 1853, this campaign was lauded as one of the successes of the administration. The Thagi and Dakaiti Department estimated that between 1832 and 1852, more than a 1,000 murders had been committed by nearly 1,414 'thugs', of which more than half had been arrested in the early 1850s.[5]

The anti-'thugee' crusade had ended and laurels had been distributed.

However, an interesting feature of this campaign was that neither the Punjab administrators nor the Thagi and Dakaiti Department were really clear whether these cases in Punjab, were 'thagi' at all. Larkins had based his assessment on the accounts of the Thagi and Dakaiti Department. Yet, as recent research has highlighted, even the definition of the offence of 'Thuggee' as described under Act XXX of 1836 was imprecise.[6] The 'reality of thuggee' or the 'knowledge' of it, was based simply on the accounts of old approvers.[7] Even in 1848, both Larkins and Sleeman had acknowledged that the Punjab 'thugs', were found to be a class unique to Punjab and altogether unconnected with any of the older associations.'[8] Sleeman had even admitted to the Board of Administration in 1850, that he did '. . . not possess any information', as to 'whether thuggee / properly so-called / exists in Punjab.'[9]

Thuggee in 'Hindostan' had been associated with the features such as 'dark superstition', 'sacred ceremonies', 'mysterious bond of union', 'religious faith',[10] and all these seemed absent in Punjab's 'thugs', derived mainly of the Mazhabi caste of Sikhs. Dalhousie, who in his Minute in 1856 even conceded that these Punjab 'thugs' were merely an organized body of highwaymen, and murderers, rude, ferocious and desperate.'[11]

The fact that the Punjab Mazhabi 'thugs' did not share many of the features associated with those of older thugs did not unduly perturb the Punjab officers. Nor did it stop them from pursuing the 'suppression' of thagi cases and subsequently in placing the Mazhabi caste under surveillance. This was because Punjab's Mazhabi 'thugs' did share certain basic features associated with the 'professional' criminal groups elsewhere. These Mazhabi 'thugs' were identified as 'fraternities' or hereditary associations with wide organized networks. These characteristics made them an out-of-the ordinary criminal threat to British authority that was to be treated by special measures.

The mere existence of these thagi cases, long considered extinct, was viewed as a violation of the 'order' and an affront to the 'good government' that the British claimed to have introduced in the 'Punjab of British Rule'. Captain Larkins conveyed this reaction in a letter to the Thagi and Dakaiti Department. 'It is strange,' he wrote, 'there our operations for the suppression of thuggee should have been so long in force, and to such an extent, and that the fact of the thuggee being in existence in these territories which have in a measure been made our rule and protection for a long period, and for the last two years completely under our control and administration should not have been disclosed before.'[12]

Closely linked with these insecurities and threat perceptions of 'thug' fraternities was a more general problem facing the Punjab administrators. The uneasiness arose from knowing that their ideas of 'good government', definitions of crime and criminality were frequently at variance with the norms in the Punjabi society.

Native rulers past and present had tolerated and even protected 'thug' and other criminal fraternities. Various histories that were drawn up of Punjab's 'thagi' indicated that this crime and its association had flourished 'at the time when Runjeet Singh was rising into eminence.'[13] Even after annexation, many smaller native chiefs were often accused in Police Reports of fostering 'organized gangs'.

It was not only the native rulers but the population at large in Punjab, according to some officers, that exhibited a 'social weakness,'[14] a lack of discrimination between the criminal and the non-criminal that needed to be curbed.

A Chief Commissioner, Punjab wrote in 1854 that criminals in Punjab were '. . . not comparatively much more depraved than the mass of the people . . .[15] theft among most classes is looked on as a very menial offence – Indians of the highest class, and almost universally the heads of villages used to protect robbers and thieves and share their illegal gains.'[16] He added that petty crimes like burglary, forgery, cattle stealing 'were hardly considered as crimes, certainly seldom punished as such under Native Rule.' Even heinous crimes were committed and tolerated not only in the border districts but even among the ranks of the Native Police.

It was perhaps with these apprehensions in mind that the Chief Commissioner of Cis and Trans Sutlej decided that the thuggee cases would not be transferred to Agra but tried in Punjab courts. He agreed with Larkins and the civil and sessions judge who had argued that some 'examples' were required to be made and that the 'effect' of the trials 'would be felt much more if carried out in the courts of the Districts where these thugs have been carrying on their system of thuggee.'[17]

These concerns, as well as related insecurities regarding criminal collectivities that threatened order, motivated the urgent suppression of 'thagi'. Once the cases of 'thagi' were declared 'extinct', the Punjab authorities turned their attention to the Mazhabi or Rungretta Sikhs who had been identified in an overwhelming number of 'thagi' cases. Punjab's Mazhabi Sikhs were placed under surveillance and some measures were suggested to offer them alternative employment so as to keep them out of 'mischief'. George Campbell,[18] a Punjab officer, urged the government to reclaim these 'Mazhabis' to 'honest life' and put forward a spirited defence on their behalf. Campbell wrote that the 'Rungrettas' or low caste Sikhs had originally either been cultivators or professional soldiers. As mercenary soldiers, they had been in 'great estimation with the Sikh chiefs' and had been 'constantly employed by them.' Since annexation, he alleged, the Rungrettas had been unable to find employment as regular soldiers owing to their low caste status. As for returning to cultivation, the Rungrettas, claimed Campbell, had been 'ousted' by British settlement officers because of their inability to 'prove that in the day of their power they acquired . . . (land) by strictly legal / in our sense of the term means . . .' lacking all 'honest employment' therefore, they had turned to 'violent crime'. Campbell pleaded that this be remedied immediately, by allowing this community to enter the Sikh Regiments.

Campbell's defence of the Rungrettas was a plea that they were entirely 'reclaimable' and could be returned without qualifications to the mainstream; even into the ranks of that holiest of cows, the British Indian Army.

Yet in an indirect, implicit way, Campbell defended the Rungrettas without ever rejecting the understanding of the 'professional' criminality of certain groups. He redeemed the Rungrettas by tracing a respectable, 'honest' ancestry; he then denied that they were criminals by 'profession' but only by a particular displacement as a result of the British annexation of Punjab.

Both Campbell's explanation of the Rungretta's background, as well as the reform measures that he suggested, were rejected by the authorities at Fort William. In 1853, it was decided to form 'companies'[19] of Mazhabi Sikhs as 'pioneers'[20] employed on the Multan canals. However, the 'companies' were to be formed only after appointing the necessary superintendence and making arrangements for their security.[21]

Two years later, some Mazhabi 'thug' approvers were placed in a special School of Industry at Lahore in 1855. The avowed aim was to model it on an earlier experiment in Meerut by training them in manufacturing trades and allowing them subsequently to practise their trades independently.

Yet the wariness and insecurity of 'professional' criminals and their 'calling' was such that even in 1880 a proposal to allow the aged 'thug' inmates to live in a neighbouring village under ticket-of-leave rules was rejected.[22] The officiating commissioner was unwilling to abandon surveillance of these inmates. He was of the opinion that 'the location of these men in a village where they will be at large, and seen and spoken to daily by young and old,' was, 'objectionable'. He suggested, instead, these approvers be relocated '. . . in a few *katcha* houses which might be built for them near the Central Jail.[23]

Simultaneously, as measures of surveillance and related 'reclamation' steps were being instituted for the Mazhabis, another group of 'professional' criminals, certain 'predatory' tribes had been identified and were being controlled.

These 'predatory' tribes, were understood to have possessed the same essential features as the Mazhabi 'thugs', which made them bands of unsettled, organized, criminals by birth. With these tribes, as with the Mazhabi 'thugs', the Punjab officers felt compelled to initiate some informal measures of surveillance and crime deterrence. George Campbell's Report in 1850[24] makes one of the early references to 'this vagrant and criminal class.' His account focused on the Baurias. He put forward what would be an oft repeated complaint from the Punjab executive in subsequent years. He mentioned that a scheme had been initiated to collect Baurias in separate villages since they were difficult to 'treat'. It had been impractical to keep them continually in jail as bad characters or to make them 'work at honest trades'.

By 1856, more concrete measures were devised for the surveillance of these tribes. Based on similar methods initiated in the North-Western provinces, the Judicial Commissioner prepared Circular-18[25] regarding the coercive measures to be adopted vis a vis certain criminal classes such as the 'Sansiahs, Harnees and Bouriahs.' The Judicial Commissioner proposed six measures of check that would be applied to these three tribes. These included rules such as the registering of these tribes in local *thanas* and enforcing ticket-of-leave regulations so as to keep local authorities informed of their whereabouts. Aware that the police alone would be unable to enforce this surveillance, the circular included local headmen within its ambit. The 'thanedars' were enjoined to take security from the headmen of the villages and the latter were made answerable for the conduct of these tribes and report their movements.

This circular order was made out to be similar to the surveillance measures enforced over the Mazhabi caste. It was portrayed as a 'temporary' measure that would settle these tribes to a life of honesty and accountability yet, little was done to foster the latter except a formal directive to landholders to employ them.

The circular also did not remain merely a temporary measure as promised. It was only the first of a series of measures of its kind by which the Punjab Executive, along with other authorities, attempted to control and deter 'professional' criminals. Even the initial reports from Punjab Field Officers in the 1860s praised the success of reformatory settlements in Amritsar and Sialkot and asked for the circular to be expanded to include other 'predatory' tribes.[26]

In November 1867, a verdict of the Punjab Chief Court brought the operation of the circular to an abrupt halt by declaring that 'there was no order in legal force which prohibited a person from leaving his village without ticket-of-leave or the permission of police.'[27]

The setting aside of executive orders of this nature by court verdicts, had meanwhile also occurred in the North Western Provinces. Officers from both provinces then pressed the Legislative Department to consider passing a Criminal Tribes Act that would formalize such measures.

Punjab was an active participant in the debate that followed over the

Criminal Tribes Bill and its Executive submitted two of the three drafts that were considered by the Legislative Department.

The debate over the Bill in Punjab is interesting for the purposes of our account since it clarifies the perception of the 'problem' of criminal tribes as viewed by both the Punjab Executive and Judiciary, and the respective policies that they advocated.

The Punjab Judiciary was by and large against the passing of an out-of-the ordinary legislation of the kind proposed. They were of the view that existing provisions in the Indian Penal Code and Criminal Procedure Code 'would be sufficient to enable the magistrate and the police effectually to control persons of bad character, whether Sansi, Harnee, Bauria or members of any other wandering or thieving tribe.'[28]

By rejecting the need for special, deterrent legislation, judges of Punjab's newly formed Chief Court, were putting forward an alternative view of these tribes. Without denying that these tribes were frequently involved in petty crime they attempted to explain their involvement in crime related irregularities.

Some judges pointed out that criminal tribes like the Harni villages in Sialkot had taken to crime because of infertile land.[29] On the other hand, many like the Harnees in the Amritsar area possessed land and led the life of innocuous cultivators.[30] By focusing on factors like the socio-economic context to criminal activities, the Judiciary set aside the need for special laws that understood certain groups as possessing inherent criminal inclinations.

The Punjab Executive in turn, put forward views that elaborated earlier complaints made by Campbell in the 1850s. In their opinion, these 'criminal' tribes could not be treated by ordinary laws since they were not merely routine criminals. Ordinary laws and procedures did not possess the scope to control 'organized' crime since they were not framed to treat criminals by birth whose latent tendencies needed to be watched and deterred.

A key participant in this debate, Punjab's Inspector General of Police, commented that while the Chief Court's system sought 'to deter from crime by inflicting punishment, after a man is proved to be so bad that you must either take security from him or give him imprisonment with hard labour'; the old Punjab system of the circular with '. . . infinitely more mercy to the criminal tribes sought by a system of roll-call and ticket-of-leave to incapacitate . . . the man from crime, since it only punished him after its preventive measures failed.'[31] Many others, like a former Lieutenant Governor, supported this view that a 'special mode of treatment' based on 'measures of constraint and control' were needed, since the aims and experience of the Judiciary were 'confined to deal with crime after its has been committed.'[32]

While asking for special, deterrent legislation for these tribes, the Executive supported their case by recourse to the thagi analogy and the separate forms and institutions that had been employed to treat this 'evil'.

One memorandum stressed that the Thagi and Dakaiti Department had employed 'measures opposed to accepted usage'[33] and that there was every reason to resurrect and legalize the same treatment with regard to the criminal tribes. Referring to these tribes, it stated:

> If their warfare with their neighbours is less murderous than that of the thugs, it is more insidious, more universal, and equally demoralizing to themselves. Their own interests and those of society at large require that restrictive measures of a special character should be directed against them. Even, the existence of such a criminal class. Living notoriously on robbery, it added, (was an) outrage on civilized society.[34]

There were some who question this analogy. The sole instance of this kind that incisively debunked this comparison originated in a note from the Central Provinces.[35] This note stated that to compare the thugs to the criminal tribes was to confuse actual criminals sharing a murderous profession; to potential criminals of the same caste who were merely involved in petty crime. This observation was ignored since it displayed an inadequate understanding of 'professional', 'organized' criminal groups. Those identified in this category were criminals by inherent vocation and therefore the difference between actual and potential culpability did not exist. Due to this understanding of 'professional' criminals, later administrators would not with any seriousness put forward the 'proof' of criminal offences as would be required before notification and registration under the Criminal Tribes Act of 1871.

The Punjab Executive's stand was further clarified in one of the Draft Bills that was submitted by Hutchinson, its Inspector General of Police. This Draft Bill[36] was titled as an 'Act to legalize the surveillance of hereditary vagrants and criminals' and put forward as a measure that was merely intended 'to legalize the measures heretofore enforced under the Judicial Commissioner's Circular 18 of 1856.'[37]

However, this Bill suggested measures regarding both criminal tribes as well as Mazhabis, that were far more severe and rigorous than the Circular of 1856 had been. It provided that these groups be kept under a rigid police surveillance solely by appearing to have 'no sufficient ostensible means of subsistence; or by the common reputation in which they are held in the neighbourhood.'[38] Based on this, the local police, with few checks of any kind, could control these groups without even any of the formal responsibilities of reclamation that the earlier circular had suggested.

Based on their experience since the 1860s, the Punjab officers were thus pressing for a legislation that would be a severe elaboration and not only a simple revival of the Circular of 1856. The measures of surveillance imposed upon certain groups such as the Minas of Shahjahanpur had not been altogether successful. The Minas had on many occasions absconded and been involved in dacoities outside Punjab, especially in Rajputana.[39]

To the Punjab officers, this seemed indication enough that not only was surveillance necessary, but it needed to be reinforced by further deterrent punishment as well as by interprovincial coordination.

The Criminal Tribes Act of 1871, when passed, embodied these objectives as voiced in Punjab and the North Western Provinces. This Act provided a network of coordination between various local governments for the purpose of providing 'for the registration, surveillance and control of certain criminal tribes. . . .'[40] The Thuggee and Dacoity Agency had been relegated to the native states in 1863. By this Act, an entire set of legal procedures and provisions were created to fill that vacuum so as to control absconding groups who were involved in 'organized' or 'systematized' crime.

This interprovincial coordination of surveillance measures was supported by detailed procedures at the level of the two local governments concerned with its implementation, the Government of Punjab and North-Western Provinces. It was left to the initiative of the local government to state that it had reason to believe that 'any tribe, gang or class of persons,' was, 'addicted to the systematic commission of non-bailable offences.'[41]

It had to report this to the Supreme Government, and with its sanction, could proclaim such a tribe, gang or class to be a 'criminal' and make detailed local rules with regard to its registration, surveillance and control.

However, as a prefix to the introduction of these surveillance measures, the Criminal Tribes Act of 1871 also chose to enforce certain responsibilities towards 'reclamation' or 'reform' upon local authorities. During the debates over the Criminal Tribes Bill, members of the Legislative Department as well as some members of the Punjab Executive had spoken of the responsibility and mission to provide these groups with a settled means of honest livelihood. Accordingly, the Criminal Tribes Act laid down that before notifying the gang or class as a 'criminal' tribe', the local government had also to indicate in a Report to the Supreme Government as to 'the arrangements which are to enable them to earn their living.'[42] In the case of a wandering group, provisions had also to be made to settle the group concerned in a particular area or in a reformatory or *kot*.

By these 'reclamation' provisions, the Criminal Tribes Act of 1871 chose to address the problem of controlling these 'criminal groups' by attempts at reforming these groups in lifestyle, and habit, to norms dictated by colonial authorities; as well as by means of physical restrictions and surveillance. In this sense, it was a departure from the Punjab Circular of 1856. It not only enhanced deterrent punishment as the Punjab officers had wished, but also chose to tie together reform and surveillance unlike the now defunct circular or Hutchinson's Draft Bill.

Once the Punjab Government had framed its Rules under the Criminal Tribes Act in 1872, it initiated the process of 'notifying' or 'proclaiming' certain 'criminal tribes' and to implement the measures of control.

A recurring theme in the study of this 'proclamation' procedure is that the Punjab Government, with implicit tolerance of the Supreme Government, rarely met two of the crucial provisions that the Criminal Tribes Act laid down in this procedure. These concerned, providing 'proof' that the groups concerned were habitual criminals as well as convincing the Supreme Government that these groups would be provided with a means to earn an honest livelihood once declared 'criminal'.

In 1872 for instance, the Punjab Government made a request for permission to declare 6 tribes – the Sansis, the Harnis, the Pakhiwars, the Bauryas, the Gurmang and the Bithuchis as 'Criminal Tribes'.[43] For all these tribes, the proof of their alleged criminality was based largely on local notoriety, tribal legend, mere absence from home and the lack of a settled lifestyle. The Punjab authorities were aware of the deficiencies in the Report to the Supreme Government. Yet they passed it off saying that it was 'hopeless to search yet further among judicial and police proceedings for more evidence on this point,' since these tribes were dexterous in concealing their identity, and 'not one thousandth part of the crime they commit can be brought home to them'. With an economy of explanation, they reiterated that 'the criminal character of these tribes' was 'notorious' and that it had 'always, everywhere and by all persons been declared highly criminal.'[44]

Similarly, the Punjab Government's report was equally opaque in the matter of establishing that these tribes would be provided with an alternative means of livelihood. District officers' reports, in fact, highlighted that these tribes were 'almost entirely superfluous to the agricultural community' and that the *lambardars* had declined to be responsible for them or even offer them wasteland.[45]

A similar attitude prevailed in 1873, when the Punjab Government proposed to deport the Minas of Gurgaon to a proposed Reformatory Settlement at Shahpur.[46] The Supreme Government had so far turned a blind eye and cooperated with local proclamation initiatives. However, in this instance, even the Home Department felt compelled to point out that the 'reclamation' by settlement in a Reformatory amounted 'to constituting a penal settlement with hard labour indefinitely, and with prison rules.'[47]

These comments apart, the Supreme Government never turned down any of the 'notification' proposals of the Punjab Government. The Punjab authorities in turn operated the Act taking the criminality of these groups as 'given'. As for measures of reform, they were rarely implemented with any sincerity and tended to be overshadowed by the insecurities of surveillance.

Nearly two decades after the passing of the Act, it was easily admitted by the government both of the North-Western Provinces and Punjab, that the Criminal Tribes had not been a success. Following these conclusions, a proposal was made by the Lieutenant Governor of North-Western Provinces to amend the Criminal Tribes Act in such a way as to emphasize 'suppression' and to follow it with 'reform by coercion.'[48] These proposals found a positive response in Punjab and in 1897 the Act was amended by enhancing the deterrent punishments that it prescribed. A provision was also made for the establishment of Juvenile Reformatories, where the children of these 'criminal classes' were to be segregated and trained in the trades.

Interestingly, in Punjab, the officials had been aware for many years that both surveillance as well as reform measures had proved to be a failure. At Sialkot for instance, the Punjab Government had been maintaining five Reformatory settlements for the Sansis for many years. Officers had frequently complained about the inadequacies of this experiment. In 1877–78, officers at Sialkot had assessed that the cause for a large amount of absenteeism in these settlements was because they limited the area within which the Sansis could 'gain some livelihood by begging and hunting.'[49] Advice had followed that the Sansis be removed from the strict confinement of these *kots* and be reclaimed by offering them other forms of livelihood. The local Deputy Commissioner heard these suggestions sympathetically but refused to envisage any tempering of surveillance. Instead, he professed that any 'amelioration in the habits and characters,' of these Sansis would be a slow process, 'imperceptible to . . . rulers of this generation.'[50] The government would therefore support and maintain the present generation of Sansis in confinement.

This approach remained unchanged in 1897, when the proposals from the North-Western Provinces were under consideration and were subsequently approved. Members of the Executive accepted the 'additional severities'[51] imposed by the amendment, though some also commented that these measures would 'have the effect of keeping the offending members of the proclaimed tribes in jail for longer periods.'[52]

In 1897, the Punjab officials set priorities that emphasized deterrent measures of control. All reform measures were subsidiary to this priority. Their concern was to make surveillance more effective. They ignored the advice of some Judges of the Chief Court that the solution lay in better implementation of existing surveillance provisions along with the establishment of viable livelihood options for these tribes. Within a few years however, the need was again felt to provide for more executive force to the Criminal Tribes Legislation.

At the turn of the century, the Police Reports revealed high levels of absenteeism amongst registered tribes. A typical Police Report in 1898[53] reported 908 absentees out of about 3,400 registered persons under the Criminal Tribes Act. Absenteeism was always a source of worry since all absentees were believed to be 'living by habitual crime'. The DIG Police of Sialkot echoed commonly voiced frustration when he wrote:

> The Criminal Tribes Act is a very difficult one to work. If it is very strictly enforced the persons subject to it leave their homes. If any slackness is permitted the members of the tribe depredate the neighbourhood of their homes.[53]

Faced by this delemma, the Punjab Government decided to make explicit the priorities that had guided their acceptance of the amendment to the Criminal Tribes Act in 1897. They were also encouraged in asking for what was to be an 'important change in policy'[54] by the rationalization of crime controlling agencies that was being generally effected as a result of rise in 'serious crime' and lawlessness in the state in the 1890s. Moreover, the Report of the Police Commission in 1900 had also recommended the need to obtain more information about these criminal collectivities so as to guide a policy of effective control and restraint.[55]

The Punjab Government thus framed a request in October 1902, regarding 'the surveillance and control of habitual criminals belonging to wandering gangs or tribes.' Punjab's Lieutenant Governor proposed 'that power should be taken to proclaim and register such tribes and gangs without insisting upon their being first settled by Government and provided with means of living.'[56]

The Punjab authorities claimed that it was the 'financial stringency' that compelled it to make such a request. However, not even members of the Home Department were willing to accept such an excuse. They concluded that the Punjab Government seemed to wish 'to be empowered to apply all the restrictive measures (which have been made more stringent by amending the Act of 1897) without incurring the corresponding obligations.'[57] The Punjab Government had also added that the registered groups would be allowed to move around a wide area so as to enable them to earn a livelihood, but few believed that this was feasible.

The implementation of reclamation measures had never been a matter of serious concern for the Punjab Government. As its needs for reinforcing measures of surveillance became more urgent, it now sought formally to set aside all reclamation responsibilities so as to implement more comprehensive surveillance based on 'simple registration'[58] of all 'professional' criminal classes. These proposals were accepted and embodied in the Criminal Tribes Act III of 1911. For the next decades the Punjab Government was free to pursue its priorities, armed with enhanced powers of control and no attendant responsibilities.

NOTES AND REFERENCES

1. No. 124, 13 April 1848, Foreign Policy Progs. 1091A, 24 June 1848.
2. P. 139, R. Singha 'Providential Circumstances . . .' *Modern Asian Studies,* 27, 1993, pp. 83–146.
3. No. 128, 14 March 1848, Foreign Policy Progs., 24 June 1848.
4. No. 82, 21 April 1848, Foreign Policy Progs., 24 June 1848.
5. Selections from Public Correspondence, Vol. IV, pp. 51, NAIL.
6. P. 84, R. Singha MAS 27, 1993, pp. 83–146.
7. *Ibid.*
8. No. 124, 13 April 1848, Foreign Policy Progs. No. 1091A, 24 June 1848.
9. *Ibid.*
10. Selections from the Records of the Government of India Home Department (28 February 1856), p. 61.
11. *Ibid.*, 28 February 1856 (Minute by Governor General).
12. No. 124, Foreign Progs. 1901A, 24 June 1848.
13. Selection from Public Correspondence Report on Thuggee Operations, November 1852.
14. No, 227 from Chief Commissioner Punjab, 1 September 1854, 227–29 F.C.
15. *Ibid.*
16. *Ibid.*
17. No. 82, Foreign Policy Progs., 24 June 1848.
18. No. 107, Foreign Policy Progs., 10 January 1851.
19. No. 533–35, Foreign Policy Progs., 4 March 1853.
20. *Ibid.*
21. *Ibid.*
22. No. 46–47, Home Judicial, September 1880.
23. *Ibid.*
24. No. 107, Foreign Policy Progs., 10 January 1851.
25. Letter No. 83, 5 April 1856, Selections from Public Correspondence, Vol. IV, 1859–65.
26. *Ibid.*, pp. 42–43.
27. No. 67, November 1871, Legve. Progs. (Nos. 44–127).
28. *Ibid.*
29. *Ibid.*
30. *Ibid.*
31. No. 88, Legve. Progs. November 1871 (Nos. 44–127).
32. No. 67, Legve. Progs. November 1871 (Nos. 44–127).
33. *Ibid.*
34. *Ibid.*
35. Home Judicial, 30 July 1870.
36. No. 67, Legve. Dept. November 1871 (Nos. 44–127).
37. *Ibid.*
38. *Ibid.*

39. Papers Related to Act XXVII of 1871.
40. *Ibid.*
41. *Ibid.*
42. *Ibid.*
43. No. 194, Home Judicial A September 1872.
44. *Ibid.*
45. No. 73–75, Home Judicial A December 1873.
46. No. 3–11, Home Judicial A February 1874.
47. *Ibid.*
48. No. 1, Legve. Dept. K.W., February 1897 (No. 1–28).
49. No. 120, Home Judicial A February 1880.
50. No. 134, *ibid.*
51. Appendix Legve Dept. K.W, February 1897 (No. 1–28).
52. *Ibid.*
53. Report on Police Administration in Punjab for 1898 N.A. I. Library.
54. Nos. 53, Home Police A March 1911 (53–79).
55. *Ibid.*
56. No. 24, Home Police Progs. A February 1904 (No. 24).
57. No. 91, Home Police Progs. A December 1903.
58. No. 53, Home Police Progs. A March 1911 (53–79).

FIFTEEN

Gandhi and the Jallianwala Bagh Tragedy: A Turning Point in the Indian National Movement

S. R. SINGH

POST WORLD WAR I India was a seething cauldron of discontent – economic, social, political and religious. India was in a state of suppressed excitement, industrialism had spread and the capitalist class had grown in wealth and power; the handful at the top had prospered and were greedy for more power and opportunity to invest their savings and add to their wealth, but the great majority were not so fortunate and were looking forward to lightening their burden that crushed them. Among the middle classes there was everywhere an expectation of great constitutional changes which would bring a large measure of self-rule, thus improving their lot by opening out many fresh avenues of growth to them. Political agitation, peaceful and wholly constitutional as it was, seemed to be working itself to a head and people spoke with assurance of self determination and self-government. Some of this unrest was visible also among the masses, especially the peasantry. In the rural areas of the Punjab the forcible methods of recruitment were remembered with bitterness and the fierce suppression of the Komagata Maru people and others by conspiracy trial added fuel to the widespread resentment. The soldiers back from active service on distant fronts were no longer the subservient robots that they used to be. They had grown mentally and so there was much discontent among them. Among the Muslims there was widespread anger over the treatment meted out to Turkey. The dominant note all over India was one of waiting and agitating. People were full of hope and yet tinged with fear and anxiety.

Such a volcanic situation was not to be treated as a case of law and order, but to be diagnosed as a social malady and to be solved accordingly. The bureaucracy of an alien power was incapable of finding such a remedy and a red rag was flanked to the bull in the form of the Rowlatt Bills with drastic provisions for arrest and trial, without any of the checks and procedural formalities which the law is supposed to provide. A wave of intense anger greeted them all over India. The entire non-official block in the Imperial Legislative Council vehemently opposed the bills. To name only a few, they were eminent leaders of public opinion like V.J. Patel,[1] M.A. Jinnah,[2] G.S. Khaparde,[3] T.B. Sapru,[4] Mazharul Haque,[5] S.N. Banerjee,[6] M.M. Malaviya,[7] etc. Despite such widespread resistance, the bills were pushed through by the official block and became law. The only concession that was made to the public opinion was that the operation of the law was limited to three years.[8] The irony was that the laws were never used even once during the span of three years, the years of unrest and the most troubled years that India had known since 1857. Nehru noticed another interesting fact – that fifteen years thereafter, there were any number of harsher laws on the statute book than these and compared to them, the Rowlatt Bills appeared to be the charter of liberty.[9]

The newspapers were also breathing unrest. According to one, Bolshevism appeared in every country and Lord Chelmsford and his colleagues had an invitation to this struggle by the introduction of the Sedition Bills. The self-respecting and progressive Indians demanded that this was to be replied in a thoughtful and courageous manner. Indians owed devotion to the King-Emperor, but not to the bureaucracy. They wanted to remain in the British Empire, but contemporary not under arbitrary Government. The inhuman measures were to be met by passive resistance.[10] Thus the country was goaded into rebellion.

Gandhi had shown loyalty to the British Constitution while fighting against the helotry imposed on Indians in South Africa. He had faith in the British sense of justice. But Gandhi's faith was now on trial. From an enforced rest of about six months, from August 1918 to January 1919, he was thrown by circumstances into the thick of the national struggle and assumed the leadership of the anti-Rowlatt Bill agitation. The country took the Rowlatt Bills as an attack on national self-respect and Gandhi worked actively to give organized expression to popular resentment. He pledged himself and his co-workers to determined agitation against the proposed legislation through civil disobedience of laws, if need be. Though physically weak, he undertook an extensive tour of the country and to demonstrate the strength of popular feeling against the Bills, issued a call to the nation to observe 6 April as satyagraha day to be observed with prayers and fasting, and taking the pledge of civil disobedience. The day passed off peacefully in Bombay, but there were reports of ominous troubles in the Punjab. Gandhi set out on 8 April from Bombay to work for peace in the province, but he was prevented from entering the Punjab and this triggered off violence in certain parts of the country. The atmosphere was charged with suspense and fear and the countrywide tension culminated in the fateful shooting at Amritsar on 13 April, the Baisakhi day. This was followed by the imposition of Martial Law in the Punjab and the infliction of cruel indignities on citizens .

Much light has been thrown on the details of the Jallianwala Bagh tragedy and several books have been written on different aspects of the subject. Many controversies are still raging and there is no likelihood of them coming to an end.[11]

What is of significance to historians is that the Jallianwala Bagh massacre provoked strong public reaction both in India and England. It created a wide gulf between the colonial power and the natives. Fierce arguments and counter-arguments followed Dyer's inhuman massacre which fostered ill-will between the rulers and the ruled. While reflecting on Jallianwala Bagh, one S.K. Datta, burst out with tears in his eyes: 'This ends the British connection with India'.[12] The administration of Michael O'Dwyer who had approved Dyer's action came under fire. Jawaharlal Nehru, in his conversation with Lord Montgomery, said later that the Jallianwala tragedy marked a turning point in Anglo-Indian relations.[13] The event left deep scars on the face of India.

But Gandhi maintained his balance and tried to give the culprit time to mend. He candidly admitted his Himalayan miscalculation in that he could not judge the public mood. He did not minimize the scale and strength of the provocation, but at the same time, he strongly condemned the people's loss of self-control and announced a seventy-two hour fast. He also issued a statement to the press and temporarily suspended the civil disobedience part of satyagraha. In his letter to the Private Secretary to the Viceroy, he categorically affirmed his continued reliance upon satyagraha and his hope that in the course of time it would be accepted both by the people and the government. The suspension of civil disobedience, therefore, did not mean abandoning satyagraha itself, but it meant only a change of approach. He deprecated the orders against his entry into Delhi, Amritsar and Lahore. His presence would have prevented or minimized violence as elsewhere. He pleaded for justice to the Muslims in connection with the Khilafat question and referred to the great discontent which was agitating the Muslim mind and threatening to break into violence. He pleaded for the withdrawal of the Rowlatt legislation in deference to Indian public opinion and added that this would add to the prestige of the Government.[14]

Gandhi now devoted himself to educating public opinion in the art and science of satyagraha. In a series of satyagraha leaflets and through his speeches and public statements, he tried to explain the meaning of satyagraha as a weapon of moral force. Civil disobedience of laws was, he explained, only incidental to the practice of satyagraha, which was essentially a process of self-purification. He insisted that its votary is to follow swadeshi which was the most natural expression of one's concern for the welfare of one's neighbour. After the event of April, he took it up with increasing earnestness as the most effective expression of healthy and constructive patriotism.[15]

On the deportation of B.G. Horniman, the editor of *The Bombay Chronicle* and a fearless champion of the nationalist cause, Gandhi gave a call for a peaceful *hartal* on 2 May 1919. With his trust in the authorities, he continued to plead with them for justice and reason. On 4 May, he wrote to Andrews that in the midst of carnage, persecutions, Martial Law, military dispositions, he (Gandhi) found, the law of love answering fully and abundantly proved. He appealed for an independent 'inquiry to examine the cause of disturbance in the Punjab and the administration of Martial Law in the province, including the sentence passed by the Martial Law Tribunal.'[16] Failing redress on these matters, he was ready to revive civil disobedience and gave an intimation of his intention to the Viceroy. He went on in June with preparation for its resumption, carrying on simultaneously intensive propaganda for swadeshi. Finally, in July he decided on an indefinite suspension of civil disobedience and explained his reasons for doing so in a statement to the press. 'If my occasional civil resistance be a lighted match, Rowlatt legislation and persistence in retaining it on the statute book are a thousand matches scattered throughout India and the only way to avoid civil resistance altogether is to withdraw that legislation. I have thus suspended civil resistance to hasten the end of that legislation. But satyagrahis will pray for its removal by their life if it cannot be removed by lesser means.'[17]

In 1919, Gandhi was convinced thus:'. . . we are faced with despair everywhere. It was confidently hoped that at the close of the War, India would get something substantial, but the hope turned out to be false. For aught we know the reforms may not come. Even if they do, will be worthless . . . we have to wait and see. The Punjab has been a scene of most revolting episodes. Innocent lives have been lost. . . . The gulf between the rulers and the ruled has widened.'[18] The only silver lining, according to Gandhi, 'to the thick dark cloud of despair' was the dawn of satyagraha.

The Rowlatt Act which had been the cause of the upheaval in April 1919, was repealed. Gandhi asked in distress whether the will of the people was to prevail or that of the Government.[19] For securing its repeal, he tried in the first instance,[20] the old method of sustained and orderly agitation and mobilization of public opinion. He recommended a petition after the style of the Congress-League scheme memorial. When the All-India Home Rule League drew up this petition, he appealed to all the people to sign it.[21] But Montagu was reported to have declared that the Rowlatt Act would never be repealed. To this, Gandhi's retort was that General Smuts had said the same with regard to the Transvaal

Asiatic Law, but the Indians' satyagraha had compelled him to remove the racial bar from the Immigration Law in 1914. Official intransigence stifled Gandhi's attitude and he soon realized that the only answer to the Rowlatt Act was civil resistance and that constitutional measures like a petition were totally ineffective.[22]

Convinced of the excesses of the Martial Law cases, Gandhi demanded review, revision and reversal of the cruel sentences imposed on innocent people. He was convinced that Kitchlew and Satyapal, the deported leaders, were levelled with all sorts of charges they were not guilty of.[23] It was difficult for him to remain outside prison walls when so many in Punjab were suffering behind the bars for no fault of theirs.[24] The best that could be done in the circumstances was to have an impartial inquiry into the happenings in the Punjab. Writing on 7 September regarding the appointment of the Hunter Inquiry Committee, Gandhi hoped that justice would be done and called upon experienced men everywhere to present facts fearlessly before it. On 2 October, he urged Swami Shraddhananda, the Arya Samaj leader, to set up a central body to collect facts and tender evidence.

On 29 October, along with C.F. Andrews, Gandhi met Lord Hunter, the Chairman of the Disorders Inquiry Committee, which held its first sitting in Delhi in November.[25] Gandhi wrote to the Lieutenant Governor of the Punjab demanding recognition of the right of the public bodies to lead evidence before the Hunter Committee for this purpose. The Punjab Government's refusal to let imprisoned leaders appear before the Committee amounted, in Gandhi's opinion, to the rejection of a right to which any criminal was entitled. So he conveyed to the Punjab Government the decision of the setting up of a Congress Sub-Committee, which was set up to enquire into the Punjab disturbances and to boycott the Hunter Committee. Madan Mohan Malaviya, Motilal Nehru, Rasbihari Ghosh, Syed Imam, B. Chakravarti, C.R. Das, Kasturi Ranga Ayyangar, Umar Sobhani and Gokaran Nath Mishra were the members of the Congress Sub-Committee. Gandhi was co-opted to it in mid-October. In the Punjab the Committee was assisted by C.F. Andrews. Gandhi played the most vital role in the preparation of the report.[26] At first C.R. Das supervised the work; later Gandhi and M.R. Jayakar did the remaining work on the report, of which Gandhi was the dominant partner.

Another issue which provoked controversy was the Indemnity Bill passed by the Government on 25 September 1919.[27] It was aimed at protecting officers who had acted outside the letter of the law while confronting the difficult situation during the disturbances. This Act also excited public resentment, but Gandhi supported it even in the face of strong public opinion against it. This provides clear proof that he did not take undue advantage of the embarrassment faced by the Government and supported the Government where it was justified.

To the widespread resentment over the continuance of the Rowlatt Act was added another grievance. The Muslim demand for the continuance of the Khilifat's control on Arabia and the holy places of Islam was one of the issues which dominated the political landscape during this time. On 18 September, Gandhi addressed the Khilafat meeting in Bombay, which adopted a resolution expressing anxiety over the dismemberment of Turkey and demanded the fulfilment of British promises. October 17 was observed as 'Khilafat Day'. Gandhi wrote letters to the press and stressed in *Navjivan* the significance of the 'Day'. He also considered it necessary for Indians to dissociate themselves completely from the peace celebrations announced for mid-December so long as the Muslim demand was not granted. He emphasized that the Khilafat claim was backed by justice, the declarations of British ministers and the united strength of Hindu and Muslim opinion. He made the 'Khilafat' a plank for Hindu-Muslim unity, believing as he did, that if the Hindus befriended the Muslims in the hour of their trial, the two communities would draw closer together.

But despite public resentment over all these questions, Gandhi continued to believe in British cooperation. When in the first week of December 1919, the Reform Bill had its third reading in the House of Commons, Gandhi was against rejecting the Reforms, as they, in his opinion, conceded important rights for which thanks were due to Mr Montagu. Gandhi saw behind the Act the hand of Lord Sinha (the Under-Secretary of State for India then) and it lent a ray of hope.[28] The country had to send honest and competent representatives to the legislature and secure justice vis-a-vis the Rowlatt Act and the Punjab. In the last resort, they had the weapon of satyagraha.[29]

When the Royal Proclamation was issued on 24 December, Gandhi described it as evidence of the British intention to do justice. He considered it the duty of the country to work the reforms in order 'to make them a thorough success and thus anticipate the time for a full measure of responsibility'.[30] A logical corollary to this was Gandhi's moving the Reforms Resolution at the Amritsar Congress which inter alia, hoped that 'the authorities and the people will cooperate so to work the reforms as to secure an early establishment of full responsible Government.'[31]

Jawaharlal Nehru has called the Amritsar Congress the first Gandhi Congress. Lokmanya Tilak took a prominent part in the deliberations, but there was no doubt that the majority of the delegates, and even the great crowds outside, looked to Gandhi for leadership. The slogan *Mahatma Gandhi ki Jai* began to rent the Indian political horizon. The Ali Brothers, recently discharged from internment, immediately joined the Congress, and the National Movement began to take a new shape and a new orientation.[32]

According to Gandhi himself, his real association with the Congress began at Amritsar. Upto this time, his share in the annual proceedings of the Congress was confined to the constructive advocacy of Hindi. He made his speech in the national language and and presented the case of the Indians overseas. Nor did he expect to be called upon to do anything at Amritsar. But, as had happened on many previous occasions, responsibility fell on him all of a sudden. Gandhi felt that though the reforms were not entirely satisfactory, they could be accepted for the time being. The stalwarts of the Congress (for example, the Lokmanya and the Deshbandu) were not in favour of the Reforms. After a good deal of confabulations, a compromise resolution was passed on the Reforms to the joy of all present.[33]

Gandhi regarded his participation in the Congress proceedings at Amritsar as his real point of entrance into the Congress politics. His attendance in previous Congress sessions was nothing more than the annual renewal of allegiance to the party. He never felt on these occasions that he had any specific duty cut out for him except that of a mere private member. Nor did he desire more. His experience of Amritsar had shown that there were one or two things for which he had an aptitude and which could also be useful to the Congress. He could also see that the Lokmanya, the Deshbandu and Pandit Motilal Nehru and other leaders were pleased with his work in connection with the Punjab inquiry. They used to invite him to their informal gatherings where resolutions for the Subjects Committee were conceived.[34]

In the coming years there were two things in which Gandhi was interested and for which he had special aptitude. One of these was the memorial of the Jallianwala Bagh massacre for which the Congress had passed a resolution with great enthusiasm and for which a fund of about five lakhs was to be collected. As one of the trustees, Gandhi assumed the responsibility of collecting the fund and a handsome amount was collected to sanctify which Hindus, Muslims and Sikhs mingled their blood. But the memorial could not be erected at that time. Gandhi's other aptitude which the Congress could utilize was as a draftsman. The old constitution as drafted by Gokhale was not adequate to serve the purpose of the Congress under the new circumstances. Therefore, the need for redrafting the constitution was felt by everybody. The responsibility of framing a new constitution was entrusted to Gandhi which he accepted on condition that either Lokmanya and the Deshbandu, or two of their representatives should be on the Committee. With the assumption of this responsibility, Gandhi could be said to have made his real entrance into the Congress politics.[35]

While Gandhi was closely associated with the Congress at Amritsar, he had been all the time making patient efforts to educate public opinion on the meaning of satyagraha; the events of April 1919 had convinced him of the absolute necessity of such education. Neither the people nor the Government had understood that Gandhi conceived satyagraha not merely as a political weapon, but as a technique of employing soul-force for solving all the problems of life. It could be applied for almost any reform in any sphere.[36] Essentially it meant resistance of wrong by quiet and dignified suffering.[37] It encompassed the spheres of swadeshi, political and social reforms. The permanence of these reforms was ensured only so far as these were based on satyagraha.[38] He declared it was his intention to demonstrate that the strongest physical force bends before moral force when it is used in the defence of truth.[39]. . . In his view, satyagraha was nothing but a moral revolution and civil resistance was only a necessary part of it.[40] In his rejoinder to Lokmanya Tilak's interpretation of the *Bhagavadgita*, he affirmed that the law was not to return evil for evil but good for evil.[41]

The record of Gandhi's testimony before the Disorders Inquiry Committee is an outstanding document. On 5 January 1920, he submitted a statement to the Committee in which he gave a brief exposition of the science of satyagraha and the movement against the Rowlatt Act. Referring to the developments in the Punjab and Ahmedabad, he said that he did not believe 'there was any revolutionary movement behind the excesses. They could hardly be dignified by the term rebellion'.[42]

He clarified the purpose of a general *hartal* in April 1919, criticized the restraint order served on him to turn him 'away from a mission of peace'[43] and considered the violence at Ahmedabad and Viramgam as unjustified and the work of 'half-educated raw youths.'[44] Satyagraha had been suspended not because it was unsuitable to the masses, but because it was not in the right season.[45] Gandhi affirmed that it had been neither the cause nor the occasion of the upheaval.[46] After setting out objections to the Rowlatt Act, he declared: 'But for satyagraha, India would have witnessed scenes perhaps more terrible than it has passed through.'[47]

Though Gandhi had advocated acceptance of the reforms at Amritsar, he had also accepted many other resolutions demanding the rectification of the Punjab wrongs. The Congress deprecated the Lieutenant Governor's action in not permitting even a few of the Punjab leaders undergoing imprisonment, to attend and sit even as prisoners under custody in the Committee room, to assist and instruct counsel in the same manner as the Government counsel was instructed by the officials whose conduct was under investigation. Pending final judgement, the Government of India and the Secretary of State should see to it that General Dyer was immediately relieved of his command. The

Congress placed on record that in its opinion the Government of India and the Punjab Government must be held responsible for the inexcusable delay in placing an authoritative statement of the Jallianwala Bagh massacre before the public and His Majesty's Government. The Congress called upon His Majesty's Government to relieve Sir Michael O'Dwyer of his existing duties in India as a member of the Army commission as a prelude to necessary legal action being taken against him. This was in view of the oppressive regime of Sir Michael O'Dwyer in the Punjab and endorsement of General Dyer's massacre at the Jallianwala Bagh. The Congress also gratefully thanked Sir Sankaran resigning his office as member of the Executive Council of the Governor-General of India as a protest against the policy pursued by the Government of India and the Government of the Punjab. The Congress requested the Secretary of State for India to advise His Majesty to exercise the Royal Veto to repeal the hated Rowlatt Act, the root of all troubles in India. It strongly protested against an action of the Government of India in prematurely passing the Indemnity Bill in spite of the strong opposition by the press, numerous public bodies and non-official members of the Imperial Legislative Council. It also expressed the hope and trusted that the fullest effect would immediately be given to the letter and spirit of the Royal Command. In view of the fact that Lord Chelmsford had completely forfeited the confidence of the people of India, the Congress humbly besought his Imperial Majesty to be graciously pleased immediately to recall His Excellency. The Congress further entered its strong protest against the policy of the British Government against 'Khilafat', and demanded an immediate repeal of the India Press Act. These were among the most important resolutions adopted at the Amritsar Congress.[48]

Thus India vindicated her honour at Amritsar and in spite of all the hurdles placed against his entry into the Punjab till late, Gandhi was thirsting for cooperation only if Britain showed some generous gestures.

It was during this period that Gandhi took up the publication of *Young India* and *Navjivan* under his own editorial care. He felt that he had something to give to India and he wanted to give it through his own journals[49] to educate public opinion on political matters and regenerate national life in all fields. *Navjivan* means 'renewal of life' and Gandhi sought to bring this about by activating the moral energy which the people had inherited through the ages.

Though Gandhi was very badly needed by the people of the Punjab, he was not allowed to enter the province till it was very late. Sir Michael O'Dwyer held him responsible for all that had happened in the Punjab, and some irate young Punjabis even held him responsible for the Martial Law. The latter asserted that only if Gandhi had not suspended civil disobedience, there would have been no

Jallianwala Bagh massacre. Some of them even went to the length of threatening Gandhi with assassination if he went to the Punjab.[50] But Gandhi was impatient to get there. His visit to the Punjab, however, had to be postponed time and again and every time he asked for the Viceroy's permission, he was denied it. The Hunter Committee had been, in the meantime, announced to enquire into the events under the Martial Law. C.F. Andrews had reached the Punjab, and his letters gave a heart-rending description of the state of things there, and Gandhi formed the impression that the Martial Law atrocities were in fact even worse than the press reports had indicated.[51] Andrews pressed Gandhi to come and join him immediately. At the same time, Malaviya also sent telegrams asking Gandhi to proceed to the Punjab at once. The Viceroy permitted Gandhi to enter the Punjab after 15 October 1919.[52]

The scenes that Gandhi witnessed at Lahore were to be remembered for ever. There was a mammoth gathering of the people at the station and they were over enthusiastic. Gandhi became very intimate with the people there and they made him their own. The women brought to him heaps of yarn and thus he found that the Punjab could be a great field for khadi work.[53]

As Gandhi proceeded with his inquiry into the atrocities that had been committed, he came across tales of the Government's tyranny and the despotism of its officers which filled him with deep pain. What surprised him then and what continued to surprise him ever thereafter was the fact that a province that had furnished the largest number of soldiers to the British Government during the War should have taken all these excesses lying down.[54] Gandhi went on with the work of the Congress Inquiry Sub-Committee and very meticulously completed the drafting of the report which was entrusted to him. The report gives an authentic idea of the kind of atrocities that were perpetrated on the people of Punjab. In Gandhi's opinion, there is not a single conscious exaggeration in the report anywhere and every statement made in it is substantiated by evidence. Moreover, the evidence published was only a fraction of what was in the Committee's possession. No statement about the veracity of which there was the slightest room for doubt was allowed to appear in the report, which was prepared solely with a view to bring the truth and nothing but the truth and to show to what length the British Government could go, and what barbarities it was capable of perpetrating, in order to maintain its power. So far as Gandhi was aware, not a single statement made in the report could be disproved.[55]

How Punjab was touched by the presence of Gandhi there, can better be described in the words of C.F. Andrews, an English missionary and a friend of India. On 4 November, he was at Amritsar with Gandhi, and he had the experience of scenes he had never had before. With religious devotion and ecstasy the people, especially women, received Gandhi. The women with their infants, were at every window and behind every lattice straining their eyes to have the first sight of the coming event. There was eager expectation that morning, but there was also sorrow, tragically deep, behind it. These women and children had recently seen things that could never be forgotten. The fear caused by Martial Law and punitive police many weeks ago was still fresh in people's minds. There was a strongly marked feature of cowed submission present everywhere and grew increasingly. This terror and awe had entered every nook and corner. But the advent of Gandhi effectively broke this evil spell. Indeed, his victory was so great that it extended over the police themselves. For the joyful news had spread from street to street that the police had been joining with the multitude on that day of universal rejoicing.[56]

Gandhi came. He saw. He conquered. Not as Imperial Caesar did with the might of his armed legions, but with that peaceful force of the divine soul, wherein alone Gandhi put his trust. Andrews had thought that long morning triumphal procession of tumultuous rejoicing, by which the pent-up feelings of many months of anguish were transformed into joy were one of the crowning acts of that eventful day. But there was an act to follow which was supreme. All through the long afternoon the women of Amritsar with their small children came in their thousands to pay their respects to Gandhi, a man who stood amidst them in his great simplicity, clad in white home-spun garments.[57]

But in spite of Gandhi's attempts at conciliation at the Amritsar Congress, his attempt to forget and forgive all that had happened after the first week of April 1919, the conservative elements in England and the unrepentant bureaucracy in India triumphed. The relations between nationalist India and the alien British Indian Government further worsened in the first half of 1920. The Rowlatt Act, the Punjab wrongs, the Khilafat and the swaraj remained unredeemed.

The discontent in the country swelled into a flood. In Gandhi's attitude now there was a profound change towards the Empire. He had more or less accepted the British claim that their Empire rested on moral and political principles and that India had benefited greatly by being part of it. That faith was shaken now and Gandhi wanted the country to generate sufficient moral strength to mend or end the Empire. This was to be the guiding principle of his leadership henceforth.

The idea of direct action appealed to the prevailing mood and conditions seemed favourable for Gandhi to assume the leadership of the country. The Muslim leaders who headed the Khilafat agitation welcomed his help and counsel, though they did not agree with him on the ethical base of his programme. Gandhi was, however, deeply involved in the Khilafat programme and it became his main concern in the political field. This involvement in the Khilafat problem exposed him to many doubts and questions regarding both his motives and the wisdom of his action. He was accused of wanting to unite Hindus and Muslims against the British and of exploiting an unreasonable religious sentiment to embarrass the British Government. Gandhi faced these charges with the utmost patience and forbearance and said that it was contrary to his creed to embarrass Governments or anybody else.[58] He had thrown his heart and soul into the Khilafat question because British pledges, abstract justice and religious sentiment coincided. He could conceive the possibility of a blind and fanatical religious sentiment existing in opposition to pure justice. He would then resist the former and fight for the latter.[59] He was convinced that on the Khilafat issue the Muslims were in the right.

The plea for the self-determination of the subject peoples could be reconciled with the suzerainty of the Sultan of Turkey, as demanded by Muslim religious sentiment. British pledges, as interpreted by Gandhi, had assured that this would be respected. In any case the plea was insincere as it was only designed to cloak the political designs of the Allies in the Middle East. Therefore Gandhi felt that as between the British Government and the Indian Muslims, justice was on the side of the latter, both politically and morally. For Hindu-Muslim unity it was the neighbourly duty of a Hindu to support the just cause of the Muslim unconditionally. The Hindu-Muslim unity, according to Gandhi, consisted of common purpose, a common goal and common sorrow. It would be best promoted by sharing one another's sorrows, with mutual toleration.[60]

Gandhi also refuted Annie Besants's fear that non-cooperation would lead to violence. In *Young India* (28 April 1920) he asserted that he did not fear any evil consequences for the simple reason that every responsible Muslim understood that non-cooperation would be successful only if it is totally unattended with violence.[61] He also wrote that one could not claim that violence would never occur, but having taken all precautions against its occurrence one must go ahead with the programme.[62] There was also a more practical reason for advocating non-cooperation. Gandhi was convinced that had there been no move for non-cooperation, violence would have long since broken out. The Muslims were boiling with rage, but they had kept their patience in the belief that the Hindus were with them.[63] In any case, the programme was to be implemented gradually and the people's response was to be watched carefully before the next was taken.

The disillusionment about the moral root of British rule was complete with the publication of the Hunter Committee's Report in May 1920. Needless to say that the Congress had boycotted the proceedings of the Committee as a protest against the refusal of the Lieutenant Governor of the Punjab to give a fair opportunity for the presentation of the people's case before it. But Gandhi still hoped that the Committee would arrive at the right conclusions on the basis of even the incomplete evidence placed before it. The Congress had also appointed a Committee of its own and Gandhi had prepared a report with great care. This was published in March 1920. He had worked on the report for a fortnight, confining himself to the Ashram at Ahmedabad where he had returned after a strenuous tour of the Punjab. The report is nowhere legal or a juristic piece of writing; it is a narrative of imaginative breadth; it places the Punjab tragedy in the right perspective, presenting it as the culmination of the anti-national policy followed by the Deputy Governor, Sir Michael O'Dwyer. The conclusions which it drew, and the action it recommended, were stated with moderation and dignity. The official report (majority report of the official Committee) appeared to have treated the unhappy events merely as a law and order problem and did not go beyond admitting a few errors of judgement and recommending nominal punishment of the guilty officials. The members seemed to have been plainly concerned with whitewashing official misconduct. Gandhi called this 'political free masonry' and saw in it an added reason for withdrawing cooperation from the British Government.[64]

The official report was no mere irritant, it was also an expression of racial arrogance and hauteur. How arrogant Dyer was is clear from this episode. Towards the end of 1919, Nehru travelled from Amritsar to Delhi by the night train and he entered the same compartment which was occupied by several European passengers, including General Dyer. The General in an aggressive and triumphant tone was bragging of his achievements at Amritsar, as to how the whole town was at his mercy, how he had felt like reducing the whole rebellious city to a heap of ashes, and how he took pity on it and refrained from doing so. He was returning from Lahore after giving his evidence before the Hunter Committee of Inquiry.[65]

More shocking than this was the adoration heaped by the European community on their hero. Dyer was made to leave his command and some other British officials were censured. But Michael O'Dwyer was left completely untouched as though nothing in his administration had deserved condemnation. At the Lords' debate in London, 129 peers supported Dyer and only 86 voted against him. On the initiative of Curzon and O'Dwyer *The Morning Post* set up a fund, as a testimonial to him, and collected an amount of £ 26,000. A third of it was contributed from India, where a majority of the Europeans considered that Dyer's action had indeed saved the Empire. The British support for Dyer's action and for O'Dwyer's administration outraged Indians and filled them with a sense of great humiliation.[66]

The situation was not ripe for a revolution. Gandhi made a countrywide tour of mass education in the course of which he launched a powerful attack on the British Empire and the Government of India which he described as *Ravanrajaya.* His vehement denunciation of the Government surprised many. He had waited too long for good sense to dawn on the Government, but there was no way of mending it, and so now he decided upon ending it. He had moulded the public opinion for the last one year. He was preaching non-cooperation with the evil that was the Government of India. But he took care to see that non-cooperation was with the system that was evil and not the British nation and the only way to do this was to reorder national life so as to purge it of centuries' old evils. Withdrawal of cooperation from the Government was only the first step in the process. He, therefore, repeatedly told his audience that non-cooperation as conceived by him was a movement for self-purification. Educating public opinion was a difficult task, but Gandhi did it very successfully with his wonderful knack of going straight to the heart of the people.

His attention next turned to the perfecting of his instrument of organization. He soon emerged as the national leader with the widest appeal both among the educated and the masses. He used this position to transform the Congress into an instrument of dynamic change. He said on 2 July 1920 that in drafting the Constitution he had attempted to give the Congress a representative character such as would make its demand irresistible.[67] His aim may not have been realized to the full, but the revised constitution and the mass appeal which Gandhi wielded soon changed the character of the Congress beyond recognition.

Thus with an unparalleled popularity among the people who were disgusted with the vagaries of the Government, a reorganized Congress, his boundless capacity for leadership, unity between Hindus and Muslims, Gandhi was poised for non-cooperation. With the support of the Khilafatists, Gandhi declared the inauguration of non-cooperation on 1 August 1920 in his letter to the Viceroy returning the Kaiser-i-Hind medal and the other medals granted to him for his humanitarian services during the Zulu Rebellion and the Boer War in South Africa.[68] On this very day, destiny removed the Lokmanya from the national scene and Gandhi's spontaneous admiration for Tilak's patriotism and his services to the country appeared in the form of a glowing tribute to the departed leader.[69] Tilak's death left Gandhi the undisputed leader of the nationalist forces. His programme of national non-cooperation was accepted at a special session of the Congress in Calcutta in September in the teeth of opposition from the veteran stalwarts of the Congress. Gandhi served a stern warning in reply to the *communique* of the Government on the Non-cooperation

Movement, 'when, and if, the British nation respects the wishes of India on these two points (*a full and satisfactory revision of the Khilafat terms and complete satisfaction about the Punjab*), cooperation will replace non-cooperation, and swaraj within the Empire will be the most natural consequence.

'But till that clear repentance comes, in spite of all the resolutions and all the repression that may be resorted to by the Government, so far as I can read the national mind, non-violent non-cooperation will and must remain the creed of the nation that has grown weary of camouflage, humbug, and honeyed words'.[70]

It is thus that events moulded themselves after about a year of the infamous Rowlatt Act and the Jallianwala Bagh tragedy that Gandhi emerged as the sole leader of the Congress with a new weapon, a new constitution, a new outlook and a rural base. Gandhi's fight to the finish ended only when the British were forced to quit India.

NOTES AND REFERENCES

1. Proceedings of the Imperial Legislative Council, April 1918 to March 1919, LVII, pp. 454–57.
2. *Ibid.*, p. 463.
3. G.S. Khaparde's Diary, 6 February 1919, NAI.
4. Proceedings of the Imperial Legislative Council, April 1918 to March, 1919, LVII, p. 510.
5. *Ibid.*, p. 536.
6. *Ibid.*, p. 558.
7. *Ibid.*, pp. 902–4.
8. J. Nehru, *An Autobiography* (New Delhi), 1989, p. 40.
9. *Ibid.*, p. 41.
10. *Bhavishya*, Allahabad, 28 February 1919. Report on the Native News published in the UP, 1919, p. 83.
11. (*i*) B.G. Horniman, *Amritsar and Our Duty to India* (London, 1920); (*ii*) P. Mohan, *An Imaginary Rebellion and How It Was Suppressed* (Lahore, 1920); (*iii*) Edward Thompson, *A Letter from India* (London, 1932); (*iv*) Naidis, 'The Punjab Disturbances of 1919 – A Study of Indian Nationalism' – Dissertation submitted to Stanford University, February 1950; (*v*) *Disorders Inquiry Committee Report* (Calcutta, 1920); (*vi*) V.N. Datta, *Jallianwala Bagh* (Ludhiana, 1969); (*vii*) V.N. Datta, *New Light on the Punjab Disturbances* (Simla, 1969); (*viii*) Rupert Furneaux, *Massacre at Amritsar* (London, 1963); (*ix*) S.C. Mittal, *Freedom Movement in the Punjab* (Delhi, 1977); (*x*) Sankaran Nair, *Gandhi and Anarchy* (Madras, 1923); (*xi*) Hari Singh, 'Political Disturbance in Punjab and Delhi in 1919, A Study into the Evolution of Nationalism in India,' Ph.D. Thesis, Kurukshetra University, November, 1976; (*xii*) Raja Ram, *Jallianwala: A Premeditated Plan* (Chandigarh, 1969); (*xiii*) Arthur Swinson, *Six Minutes to Sunset* (London, 1964); (*xiv*) Helen Fein, *Imperial Crime and Punishment* (Honolulu, 1977).
12. Edward Thompson, *A Letter from India* (London, 1932), p. 99.
13. *The Sunday Times*, London, 29 January 1961.

14. *The Collected Works of Mahatma Gandhi*, vol. XV (Ahmedabad, 1965), pp. 218–19. Henceforth CWMG.
15. *Ibid.*, p. 272.
16. *Ibid.*, p. 334.
17. *Ibid.*, p. 470.
18. *Ibid.*, vol. XVI, p. 259.
19. *Ibid.*, p. 23.
20. *Ibid.*, p. 53.
21. *Ibid.*, p. 23b.
22. *Ibid.*, p. 449.
23. *Ibid.*, p. 85.
24. *Ibid.*, pp. 72–73.
25. *Ibid.*, pp. 72–73.
26. Jayakar Papers (Punjab Inquiry), December 1919, NAI.
27. K.K. Chanda, M.M. Malaviya opposed or moved amendments to the Bill in the Imperial Legislative Council, Proceedings of the Council (April 1919 to March 1920), LVIII, pp. 287–93 and *Ibid.*, pp. 318–21.
28. CWMG, vol. XXXIX, p. 385.
29. *Ibid.*, vol. XVI, p. 342.
30. *Ibid.*, p. 361.
31. *Ibid.*, pp. 363–64.
32. Jawaharlal Nehru, *op. cit.*, pp. 44–45.
33. CWMG, vol. XXXIX, pp. 384–87.
34. *Ibid.*, p. 387.
35. *Ibid.*, pp. 387–89.
36. CWMG, vol. XVI, p. 123.
37. *Ibid.*, p. 317.
38. *Ibid.*, p. 260.
39. *Ibid.*, p. 23.
40. *Ibid.*, p. 49.
41. *Ibid.*, pp. 490–91.
42. *Ibid.*, p. 371.
43. *Ibid.*, p. 389.
44. *Ibid.*, p. 392.
45. *Ibid.*, p. 416.
46. *Ibid.*, p. 126.
47. *Ibid.*, p. 460.
48. AICC Papers, File No. 1/19191, N.M.M.L.
49. CWMG, vol. No. XVI, p. 92.
50. CWMG, vol. XXXIX, p. 378.
51. *Ibid.*
52. *Ibid.*, p. 379.
53. *Ibid.*, p. 379.
54. *Ibid.*
55. *Ibid.*
56. C.F. Andrews to the Editor of *The Tribune* on the Punjab affair, 7 November 1919. C.F. Andrews Papers, 1/D 28.

57. *Ibid.*
58. CWMG, vol. XVII, p. 350.
59. *Ibid.*, p. 411.
60. *Ibid.*, p. 46.
61. *Ibid.*, p. 352.
62. *Ibid.*, p. 372.
63. *Ibid.*, p. 415.
64. *Ibid.*, p. 480.
65. Jawaharlal Nehru, *op. cit.*, p. 43.
66. V.N. Dutta, *Jallianwala Bagh*, p. 1.
67. CWMG, vol. XVIII, p. 3.
68. *Ibid.*, pp. 104–6.
69. *Ibid.*, pp. 110–111.
70. *Ibid.*, p. 479, also *Young India*, 17 November 1920.

SIXTEEN ❖

Jallianwala Bagh and the Indian National Movement

K. L. TUTEJA

THE MASSACRE WHICH shocked the people of Punjab and created wide rumblings in the country occurred on 13 April 1919 at a public meeting which had been organized at Jallianwala Bagh in defiance of an official proclamation banning such gatherings. About twenty thousand persons were present at the meeting. They included some from the surrounding countryside who had come to Amritsar in connection with the soldiers to Jallianwala Bagh where the meeting was held and immediately after his arrival, ordered his men to fire. No warning was given, nor was the crowd asked to disperse. The firing continued for ten minutes; in all 1,650 rounds were fired. Dyer ordered fire to be focused where the crowd was thickest including the exits. He gave orders to cease firing only when the stock ammunition was virtually exhausted.[1] According to an official account, 379 people were killed and 1,200 wounded.[2] However, the number of casualties was actually much higher than this.[3] The massacre evoked sharp criticism both in England and India. Winston Churchill called it 'a monstrous event, an event which stands in singular and sinister isolation.' Herbert Asquith observed that it was 'one of the worst outrages in the whole of history.'[4] These responses indicate that even those who believed that the British government in India was based on justice were shocked and disturbed. In India a large number of people felt that it was a gruesome event unparalleled in history. The disturbance and anguish caused by the massacre, and what the grim event signified to the people of India were best reflected in Mahatma Gandhi's reactions when he wrote: 'We do not want to punish Dyer. We have no desire for revenge. We want to change the system that produced Dyer.'[5] The massacre deeply influenced the subsequent course of the anti-Imperialist struggle in the country and contributed in its own way to the strengthening of forces which posed a challenge to the British rule in India.

I

The Jallianwala Bagh incident has been discussed in detail in a number of writings. Some of the earlier accounts are highly polemical in nature and carry an emotional load which gives them an evidently partial colouring according to later historians. In particular, the publications which came out in India and England immediately after the incident had an obviously partisan bias and had their primary focus on the role played by General Dyer.

A more comprehensive account of the incident has been published by Professor V.N. Datta in his well documented work[6] which reconstructs the entire series of happenings, giving minute details.[7]

He rightly emphasizes that it should not be viewed as an isolated incident but understood in the larger context of the nationalist confrontation with the British Raj which had been gaining strength in the country around this period and was also visible in Punjab.[7]

In this paper, my concern in not to review Dyer's role or that of any other British official involved in this massacre. The object here is not limited to fixing the responsibility for the massacre on any individual or merely to rest with condemnation of the firing but to make an attempt to understand the precise nature of the social phenomenon of which this particular incident formed a part. My purpose is primarily to attend to the issues involved in the Jallianwala Bagh massacre when viewed as a part of the larger historical process taking place in the society and politics of Punjab, as also in the larger domain of the anti-colonial struggle, spearheaded by the Congress at the all India level.

II

The Punjab was annexed by the East India Company in 1849. When the British came to this region, they did not do so merely as traders. Instead, they came, to quote Kenneth W. Jones, with 'mature Imperial consciousness',[8] which indeed determined their policies in the newly acquired province.

The Punjab also became crucial for the imperial system of control because the British army made its home in this province after 1880. The British government was dependent on the army which it needed not only to defend the frontier, but also to maintain its authority within the empire. In Punjab, a sizeable number of people belonging to the peasantry began to join military service, and soon their number swelled. Before the outbreak of the First World War, the soldiers from Punjab constituted three-fifth of the total army in India. The recruitment was made in maximum number from particular sections of Punjab society which were supposed to be imbued with strong martial traditions'. Ian Talbot has observed that actually the British policy of drawing recruits from Punjab was based on 'sound pragmatic grounds' but it was 'consciously enshrined in the mythology of martial caste theory' which maintained that 'ethnic origins and racial characteristics of the main groups of Punjabi recruits particularly fitted them for military service.'[9] In order to ensure a regular supply of manpower for recruitment, the government considered it essential to maintain its dominant hold over the rural society. Any attempt to disturb its hegemony was perceived by the British officials as 'seditious' activity which needed to be ruthlessly suppressed.[10] Already in this province, since the beginning of colonial rule, a distinct ideology described as the 'Punjab School Ideology' was developed which 'emphasized firm paternal rule by an elite of self-confident administrators who conceived their duty as that of bringing order and prosperity to a contented peasant society'.[11] Apart from paternalism, it also embodied the necessity of taking firm action against the people if they ever tried to pose a challenge to the authority of British rule. This framework of colonial ideology was best reflected in the statue of Lord Lawrence built in Lahore with sword in one hand and pen in the other. The inscription engraved on the statue mentioned, 'Will you be governed by the sword or the pen'?[12] The application of repressive methods whenever necessary constituted a major element of administration in Punjab.

The colonial state tried to strengthen its grip on rural society in Punjab by making an 'informal alliance' with the rich landed classes which held dominant influence over the local rural societies through social and economic ties. The landlords who were described as 'natural leaders' by the British officials, willingly acted as intermediaries between the state and the rural masses. This section of society, by and large, remained loyal to the government. The latter also nurtured and deepened their loyalty by extending patronage to them. But a significant step by which the government intended to win over the rural masses was the Land Alienation Act (1900). The new legislation disallowed permanent alienation of land owned by the agriculturist castes to the non-agriculturist moneylenders which included persons belonging to the Khatri, Arora and Bania castes. Later Michael O'Dwyer, who harboured strong prejudices against the urban middle classes granted agriculturists a 'preferential right of recruitment in the government service.'[13] This attitude of favouring agriculturists became further evident when the Montagu-Chelmsford Report recommended higher representation for them in the Punjab Legislative Council.[14]

Of course, the logic behind the pro-agriculturist policy followed by the British in Punjab underwent a change at the later stages of its rule. In the earlier phase, as stated above, the government through this policy endeavoured to maintain its hold over rural society in order to ensure regular export of agrarian products needed for the metropolis, and also to ensure the supply of manpower for the army. But, when the anti-imperialist forces started gaining strength after the turn of the century, the government realized that an ideology which projected agriculturists against non-agriculturists could also be an effective device to frustrate the attempts made by the nationalists to bring unity of all Indians against their rule in this province.[15]

The urban society in Punjab also underwent a major transformation following the establishment of colonial rule. The economic and social changes which took place during this period threw up new social classes with their distinctive interests and assertions. First of all, a large trading class which included big traders, moneylenders and petty shopkeepers sprang up as a powerful section of society. In particular, the urban Hindus belonging to the intermediate castes such as Khatris, Aroras and Aggarwals formed a major component of this class. Some Khatri and Arora Sikhs, and Khoja and Piracha Muslims also constituted a small section of the emergent trading community.[36] In the pre-colonial Punjab too, the merchant class which primarily included Hindus of the intermediate castes had formed an important segment of the urban population of leading commercial and administrative towns such as Lahore, Amritsar, Multan and Sialkot.[17] Soon after the annexation of Punjab by the British, the system of transportation made fast progress because of the massive employment of capital in railways. The rail link from Lahore to Amritsar was established in the early 1860s. Later, railway lines were spread over the province, and leading towns such as Lahore were connected through railways with Presidency towns and port cities.[18] Similar developments were also witnessed in the road transportation system.[19] The newly constructed roads helped in establishing closer links between the urban areas and the countryside. This development in the means of transport significantly expanded the trade which included large exports of agrarian products to the overseas market.[20] At the same time, machine made products, particularly cotton piece goods from England began to arrive in Punjab in large quantities, and were easily available both in big and small urban centres.[21]

Regarding the industries in Punjab, it is well known that the handicraft goods were manufactured generally by the Muslim artisans at the urban centres. For instance, there were 2,000 shops and manufacturers of shawls in Amritsar towards the close of Ranjit Singh's artisans.[22] But since the late nineteenth century, the economic condition of the Kashmiri artisans began to deteriorate because of the decline in the demand of Pashmina shawls produced by them for the overseas market.[23] Therefore, Ibbetson recorded that Kashmiri artisans were 'miserably poor'.[24] In fact, with the increasing import of manufactured products like cotton piece goods, the condition of artisans as a class worsened, and some of them were forced to quit their artisanal profession. Still at the turn of the twentieth century, a number of artisans lived in Amritsar and Lahore, and made small earnings through their traditional profession. According to Sumit Sarkar, the process of de-industrialization which caused acute hardship to the artisans 'occasionally led to urban and rural explosions of various types'.[25] This perhaps explains why a large number of artisans living in urban areas took active part in the Rowlatt Satyagraha in 1919.

After the turn of the twentieth century, the Punjab also witnessed the growth of some modern industries. The initial capital which was invested in the industries came from the local trading class.[26] However, the growth of industrialization in Punjab was on a very limited scale which, according to A.K. Bagchi, was 'due to lack of power resources owing to an almost total absence of coal and inadequate development of hydro-electricity in this area.'[27] Industries in Punjab were established with very limited capital. Most of them were related to the processing of agricultural products or mineral resources meant primarily to cater to the local needs. The Hindus belonging to the intermediate castes which have been mentioned above owned most of the industries. In view of slow progress of capitalist development, the industrial bourgeoisie could not take shape as a distinct formation and play a leading role in giving direction to the social and cultural life of the urban bourgeoisie as a whole. The entrepreneurial class in this province at the beginning of the twentieth century, does not in any case qualify to be described as industrial bourgeoisie with its own distinctive character and can at best be classified as a segment of the newly assertive middle classes. Further, since the industrialists in Punjab were organically linked with the trading classes at the social and economic levels, it is logical to believe that there were many similarities in the ideology and belief system of these two sections of the urban middle class, which perhaps led Richard Fox to describe them in a broad category of 'petite-bourgeoisie.'[28]

The most significant change in Punjab came as a result of the growth of education in the late nineteenth century. A number of schools and colleges were established in different parts of the province.[29] Lahore, the capital of Punjab, became a leading centre of education attracting students from all parts of north India. The Punjab University was established in 1882. The other premier institutions of higher education at Lahore were Government College, DAV College, Islamia College and Dyal Singh College which imparted education both in the humanities and sciences. Moreover, Medical College and Law College were set up for professional education. With the proliferation of schools and colleges in Punjab, particularly in Lahore, Sialkot, Gujranwala and Rawalpindi the number of literates in urban society significantly increased in the late nineteenth and early twentieth centuries. The establishment of the British colonial regime created opportunities for the newly educated sections in the form of government jobs and in other liberal professions. It is important to note that the urban Hindus who formed the largest of literates in Punjab gained ascendancy in jobs and professions.[30] On the other hand, only a small number of Muslims could find a place for themselves in these professions primarily because of a slow rate of growth of education among them and their primary engagement with agricultural activity.[31] Besides, the number of educated Sikhs, belonging to the Khatri and Arora castes also remained limited in these professions.

III

It is well known that the middle classes particularly residing in the presidency towns began to assert themselves in the social and political life towards the last quarter of the nineteenth century.[32] In Punjab, this section of society, though comparatively small in number, first took a deep interest in the religious reform / revivalist movements of the period.

It is important to understand how these sectarian communities constructed on the basis of religious identities started interacting with one another in the socio-political sphere in the last three decades of the nineteenth century. The colonial state adopted during this period a policy of extension of opportunities for participation in administration and transfer of initiative to a certain extent to Indians in the newly established municipalities and district boards. In such conditions a fervid sense of competition on matters relating to government jobs and seats in the municipalities among the middle and upper class Hindus, Muslims and Sikhs in Punjab, determined to a large extent the functioning of these sectarian communities and shaped their communitarian consciousness. The competition for wresting concessions in civil society heightened a sense of rivalry between the Hindus and Muslims to such an extent that it often created bitterness and hostility among them. This issue has been discussed in detail elsewhere.[33]

In view of the increasing competition in civil society, the different sectarian communities started consolidating themselves by setting up organizational networks, and expanding their propaganda activity. Among the Muslims, the pioneer organizations were *Anjuman-i-Islamia* and *Anjuman-Himayat-i-Islam.* These bodies and other similar local societies in different towns worked for the promotion of Islamic unity for a more self-conscious assertion among the Muslims as a sectarian community.[34] After the turn of the twentieth century, a prominent Muslim leader of Punjab, Fazl-i-Husain planned to form a provincial body of the Muslims which was called the 'Muslim League'.[35] A similar type of organization called the 'Muslim Association' was established under the leadership of Mian Mohammad Shafi, a political opponent of Fazl-i-Husain. Later, under the guidance of the All India Muslim League, both these bodies were merged into a single organization which began to function as the provincial Muslim League in Punjab.[36]

Among the Hindus, the Punjab Hindu Sabha was formed on 16 December 1906. It included prominent Hindus like Lala Lajpat Rai, Ruchi Ram Sahni, Harkishan Lal and Ram Bhaj Dutta Chaudhary.[37] The ideological differences between the Brahmo Samaj, Arya Samaj and Sanatan Dharma were papered over with comparative ease on account of the need for collective assertion of broad sections of Hindus with middle class aspirations as a consolidated sectarian community. An increasing shift of emphasis among various sectarian communities in Punjab from spiritual to economic, social and political issues took place around this period and the logic of this shift necessitated a broadening of numbers and a greater amount of consolidation and cohesiveness within them. Within the Sikhs, the Singh Sabhas were already working as communitarian organizations. These Sikh bodies took up religious, social and political issues concerning not only the Sikh middle class elements but also people belonging to other classes among the Sikhs. The major emphasis of the Singh Sabha movement in this phase was to posit all the Sikhs as a sectarian socio-religious community distinct from the Hindus.[38] Later in 1902, a central organization called Chief Khalsa Diwan was formed and all the Singh Sabhas were affiliated to it.

The majority of the people actively participating in these sectarian communitarian formations, however, belonged to the middle and upper classes. The communitarian organizations set up during the period were primarily concerned with issues considered by the middle class leadership as relevant to the 'interests' of the communities at the local and provincial levels. In view of the competitive politics of wresting concessions which defined the substance and scope of these community interests, the communitarian consciousness sometimes assumed, particularly between the Hindus and Muslims, an aggressively assertive and abrasive character verging on communal hatred and confrontation. Incidents of communal violence took place occasionally. However, it is essential to note here that the communal violence was not a pervasive phenomenon in Punjab during the pre-1919 period.[39]

In some recent writing, however, it has been argued that the national movement in Punjab was weak in this phase because the provincial leadership became more interested in issues which concerned the interests of their sectarian communities than the issues of larger national concern.[40] This observation is based on the assumption that communitarian consciousness is invariably and in all cases incompatible with a nationalist perspective which grows out of consistent and systematic anti-colonial struggle. In fact, the communitarian consciousness which had emerged in Punjab during the last three decades of the nineteenth century had a real potential for the evolution of a nationalist perspective which could manifest itself quite emphatically during certain stages and phases of its development. The relationship between communitarian assertions during the colonial period and the nationalist struggle is actually defined by the specific historical context. It is indeed true that Gandhi was the first national leader who consciously intended to achieve an effective linkage between communitarian loyalties in the political field with commitment to the larger collectivity of the nation that had gradually emerged in the course of a common confrontation of all sectarian communities with the colonial regime.[41] In Punjab the transformation of communitarian consciousness and its assuming a form where without ceasing to be communitarian, it could also acquire a nationalist perspective had already started taking place in the pre-Grandhian period.[42]

IV

During this period, the Punjab also witnessed the participation of the urban middle and lower middle classes in the nationalist activities. The first nationalist organization known as the Lahore India Association was established in Lahore on the advice of Surendra Nath Banerjee who visited this province in 1877.[43] It was, however, only after the formation of the Congress in 1885, and the subsequent setting up of its provincial and district branches that the social base of the national movement widened in the urban society of Punjab. However, the provincial and local leadership in the early phase was largely selected by the criteria of education and social status.[44] The growing popularity of the Congress was clearly revealed when for the first time the session of the Congress was held in Lahore in 1893, the pavilion having the capacity for seating 4,000 persons, remained filled with 'visitors' during all the days of the session.[45] In 1900, when the Congressmen assembled here again for the sixteenth session of this all India organization, a new building known as Bradlaugh Hall was constructed exclusively for holding the Congress meeting. Kali Rasanna Ray, Chairman, Reception Committee, mentioned with great admiration that the funds for constructing this building came primarily from the 'middle classes and masses'.[46] However, similar enthusiasm was not witnessed among the urban people in Punjab when the Congress session took place here in 1909. The number of Punjabi delegates who participated in this session was 76, whereas in 1893 their strength was 421.[47] This slackness on the part of the Punjabi urban people in nationalist activities was largely the result of the fear of repression which prevailed in Punjab following the decision by the government to punish Lajpat Rai and others for their participation in the agrarian movement of 1907.[48] At the same time, some Hindu middle class persons were seriously perturbed when the Muslims were assured of separate communal representation under the Morley-Minto reform scheme. A prominent Hindu leader Lal Chand even suggested the substitution of Hindu Sabhas for Congress Committees in Punjab.[49] For the next few years the popularity of the Congress was at a low ebb in this region, and the activities of the provincial Congress did not 'amount to anything more than annual gatherings in which a few interested in the movement participated.'[50]

The main thrust of Congress at the time was to build up an anti-Imperialist consciousness as a long term objective. But at the same time, the Congress took up issues like the larger representation of Indians in local and legislative bodies, and greater employment opportunities for them in government jobs. In other words, the immediate object of the Congress was to secure some concessions for the Indians in the existing politico-administrative structure. Thus, the Congress provided space to all those who, without giving up the anti-Imperialist framework believed in the politics of securing concessions as a short term objective. The primary aspect of the politics of the Congress was to pursue the nationalist goal of carrying on the united struggle against the colonial rule and to enlist support for this purpose from all sections belonging to different communities. That is why from its very inception the Congress maintained a broad character and carried within its fold active members and leaders who had also some time pronounced communitarian leanings.[51] The Congress, however, always took care to project itself as a secular organization, and the Muslims, in particular, were assured that by joining it their interests would be protected.[52] It is a fact that in Punjab the majority of its members came from the Hindu urban middle classes particularly to the Arya Sabha which took part in the cow slaughter riots of the 1880s and 90s. But an overall perspective of the Congress in Punjab remained secular permitting the unity of Hindus, Muslims and Sikhs in the nationalist movement without giving up the pursuit of sectional interest at local and provincial levels.

In other words, the domnant form of political consciousness in Punjab at this juncture was nationalist and communitarian at the same time. It is because of this reason that at the time of the Rowlatt Satyagraha in Amritsar, the Muslim League and the Congress were closely associated with each other. Saifuddin Kitchlew was office bearer of both local Congress committee and branch of the Muslim League in Amritsar.[53] Dr Satyapal, another activist of the Rowlatt Satyagraha had a close association with the local Hindu Sabha and the District Congress Committee at the same time. It does not, however, mean that the nationalist discourse outside the communitarian perspective did not exist at all. As a matter of fact, a section of people belonging to all communities had been taking part in the anti-imperialist movement without being in any way bound by the horizons of a communitarian perspective. In particular, the Ghadarites had forged a supra-communal identity, and their ideology remained secular. During the war period, the nationalist activities were curtailed for some time on account of the repressive policy followed by O'Dwyer. But in 1917, the ban on political activities was lifted at the insistence of Montagu, the Secretary of State. As a result, participation of people in the nationalist programme of the Congress again became possible. In Amritsar, a local Congress committee was founded in 1917. The growing anti-imperialist consciousness in both its secular and religious communitarian variants was evident from the fact that the Punjab Provincial Congress Committee extended an invitation to the Congress in 1918 to hold its session in Amritsar the following year. The resurgence of nationalist activities under the leadership of the following provincial Congress was noted with satisfaction by *The Tribune.* It wrote:[54]

> Happily the tide has now turned as it was bound to turn. During the last few months a considerable number of Congress Committees have come into existence, and judging . . . from the large contingent of delegates which the Punjab was able to send to the Congress, from the part which these delegates generally, and the more prominent among their leaders in particular took in the deliberations of the Congress, and above all from the readiness and the enthusiasm with which the Punjab has invited the next session of the national assembly this committee (provincial Congress) appears to have done valuable work.

In other words, there was a groundswell of national sentiments in Punjab, and this led to a massive participation of urban people in the Rowlatt Satyagraha in 1919. The economic hardships which the people in Punjab had suffered during the War also served to heighten their anti-colonial consciousness. The first major issue of common concern was the steep rise in the prices of essential commodities in this Province. For instance, there was 100 per cent price rise in the case of foodgrains between 1917 and 1919 but the wages of the artisans and workers increased only by 20–25 per cent.[55] It caused deep economic distress to the lower middle classes, artisans, workers and other fixed income groups living in the cities. Particularly in Amritsar, the artisans including large sections of Kashmiri Muslims and petty shopkeepers, who formed the poorer section of the urban society, were hit hard by the rise in prices.[56] The professional and commercial middle classes in Punjab also strongly resented war-time taxes, and in particular, the recent amendments made in the rules of Income Tax. Under the new rules, the tax collectors were empowered to conduct house to house survey which was perceived by the middle classes as 'a design on the part of the government to confiscate property'.[57] As a consequence of the new mode of assessment, the tax returns went up by 55 per cent in Amritsar city in 1918–19.[58] The trouble for a section of the merchant class was further aggravated because of the slump in piece goods trade. By this, the merchants in Amritsar which was the major centre of the piece goods trade in Punjab were seriously affected. Above all, Michael O'Dwyer as Lieutenant Governor of Punjab adopted a very hostile attitude towards the urban middle class. He disliked Harkishan Lal, who was a leading businessman and an active political leader in Punjab. In 1919, the commercial empire of Harkishan Lal suddenly collapsed because of his rivalry with some other businessmen. This financial crash also caused economic loss to a number of middle class persons who were associated in one way or the other with Harkishan Lal's business establishments. These adversely affected persons, according to Professor Ravinder Kumar, 'ascribed the crash solely to O'Dwyer's hostility towards them, and to his partiality to English financial interests.'[59] In other words, the trading classes in Punjab because of their economic discontentment developed a strong anti-imperialist consciousness which indeed influenced their decision to participate in the Rowlatt agitation.[60]

However, to explain the large scale participation of the urban people as a direct result of economic discontentment would not be correct. Similar economic hardships had been faced by the urban social classes earlier too, but they could not transcend the politics of wresting concessions at that time because of the absence of the vital factor of nationalist fervour. As a matter of fact, economic hardships served the cause of strengthening anti-colonial orientation which had been gaining strength in the people of Punjab. George Rude who made a study of popular uprisings in eighteenth and nineteenth century Europe, recognizes the relationship of economic discontent with the popular outbursts. He, however, rightly contends that the economic conditions did not automatically 'trigger' off a movement.[61] In a similar manner, Sumit Sarkar while recognizing the importance of economic structures and junctures, argues that growing miseries did not mechanically lead to any popular action in late colonial India. A real link between the social, economic and political factors and an 'event' has to be sought in the formation of 'collective mentalities' (what George Lefebvre has called 'collective frame of mind') at the popular level.[62] Therefore, it is important to underline the primary significance of the crucial shifts which had been taking place in the mentalities of the urban people in Punjab during this period.

V

In 1917, the Government of India had appointed a committee headed by Justice Sydney Rowlatt to investigate 'revolutionary crime' in the country and make recommendations for its suppression. The Rowlatt Committee proposed a series of changes in the machinery of law to enable the British government to deal effectively with 'seditious' activities. On the basis of these recommendations, the Government of India drafted two bills and presented them in the Imperial Legislative Council on 6 February 1919. Despite opposition by all Indian members, the Government of India, hurriedly passed only the first bill on 18 March 1919. It was named the Anarchical and Revolutionary Crime Act. The new legislation intended to make war time restrictions permanent. It provided the trial of offenders by three high court judges *in camera* with no jury or right to appeal. Further the Act gave the authority to the government to arrest or search any Indian without warrant or confine suspects without trial for renewable periods of upto a year.

Immediately, after the introduction of the Rowlatt Bills in the Council, the people in different parts of the subcontinent made a strong protest against it by organizing local meetings and writings in the press. However, it was only under the leadership of Mahatma Gandhi that this protest against the Rowlatt legislation soon turned into a major struggle against the colonial state. Gandhi saw the new legislation as a national 'wrong' and opposed it on the ground that the government was taking away from the people their 'God-given rights'.[63] In other words, Gandhi challenged on moral grounds the Government's attempt to impose checks on the civil liberties of the Indian people. In this manner, he intended to seek support of all sections of the people irrespective of caste, class and religion. Gandhi formed a Satyagraha Sabha in Ahmedabad and its members were asked to sign the pledge that they would refuse 'civilly to obey' the Rowlatt legislation.[64] More Satyagraha Sabhas were established in a number of prominent cities, and these Sabhas carried an active campaign against the Rowlatt legislation by publishing and distributing literature against it. Gandhi himself travelled to Delhi, Allahabad, Lucknow and some southern towns to mobilize public opinion. On 26 March, Gandhi decided to broaden the movement of protest by calling upon his countrymen to observe a day of *hartal* against the Rowlatt Act. The *hartal* was fixed for 30 March, but later it was postponed to 6 April.

In Punjab, the protest against the Rowlatt legislation began much before Gandhi had formally decided to launch an agitation. Both the English and vernacular press in the province published many articles and editorials criticizing the Rowlatt bills and appealed to the government to withdraw then. But more important was the large number of public meetings which were held in many towns of Punjab against the bills. The first protest meeting was organized in early February in Lahore.[65] Another largely attended meeting took plac at Bandemataram Hall in Amritsar on 5 February. *The Tribune* reported: 'The hall was packed with people of all classes and a large number had to stand outside.'[66] Similar meetings were held at Ludhiana, Sialkot, Rawalpindi and in other towns in the middle of February.[67] In Lahore, Fazl-i-Husain presided over a 'huge public meeting of the citizens' organized at Bradlaugh Hall on 9 March 1919. But when he attempted to restrain another speaker, Habib Shah from making a provocative speech, he was 'barracked' by the people present at the meeting.[68] About this massive enthusiasm, and the anti-imperialist consciousness which was witnessed at these public gatherings, a CID report mentions:[69]

> It appears that these meetings (of protest) were attended by upwards of 30,000 persons and caused much enthusiasm. There was general closing of shops and many persons were seen wearing black ribbons. Some who were asked the reason replied, '*Badshaha mar gaya*' (The King has died). Shopkeepers were heard expressing their approval of the speeches. . . .

The meetings were generally addressed by provincial and local leaders which included Saifuddin Kitchlew, Satyapal, Rambhaj Dutt, Pir Tijuddin, Sardul Singh Cavsheer, etc. In their lectures, the leaders criticized the Rowlatt legislation, and the resolutions were passed against it within the broad framework of the anti-imperialist struggle. Another significant feature of these meetings was the emphasis on communal unity. The slogans like 'Hindu-Muslim ki Jai' were raised several times at these gatherings. This indeed was an expression of communitarian-nationalist perspective which had gained much strength in Punjab by this time. Thus, it is quite evident that the masses in Punjab towns were fully prepared for a struggle against the government before Gandhi gave the call for *hartal.*

Mahatma Gandhi could not visit Punjab before or during the Rowlatt agitation. The activities of the Satyagraha Sabha too were limited in this province as not more than a dozen people signed the Satyagraha pledge. Moreover, there were not many Home Rule leaguers who could provide the cadre to Gandhi's movement in Punjab as they did in Gujarat and Bombay.[70] Above all, Gandhi enjoyed very 'little power in Indian politics when he issued the call for hartal on 6 April 1919.[71] Yet, as is well known, Gandhi's appeal evoked a massive response from the urban people in Amritsar and in other cities of Punjab. What actually proved decisive was the popular perception of Gandhi's charisma and strength. By this time he already carried an image of a 'saviour' or 'Messiah' for the common masses which indeed deeply influenced the movement led by him. Sumit Sarkar has rightly observed: '. . . varied sections of the Indian people seem to have fashioned their own images of Gandhi, particularly in the earlier days when he was still to most people a distant, vaguely glimpsed or heard-of tale of a holy man with miracle-working powers'.[72] This deified image of Gandhi had already captured the popular imagination in Punjab before the commencement of the Rowlatt agitation. There was a repeated raising of the slogan 'Gandhi ki Jai' both by the speakers and the audience at the public gatherings organized against the Rowlatt legislation. At times, Gandhi's portrait headed the processions which were organized against the government.[73] In the local press and meetings, Gandhi was usually described in religious terms like 'Rishi and Wali' and was often compared 'to the coming of Christ to the coming of Muhammad and to the coming of Krishna'.[74] At one of the meetings, Maulivi Ghulam Mohy-ud-Din remarked that Gandhi was ready to take the 'sufferings and afflictions of the enemy (government) on his own head'.[75] Further it was believed that Gandhi's inifinite reserves of spiritual strength would eventually 'break the power of the bureaucracy' and his new device of Satyagraha would ultimately 'relieve the people of the burden with which they were threatened'.[76] They were convinced that Gandhi being their leader, there was no need to fear the colonial state. In other words, Gandhi's deified image and the popular perception of his charisma proved very effective in breaking the hegemony of the colonial state and exposing its lack of legtimacy.

An important aspect of the agitation was the meaning given to the Rowlatt legislation. The government always maintained that the new legislation was a temporary measure which aimed at preventing seditious crimes. Moreover, in order to remove the fears of the common people, it emphasized that this legislation was primarily directed against political activists, and was not going to affect the ordinary citizens in any manner.[77] Nevertheless, the press and political leadership in Punjab very emphatically pronounced it as a coercive and undermocratic measure which would deprive the people of their civil liberties and was utterly inconsistent with the spirit of Montagu's declaration of August 1917.[78] In other words, like many other liberals in the country, the educated middle class leadership in Punjab believed that the Rowlatt legislation would, above all, violate their basic civil rights. While speaking at public meetings, the leaders often expressed their meaning of the Rowlatt legislatiion in metaphorical language, or recited poems to bring home to the people its unusually draconian character which according to them, would make the life of the common people miserable. It was natural for the common people to detest the government's attempt to strengthen the hands of the police 'considering its notoriety everywhere as petty oppressors.'[79] But important was the apprehension which the people began to develop that the Rowlatt legislation was going to impose restrictions of a serious nature in their daily lives. It was, for instance, anounced that four perons would not be allowed to assemble at a social gathering; tax would be levied on every marriage; marriages and funerals would be held under the control of police, income tax would be arbitrarily raised, etc.[80]

In the official accounts, the popular meanings of the Rowlatt legislation were proclaimed as baseless 'rumours' which had no substance in them. But the masses had come to think of these 'rumours' as a true account of the real character of the Rowlatt legislation. In fact, the verbal exchanges which took place at bazaars and social gatherings played an important role in the construction of popular understanding concerning the legislation. Recently Ranjit Guha in his study of peasant insurgency has argued that 'rumour' is not to be dismissed as 'lies of bazaar' but needs to be understood as a social phenomenon. In a predominantly illiterate society, rumour represents 'non-graphic signals of communication among the subaltern people'. According to Guha, verbal exchange taking place in the market and other places concerning issues in the period of social tension 'constitute transitive function of rumour'. And in this manner rumour 'comes to affirm its own identity as a type of popular discourse'.[81] Further, it is contended that rumour helps to bring people together, 'because the communication of a report to other members of the group implies an underlying bond of unity.'[82] In other words, it contributes in evoking a 'comradeship response' among the masses against those who oppress them. Thus, it can be concluded that the rumours prevalent in this period actually constituted a type of popular discourse relating to the Rowlatt legislation. The spread of rumours among the lower sections of society including artisans and shopkeepers helped to create a 'bond of community' against the colonial rule.

The agitation against the Rowlatt legislation in Punjab took a major turn when the people observed a *hartal* in large numbers on 30 March and 6 April. On both days, the *hartal* passed off peacefully and according to the Hunter Report, 'Europeans could and did walk unmolested among the crowd'.[83] On 9 April, the Punjab Government took the decision of deporting two popular leaders of Punjab, Saifuddin Kitchlew and Satyapal. They were earlier prohibited to make speeches in public or to issue any statement to the press. On 10 April, these two leaders were deported to Dharmshala with a police escort. The people in Amritsar were agitated when they came to know about this, and also of the arrest of Gandhi on the previous day at Palwal railway station. Immediately shops were closed and people started moving in large numbers towards Civil Lines, to signify their mass protest in a most peaceful manner against the deportation of their local leaders. They did not attack government property nor did they molest any European whom they happened to see on their way to Civil Lines where the Europeans chiefly resided. However, the ordinary people not being fully attuned to the logic of peaceful mass agitation could easily lose their patience at the sight of an array of troops seeing in them flaunted symbols of the repressive colonial regime.[84] When they were prevented by the police at two of the bridges separating the Civil Lines from the city, they started stoning the troops. Some middle class persons present on the occasion tried to pacify the masses but before their initiative could produce the desired effect, the troops resorted to firing. According to the Hunter Report, the total number of persons killed was ten and those wounded larger. The people in retaliation attacked the government property which included banks, telegraph office, post office and railway station. A few Europeans were also killed. The most serious case was an assault on Miss Sherwood, Manager of the City Missionary School. The people who took part in the agitation were from the lower classes of the city. According to an official report, they included the Kashmiri Muslims, and the Khatri and Arora Hindus of the poorer classes. Their participation, however, was not controlled from above because of the absence of any recognized leader who could supervise their activities or dictate the programme of action to them. In such conditions, the masses selected their own course of action which was not necessarily in accordance with the programme of Satyagraha given by the nationalist leadership. For instance, according to an official evidence, the masses while looting offices and banks raised shouts of 'Gandhi ki Jai' and 'Maro luto' (kill and loot).[85] It is interesting to note that the participants did not find anything abnormal in expressing a desire to kill the Europeans and hailing Gandhi as a triumphant leader at the same time! It was this characteristic of mass upsurge that led the subaltern historiography to observe that the Rowlatt Satyagraha was one of the 'instances of popular initiative asserting itself in the course of nationalist campaigns in defiance or absence of elite control'.[86]

The British officials in their evidence before the Hunter Committee have used the words 'mob' or 'crowd' for the participants. In some of the CID reports, these individuals have been described as 'hooligans'. The officials and the Hunter Report intended to convey the impression that the participants were 'passive' instruments of outside agents – opportunistic leaders – and were being prompted by motives of loot or merely the need to satisfy some lurking criminal instincts. George Rude has rightly rejected this type of meaning ascribed to the crowd who participate in an agitation or a riot. According to him, the crowd is not a 'disembodied abstraction' but 'an aggregate of men and women of flesh and blood'.[87] The defining characteristic of their behaviour should be social rather than psychological. Rude believes that the crowd in agitations in pre-industrial society constituted lower classes or 'menu people' led by some persons as leaders. They were 'fired as much by memories of customary rights or a nostalgia for past utopias as by present grievances or hopes of material improvement'.[88] The people who participated in the Rowlatt agitation in Amritsar have also to be recognized in these concrete terms. They included persons from lower sections of society such as petty traders, artisans and workers all of whom had scarred memories of humiliations and wrongs suffered at the hands of the new dispensation which had emerged with the British rule. Only a small number of middle class leaders were present among them. Their activities were not determined by any instinct of hooliganism. In fact, they were motivated by a strong anti-imperialist consciousness. Before 10 April, we do not witness any incident where the property was destroyed or any European assaulted. It was only after the killing of some of their compatriots by the troops on 10 April that the participants began to see every Britisher as an 'oppressor' and the government offices and buildings assumed for them the character of the 'oppressive' colonial state. Miss Sherwood was assaulted in this mood of provocation simply because she happened to be an English woman. While assaulting her, some persons shouted 'Maro Angrej' (A Britisher, kill her).[89] Similarly, when the banks were attacked in Amritsar, they said 'Sarkari mal hai, loot lo' (It is a government property, take it away).[90] These incidents by no means reflect endemic motives of loot or criminal instances. Instead, the actions were motivated by growing hatred for the British rule and the strengthening of anti-Imperialist consciousness[91] – a consciousness, however, which was still in the form of a raw and aching wound, and carried an element of rashness and desperation.

The killing of Europeans and destruction of official property on 10 April was viewed by the masses as their victory over the government. According to Miles Irving, the Deputy Commissioner of Amritsar, 'the people . . . thought for some reason or the other that the arm of the government was paralysed. The inaction of the police when the National Bank was burned lent some colour to the belief . . . that government could do nothing. . . .'[92] In the old Amritsar city, except the Kotwali, the government had practically lost its control. Later Irving conceded this fact and informed the Hunter Committee: 'It was freely said that it might be the Raj of Sarkar outside, but inside the city it was *Hindu-Musalman ki Hakumat*'. (It means that the government might be governing outside, the local Soviet were ruling within).[93] In a similar vein, the people in the city often said that 'now government is ours' (*Hon sada raj ho gaya*).[94] All this made the British government believe that it had lost its hegemonic authority over the urban masses in the city. This erosion of ideological hegemony of the colonial rule was perceived by the British officials as 'dangerous' and, therefore, they began to describe the Rowlatt agitation as a 'rebellion' against the state. In such a situation, the primary issue for the government was to restore 'order', and also to ensure safety of Europeans residing in Amritsar. It was with this purpose that General Dyer along with a big contingent of soldiers was sent to the city on 11 April. He took over the control from the civil authorities and along with his soldiers marched around the city. A proclamation was made that all meetings and gatherings were hereby prohibited, and were to be dispersed under military law. But the urban masses were now hardly overawed by the repressive machinery of the colonial state. On the contrary, their morale was further boosted when from the neighbouring towns of Kasur and Lahore, news trickled in informing them that mass agitations in these cities too had seriously undermined the authority of the colonial state. In such conditions the attitude of the masses became all the more 'defiant'. This overconfidence in their own strength and under valuation of the power of the repressive regime is a natural consequence of the sense of liberation experienced by an oppressed mass at the initial stage of breach of the hegemonic control of such a regime. Both the strength and weakness of the national movement at this initial stage of acquiring a mass character are visible in the conduct of the protesters at Amritsar during the crucial days immediately before the Jallianwala Bagh massacre. They even believed that the threat given by Dyer of dispersing the public gatherings by use of military force was merely a 'bluff'.[95] Therefore, some local leaders decided to hold a public meeting on 13 April at Jallianwala Bagh defying the prohibitory orders. The urban masses responded with enthusiasm, and about 20,000 persons collected in active defiance of the proclamation, taking a deliberate risk. The naivety of this popular upsurge can, however, be gauged from the fact that no serious thought was given to the need for taking precautionary measures against some possible repressive action by the British regime in that mood of euphoria and breezy confidence. The majority of those who came to the meeting were imbued with deep anti-imperialist consciousness.[96] They did not bother when Dyer entered the Bagh, and proceedings of the meeting continued. Even when soldiers started firing many people did not pay any attention believing that bullets were blank (*Phukian, Phukian*).[97] The die was cast, and within minutes hundreds of persons were found lying on the ground, killed or wounded.

General Dyer's role and the policy of the British government have been discussed in a number of writings. However, it is necessary to briefly mention two points. First, the challenge to the colonial state in Amritsar, Lahore and other cities since early April had eroded its hegemonic authority in Punjab. It was because of this reason that the meeting held at Jallianwala Bagh was described by the Secretary of the Government of India as 'direct defiance and challenge to its authority'.[98] But the more important issue in the British attitude towards Indians was the syndrome of 'repression.' In fact, the dangerous potential that the Satyagraha form of agitation had for he British Raj, impelled the dominant section of the British officials to adopt the policy of ruthless repression as the only viable response to the situation. Dyer's action at the

Jallianwala Bagh was to some extent in consonance with the existing framework of imperial control in Punjab. As stated above, this system of administration embodied not only the paternalistic approach, but also the application of force, if necessary, against those elements who dared to undermine the hegemony of the colonial rule. In the past the Punjab government had once blown over a large number of Kukas by guns for their involvement in anti-government activities. In other words, application of force (i.e. repression) against the 'rebels' was considered justified for the restoration of 'order' and 'peace' in the province. That is why a large number of Britishers in Punjab and the official press approved Dyer's use of military force on civilians, since, according to them, it restored 'order and normalcy' in the province. It may be mentioned here that after the Revolt of 1857, the notion of 'repression' as an effective preventive measure became a prominent feature of the thinking of British officials. The spectre of 1857 haunted the British officials so much that they feared that there might be cases of assaults on the British living in India and attack on government property suddenly and unpredictable at any moment of time. On account of this fear, the British officials in Amritsar on 10 April shifted their families to a safer place. The Revolt of 1857 was remembered by the British ruling classes for the use of excessive force as the only effective measure in situations of such a revolt. If the revolt of 1857 was suppressed with brutal force, there was a rationale for adopting the same in any situation of a feared uprising. This compulsive logic of resorting to repression to deal with what was perceived as mass uprising was not recorded as a part of the policy followed in India. However, this 'unrecorded' way of dealing with crisis continued to form a major part of the thinking of officials working in India till the second decade of the twentieth century. This offers a better explanation of the brutal use of force made by Dyer at Jallianwala Bagh than all references to Dyer's abnormal psychology which loom large in the liberal versions of the colonialist apologia for what happened at Jallianwala Bagh on 13 April 1919.

It is also important to understand the nature of communal unity which was established during this agitation in Punjab. As already stated, in all public meetings held against the Rowlatt legislation in Punjab, the leaders emphasized the necessity of maintaining communal harmony. The people responded to their appeals enthusiastically and fraternal amity and solidarity was demonstrated by repeated raising of slogans, particularly about the Hindu-Muslim unity. The incident of Ram Navmi day of 9 April in Amritsar is well-known when a sizeable number of Muslims participated in it as a national festival and fraternized with Hindus. Both the Hindus and Muslims expressed unity between the two communities by sharing the same water vessels. Mahatma Gandhi recorded with deep satisfaction in his autobiography that the 'Hindus and Musalmans seemed united as one man'.[99] In a similar vein, the Congress Punjab Inquiry Committee appointed to look into atrocities committed in Punjab, praised the fraternization between the communities during the course of the agitation. Later, Swami Shradhanand, described the unity of Hindus and Muslims witnessed on Ram Navmi day as a 'veritable confluence of Ganga and Yamuna'.[100] There was, of course, an element of romanticization of the manifestation of communal unity in the accounts given by the Congressmen, but as a social phenomenon it was an inevitable consequence of the communitarian nationalist perspective which as stated above had gained ascendancy at this point of time in Punjab.

The British government tried to give an entirely different view of Hindu-Muslim fraternity and belittled its significance. The Hunter Committee reported that this was purely a temporary phenomenon and the efforts towards unity had been made largely indeed in 'political interest', that is to oppose the British government and had no lasting significance, being a purely expedient move. This observation fully echoed the views expressed by a number of officials, including Michael O'Dwyer in their evidence before the Hunter Committee. The perception of British officials regarding Hindu-Muslim relations was influenced by two factors. First, the British in India always accepted the Orientalists' views about Indian society according to which the Hindus and Muslims were both monolithic communities fundamentally opposed to each other in their social as well as religious life. The Hindus and Muslims have, accordingly, been described in the Hunter Report as 'warring creeds'.[101] Michael O'Dwyer makes an identical observation regarding Hindu-Muslim relations. It was because of such assumption that the display of unity on Ram Navmi day was not seen as a sign of real communal harmony between the people of two communities under the impact of a growing nationalist sentiment. The uprising of 1857 was a potent factor in shaping the attitude of the British officials towards this phenomenon of Hindu-Muslims unity. As mentioned earlier, this uprising loomed large in their minds at the time of the Rowlatt agitation. They held the view that despite fundamental differences between the people of two communities they had formed 'a political alliance' or temporarily joined hands in 1857 to fight against the government. Therefore, the unity of Hindus and Muslims at this juncture was also perceived in similar terms as an expedient measure in a moment of dire political need. In their evidence before the Hunter Committee, Michael O'Dwyer and the Punjab government, made a special reference to this issue of Hindu-Muslim unity in order to convey that like 1857, the Hindus and Muslims had joined hands merely for the purpose of political agitation or for organizing 'rebellion'.[102]

The upper class leadership in each community which had not gone through the experience of communitarian-nationalist consciousness was also of the view that the communal unity manifested during the agitation was not real and was a politically motivated expedient measure to oppose the government. Raja Narendra Nath, a leader of the Punjab Hindu Sabha, described this manifestation of unity as 'superficial'.[103] Mian Mohammed Shafi and Malik Umar Hayat Khan Tiwana contended that this unity was a temporary phenomenon because there were permanent differences between the people of the two communities. Since these upper class leaders did not share the communitarian nationalist perspective, they were not prepared to accept that the Hindus and Muslims would genuinely join hands in the nationalist struggle when its anti-imperialist character gained a sharper edge and became visibly consistent. They shared the official perspective of the colonial regime because it converged with their own nature of politics based on wresting concessions and gains from the colonial state by putting special stress on the distinct position of their community as fundamentally opposed to the other communities. It is the perspective of this leadership in different communities which eventually led to the growth of communalism in the country and befuddling of the nationalist perspective of a united struggle against British colonial rule over India.

VI

The Jallianwala Bagh tragedy, as mentioned above, was made an icon in the nationalist discourse in the subsequent phase of the anti-colonial struggle. This was a legitimate use of this exceptional moment of mass protest against the British regime and liberation from its hegemonic stranglehold. Immediately after the incident when the Congress decided to constitute a Jallianwala Bagh memorial the people responded with zeal, and in a short span Rs 776,780 was collected for this purpose.[104] In other words, the incident came to symbolize that supreme sacrifice made by the people for the cause of India's liberation. Moreover, the potency of Jallianwala Bagh as an icon can be gauged from the fact that it could be invoked with great effect time and again during the course of Gandhian movements to arouse the sentiments of the Indian masses and at the same time to expose and denounce the foreign rule. For instance, in Andhra Pradesh in the days of the Non-Cooperation Movement (1920–22) this episode was used in several dramas, nationalist songs, novels and other forms of popular arts to 'demonize the British and undermine the moral and civilizational claims of the colonial masters'.[105] But there was also an inherent weakness in this iconic invocation of an incident which was of crucial significance in understanding the process of growth of the nationalist struggle against the British regime. Such an invocation became an obstacle in going deeper into the meaning of the Jallianwala Bagh incident and analysing its basic attributes as a social phenomenon.

Before highlighting the basic features of the social phenomenon which led to the Jallianwala Bagh protest meeting and the massacre, it may be necessary to see how the incident was perceived at the popular level throughout the subcontinent. The question is enormously difficult since it implies the discerning of sentiments of non-literates who formed the majority of Indian people at that time. However, it can be said that the tragedy registered in popular consciousness as an example of brute suppression by the colonial state. Further, it was viewed that Gandhi as Mahatma (a deified image) could alone protect them from such a repressive state. In other words, it was the experience as well as the fear of suppression which not only established a bond of unity but also led the common people to identify themselves with the anti-colonial struggle spearheaded under the leadership of Gandhi. This is how after the Jallianwala Bagh tragedy the elite and popular anti-colonial consciousness converged in India.[106] This is an important after effect of the Jallianwala tragedy, the logic of which was already inherent in the initiative Gandhi had taken to give mass character to the national movement by involving the lower middle class groups as well as rural peasantry and the workers.

As mentioned at the beginning, Gandhi was deeply hurt by the killings of innocent people by General Dyer. But he was also critical of the incidents of violence in which Indians took part. Gandhi's remonstrance was natural, eruption of such incidents in the wake of the Rowlatt agitation being contrary to his creed of non-violence. He was even compelled to do some introspection about his decision of launching the civil disobedience movement and came to the conclusion that it was a 'mistake which seemed to be of Himalayan magnitude'.[107] The extent of his anguish can be gauged from his statement disowning this turn of events completely and declaring that the 'recent events in Punjab are unconnected with the Satyagraha movement'.[108] This attitude of Gandhi raises an important issue. It reveals that his Satyagraha as a mode of political assertion was different in character from the mass protest which was being witnessed in Punjab. Gandhi's Satyagraha, both in theory and practice, has been exhaustively examined by scholars and does not require any detailed discussion here. However, it is necessary to record briefly what Gandhi himself said about Satyagraha in order to highlight an important feature which is pertinent to the point at issue. According to him as a mode of political action, it does not merely involve eschewing of violence but is also based on the assumption that any show of force or any undue pressure is 'unethical' and against 'the fundamental laws of society.'[109] This emphasis on the moral aspect of non-violence was an essential part of the long-term strategy Gandhi had evolved to build up resistance against colonial rule. An overview of Gandhi's programme and strategy reveals that his primary object was to gradually weaken the legitimacy of the British rule, and to erode the hegemonic dominance of imperial authority over the minds of the Indian people.[110] This objective, he felt, could be achieved only if a sustained non-violent mass struggle with an unflinching moral rectitude was carried on against the colonial regime. If an attitude of violent confrontation was adopted against the government, the latter would get an opportunity to ruthlessly suppress the movement through its military and police apparatus, and this could cause a grave setback to the aim of building up popular resistance on the basis of breaking the hackles of fear from the minds of the common people and weakening the ideological conditioning which commanded obedience from them. As the situation in Punjab seemed to him leading to such a breaking point, he started pleading that the restoration of peace and order was the most urgent necessity at that juncture.

The Punjab government after the massacre in Amritsar had already imposed Martial Law in the province. Numerous cruelties were inflicted upon the inhabitants of the towns in which the Rowlatt agitation was being actively carried on. The imposition of Martial Law was justified by Michael O'Dwyer, the then Lieutenant Governor of Punjab, on the ground that it was required to control the 'turbulent' people and to bring back normalcy in the region.[111] Actually the government through its coercive and intimidating tactics, intended to reassert its dominant-hegemonic authority which had been undermined considerably during the Rowlatt agitation. Surprisingly, Gandhi despite his strong sympathies with the people of Punjab as victims of excesses inflicted upon them by the British, expressed his desire to support the colonial state in restoring peace and order in the province. He stated that his Satyagraha 'now consists in ceaselessly helping the authorities to restore order and curb lawlessness.'[112] Gandhi's willingness at this point to support the government for restoring 'order' or curb lawlessness, should not, however, be seen as a major shift in his attitude towards the colonial state. His main purpose was to prevent further escalation of violence for the reason mentioned above. He considered such as check on violence and lawlessness essential on moral as well as political-grounds. Despite an apparent similarity between Gandhi's position at this particular juncture and the proclaimed policy of the government, it is important to remember that the aims and purposes in the two cases were entirely different. It would be wrong to draw the conclusion that Gandhi had temporarily lapsed into the role of collaborating with the government on the issue of restoring peace in the province. This difference in meanings attributed to peace and perceptions regarding restoring order came out quite clearly when at a later stage Gandhi condemned the imposition of Martial Law which by then had become a nakedly brutal measure of committing atrocities on the people of the province by the British regime.

What happened at Jallianwala Bagh and in other towns of Punjab sharply revealed an important facet of the mass resistance which emerged as a part of the national movement under Gandhi's leadership at that particular stage. The common masses who participated in the movement did not strictly adhere to Gandhi's principle of Satyagraha, because their idea of opposing the British regime did not often tally with Gandhi's perspective. It is evident from the above study that once the fear of mighty British rule was removed from the minds of the people through the influence of Gandhi's idea of offering resistance to the arbitrary authority of the colonial regime, they quickly experienced a sense of liberation and were filled with a confidence which impelled them to underestimate the power of the regime. This produced in them a strong desire to take on its might and overthrow it with one strong push. This overconfidence and impatience made them transgress the limits of the Gandhian idea of resistance, and they did not hesitate to resort to violent means in retaliation against the oppression being carried on by the colonial state. Gandhi's Satyagraha Sabhas, which were constituted especially to organize the Rowlatt agitation, and the Congress as a body, were not organizationally strong enough to provide effective leadership and carry on the movement strictly in accordance with Gandhi's aims and objectives. In such a situation, the masses were left to select their own course of action according to their spontaneous perceptions and understanding of the prevailing conditions. They often became 'turbulent' in the sense that they worked under the psychology not merely of exposing the arbitrariness of the authority of the British regime but of immediately overthrowing it.

This divergence between Gandhi's perspective and the mindset which often governed the mass upsurge conveyed the message to him that in the absence of an adequate organizational network which could control and provide direction to the people from above, it would not be possible to carry a sustained anti-imperialist struggle in accordance with his perspective of non-violent Satyagraha. Later on, when Gandhi launched the Non-Cooperation Movement in 1920, he decided to make use of the Congress orgnization in an effective manner, and it was mainly for this purpose that the constitution of this all-India body was amended in 1920. A large number of local branches of the Congress were formed which became instruments of control from above for the nationalist leadership. They were now able to maintain strong linkages in a vertical manner to the lowest level of society in the villages. The new set-up of the Congress proved immensely useful not only in bringing large sections of the Indian masses to the fold of the anti-imperialist struggle, but also in providing a network to control and guide their activities in accordance with the programme laid down at the national level. Gandhi's emphasis on a constructive programme for reforms in society which emerged in a concrete form in the 1920s also slowly built up an extensive network of supporters at the grassroots level in different parts of the country. They became carriers of his perspective of non-violent Satyagraha whenever a mass action of resistance against the British regime was launched later.

This change at the organizational level and inclusion of constructive activity during the periods when no mass action of Satyagraha was being undertaken served to remove another weakness which became apparent during the Rowlatt agitation and the Jallianwala Bagh type of mobilizations. Despite large scale participation in urban areas, this movement remained limited to Delhi, Bombay, and some parts of Gujarat and Punjab. The movement was not sufficiently widespread and many parts of the subcontinent remained untouched. In such conditions the British government was required to deal with the agitators only at a few centres where the political activities were at a high pitch. The experience of Amritsar brought a clear massage that the government was able to use brute force primarily because it did not have to face simultaneously a similar situation all over the country. This made Gandhi realize that in order to be a real challenge, the anti-imperialist movement needed to be spread out throughout the country. Only when the mass upsurge is not limited to a few pockets, it would become difficult for the government to resort to repressive tactics adopted at Jallianwala Bagh.

It is an indisputable fact that Gandhi's charismatic leadership proved decisive in making the Rowlatt Satyagraha a popular upsurge against the colonial rule. But his mode of mobilizing the masses was at that stage largely emotive in character. It certainly produced results as large sections of people responded enthusiastically to his appeal. But this enthusiasm could neither gain sufficient momentum nor be sustained for long unless it was linked as it happened in Punjab with deep seated anti-imperialist consciousness which had grown out of the difficulties faced by the common people in their day-to-day material life. The disenchantment of different social classes and groups against the government had finally coalesced here with the sentiments aroused by the Rowlatt agitation. This provided a real strength to the movement launched by Gandhi. The strong character of the Rowlatt Satyagraha witnessed in Punjab was, in other words, the result of emotive appeal made by Gandhi combining with the strong resentment which existed among the people on account of issues related to their social and economic life. This feature of the Rowlatt Satyagraha in Punjab was not a product of a deliberate plan but an accidental coalescence of national fervour with the material interests of the people. After 1919, however,

Gandhi and the Congress made some efforts to create such a linkage between the anti-imperialist sentiment based on the issues of national dignity and specific material interests of different groups of society. The constructive programme adopted by Gandhi proved to be an initial step in this direction. But this linkage, as it was visualized and effected, did not prove to be adequately strong.

NOTES AND REFERENCES

(This is a revised and enlarged version of the Presidential Address (Modern section) delivered at the Punjab History Conference, Patiala in March 1995. I am grateful to Professor O.P. Grewal who read the earlier draft of this paper. His critical comments modified many of my ideas and helped me in building the analytical framework. For the shortcomings, I am alone responsible.)

1. Derek Sayer, 'British Reactions to the Amritsar Massacre, 1919–30' in *Past and Present*, Winter, 131, May 1991, pp. 130–64. Also see, *The Congress Punjab Enquiry, 1919–20* (Bombay, 1920), reprinted as *Punjab Disturbances 1919–20*, Vol. II (Delhi, 1978), pp. 54–56.
2. *Disorder Inquiry Committee, 1919–20, Report* (Calcutta, 1920), reprinted as *Punjab Disturbances 1919–20*, Vol. II (Delhi, 1978), p. 47.
3. V.N. Datta, *Jallianwala Bagh* (Ludhiana, 1969), pp. 104–5.
4. Quoted in Derek Sayer *op. cit.* However, it is necessary to mention that the firing at Amritsar also received widespread support throughout the services. In England, General Dyer's role was acclaimed in the House of Lords, and a special fund of £ 26,000 was raised for him.
5. Quoted in V.N. Datta, 'Perceptions of the Massacre', unpublished paper presented at the ICHR Seminar on 'Jallianwala Bagh Tragedy and its Impact on the Indian National Movement' held in New Delhi, 14-16 April 1994.
9. V.N. Datta, Jallianwala Bagh.
10. Ian Talbot, *Punjab and the Raj* (New Delhi, 1988), p. 43. However, it is important to note here that the peasants' decision to join the army was largely influenced by the socio-economic factors. The salaries which they received as soldiers substantially augmented their meagre financial income coming from agriculture. Moreover, they expected to get some land in the fertile region of canal colonies because the government in the 1890s had decided to distribute land grants to the ex-soldiers. At the same time, military service provided to the lower caste persons was an opportunity for upward social mobility.
11. This aspect of British rule in Punjab is sharply revealed in the repressive policy followed by Michael O'Dwyer, Lieutenant Governor of Punjab against the Ghadar movement which was considered as a serious threat to the safety of the British empire in India during the First World War. Michael O'Dwyer, *op. cit.*, pp. 190–212.
12. Thomas R. Metcalf, *The New Cambridge History of India: Ideologies of the Raj* (New Delhi, 1995), p. 288.
13. Regarding this statue which was built in the 1880s, a British official noted: 'The pose has been not infelicitously described as that of a foreman haranguing a gang of coolies'. (File No. 53/1923 *Home Political*) cited in David Gilmartin, *Empire and Islam* (Delhi, 1989), p. 11.
14. Ian Talbot, *op. cit.*, p. 57.

15. See, Virinder Singh, *Dyarchy in Punjab* (New Delhi, 1991), ch. II.
16. For this view, see Prem Chaudhary, *Punjab Politics: The Role of Sir Chhotu Ram* (New Delhi, 1984).
17. In the late nineteenth century, the Hindus formed the majority of traders with 5,57,000 engaged in this occupation. The number of Sikh and Muslim traders was 73,000 and 30,000 respectively. S.S. Thornborn, *Musalmans and Moneylenders in the Punjab* (London, 1886), p. 36.
18. J.S. Grewal, 'Business Communities of Punjab' in *Business Communities in India*, edited by Dwijindra Tripathi (New Delhi, 1984, pp. 209–23).
19. H. Calvert, *The Wealth and Welfare of the Punjab* (Lahore, 1936), p. 134. See also Ian J. Kert, *Building the Railways of the Raj* (Delhi, 1995).
20. *Punjab Census Report*, 1921, pt. 1, p. 17.
21. H. Calvert, *op. cit.*, pp. 102–48.
22. At the beginning of the twentieth century, cotton piece goods worth Rs 423 lakhs were imported in Punjab, J.S. Grewal *op. cit.*, p. 218.
23. *Ibid.*
24. For the decline of the shawl industry in Amritsar, see V.N. Datta, *Amritsar, Past and Present* (Amritsar, 1967). p. 138.
25. D.C.J. Ibbetson, *Punjab Castes*, reprint (Patiala, 1970), p. 194.
26. Sumit Sarkar, *Modern India* (Delhi, 1983), p. 30.
27. Ravinder Kumar, *op. cit.*, p. 253.
28. Amiya K. Bagchi, *Private Investment in India* (London, 1976), p. 436. For industrial development in Punjab, also see H. Calvert, *op. cit.*, pp. 287–385; *Punjab Census Report*, pt. 1, 1921; A.C. Badenoch, *Punjab Industries* (Lahore, 1917).
29. Richard Fox, 'Urban Class and Communal Consciousness in Colonial Punjab: The Genesis of India's Intermediate Regime' in *Modern Asian Studies*, 18, 3 (1984), pp. 459–89.
30. See H.R. Mehta, *A History of the Growth and Development of Western Education in the Punjab, 1846–84* (Lahore, 1929).
31. Among the urban Hindus the increase of literacy was at a high rate. In 1819, they accounted for 89 per cent of the total literate in Punjab. Among the English knowing literates, the number of Punjabi Hindus was 82 per cent. This gave educated Hindus a special advantage over others in securing higher jobs for which knowledge of English had been made essential by the government. They held more than 80 per cent 'superior appointments' carrying a salary of Rs 75 or more per month.' Besides, the educated Hindus also dominated in professions like teaching, law, medicine, engineering and journalism. N.G. Barrier, Punjab Politics and the Disturbances of 1907' Ph.d. thesis, Duke University, 1966, pp. 16–17; Kenneth W. Jones, *op. cit.*, pp. 59–60.
32. N.G. Barrier, 'Punjab Politics and the Disturbances of 1907', p. 16; also see Peter Hardy, *The Muslims in British India* (Cambridge, 1972), pp. 92–93.
33. See Anil Seal, *The Emergence of Indian Nationalism: Competition and Collaboration in the Later Nineteenth Century* (Cambridge, 1968).
34. K.L. Tuteja and O.P. Grewal, 'Emergence of Hindu Communalism in Early Twentieth Century Punjab' in *Social Scientist*, 20, 7–8 July-August 1992, pp. 1–28. In the late nineteenth century, the Punjab administration decided to make reservation of government jobs, and seats in the municipal committees for the Muslims. This decision obviously hurt the interest of the Hindus middle classes in Punjab since they had earlier gained a position of dominance and wanted to retain it at all cost. For the next few years, this issue of competition for securing jobs and seats remained a major issue of discussion in the Punjab

press, and this served to consolidate an assertive and abrasive form of sectarian community consciousness among the Hindus.

35. K.L. Tuteja, 'Muslim Communitarian Consciousness in Punjab in the Late Nineteenth and Early Twentieth Centuries; unpublished paper, presented at the seminar organized by the Department of History, Punjab University, Chandigarh in January 1995.
36. Azim Husain, *Fazl-i-Husain, A Political Biography* (Bombay, 1946), p. 96.
37. *Ibid.*, p. 97.
38. *The Tribune*, 19 and 23 December 1906.
39. See Kahan Singh, *Ham Hindu Nahin* (Amritsar, 1899).
40. The Punjab witnessed aggravation of communal tension over the issue of cow slaughter in the 1880s and 90s. Later a prominent leader of the Arya Samaj, Lekh Ram was assassinated by a fanatic Muslim in 1897. But, it is important to note that no major incident of communal violence occurred in Punjab in the first two decades of the twentieth century. When in 1917 fierce communal riots broke out between the Hindus and Muslims over the issue of cow slaughter in some parts of U.P. and Bihar, no such incident of violence took place in Punjab. This fact was later brought to the notice of the Hunter Committee by the Punjab government. It reported: 'The relations between the two religions which have led to outbreaks such as those at Shahabad in Bihar or of Kartarpur have been less marked in the Punjab'. V.N. Datta (ed.) *New Light on the Punjab Disturbances*, vol. I (Shimla, 1975), p. 246.
41. Kenneth W. Jones, *op. cit.*, pp. 280–303; N.G. Barrier, 'The Arya Samaj and Congress Politics in Punjab, 1894–1904' in *Journal of Asian Studies*, 1, 26, (1966–67), pp. 365–77.
42. Ravinder Kumar contends that Gandhi clearly understood that Indian society was a 'loose constellation of classes and communities and religious groups' and on the basis of this understanding he was able to 'super-impose over existing loyalties in India loyalty to the concept of nation'. Gandhi was successful in his objective because, according to Ravinder Kumar, the 'privileged communitarian at the cost of class identities leading became an integral part of the political scene'. Ravinder Kumar, *Essays in the Social History of Modern India* (New Delhi, 1963); pp. 47–48. Also see his keynote paper 'The Jallianwala Bagh Tragedy, the Rowlatt Satyagraha and the Character of the Nationalist Struggle in India: Some Reflections', presented at ICHR seminar held in April 1994.
43. K.L. Tuteja and O.P. Grewal, *op. cit.*
44. Azim Husain, *op. cit.*, p. 71.
45. See Gopal Krishna, 'The Development of the Indian National Congress as a Mass Organization, 1918–23' in *Journal of Asian Studies*, xxv, 3 May 1966, pp. 413–30.
46. A.M. and S.G. Zaidi, *The Encyclopaedia of the Indian National Congress: Gathering Storms*, vol. 3, 1896–1900 (New Delhi, 1977), pp. 499–502.
47. Annie Besant, *How India Frought for Freedom* (Adyar, 1915), pp. 162, 311, 491.
48. See Shyamala Bhatia, *Social Change and Politics in Punjab*, 1898–1910 (New Delhi, 1987).
59. Lal Chand, *Self Abnegation in Politics* (Lahore, 1939).
50. Duni Chand, *The Ulster of India* (Lahore, 1936).
51. *Ibid.*
52. At its session of Lahore in 1900, the Congress decided not to take up the issue of the Land Alienation Bill because it feared that such a step would alienate a section of Muslims in Punjab.
53. *File Nos. 32-41, Home Political B*, November 1909, NAI.
54. Toufique Kitchlew, *Saifuddin Kitchlew* (New Delhi, 1987), p. 11.
55. *The Tribune*, 9 January 1919.

56. Ravinder Kumar, 'The Rowlatt Satyagraha in Lahore', pp. 236–97; also see Brij Narain, *Eighty Years of Food Price, 1841–1921,* (Lahore, 1926).
57. V.N. Datta, *Jallianwala Bagh*, pp. 20–21.
58. *Ibid.*, p. 23.
59. V.N. Datta (ed.), *New Light on Punjab Disturbances* (Shimla, 1975), vol. 1, p. 105.
60. Ravinder Kumar, *op. cit.*, pp. 236–97.
61. D.A. Low provides an illuminating account of the role of trading classes in the Rowlatt agitation in Punjab in his paper ' Forgotten Bania: Merchant Communities and Indian National Congress', D.A. Low (ed.), *The Indian National Congress: A Centenary Hindsight* (Delhi, 1978) pp. 129–54.
62. George Rude, *The Crowd in History, 1730–1848* (London, 1981), p. 218.
63. Sumit Sarkar, *'Popular' Movements and 'Middle Class' Leadership in Late Colonial India* (Calcutta, 1983), p. 40.
64. Judith Brown, *Gandhi's Rise to Power* (Cambridge, 1972), p. 164.
65. *The Collected Works of Mahatma Gandhi*, vol. XXI, (Ahmedabad, 1965).
66. *The Tribune*, 7, 11 February 1919.
67. *Ibid.*, 11 February 1919.
68. *Ibid.*, 13, 14 and 16 February 1919.
69. *The Tribune*, 11 March 1919, *Home Political Deposit*, 48, April 1919 (NAI). Later, when Gandhi gave a call for *hartal*, Fazl-i-Husain decided to dissociate himself from the agitation. According to an official report, 'he refused to sign the notice of the meeting for the 30th nor agreed to preside over it'. *Home Political Deposit No. 49*, 1919 (NAI).
70. *Home Political Deposit No. 49*, 1919 (NAI).
71. See H.F. Owen, 'Organizing the Rowlatt Satyagraha of 1919' in Ravinder Kumar, *Essays on Gandhian Politics*, pp. 64–92.
72. Ravinder Kumar's Introduction, in *Essays on Gandhian Politics*, p. 4.
73. Sumit Sarkar, *Modern India*, p. 181; also see Shahid Amin 'Gandhi as Mahatma', in Ranjit Guha (ed.), *Subaltern Studies*, vol. III (Delhi, 1984), pp. 1–59.
74. V.N. Datta, *Jallianwala Bagh*, p. 34.
75. *New Light on Punjab Disturbances*, vol. 1, p. 36; *The Tribune*, 12 March 1919.
76. *The Tribune*, 12 March 1919.
77. *New Light on Punjab Disturbances*, vol. 1, p. 36.
78. Government Communique in *Civil and Military Gazette*, 8 April 1919.
79. See the speeches made by the leaders of Punjab at the protest meetings held in Lahore and Amritsar. *The Tribune* 7 and 8 March 1919.
80. Sumit Sarkar, *Modern India*, p. 187.
81. Statement of Miles Irving, *Disorder Inquiry Committee*, vol. III, p; *Civil & Military Gazette*, 17 April 1919; V.N. Datta, *Jallianwala Bagh*, pp. 42–43.
82. Ranjit Guha, *Elementary Aspects of Peasant Insurgency in Colonial India* (New Delhi, 1983), pp. 256–61.
83. J. Prasad, 'The Psychology of Rumour' cited in *Ibid.*
84. *Disorder Inquiry Committee Report*, p. 29.
85. Regarding this violence, the Hunter Committee (Minority Report) recorded '... although the excesses were altogether inexcusable and without justification, the mob had not any previous fixed intention of committing excesses, but after the firing lost their heads and were seized by a mob frenzy.' *Ibid.*, p. XIX.
86. *New Light on Punjab Disturbances*, vol. I, p. 275.
87. Ranjit Guha's Introduction, *Subaltern Studies*, vol. I (Delhi, 1982), p. 3.

88. George Rude, *op. cit.*, p. 9.
89. *Ibid.*, p. 6.
90. *Home Political Deposit No. 28,* October 1919 (NAI).
91. *Ibid.*
92. J.P. Thompson, Chief Secretary, accepted this point later. See his evidence before the Disorder Inquiry Committee, *New Light on Punjab Disturbances*, vol. I, p. 49.
93. *Disorder Inquiry Committee, Evidence*, vol. III, p. 7.
94. *Ibid.*, p. 6.
95. *Home Political Deposit No. 28,* October 1919 (NAI).
96. V.N. Datta, *Jallianwala Bagh*, p. 96.
97. It is difficult to agree with the contention that the massacre at Jallianwala Bagh was a conspiracy hatched by the local administration in connivance with Hans Raj who, it is claimed, cleverly arranged this meeting so that Dyer could punish the people for their 'rebellious' attitude. As our study clearly shows most of the people had assembled at Jallianwala Bagh out of their strong feeling of protest against the recent incidents of repression. A large crowd of about 20,000 persons could not have been arranged only by the machinations of a conspirator, however, ingeniously active he might have been at that time. As Lord Granville in a different context of the popular disturbances of 1736 rightly said in the House of Lords in February 1737: 'The people seldom or never assemble in any riotous or tumultuous manner, unless they are oppressed or at least imagine they are oppressed'. Quoted in George Rude, *The Crowd in History*, p. 7.
98. *Report and Evidence of the Sub-Committee of the Indian National Congress*, p. 70, cited in *Ibid.*
99. *Home Political B*-January 1920, 513, NAI.
100. Derek Sayer, *op. cit.*, pp. 130–64.
101. M.K. Gandhi, *An Autobiography or The Study of My Experiments with Truth* (Ahmedabad, 1927), p. 349.
102. Speech by Swami Shradhanada at the Amritsar Congress Session, 1919. A.M. and S.G. Zaidi, *The Encyclopaedia of the Indian National Congress: Emergence of Gandhi*, vol. VII (Delhi, 1979), pp. 456–69.
103. *Disorder Inquiry Committee Report*, p. 29.
104. Evidence of Michael O'Dwyer in *New Light on Punjab Disturbances*, vol. I, pp. 124–233.
105. Narendra Nath to S.P. O'Donnell, 20 March 1920, *File No. 1904, Franchise B, April 1920* (NAI).
106. *The Hindu*, 9 January 1921, quoted in Gopal Krishna, *op. cit.*, p. 426.
107. Atluri Murali, 'Demonizing the 'Other' and Mythifying History: Jallianwala Bagh Tragedy and Andhra Nationalists' (Unpublished paper) presented at the ICHR Seminar held in April 1994.
108. Eric Hobsbawm draws our attention to particular circumstances under which nationalism gains strength through such a convergence of the perception of elite and popular consciousness. E.J. Hobsbawm, *Nations and Nationalism Since 1780* (Cambridge, 1990).
109. D.G. Tendulkar, *Mahatma*, vol. I (Delhi, 1951), pp. 251–64.
110. *Ibid.*
111. *The Collected Works of Mahatma Gandhi*, vol. XXIII, pp. 231–33.
112. See Bipan Chandra, *Indian National Movement: The Long Term Dynamics* (New Delhi, 1988).

Appendix

SIR RABINDRANATH TAGORE TO LORD CHELMSFORD ON THE RENUNCIATION OF HIS TITLE* 31 MAY 1919

YOUR EXCELLENCY,

The enormity of measures taken by the Government in the Punjab for quelling some local disturbances has, with a rude shock, revealed to our mind the helplessness of our position as British subjects in India. The disproportionate severity of punishments inflicted upon the unfortunate people and the methods of carrying them out, weare convinced, are without parallel in the history of the civilized government, barring some conspicuous exceptions, recent and remote. Considering that such treatment has been meted out to a population, disarmed and resourceless, by a power which has the most terribly efficient organization for destruction of human lives, we must strongly assert that it can claim no political expediency, far less moral justification. The accounts of insults and sufferings undergone by our brothers in the Punjab have trickled through the gagged silence, reaching every corner of India and the universal agony of indignation roused in the hearts of our people has been ignored by our rulers – possibly congratulating themselves for what they imagine as salutary lessons. This callousness has been praised by most of the Anglo-Indian papers, which have in some cases gone to the brutal length of making fun of our sufferings, without receiving the least check from the same authority, relentlessly careful in smothering every cry of pain and expression of judgement from the organs representing the sufferers. Knowing that our appeals have been in vain and that the passion of vengeance is blinding the nobler vision of statesmanship in our Government, which could so easily afford to be magnanimous as befitting its

*Chelmsford Papers, 1919, Vol. 22, Roll No. 10, No. 554(a).

physical strength and moral tradition, the very least that I can do for my country is to take all consequences upon myself in giving voice to the protest of the millions of my countrymen suppressed into a dumb anguish of terror. The time has come when badges of honour make our shame glaring in their incongruous context of humiliation, and I, for my part, wish to stand, shorn of all special distinctions by the side of those of my countrymen who, for their so-called insignificance, are liable to suffer degradation not fit for human beings.

These are the reasons which have painfully compelled me to ask Your Excellency with due deference and regret, to relieve me of my title of Knighthood, which I had the honour to accept from His Majesty the King at the hands of your predecessor, for whose nobleness of heart I still entertain great admiration.

THE SATYAGRAHA PLEDGE

Ahmedabad,
24 February 1919

Being conscientiously of opinion that the Bills known as the Indian Criminal Law (Amendment) Bill No. I of 1919 and the Criminal Law (Emergency Powers) Bill No. II of 1919 are unjust, subversive of the principle of liberty and justice, and destructive of the elementary rights of individuals on which the safety of the community as a whole and the State itself is based, we solemnly affirm them, in the event of these Bills becoming law and until they are withdrawn, we shall refuse civilly to obey these laws and such other laws as and committee to be hereafter appointed may think it and we further affirm that in this struggle we will faithfully follow truth and refrain from violence to life, person or property.

MOHANDAS KARAMCHAND GANDHI,
Satyagraha Ashram, Sabarmati

VALLABHBHAI J. PATEL, BAR-AT LAW,
Ahmedabad

CHANDULAL MANILAL DESAI, L.D.S.,
Ahmedabad

KESARIPRASAD MANILAL THAKOOR,
Ahmedabad

(BEHN) ANASUYABAI SARABHAI,
Secretary, Women's Branch of
the Home Rule League,
Ahmedabad and OTHERS

New India, 3 March 1919

COLONEL WEDGEWOOD ON THE JALLIANWALA BAGH MASSACRE

Colonel Wedgewood (later on the adjournment): I rose because I wanted to raise a question which is different from the Irish question in locality but very similar to it in general characteristics.

I want to raise the question of the Amritsar massacre, and the duty of this country towards India in that respect. The details of the massacre are, unfortunately, too well-known to us. The English Press, with a few exceptions, has taken the English view of the matter. The whole country has been horrified at what took place. Let me remind the House of what took place, and not from hearsay, but on the evidence given by the principal actor. Here enquiry will result in some trivial action. The thing must be put right. What happened? There was a religious festival and thousands of Punjabis had gone into Amritsar. The British officials were anxious and the Deputy Commissioner on April 9 surrounded the notorious Dr Satyapal and Kitchlew and carried them off. The news got about and their followers sent a massed deputation to the Deputy Commissioner demanding their release. The deputation was stopped, apparently by troops; it was only armed with sticks and as a result the troops fired and shot some of the demonstrators. Speeches were made over the bodies, and the mob turned and murdered three Englishmen and beat a lady. No one would excuse riots of that sort. On the evening of the 10th, General Dyer arrived at Amritsar, and the Deputy Commissioner handed over the civil power to him. He issued a proclamation by word of mouth that no meetings should be held. Two days later, after there had been no sort of riot nor murder, General Dyer heard that a meeting was to be held at the Jallianwala Bagh. He proceeded there with about 50 troops, half British, half Indian, and a certain number of Gurkhas armed with their kukris. The Jallianwala Bagh is an open space, half a mile square, which has one entry wide enough for three persons. The troops got in and lined up on a mound of debris. The walls, seven feet high, and the surrounding houses enclosed the people. There were, too, three alleys through which the people might have been able to pass. Within 30 seconds of the troops getting in, General Dyer gave orders to fire, and the crowd of people, estimated at anything from 5,000 to 20,000, who were sitting on the ground, peacefully listening to the mob oratory, were fired on. The result of the troops' fire into the mass of people we do not know. But we do know that Dyer's own estimate of the casualties resulting from ten minutes' continual individual firing was 400 to 500 killed and 1,500 wounded. What were the people to do? They could not escape. They were people who had not offered any violence and who had not been warned. These people were shot down. After ten minutes the ammunition was exhausted and the troops marched off, and they left 1,500 wounded there. There were men lying there for two days, dying of thirst, eating the ground, bleeding to death and nobody to look after them. Those relations who lived near came and carried away some of the wounded from among the dead and dying, but the unfortunate country people died there miserably of their wounds. This is what was done in 1919 in British India. An English sportsman would take any amount of trouble or time to see that a wounded partridge was put out of its misery, but these wounded people were lying there for two days dying slowly. Think what this means. There has never been anything like it before in English history, and not in the whole of our relations with India has there have been anything of this magnitude before. If you are to find anything so damning to the British reputation you have to go back centuries. In the ordinary English primer the only thing the ordinary person learns about British rule in India is about the Black Hole of Calcutta, and the massacre of Cawnpore, where there was a well chocked with corpses. Centuries hence you will find Indian children brought up to this spot, just as they visit now the Cawnpore well, and you can imagine the feelings of these Indians for generations over this terrible business.

JAWAHARLAL NEHRU ON JALLIANWALA BAGH

Satyagraha Day – all-India *hartals* and complete suspension of business – firing by the police and military at Delhi and Amritsar, and the killing of many people – mob violence in Amritsar and Ahmedabad – the massacre of Jallianwala Bagh – the long horror and terrible indignity of Martial Law in the Punjab. The Punjab was isolated, cut off from the rest of India; a thick veil seemed to cover it and hide it from outside eyes. There was hardly any news, and people could not go there or come our from there.

Odd individuals, who managed to escape from the inferno, were so terror-struck that they could give no clear account. Helplessly and impotently, we, who were outside, waited for scraps of news and bitterness filled our hearts. Some of us wanted to go openly to the affected parts of the Punjab and defy the Martial Law regulations. But we were kept back, and meanwhile a big organization for relief and enquiry was set up on behalf of the Congress.

As soon as Martial Law was withdrawn from the principal areas and outsiders were allowed to come in, prominent Congressmen and others poured into the Punjab offering their services for relief or enquiry work. The relief work was largely directed by Pandit Madan Mohan Malaviya and Swami Shraddhananda; the enquiry part was mainly under the direction of my father and Mr C.R. Das, with Gandhiji taking a great deal of interest in it and often being consulted by the others. Desbandhu Das especially took the Amritsar area under his charge and I was deputed to accompany him there and assist him in any way he desired. That was the first occasion I had of working with him and under him and valued that experience very much and my admiration for him grew. Most of the evidence relating to Jallianwala Bagh and that terrible lane where human beings were made to crawl on their bellies, that subsequently appeared in the Congress Inquiry Report, was taken down in our presence. We paid numerous visits to the so-called Bagh itself and examined every bit of it carefully.

A suggestion has been made, I think by Mr Edward Thompson, that General Dyer was under the impression that there were other exits from the Bagh and it was because of this that he continued his firing for so long. Even if that was Dyer's impression, and there were in fact some exits that would hardly lessen his responsibility. But it seems very strange that he should have such an impression. Any person, standing on the raised ground where he stood, could have a good view of the entire space and could see how shut in it was on all sides by houses several storeys high. Only on one side, for a hundred feet or so, there was no house, but a low wall about five feet high. With a murderous fire mowing them down and unable to find a way out, thousands of people rushed to this wall and tried to climb over it. The fire was then directed, it appears (both from our evidence and the innumerable bullet-marks on the wall itself) towards this wall to prevent people from escaping over it. And when all was over, some of the biggest heaps of dead and wounded lay on either side of this wall.

Towards the end of that year (1919), I travelled from Amritsar to Delhi by the night train. The compartment I entered was almost full and all the berths, except one upper one, were occupied by sleeping passengers. I took the vacant upper berth. In the morning I discovered that all my fellow passengers were military officers. They conversed with each other in loud voices which I could not help overhearing. One of them was holding forth in an aggressive and triumphant tone and soon I discovered that he was Dyer the hero of Jallianwala Bagh, and he was describing his Amritsar experience. He pointed out how he had the whole town at his mercy and he had felt like reducing the rebellious city to a heap of ashes, but he took pity on it and refrained. He was evidently coming back from Lahore after giving his evidence before the Hunter Committee of Inquiry. I was greatly shocked to hear his conversation and to observe his callous manner. He descended at Delhi station in pyjamas with bright pink stripes, and a dressing-gown.

MAHATMA GANDHI ON JALLIANWALA BAGH

There was an unfortunate hitch about the purchase of this Bagh for the nation. Thanks to the efforts of the Hon'ble Pandit Madan Mohan Malaviya, Sannyasi

Swami Shri Shraddhanand and the local leaders, it has now become the property of the nation subject to the full payment of the purchase price within three months from the 6th instant. The purchase price is Rs 5,36,000. And the amount must be raised within the prescribed period.

It is, therefore, necessary to examine the propriety of making this purchase on behalf of the nation, especially as it has been questioned even in enlightened quarters. With the Cawnpore Memorial before us the attitude is not to be wondered at. But with all respect to objectors, I cannot help saying that if the Bagh had not been acquired, it would have been a national disgrace. Can we afford to forget those five hundred or more men who were killed although they had done nothing wrong either morally, or legally? If they had died knowingly and willingly, if, realizing their innocence they had stood their ground and faced the shots from the fifty rifles, they would have gone down in history as saints, heroes and patriots. But even as it was, the tragedy became one of first-class national importance. Nations are born out of travail and suffering. We should forfeit all title to be considered a nation, if we failed to treasure the memory of those who in our battle for political freedom might, innocently or for the crimes of others, lose their lives or otherwise suffer. We were unable to protect our helpless countrymen when they were ruthlessly massacred. We may decline, if we will, to avenge the wrong. The nation will not lose if we did. But shall we – can we afford to – decline to perpetuate the memory and to show to the surviving members of the families of the dead that we are sharers in their sufferings, by erecting a national tombstone and by telling the world thereby that in the death of these men each one of us had lost dear relations? If national instinct does not mean at least this much kinship, it has no meaning for me. I hold it to be our duty to tell the generations yet unborn that in our march towards true freedom we must be prepared for repetitions of the wrongs such as the Jallianwala Bagh massacre. We must provide against them; we must not seek them, but we must be ready to face them if they come again. I would not have us flinch from the battle of national life. The supreme lesson of the Amritsar Congress was that the sufferings of the Punjab did not dishearten the nation but the nation treated them as a matter of course. Some of us made stupid mistakes and the innocent suffered for them. We must in future try to avoid the mistakes but in spite of our best effort, we may fail to covert everyone to sanity. We must, therefore, be ready for the repetition of the sufferings of the guiltless by telling the country now that they and theirs shall not be forgotten but that the memory of the innocent dead shall be regarded as a sacred trust and that the surviving relations shall have the right to look to the nation for maintenance in case of need. This is the primary meaning of the memorial. And has not the blood of the Mohammedan mixed with that of the Hindu? Has not the blood of the Sikh mixed with that of the Sanatanist and the Samajist? The memorial should be a national emblem of an honest and sustained effort to achieve Hindu-Muslim unity.

But the objector's objection still remains unanswered. Will not the memorial also perpetuate bitterness and ill will? It will depend upon the trustees. And if I know them, I know that is not their intention at all. I know that such was not the intention of the vast assembly. I do not wish to convey that bitterness was not there. It was there – not in any way suppressed. But the idea of the memorial had nothing of bitterness in it. The people want to, they must be encouraged to, forget the doer and his madness. What General Dyer did we may all do if we had his irresponsibility and opportunity. To err is human and it must be held to be equally human to forgive if we, though being fallible, would like rather to be forgiven than punished and reminded of our misdeeds. Nor does this mean that we may not ask for General Dyer's dismissal. A lunatic cannot be kept in a position from which he can do harm to his neighbours. But just as we do not bear ill will towards a lunatic, so too may we not bear ill will even towards General Dyer. I would therefore eschew from the memorial all idea of bitterness and ill will but treat it as a sacred memory and regard the Bagh as a place of pilgrimage to be visited by all irrespective of class, creed or colour. I would invite Englishmen to appreciate our feeling in the matter, ask them by subscribing to the memorial in the spirit of the Royal Proclamation to make common cause with us in our endeavour to regain consciousness, to realize the same freedom that they enjoy under the same constitution and to realise Hindu-Muslim unity without which there can be no true progress for India.

Young India, 18 February 1920.

THE ROWLATT ACT: THE ROWLATT ACT AS PASSED IN THE IMPERIAL LEGISLATIVE COUNCIL, 18 MARCH 1919

(Passed by the Imperial Legislative Council)
(Received the assent of the Governor-General on 21 March 1919)

An Act to cope aita anarchical and revolutionary crime

Whereas it is expedient to make provision that the ordinary criminal law should be supplemented and emergency powers should be exercisable by the Government for the purpose of dealing with anarchical and revolutionary movements;

And whereas the previous approval of the Secretary of State in Council has been accorded to the making of this law; it is hereby enacted as follows:

1. *Short title, extent and duration:* (1) This Act may be called the Anarchical Revolutionary Crimes Act, 1919;

(2) It extends to the whole of British India; and

(3) it shall continue in force for three years from the date of termination of the present war.

2. *Definitions:* (1) In this Act, unless there is anything repugnant in the subject or context:

'Court Justice' means the Judge of highest rank in a High Court;

'The Code' means the Code of Criminal Procedure, 1898;

'High Court' means the highest Court of criminal appeal or revision for any local area;

'Scheduled Offence' means any offence specified in the schedule.

(2) All words and expressions used in this Act and defined in the Code, and not herein before defined, shall be deemed to have the meanings respectively attributed to them in the Code.

PART I

3. *Condition of application of Part I:* If the Governor-General in Council is satisfied that, in the whole or any part of British India, anarchical or revolutionary movements are being promoted, and that scheduled offences in connection with such movements are prevalent to such an extent that it is expedient in the interests of the public safety to provide for the speedy trial of such offences, he may, by notification in the Gazette of India, make a declaration to that effect, and thereupon the provisions of this Part shall come into force in the area specified in the notification.

4. *Initiation of proceedings:* (1) Where the Local Government is of opinion that the trial of any person accused of a scheduled offence should be held in accordance with the provisions of this Part, it may order any officer of Government to prefer a written information to the Chief Justice against such a person.

(2) No order under sub-section (1) shall be made in respect of, or be deemed to include, any person who has been committed under the Code for trial before a High Court or a Court of Session, but save as aforesaid, an order under that sub-section may be made in respect of any scheduled offence whether such offence was committed before or after the issue of the notification under Section 3.

(3) The information shall state the offence charged and so far as known the name, place of residence, and occupation of the accused, and the time and place when and where the offence is alleged to have been committed and all particulars within the knowledge of the prosecution of what is intended to be provided against the accused.

(4) The Chief Justice may by order require any information to be amended so as to supply further particulars of the offence charged to the accused, and shall direct a copy of the information or the amended information, as the case may be, to be served upon the accused in such manner as the Chief Justice may direct.

5. *Constitution of Court:* Upon such service being effected, and on application duly made to him, the Chief Justice shall nominate three of the High Court Judges (hereinafter referred to as the Court) for the trial of the information, and shall fix a date for the commencement of the trial;

Provided that when the total number of Judges of the High Court does not exceed three, the Chief Justice shall nominate not more than two such Judges, and shall complete the Court by the nomination of one or, if necessary, two persons of either of the following classes, namely:

(*a*) persons who have served as permanent Judges of the High Court; or

(*b*) with the consent of the Chief Justice of another High Court, persons who are Judges of that High Court.

6. *Place of sitting:* The Court may sit for the whole or any part of a trial at such place or places in the provinces as it may consider desirable:

Provided that if the Advocate-General certifies to the Court that it is in his opinion necessary in the interests of justice that the whole or any part of a trial shall be held at some place other than the usual place of sitting of the High Court, the Court shall, after hearing the accused, make an order to that effect, unless for reasons to be recorded in writing it thinks fit to make any other order. It shall not be necessary for the certificate of the Advocate-General to be supported by any affidavit, nor shall he be required to state the grounds upon which such a certificate was given.

7. *Application of Code of Criminal Procedure subject to this Part:* The provision of the Code shall apply to proceedings under this Part, in so far as the said provisions are not inconsistent with the provisions of this Part, and such proceedings shall be deemed to be proceedings under the Code, and the Court shall have all the powers conferred by the Code on a Court of Session exercising original jurisdiction.

8. *Trial:* (1) The trial shall be commenced by the reading of the information. And thereafter the prosecutor shall state shortly by what evidence he expects to prove the guilt of the accused.

(2) The Court shall then, object to the provisions of this Part, in trying the accused, follow the procedure prescribed by the Code for the trial of warrant cases by the Magistrate.

9. *Adjournment:* If a charge is framed, the accused shall be entitled to ask for an adjournment for fourteen days, or any less period that he may specify,

and the Court shall comply with his request, but subject to the adjournment provided for by this section, the Court shall not be bound to adjourn any trial for any purpose, unless such adjournment is in its opinion necessary in the interests of justice.

10. *Record of evidence:* The Court shall cause the evidence of each witness who is examined to be recorded in full in such manner as the Court may direct.

11. *Prohibition or restriction of publication of trial:* The Court, if it is of opinion that such a course is necessary in the public interest or for the protection of a witness, may prohibit or restrict in such way as it may direct the publication or disclosure of its proceedings or any part of its proceedings.

12. *Examination of accused:* (1) No questions shall be put by the Court to the accused in the course of a trial under this Part until the close of the case for the prosecution. Thereafter, and before the accused enters on his defence, the Court shall inform the accused that he is entitled, if he so desires, to give evidence on oath on his own behalf, and shall at the same time inform him that if he does so, he will be liable to cross-examination. Unless the accused then states that he desires to give evidence on oath, the Court may at any time thereafter question the accused generally on the case in accordance with the provisions of Section 342 of the Code.

(2) If, when so called upon, the accused states that he desires to give evidence on oath, the Court shall not at any subsequent stage put any question to him:
Provided that if the accused does not so give evidence, then, after the witness for the defence has been examined, the Court may question the accused generally on the case in accordance with the provisions of the said section.

(3) The failure of the accused to give evidence on oath shall not be made the subject of any comment by the prosecution, nor shall the Court draw any inference adverse to the accused from such failure.

(4) If the accused gives evidence on oath, the following rules shall be observed, namely:

(*a*) He may be asked any question in cross-examination notwithstanding that it would tend to criminate him as to the offence charged.

(*b*) He shall not be asked, and if asked shall, not be required to answer, any question tending to show that he has committed or been convicted of, or has been charged with, any offence other than that with which he is then charged, or has a bad character, unless:

(*i*) proof that he has committed or been convicted of such other offence is admissible in evidence to show that he is guilty of the offence with which he is then charged, or (*ii*) witnesses for the prosecution have been cross-examined with a view to establish his own good character, or he has given evidence of his good character or the nature or the conduct of the defence is such as to involve imputations on the character of the witnesses for the prosecution, or

(*iii*) he has given evidence against any other person charged with the same offence.

(*c*) Unless otherwise ordered by the Court, he shall give his evidence from the witness-box or other place from which the other witnesses give their evidence.

13. *Right of reply:* If the accused or any one of the accused calls and examines any witness, the right of final reply shall lie with the prosecution, but in all other cases with the accused.

Provided that the examination of the accused as a witness shall not of itself confer the right of final reply on the prosecution.

14. *Differences of opinion:* In the event of any difference of opinion among the members of the Court, the opinion of the majority shall prevail.

15. *Accused may be convicted of any offence referred to in the Schedule:* At any trial under this Part the accused may be charged with and convicted of any offence against any provision of the law which is referred to in the Schedule.

16. *Sentence:* The Court may pass upon any person convicted by it any sentence authorized by law for the punishment of the offence of which such person is convicted, and no order of confirmation shall be necessary in the case of any sentence passed by it:

Provided that a sentence of death shall not be passed upon any accused person in respect of whose guilt there is a difference of opinion among the members of the Court.

17. *Exclusion of interference of other criminal Courts:* The judgement of the Court shall be final and conclusive and, notwithstanding the provisions of the Code or of any other law for the time being in force, or of anything having the force of law by whatsoever authority made or done, there shall be no appeal from any order or sentence of the Court, and no High Court shall have authority to revise any such order or sentence or to transfer any case from such Court, or to make any order under Section 491 of the Code or have any jurisdiction of any kind in respect of any proceedings under this Part:

Provided that nothing in this section shall be deemed to affect the powers of the Governor-General in Council or of the Local Government to make orders under Section 401 or Section 402 of the Code in respect of any person sentenced by the Court.

18. *Special rules of evidence I of 1872:* (1) Notwithstanding anything to the contrary contained in the Indian Evidence Act, 1872,where:

(*a*) the statement of any person has been recorded by a Magistrate, and such statement has been read over and explained to the person making it and has been signed by him, or

(*b*) the statement of any person has been recorded by the Court, but such person has not been cross-examined.

Such statement may be admitted in evidence by the Court if the person making the same is dead or cannot be found or is incapable of giving evidence, and it is established to the satisfaction of the Court that such death, disappearance or incapacity has been caused in the interests of the accused.

(2) Depositions recorded under Section 512 of the Code may, in the circumstances specified in that section, be given in evidence at the trial of an accused under this Part I.

19. *Recall of witness on reconstitution of Court:* In case of any reconstitution of the Court during the trial, the Court so reconstituted shall, if the accused so desires, recall and re-hear any witness who has already given evidence in the case.

20. *Power to make rules:* The Chief Justice may from time to time make rules providing for:

(1) the appointment and power of a President of the Court, and the procedure to be adopted to complete the Court in the event of any Judge of the Court being prevented from amending throughout the trial of an accused, and

(2) any matters (including the intermediate custody of the accused and his release on bail) which appear to him necessary for carrying into effect or supplementing the provisions of this Part preliminary or ancillary to trials.

PART II

21. *Condition of application of Part II:* If the Governor-General in Council is satisfied that anarchical or revolutionary movements which are, in his opinion, likely to lead to the commission of scheduled offences are being extensively promoted in the whole or any part of British India, he may, by notification in the Gazette of India, make a declaration to the effect, and thereupon the provisions of this Part shall come into force in the area specified in the notification.

22. *Powers exercisable when Part II is in force:* (1) Where, in the opinion of the Local Government, there are reasonable grounds for believing that any person is or has been actively concerned in such area in any movement of the

nature referred to in Section 21, the Local Government may place all the materials in its possession relating to his case before a judicial officer who is qualified for appointment to a High Court and take his opinion thereon. If, after considering such opinion, the Local Government is satisfied that action under the provisions of this section is necessary, it may by order in writing contain a declaration to the effect that such person is or has been actively concerned in such area in any movement of the nature referred to in Section 21, give all or any of the following directions, namely: that such person:

(*a*) shall, within such period as may be specified in the order, execute a bond with or without sureties undertaking, for such period not exceeding one year as may be so specified, that he will not commit, or attempt or conspire to commit, or abet the commitment of, any offence against any provision of the law which is referred to in the Schedule;

(*b*) shall notify his residence and any change of residence to such authority as may be so specified.

(*c*) shall remain or reside in any area in British India so specified: Provided that, if the area so specified is outside the province, the concurrence of the Local Government of that area to the making of the order shall first have been obtained;

(*d*) shall abstain from any act so specified which, in the opinion of the Local Government, is calculated to disturb the public peace or is pre-judicial to the public safety; and

(*e*) shall report himself to the office in charge of the police-station nearest to his residence at such periods as may be so specified.

(2) Any order under clauses (*b*) to (*e*) of sub-section (1) may also be made to take effect upon default by the person concerned in complying with an order under clause (*a*) of that sub-section.

23. *Service of orders under Section 22:* An order made under Section 22 shall be served on the person in respect of whom it is made in the manner provided in the Code for service of summons and upon such service such person shall be deemed to have due notice thereof.

24. *Enforcement of orders:* The Local Government and every officer of Government to whom a copy of any order made under Section 22 may be directed by or under the general or special authority of, the Local Government, may use all means reasonably necessary to enforce compliance with the same.

25. *Interim nature of order made by Local Government:* An order made under Section 22 shall only continue in force for a period of one month, unless it is extended by the Local Government as hereinafter provided in this Part.

26. *Reference to investigating authority:* (1) When the Local Government

makes an order under Section 42 such Government shall, as soon as may be, forward to the investigating authority to be constituted under this Act a concise statement in writing setting forth plainly the grounds on which the Government considered it necessary that the order should be made, and shall lay before the investigating authority all material facts and circumstances in its possession relevant to the inquiry.

(2) The investigating authority shall then hold an inquiry in camera for the purpose of ascertaining what, in its opinion, having regard to the facts and circumstances adduced by the Government, appears against the person in respect of whom the order has been made. Such authority shall in every case allow the person in question a reasonable opportunity of appearing before it at some stage in its proceedings and shall, if he so appears, explain to his the nature of the charge made against him and shall hear any explanation he may have to offer, and shall make such further investigation (if any) as appears to such authority to be relevant and reasonable:

Provided that:

(*a*) nothing in this sub-section shall be deemed to entitle the person whose case is before the investigating authority to appear or to be represented before it by pleader, nor shall the Local Government be so entitled.

(*b*) the investigating authority shall not disclose to the person in question, any fact the communication of which might endanger the public safety or the safety of any individual;

(*c*) if the person in question requests the investigating authority to secure the attendance of any person or the production of any document or thing, such authority shall, unless for reasons to be recorded in writing it deems it necessary so to do, cause such person to attend or such document or thing to be produced, and for that purpose shall have all the powers conferred on a District Magistrate in respect of those matters by the Code.

(3) Subject to the provisions of sub-section (2) the inquiry shall be conducted in such manner as the investigating authority considers best suited to elicit the facts of the case; and in making the inquiry, such authority shall not be bound to observe the rules of the law of evidence.

(4) Any statement made to an investigating authority by any person other than the person whose case in under investigation shall be deemed to be information given to a public servant within the meaning of Section 182 of the Indian Penal Code.

(5) On the completion of the inquiry, the investigating authority shall

report in writing to the Local Government the conclusions at which it has arrived, and shall adduce reasons in support thereof. In so reporting the investigating authority shall state whether or not, in its opinion, the person whose case is under investigation is or has been actively concerned in any movement of the nature referred to in Section 21.

(6) If the investigating authority has not completed the inquiry within the period for which the duration of the order is limited by Section 25, such authority may recommend to the Local Government that the period of duration of the order shall be extended for such period as it may consider necessary, and on such a recommendation the Local Government may extend the duration of the order accordingly.

27. *Disposal of report of investigating authority:* (1) On receipt of the report of the investigating authority, the Local Government may discharge the order made under Section 22, or may make any order which is authorized by that section:

Provided that:

(*a*) any order so made shall recite the conclusions of the investigating authority as reported by the authority; and

(*b*) a copy of such order shall be furnished to the person in respect of whom it is made.

(2) No order made under sub-section (1) shall continue in force for more than one year from the date of the order made under Section 22.

(3) On the expiry of an order made under sub-section (1), the Local Government may, if it is satisfied that such a course is necessary in the interests of the public safety, again make in respect of the person to whom such order related any order which is authorized by Section 22:

Provided that, before an order is made under this sub-section, a copy of the order which it is proposed to make shall be furnished to the person concerned, who may submit to the Local Government a representation in regard to such order. Any such representation shall be forwarded by the Local Government to the investigating authority for inquiry and report, and such authority after inquiry conducted in accordance with the provisions of Section 26, shall report thereon, and the Local Government shall consider such report:

Provided further that no order made under this sub-section shall continue in force for more than a year from the date on which it was made.

(4) Another order made under this section may at any time be discharged or may be altered by the substitution of any other order authorized by Section 22:

Provided that no such alteration shall have the effect of prolonging the period for which such order would have been in force.

(5) *Penalty for disobedience to order:* The provisions of Section 24 shall apply to the enforcement of orders made under this section.

28. If any person fails to comply with, or attempts to evade, any order (other than an order to furnish security) made under Section 22 or Section 27, he shall, on conviction by a Magistrate, be punishable with imprisonment for a term which may extend to six months, or with fine, which may extend to five hundred rupees, or with both.

29. *Provisions as to bonds:* The provisions of Section 514 of the Code shall apply to bonds executed under the provisions of this Part, with this modification that the powers conferred by the section on the Court shall be exercisable by any District Magistrate or Chief Presidency Magistrate, on application made on behalf of the Local Government.

30. *Investigating authority:* (1) As soon as may be after a notification has been issued bringing this Part into force, the Local Government shall appoint one or more investigating authorities for the purpose of this Part, and may appoint additional investigating authorities when necessary.

(2) Every investigating authority shall be appointed by order in writing, and shall consist of three persons, of whom two shall be persons having held judicial office not inferior to that of a District and Sessions Judge, and one shall be a person not in the service of the Crown in India.

(3) The Local Government may by like order appoint persons to fill casual vacancies occurring by reason of death, resignation of office or otherwise on any investigating authority, but in so doing shall observe the provisions of sub-section (2).

31. *Visiting Committees:* (1) The Local Government shall by order in writing appoint such persons as it thinks fit to be Visiting Committees to report upon the welfare and treatment of persons under restraint under this Part, and shall by rules prescribe the functions which these Committees shall exercise:

Provided that, in making such rules, provisions shall be made for periodical visits to persons under restraint under the provisions of this Part:

Provided further that a person in respect of whom an order has been made under Section 22 or Section 27 requiring him to abstain from any specified act or to report himself to the police shall not be deemed to be under restraint for the purposes of this section.

(2) All rules made under sub-section (1) shall be published in the local official Gazette, and on such publication shall have effect as if enacted in this Part.

32. *Power to make rules by Local Government:* (1) The Local Government may make rules prescribing the authorities before whom and the manner in which bonds under this Part shall be executed, and providing for the procedure to be followed regarding the notification of residence and reports to the police by persons in respect of whom orders have been made under Section 22 or Section 27.

(2) All rules made under sub-section (1) shall be published in the local official Gazette, and on such publication shall have effect as if enacted in this Part.

PART III

33. *Condition of application of Part III:* If the Governor-General in Council is satisfied that in the whole or any part of British India anarchical or revolutionary movements are being promoted and that scheduled offences in connection with such movements are prevalent to such an extent as to endanger the public safety, he may, by notification in the Gazette of India, make a declaration to that effect, and thereupon the provisions of this part shall come into force in the area specified in the notification.

34. *Powers exercisable when Part III is in force:* (1) Where, in the opinion of the Local Government, there are reasonable grounds for believing that any person has been or is concerned in such area in any scheduled offence, the Local Government may place all the materials in its possession relating to his case before a judicial officer who is qualified for appointment to a High Court and take his opinion thereon. If after considering such opinion the Local Government is satisfied that such action is necessary; it may make in respect of such person any order authorized by Section 22, and may further by order in writing direct:

(*a*) the arrest of any such person without warrant;

(*b*) the confinement of any such person in such place and under such conditions and restrictions as it may specify:
Provided that no such person shall be confined in that part of a prison or other place which is used for the confinement of convicted criminal prisoners as defined in the Prisons Act, 1894 (IX of 1894); and

(*c*) the search of any place specified in the order which, in the opinion of the Local Government, has been, is being, or is about to be, used by any such person for any purpose connected with any anarchical or revolutionary movement.

(2) The arrest of any person in pursuance of an order under clause (*a*) of sub-section (1) may be effected at any place where he may be found by any police officer or by any other officer of Government to whom the order may be directed.

(3) An order for confinement under clause (*b*) or for search under clause (c) of sub-section (1) may be carried out by any officer of Government to whom the order may be directed, and such officer may use all means reasonably necessary to enforce the same.

35. *Arrest:* Any person making an arrest in pursuance of an order under clause (a) of sub-section (1) of Section 34 shall forthwith report the fact to the Local Government and, pending receipt of the orders of the Local Government may by order in writing commit any person so arrested to such custody as the Local Government may by general or special order specify in this behalf:

Provided that no person shall be detained in such custody for a period exceeding seven days unless the Local Government so directs, and in no case shall such detention exceed fifteen days.

36. *Search:* An order for the search of any place issued under the provisions of clause (c) of sub-section (1) of Section 34 shall be deemed to be a search warrant issued by the District Magistrate having jurisdiction in the place specified therein, and shall be sufficient authority for the seizure of anything found in such place which the person executing the order has reason to believe is being used, or is likely to be used, for any purpose pre-judicial to the public safety, and the provisions of the Code, so far as they can be made applicable, shall apply to searches made under the authority of any such order and to the disposal of any property seized in any such search.

37. *Application of Part II procedure:* Where an order (other than an order for arrest or search) has been made under Section 34, the provisions of Section 25 to 27 shall apply in the same way as if the order were an order made under Section 22, save that, on receipt of the report of the investigating authority, the Local Government may, subject to the conditions prescribed by Section 27, make any order which is authorized by Section 34, and Sections 23 to 27 and 29 to 32 shall be deemed to be included in this Part.

PART IV

38. *Persons already under executive control:* (1) On the expiration of the Defence of India (Criminal Law Amendment) Act, 1915, every person in respect of whom an order under Rule 3 of the Defence of India (Consolidation) Rules

1915 (IV or 1915), was in force immediately before the expiration of that Act, and who has in the opinion of the Local Government been concerned in any scheduled offence, shall be deemed to be a person resident in an area in which a notification under Section 21 is in force, and the provisions of Part II shall apply to every such person accordingly; and every person who is on such expiration in confinement in accordance with the provisions of the Bengal State Prisoners Regulation, 1818 (III of 1818), shall be deemed to be a person resident in an area in which a notification under Section 33 is in force, and the provisions of Part III shall apply to every such person accordingly:

Provided that, within one month from the expiration of the Defence of India (Criminal Law Amendment) Act, 1915 (IV of 1915), the Local Government may, subject to the conditions prescribed in the first proviso to sub-section (3) of Section 27 as made applicable by Section 37, make any order of restraint which is authorized by Part III in respect of any person who is in confinement in accordance with the provisions of the said Regulation, and if such an order is so made it shall be deemed to be an order made under sub Section (3) of Section 27 as made applicable by Section 37, and the provisions of that Part regarding such an order shall apply accordingly.

(2) On the expiration of the Ingress into India Ordinance, 1914 (V of 1914), as continued in force by the Emergency Legislation Continuance Act, 1915, any person in respect of whom an order was in force immediately before such expiration under Section 2 of that Ordinance read with clause (b) or clause (c) of sub-section (2) of Section 3 of the Foreigners Ordinance, 1914 (III of 1914), shall be deemed to be a person resident in an area in which a notification under Section 21 is in force, and the provisions of Part II shall apply to every such person accordingly:

Provided that, within one month from the expiration of the Ingress into India Ordinance, 1914 (V of 1914), the Local Government may, subject to the conditions prescribed in the first proviso to sub-section (3) of Section 27, make any order of restraint which is authorized by the Part in respect of any such, person, and if such an order is so made it shall be deemed to be an order made under sub-section (3) of Section 27, and the provisions of the Part regarding such an order shall apply accordingly:

Provided that, within one month from the expiration of the Ingress into India Ordinance, 1914 (V of 1914), the Local Government may, subject to the conditions prescribed in the first proviso to sub-section (3) of Section 27, make any order of restraint which is authorised by the Part in respect of any such person, and if such an order is so made it shall be deemed to be an order made under sub-section (3) of Section 27, and the provisions of the Part regarding such an order shall apply accordingly.

PART V

39. *Effect of Cancellation of notifications under Sections 3, 21, or 33:* When a notification issued under Section 3 and Section 21 or Section 33 is cancelled, such cancellation shall not affect any trial, investigation or order commenced or made under this Act, and such trial, investigation or order may be continued or enforced, and on the completion of any such investigation, any order which might otherwise have been made, may be made and enforced, as if such notification had not been cancelled.

40. *Effect of orders made under Parts II and III outside notified area:* (1) an order made under Part II or Part III directing a person to remain or reside in any area in British India outside the area in which such Part is in force, shall be as valid, and enforceable in like manner, as if such Part were in force throughout British India.

(2) An order made under clause (a) of sub-section (1) of Section 34 for the arrest of any person may be executed at any place in British India outside the area in which Part III is in force, and the same procedure shall be followed as if Part III was in force throughout British India:

Provided that, if the arrest is made outside the province of the Local Government which made the order, the report required by Section 35 shall be made to that Local Government, and the maximum period of detention limited by the proviso to that section shall be extended to twenty-one days.

41. *Orders under this Act not to be called in question by the Courts:* No order under this Act shall be called in question in any Court, and no suit or prosecution or other legal proceeding shall lie against any person for anything which is in good faith done or intended to be done under this Act.

42. *Power of Act to be cummulative:* All powers given by this Act, shall be in addition to, and not in derogation of, any other powers conferred by or under any enactment, and all such powers may be exercised in the same manner and, the same authority as if this Act has not been passed.

THE SCHEDULE (SEE SECTION 2)

(1) Any offence under the following Sections of the Indian Penal Code, namely: Sections 121, 121-A, 122, 123, 124, 131 and 132.

(2) Any of the following offences, if in the opinion of Government, such offences connected with any anarchical or revolutionary movement, namely:

(*a*) any offence under Section 124-A, 148, 153-A, 302, 304, 326, 327, 329, 332, 333, 335, 386, 387, 392, 394, 395, 396, 397, 398, 399,

400, 401, 402, 431, 435, 436, 437, 438, 440, 454, 455, 458, 459, 460 and 506 of Indian Penal Code (XLV of 1860);

(*b*) any offence under the Explosive Substances Act, 1908 (VI of 1908);

(*c*) any offence under Section 20 of the Indian Arms Act, 1878.

(3) Any attempt or conspiracy to commit or any abetment of any of the above offences.

Bibliography

I. GOVERNMENT OF INDIA RECORDS

Amritsar Conspiracy Case 1919, Crown Versus Saifuddin Kitchlew, Satyapal and Others. Microfilm at National Archives of India, New Delhi.

Charge Sheet, In that he at Amritsar on and between 30 March and 10 April 1919 conspired to wage war and abetted the waging of war against the king, was a member of the criminal conspiracy in the pursuit of the common object of such conspiracy, uttered sedition, used criminal intimidation, rioted and abetted the commission of arson and murder.

Amritsar Debate and O'Dwyer, Letter of 4 August 1920, Montagu to Wellingdon, Montagu Papers, Rl. no. 4, pp. 121–24.

Microfilm at NAI, O'Dwyer and Conspiracy Theory in 1919.

Amritsar Police Diary, 1919 in Amritsar Conspiracy Case, Microfilms at NAI Day-to-day happenings, along with exact time of events was noted in police diary, useful source for the study of the Rowlatt Satyagraha.

Amritsar Riot Case, 10 April 1919. Legal papers, Charge Sheet Motilal Nehru Papers, File No. 18 of 1919/B/Part-II NMML

Amritsar leaders charged with rioting and violence, *Amritsar Rioting on 10 April 1919;* Report Home Poll, 23 June 1919.

Details of mob violence on 10 April at Amritsar and murder of bank managers.

Baksh, Sheik Umar, *Martial Law in the Punjab,* Lahore, 3 pts, pp. 50, 72, 66.

A collection of various Martial Laws in the Punjab Cocks (Punjab CID). *Handbook of Punjab Revolutionaries and Other Freedom Fighters,* 1918. Punjab State Archives, Patiala.

A source for understanding the nature of revolutionary movement in the Punjab.

Collection of Martial Law orders and notices issued in certain areas of Punjab during disturbances, April–May 1919, Lahore, Supdt. Govt. Printing, 1919 (NAI).

Colonel Wedgewood on the Jallianwala Bagh, 22 December 1919. There were men lying at Jallianwala Bagh, dying of thirst, eating the ground, bleeding to death and nobody to look after them. Unfortunate country people died of their wounds. There had never been anything like this in English history and not in the whole of our relations with India has there been anything of this magnitude before.

Debate on Indian Affairs, House of Commons, 1919, 13 February to 23 December 1919, Col. 710–12, NAI.

Daily Reports for April 1919, from the Punjab Government on the disturbances in the Punjab connected with the Satyagraha Movement.

Home Political, File Nos. 148–78, May 1919, B, NAI.

Local leaders admit that they have no control over the mob. There were very few Sikhs in the mob, which was composed of Kashmiri Muhammadans and city *badmashes*. Murder of bank managers at Amritsar was the work of this element.

Disorders Inquiry Committee Report, 1919–20, Calcutta, Supdt. Govt. Printing, 1920, LII 275p. (NMML)

———, Majority Report, pp. 1–142.

———, Minority Report, pp. 143–236.

Disorders Inquiry Evidence, 7 vols., Calcutta; Supdt. of Govt. Printing, 1920 (NAI, NMML, PULP).

Consists of evidence collected at various places about the disturbances in India in April 1919.

———, vol. I, Delhi, p. 214.

———, vol. II, Bombay Presidency, p. 2929.

———, vol. III, Amritsar, p. 223.

———, vol. IV, Lahore, Kasur, p. 398.

———, vol. V, II, Gujranwala, Gujrat, Lyallpur, p. 259.

———, vol. VI and VII, Pub. Datta, V.N. (ed.), *New Light on Punjab Disturbances*, Shimla, IIAS, 1974–76, 2 vols., p. 1155.

Datta, V.N. and Mittal S.C., *Sources on National Movement, Volume I (January 1919 to September 1920), Protests, Disturbances and Defiance*, Allied Publishers and ICHR, New Delhi, 1985, pp. XXIII + 313.

Contains, official and non-official documents on Rowlatt Satyagraha, Khilafat and the Non-cooperation Movement, valuable material on the Jallianwala Bagh massacre has been incorporated. Professor V.N. Datta's introduction to the volume is authoritative.

East India (Punjab Disturbances) Reports on the Punjab Disturbances, April 1919, presented to Parliament by Command of His Majesty London, HMSO., 1920, Command 534. *Jallianwala Bagh: A Watershed in the Freedom Movement.* 75th Anniversary, 13 April 1994, Department of Information and Public Relations, Punjab, Chandigarh, 1994.

Tribute to martyrs and its importance for Indian nationalism.

———, *Jallianwala Bagh Bagh: Estimate of People Killed.*

Press reactions on Rowlatt Satyagraha, violence and Jallianwala Bagh event.

Press Communique and Official Report from the Punjab Government on Amritsar Riots. Home Poll, File No. 23, June 1919, Deposit.

———, Report on Punjab Disturbances, April 1919, London.

———, His Majesty's Stationery Office, 1920, p. 68 (NAI).

A white paper issued by the Secretary of State for India in connection with the Punjab disturbances to present to British Parliament, submitted on 11 October 1919, and was read on 18 December 1919. Discusses the disturbances upto 25 April 1919.

Puchle, F.H. D.C. Amritsar to J.P. Thompson, Chief Secretary, Punjab, Home Political, Deposit, September 1919, No. 23 and Home Political Deposit, October 1919, no. 31.

Swami Shardhanand visited Punjab and estimated 1,500 killed and M.M. Malaviya stated, 1,000 persons were killed at Amritsar. General Dyer estimated that about 200 to 300 persons were killed. Two women were killed and also 5 boys under 15, youngest being of 9 years. Seva Samiti Allahabad estimated 530 killed including 60 who could not be traced, 200 wounded.

———, House on Rowlatt Act, 1919.

———, House of Commons, Debates 22 May 1919.

———, London His Majesty's Stationery Office, 1920, vol. 116, NAI Rowlatt Act was throughout India a very unpopular Act. Still he thought that, 'Rowlatt Act was necessary, ought to have been passed and could not be avoided', p. 329.

———, *Newspaper Cuttings on Amritsar Disorders,* K.W. to Home Poll, File Nos. 347–58 A, February 1920 NAI.

II. PRIVATE SOURCES / INSTITUTIONAL PAPERS

Bharti, Sohanlal, *Jallianwala Bagh Ki Khuni Dharti aur Mere Mata Pita,* Amritsar, Elgin printers, 1983.

The author writes about his mother's account of the massacre as she saw it all happen on 13 April 1919.

———, *Bhim Sen Sachar, Oral Interview*, recorded on 15 March 1974, at Nehru Memorial Museum and Library, Transcript at MSS Section.

In April 1919 politics revolved round the intellectual class, the lawyers and other educated people. Mass meetings were held and resolutions passed. Despite Martial Law, trains were full, people would travel without tickets and say: *Mahatma Gandhi ki jai, ticket nahin hai.* The Indian railway officials were all in sympathy with them, p. 35.

———, *C.F. Andrews on Jallianwala Bagh Massacre.*

Military officers told him independently that casualties were over a thousand, in order to avoid excitement, the true Government facts were carefully concealed from the people of Amritsar. *The Statesman*, 18 June 1919, See also C.F. Andrews papers 1/D–16, NAI names of their dead or wounded relations for fear of police.

C.F. Andrews on M.K. Gandhi's visit to Jallianwala Bagh: Andrews and Gandhi visited Amritsar on 4 November 1919 huge procession, there was a brightening of eager expectation, his coming has effectively broken the evil spell of terror in Amritsar. It was a day of universal rejoicing, women with children marched with devotion. He came, he saw and he conquered by the peaceful force of divine soul.

———, *Indian Legislative Council Proceedings*, 18 September 1919, vol. LVIII. Speech of Kamini Kumar Chandra on Michael O'Dwyer's policy of advertising Punjab as the quietest province. He despised political agitation subsequently, harsh measures were adopted against political activists and the press was muzzled.

Indian National Congress 34th Session, 1919, Amritsar. Amritsar, 1919 (Report).

Punjab wrongs dominated the session and non-cooperation with the British Government mooted.

———, *Jallianwala Bagh – Number of people killed.*

Kotumal, a local leader of Amritsar estimated, 1,500 wounded and 1,000 killed.

———, Kotumal to Lala Hans Raj, 15 April 1919, Encl. 1, S. No. 6552.

———, *Gandhi Papers*, Gandhi National Museum, Library.

———, *Jallianwala Bagh, Prearranged*, Dr Muhammad Bashir's letter to *Bombay Chronicle*, 17 July 1920.

———, *Jayakar Papers*, File No. 477, NAI.

Explains Hans Raj, a vagabond was seen talking to CID inspector. He had arranged this meeting, as military arrived, he pacified the crowd waved a handkerchief and disappeared.

Gopal, S. (ed.), *The Selected Works of Jawaharlal Nehru (1903–24)*, New Delhi, vol. 1, p. 130.

Evidence shows that after killing people by the hundreds they left the dead and dying unattended, to be carted away by sorrowing relatives and men of the local Seva Samiti, *Ibid.*, pp. 148–49.

———, *Punjab atrocities, 1919.*

———, Sarojini Naidu's letter to *Bombay Chronicle*, 14 August 1920.

Bosworth Smith forcibly uncovered the faces of all women with his own stick. He repeatedly called them she asses, bitches, flies and swine.

Khaparde, G.S., Source material for a history of Freedom movement, correspondence and Diary of G.S. Khaparde, 1897–1920 Bombay, Government of Maharashtra, 1978, p. 519.

Contains valuable material of Punjab disturbances in 1919. Khanna, Guru Ditta (Amritsar).

———, *What did I see at Jallianwala Bagh on 13 April 1919?*

Criminal elements had come from outside on 13 April considering Amritsar unprotected and orphaned.

———, *Freedom Movement Papers*, NAI, File No. III 10/2. Statement sent to F.M. Committee Montagu Papers (NAI)

Montagu, E.S., Secretary of State for India, 1917–22, Reel No. III, O'Dwyer and Punjab Disturbances.

———, Reel No. IV, Hunter Committee Report. O'Dwyer's correspondence with Prime Minister.

———, Reel No. VIII, Rowlatt Bill Readings.

———, Reel No. IX, Satyagraha Demonstrations, anxiety over Civil Disobedience Movement.

Nehru, Motilal on Jallianwala Bagh, Visited on 29 June 1919, Note Book No. II, Motilal Nehru Papers, NMML.

'Saw Jallianwala Bagh- most gruesome sight. Corpses still decomposing in the big well. Shooting practice on 25,000 natives, from a raised, platform, walls pierced with bullets'.

Nehru, Jawaharlal on 'Jallianwala Bagh' Massacre,

Visited Jallianwala Bagh – walked around and saw numerous bullet marks; counted 67 on part of the wall.

Parsad, Dewan Niranjan (Oral Transcript), NMML.

———, Reflections on Jallianwala Bagh.

———, Parliamentary Debates (House of Lords), 1919–20, London, HMSO, 1920.

Punjab Disturbances Jaykar Papers, File Nos. 9–14, vol. I, Press clippings.

File Nos. 476–77, vol. II, Correspondence Punjab Inquiry, 15 April 1920 to 15 January 1920.

Report of Civil Disobedience Enquiry Committee, Madras; Ajmal Khan Committee, 1922 (NAI).

Tilak, B.C., *CID Reports on Jallianwala Bagh Massacre and Looting of Banks.* Maintains that CID reports alleged that police looted the banks. Government ignored these reports and they were also not put before the Hunter Committee.

Tilak, B.G. to G.S. Khaparde, Letter, 28 January 1920, Khaparde Papers, File No. 2–52, NAI.

III. THESIS

Fein, A. Helen, *Imperial Crime and Punishment: A Study of Sanctioning of Collective Violence* (Columbia University, Ph.D. Thesis 1971, XII, p. 425. Microfilm at Nehru Memorial Museum and Library New Delhi.

Naidis, Mark, *The Punjab Disturbances of 1919: A Study in the Indian Nationalism*, Ph.D. Thesis, Stanford University, 1951, VI, p. 254. Microfilm at NMML.

Sharma, Subash, *Sir Michael O'Dwyer, 1913–19*, Ph.D. thesis, Jammu University, Jammu, 1980, Administration, personality and responsibility for Punjab disturbances and Jallianwala Bagh episode.

Singh, Hari, *Political Disturbances in Punjab and Delhi in 1919: A Study of the Evolution of Nationalism in India*, Ph.D. thesis, Kurukshetra University, Kurukshetra, 1976, pp. 302+XX.

IV. ARTICLES

A. *Tribune.*
B. *Modern Review.*
C. Jallianwala Bagh Commemoration Volume, Patiala, 1997.
D. *Past and Present.*
E. *Bombay Chronicle.*
F. Proceedings of Punjab History Conference.
G. *Khalsa Advocate.*
H. *Blackwood Magazine* (New York).
I. *Hindustan Review.*
J. *The Times* (London).

Ahluwalia, M.L., *Jallianwala Bagh – A Tragedy or Massacre,* Jallianwala Bagh Commemoration Volume, Patiala, 1997, pp. 141–47.
Legal point of view analysed on the basis of cases, debates and Congress Inquiry Committee Report.
A member of the Indian Intelligence, *Sir Michael O'Dwyer as His Own Painter.*

———, *Hindustan Review* (Allahabad), vol. XLVIII, July 1925, pp. 360–67.

A critical assessment of Sir Michael O'Dwyer's personality and administration based on his book, *India as I Knew It, 1885–1925*.

An English Woman, *Amritsar*.

Blackwood's Magazine, New York, vol. CCVIII, April, 1920, pp. 441-46.

Jallianwala Bagh tragedy is the focus of this essay.

———, *Amritsar: Four Hundred Years, Tribune* (Special Supplement), 24 October 1977.

Articles on Freedom Movement in Amritsar by G.R. Sethi, Kirpal Singh and V.N. Datta.

Bajaj, Y.P., *Carnage at Jallianwala Bagh: The Constitutional Responsibility.* Jallianwala Bagh Commemoration Volume, Patiala, 1997, pp. 158–62.

Argues that Dyer deliberately punished the peaceful people assembled at Jallianwala Bagh, so that they did not challenge the Imperial System.

Banerjee, Kaushik and Barn Jatinder, *Verrioning Terror: Jallianwala Bagh and the Jungle*, Jallianwala Bagh Commemoration Volume, Patiala, 1997, pp. 106–27.

Analyses the civilizing terror, the norm of the British nation, white supremacy and operation of imperialism.

Chatterji, Ramanand (ed.), Mr C.F. Andrews on Punjab Atrocities *Modern Review*, vol. XXVI, December, 1919, pp. 703–4.

Comments on C.F. Andrews' views on Jallianwala Bagh who calls it a cowardly and brutal act.

———, *The Punjab Tragedy, Modern Review*, vol. XXVII, May 1920, pp. 600–2

Discusses Rabindranath Tagore's views on the Jallianwala Bagh tragedy.

———, Jallianwala Bagh Meeting, Neither Dangerous nor Rebellious, *Modern Review*, vol. XXVIII, July 1920, pp. 94–95.

Discusses the nature of the Jallianwala Bagh meeting as a peaceful assembly.

———, The Simla Archbishop's letter, *Modern Review*, vol. XXVIII, July 1920, p. 95.

A letter written in defence of General Dyer.

———, General Dyer's Punishment, *Modern Review*, vol. XXVIII, September 1920, pp. 35–51.

Highlights Lord Milner's views on Dyer's action and reaction of members of the House of Lords.

———, O'Dwyerian Theory Disapproved, *Modern Review*, vol. XXVI, December 1919, pp. 704–6.

Criticizes O' Dwyer's theory that the disturbances in Punjab were engineered by outsiders.

———, Why Dyer was Condemned, *Modern Review*, vol. XXVIII, September 1920, pp. 345–46.

Analyses General Dyer's act at Jallianwala Bagh.

———, The O' Dwyer Nair Case, *Modern Review*, vol. XXXVI, July 1924, pp. 110–12.

Explains the nature of libel suit, Sir Michael O'Dwyer vs Sir Sankarana Nair.

———, Sydenham's article, *Modern Review*, vol. XXXVI, December 1924, pp. 725–30.

Problems of India along with views on Jallianwala Bagh massacre.

———, Sir Michael O' Dwyer on the Riots and the Reforms, *Modern Review*, vol. XXXIX, June 1926, pp. 746–47.

Provides a critical estimate of Michael O'Dwyer's views on disturbances in 1919.

———, General Dyer, *Modern Review*, vol. XLII, September 1927, pp. 356–66.

Opines that General Dyer did not save India, as there was no projected rebellion.

Das, Govardhan, *Jallianwala Bagh and Martial Law in Punjab*.

He travelled to Bombay, Allahabad, Calcutta, Madras and Pondicherry contacted leaders and narrated Punjab atrocities to them. He was arrested and punished for writing a seditious article in *Bombay Chronicle* dated 18 April 1919. F.M. Papers NAI, III, 10/2.

Datta, V.N., *Jallianwala Bagh Massacre, Tribune*, 24 October 1977.

Critical Examination of General Dyer's shooting of innocent people at Amritsar.

———, *Jallianwala Bagh Tragedy and its Aftermath, Tribune*, Chandigarh, 13 April 1969.

Critical analysis of the circumstances leading to the tragedy and its impact.

———, *Could Jallianwala Bagh Massacre be Prevented?* in Mohinder Singh (ed.), History and Culture of the Punjab through the Ages Prof. Harbans Singh, Commemoration Volume, New Delhi, 1988, pp. 262–95.

Jallianwala Bagh was a consequence of complete administrative and political failure of a tactless and wilful government oblivious of the political realities of the times. Gandhi also did not foresee chances of emergence of violence in peaceful Satyagraha in 1919.

———, Introduction – *Jallianwala Bagh Commemoration Volume*, Punjabi University, Patiala, 1997.

Critical Summary of Dyer's action, aftermath in India and England, gaps in historical research and O'Dwyer vs Nair suit, pp. 1–13.

———, 'Jallianwala Bagh', in *We Fight Together for Freedom: Chapter from the Indian National Movement,* (ed.) Ravi Dayal, Oxford University Press, Delhi, 1995, pp. 78–1040.

In depth study of the Jallianwala Bagh Tragedy. Provides fresh insights.

Gauba, A., *The Amritsar Conspiracy Case, 1919 and Dr Satyapal,* Jallianwala Bagh Commemoration Volume, Patiala, 1997, pp. 180–89.

Analyses the charges on Satyapal and others critically.

Gupta, Shiv Kumar, *Jallianwala Bagh and the Raj,* Jallianwala Bagh Commemoration Volume, Patiala, 1997, pp. 170–79.

Builds up the thesis on the basis of statements of victims suffers and eye witnesses before the Congress Inquiry Committee and analyses the British attitude towards natives during the Martial Law days.

Gurcharan Singh, *Psycho-Political Compulsions of Jallianwala Bagh Massacre.* Jallianwala Bagh Commemoration Volume, Patiala, 1997, pp. 148–57.

Responsibility for the tragedy has been fixed on Dyer, O'Dwyer and even Gandhi, who were working on their own psychological compulsions.

———, *The Imperial Terrorism in Punjab: Its Nature and Implications (1919–25).* Jallianwala Bagh Commemoration Volume, Patiala, 1997, pp. 205–17.

Analyses Dyers terrorism in Amritsar and how Dyer's baptism as honorary Sikh irked Sikh masses leading to Gurdwara Reform movement and the rise of Akalis in Nationalist politics.

Hans, Surjit, *The Construction of a Nationalist Symbol,* Jallianwala Bagh Commemoration Volume, Patiala, 1997, pp. 88–105.

Analyses the participation of various communities in Punjab, through diagrams and graphs on the basis of Martial Law punishments in 1919.

Kaur, Madanjit, *Jallianwala Bagh Tragedy: Its Impact and Emergence as National Historical Monument.* Jallianwala Bagh Commemoration Volume, Patiala, 1993, pp. 163–69.

Causes, impact and emergence of Jallianwala Bagh, a national monument have been discussed.

———, *Martial Law in Lahore and Amritsar. Dangerous Secrecy, What it Means?*

———, *Bombay Chronicle,* 20 April, 1919.

Martial Law was lawless law explains veil of secrecy to cover excesses.

———, *Michael O'Dwyer, the Incorrigible, Tribune,* 14 January 1921.

Critical assessment of the character and administration of Michael O'Dwyer, the then Lt. Governor of the Punjab.

Kumar, Raj, *Some Reflections on Jallianwala Bagh Tragedy and Annie Besant's Politics in India,* Jallianwala Bagh Commemoration Volume, Patiala, 1997, pp. 194–98.

Analyses Mrs Annie Besant's attitude to the Rowlatt Bill agitation and her fears of disorders.

Kumar, Ravinder , *The Jallianwala Bagh Tragedy, Rowlatt Satyagraha and the Character of the Nationalist Struggle in India: Some Reflections*, Jallianwala Bagh Commemoration Volume, 1997, Punjabi University, Patiala, pp. 14–22.

Studies the character of political society in 1919, Gandhian ideology and the manner it reached various sections of Indian society and how far Rowlatt agitation brought a qualitative change in the nationalist movement.

———, *Rowlatt Bills: A Colossal Blunder, Tribune*, 21 March 1919.

Challenge to the people. The Bill was an executive order, a lawless law.

Mohan, Kamlesh, *Rowlatt Act Agitation in Amritsar. Punjab History Conference Proceedings*, vol. X, February 1976, pp. 206–23.

Nature, course and impact of the Rowlatt Act agitation in Amritsar.

Natesan, G.A., *The Punjab Disorders Inquiry, Indian Review*, vol. X, no. II, November 1919, p. 736.

Analyses the debate held on Punjab disturbances in the House of Lords, London.

Naidu, Sarojini, *The Punjab 1919, Indian Review*, vol. XX, no. 9, September 1919, p. 613.

A poem written by Mrs Sarojini Naidu on the Jallianwala Bagh tragedy.

Natesan, G.A., *The Dyer Case and After, Indian Review*, vol. XXI, no. 7, July, 1920, p. 424.

Comments of *The Times, The Daily News* and the Archbishop of Canterbury.

———, *The Punjab Tragedy and Missionaries, Indian Review*, vol. XXI, no. 7, July 1920, pp. 451–52.

Narrates the protest on the Punjab tragedy made by certain missionaries in India.

Mittal, S.C., *Jallianwala Kand ke Ek Vir Senani Se Bhent* (Hindi), *JRJ*, 13 April, 1968, An Interview with Dr Gurbakash Rai

———, *Jallianwala Bagh and its Impact, Tribune*, 12 April 1981.

Discusses the impact of the great tragedy at local, provincial, national and international levels.

———, *Jallianwala Bagh: Impact on the Freedom Movement, Tribune*, 13 April 1976.

Historical survey of available literature on Jallianwala Bagh and highlights the impact of the shooting incident on public opinion.

Rai, Satya M., *Jallianwala Bagh Tragedy – Its Impact on the Political Awakening*

in India, Jallianwala Bagh Commemoration Volume, Patiala, 1997, pp. 128–40.
Analyses the causes, the tragedy, impact of massacre, political developments following the massacre and impact on Punjab legislative councillors.

Ram, Raja , *Factors Responsible for Jallianwala Bagh Tragedy,* Jallianwala Bagh Commemoration Volume, Patiala, 1997, pp. 190–98.

Santanam, K., *The Ugly Englishmam; Punjab Martial Law. Shakti,* 3(I), January 1966, pp. 43–49.
Condemns Martial Law and the attitude of British officials, *Sikhs and the Riots, 1919, Khalsa Advocate,* Amritsar, 24 June 1919.

Sayer, Derek, *British Reactions to the Amritsar Massacre, 1919–20. Past and Present,* May 1919, no. 31, pp. 130–63.

———, *British Reaction of the Amritsar Massacre 1919–20.* Jallianwala Bagh, Commemoration Volume Patiala, 1997, pp. 23–51.
Studies the British reaction to Jallianwala Bagh tragedy. Criticizes Draper for adopting Dyer's line of thinking. Dyer's testimony, Hunter Committee Report, Dyer debate in House of Commons and ultimately Maccardies arguments have been analysed.

Sethi, G.R., *Prominent Figures of Amritsar, Tribune,* 24 October 1977.
Reminiscences of prominent nationalists of Amritsar, Dr Satyapal, Dr Kitchlew, Chaudhry, Rattanchand, etc.

Singh, Hari , *The Myth of Loyalty of the Punjab during the War (1914–18).*

———, *Punjab History Conference, vol. X,* February 1976, pp. 198–205.
The deliberate circulation of loyalty myth of the Punjabis by the British has been studied on the basis of ongoing revolutionary movement and recruitment violence in the Punjab.

———, *Emergence of Violence in the Punjab Politics: A Case Study of Rowlatt Satyagraha in the Punjab.*

———, *Punjab History Conference Proceedings,* vol. XVI, March 1982, pp. 208–13.
Emergence and nature of violence during Rowlatt Satyagrah a at Amritsar on 10 April 1919.

———, *Punjab's Response to Rowlatt Bills' Agitation,* in Mohinder Singh (ed.), *History and Culture of the Punjab,* Prof. Harbans Singh Commemoration Volume, New Delhi, 1988, pp. 160–72.
Rowlatt Satyagraha in Punjab and Jallianwala Bagh. Historical forces and personality factor discussed. Socio-economic and political forces leading to violence analysed.

———, *Jallianwala Bagh, Tribune,* 13 April 1922.

——, *Lessons of Jallianwala Bagh Massacre for the People and for the British Government.*

Singh, Prem, *Jallianwala Bagh Tragedy and the National Movement. Post-War upsurge in Punjab and the Response of the National Leadership,* Jallianwala Bagh Commemoration Volume, Patiala, 1997, pp. 82–87.
Provides a brief background to the events in 1919.

Singh, Nazeer, *Amritsar, Murder and the Mahatma in 1919,* Jallianwala Bagh Commemoration Volume, Patiala, 1997, pp. 218–25.
Perspectives on Gandhi and Punjab response to Satyagraha movement.

——, *Open Rebellion in Punjab* (India), *The Times* (London), (editorial), 19 April 1919.
Explains the nature of disturbances and compares these with the rebellion of 1857. States that the murder of Englishmen at Amritsar is like repeating the incidents of 1857. Chelmsford stated that 'open rebellion' had broken out in parts of Punjab in 1919. 'On 13 April, troops came in collusion with the Mob at Amritsar and there were 200 casualties. Fraternisation of Hindus and Muslims seen as the repetition of 1857. The uprising is a deliberate attempt to overturn the British rule in India.

Singh, Sikander, *Murder of Sir Michael Francis O'Dwyer and Trial of Udham Singh,* Jallianwala Bagh Commemoration Volume, Patiala, 1997, pp. 199–204.

Singh, Udham (16) had seen the Jallianwala Bagh carnage and analyses how its was avenged by the murder of O'Dwyer in 1940.

Tuteja, K.L., *Jallianwala Bagh Tragedy: A Re-assessment,* Jallianwala Bagh Commemoration Volume, Patiala, 1997, pp. 52–81.
It is an attempt to understand the phenomena of which the particular incident formed a part. Provides the emergence of political consciousness in Punjab and the Rowlatt Bills.

IV. BOOKS

Bakshi, S.R. *Jallianwala Bagh Tragedy,* New Delhi, Capital Publishers, 1982, p. 208.
Discusses the Rowlatt Bills, firing at the Jallianwala Bagh, its reaction, Hunter and Congress Committee and finally the Amritsar Congress, 1919.

Colvin, Ian, *Life of General Dyer,* London, Blackwood, 1931.
Assesses the life of General Dyer from a structural British view point as a saviour of the Raj.

Datta, V.N., *Amritsar: Past and Present,* Amritsar Municipal Committee, 1967, p. 207.

Authoritative work on urban history of Amritsar – political (including Jallianwala Bagh tragedy) social and economic dimensions from 1577 to 1965, discussed in a lucid style.

——, *Jallianwala Bagh*, Ludhiana, Lyall Book Depot, 1969.
Pioneering critical estimate of the Jallianwala Bagh Tragedy. Expertise in analysing the multi-faceted historical forces.

——, *New Light on Punjab Disturbances in 1919*, Şhimla: Indian Institute of Advanced Study, 1976, p. 1155.
The Volume consists of Vols. VI and VII of Hunter Committee evidence which were not originally published with an introduction, situating the confidential nature of these volumes as well as the political developments in the Punjab.

Draper, Alfred, *Amritsar: The Massacre that Ended the Raj*, London, Cassel, 1981, NMML, p. 310
Analyses in detail the events of Jallianwala Bagh and Dyer's action in perspective.
Dyer's evidence and humiliation, Udham Singh – murder of Sir Michael O'Dwyer explained dramatically.

Duni Chand, *Ulster of India or Analysis of the Punjab Problems*. Lahore, the Author, 1936, p. 234.
Discusses the Punjab Problem in 1919, covers Punjab political life upto 1936.

Fein, A. Helen , *Imperial Crime and Punishment: The Jallianwala Bagh Massacre and the British Judgement, 1919–20*. Honolulu; University Press, Hawai, 1977, vol. XIX , p. 250.
Sociological interpretation of the sanctioning of violence in the Punjab, 1919.
The book revolves round the roots of the Jallianwala Bagh massacre since it has resonated in the memory of Indians for over half a century. It was the worst bloodshed in Indian history when Indians were alienated from the British rule.

Furneaux, Rupert, *Massacre at Amritsar*, London, George Allen and Unwin Ltd., 1963, p. 183.
A psychological interpretation of Dyer's action at Jallianwala Bagh and how far Dyer was justified in his stand. Discusses whether it was a riot or rebellion. Censure and libel suit against Dyer have been discussed objectively.

Garret, G.T., *An Indian Commentary*, London; Jonathan Cape, 1928.
Discontent – in India in 1919 was due to racial arrogance of Europeans and Anglo-Indians. Englishmen had learnt to look upon Indians as the

creatures, 'half-gorilla, half-negro, who appeared in contemporary *Punch* cartoons', p. 115.

Gauba, Anand, *Amritsar – A Study in Urban History* (1840–1947), Jullundur, ABS Publication, 1988.

Enriches our understanding of growth of Amritsar: Culture and economy of its people.

Ghose, Akshya K., *Lord Chelmsford's Viceroyalty; A Critical Survey*, Madras, Ganesh & Co. 1921.

O'Dwyer was a violent autocrat, offensive to educated Indians, next moment apologetic, with all the authority of British Government at his back, he generated fear in the minds of helpless and unarmed people of the Punjab since they could not love him, pp. 10–11.

He scented danger to British rule in both the Hartal and Hindu-Muslim-Unity. To him it was an anti-British combination which must be broken.

Grewal, J.S. and Puri, H.K. (eds.), *Letters of Udham Singh Amritsar*, Guru Nanak Dev University, 1975, p. 104.

Contains seven letters written from the prison in England, provides historical background and life of Udham Singh, Gursharan Singh, Parm Bakshish Singh, Verma, Devinder Kumar, Ghai, Raj Krishan (eds.), *Jallianwala Bagh, Commemoration Volume* and *Amritsar and Our Duty to India*, Patiala, Punjabi University, Publication Bureau, 1997.

Contains introduction by V.N. Datta and eighteen articles, along with the full text of the book, *Amritsar and Our Duty to India* by B.G. Horniman. This book is based on recent researches. Annotated Bibliography of articles has been given, hereafter cited as, Jallianwala Bagh Commemoration Volume, Patiala, 1997.

Gwynn, Maj-General Sir Charles, W., *Imperial Policing*, London, Macmillan & Co., 1996.

Anatomy of Rowlatt Satyagraha.

Jallianwala Bagh discussed, advocated the principle of minimum military force should be employed in anti-government protests.

Hale, H.W., *The Political Trouble in India* (1917–37) (reprint), Allahabad, Chugh Publications, 1974, p. 295.

CID interpretation of political developments in India.

Horniman, B.G., *British Administration and the Amritsar Massacre*, Delhi, Mittal Publications, 1984 (Reprint), p. 196.

Discusses causes of unrest, agitation over the Rowlatt Bills, the disturbances, and six weeks of terror in the Punjab.

——, *Amritsar and Our Duty to India*, London, T. Fisher Unwin, 1920, p. 196.

Discusses the nature of events and happenings in Amritsar in April 1919. Besides this the Indian contribution to war, Rowlatt Bill agitation, bombing of the crowds and duty of the British people has been discussed.

——, *Jallianwala Bagh*, 13 April 1919, 50 the Anniversary of Jallianwala Bagh, New Delhi, Publications Division, Government of India, 1969, p. 34.

Provides summary of the prelude, the shooting episode and impact on the Indian mind.

Jordens, J.T.F., *Josiah-i-Wedgewood: The Man and His Works*, Madras, Ganeshan & Co., n.d., p. 182.

Brief life of Col. Wedgewood. Chapter VI deals with the Punjab atrocities.

Kumar, Ravinder (ed.), *Essays on Gandhian Politics: The Rowlatt Satyagraha of 1919*, Oxford, Clarendon Press, 1971, p. 347.

A collection of nine essays on Rowlatt Bills and the Non-cooperation-Movement by eminent scholars. Detailed analysis of the movement in Gujarat, Bombay, Delhi and Lahore. It also discusses emergence of Gandhi as a national leader. Sociological dimension of pre-disposing causes has been explored.

Montagu, E.S. (Secy. of State for India 1917–22) *An Indian Diary*, London, 1930.

He wrote impulsively. Sweeping or hasty judgements modified or even contradicted a few pages later, says Venetia Montagu in her introduction. Express views on Punjab officials. P.J. Thompson, Chief Secy. Punjab and Fagan, Financial Commissioner Punjab. They were suspicious of educated Indians.

O'Dwyer, Sir Michael Francis, *The Punjab Disturbances of April 1919: A Criticism of the Hunter Committee Report*, London, Indo-British Association, London.

Mittal, S.C., *Freedom Movement in Punjab 1905–29*, New Delhi, Concept, 1977.

Traces the origin, course and character of the Freedom Movement during the period 1905–29.

Mitra, H.N., *Punjab Unrest Before and After the Rowlatt Bills*, Calcutta, Annual Register Office, 1920, pp. 128, 264.

Provides a comprehensive account of the Rowlatt Satyagraha in Punjab.

Authentic material on Hunter Report and disagreement of Indian members on certain points, specially on the theory of 'open rebellion' in the Punjab; General Dyer's conduct and Martial Law courts. Contemporary point of view presented on organization and minority report.

Mohan, Kamlesh, Sehgal, Bhupinder Singh Tasser, R.D. Sharma (eds.), *Jallianwala Bagh – A Saga of Sacrifice*, Chandigarh, Sahitya Academy, Chandigarh, 1995.

Contains twelve articles, documents and impressions on Jallianwala Bagh.

Moon, Penderel (ed.), *Divide and Quit*, London, Chatto and Windus, 1961, p. 302.

Gives an account of Punjab disturbances in 1919.

Narain, Savita, *The Historiography of the Jallianwala Bagh Massacre*, 1919, Spantech and Lancer, New Delhi, 1998, NMML, p. 76.

This work is the B.A. (Hons) degree dissertation of the University of Wales; this study looks into the events before the massacre, nature of the crowd at Jallianwala Bagh, the shooting, its aftermath, and reaction of the British, the Indians and resulted in a verdict for O'Dwyer with damages. MacCardie justified Dyer's action and the only dissenting voice in the jury was that of Professor Harold Laski.

Nundy, Alfred, Political Problems and Hunter Committee Disclosures, Calcutta, 1920.

Good comments on political situation. Masses turning to educated classes. English public opinion expressed in the *Manchester Gaurdian*. 'The shooting at Amritsar is as though a mad man has been let loose to massacre at large', p. 111. Masses believe that the country is not being run by Englishmen but by the police, p. 35.

———, *Indian Unrest, 1919–20*, Dehradun, 1921, p. 274.

Explains the factors responsible for Indian unrest in 1919 and the evolution of the Non-cooperation Movement.

———, *Revolution or Evolution*, Lahore, Tandon & Com. 1922, p. 428.

Traces Khilafat and Non-cooperation Movement. He calls Gandhi an apostle of force not of peace, who led the nation on the road to anarchy.

O'Dwyer, Sir Michael Francis, *India as I Knew It (1885–1925)*, London, Constable & Co., 1925.

———, Autobiographical Account and Perceptions of Imperial Administration of Punjab.

Peary Mohan, Pandit, (Vakil High Court), *An Imaginary Rebellion: And How It Was Suppressed*, Lahore, Kholsa Bros., 1920.

An account of the Punjab disorder and the working of Martial Law.

Collection of a variety of material, nationalist interpretation of Punjab disturbances, Martial Law orders, conspiracy case, debate in the House of Commons, specially Col. Wedgewood's speech, along with a list of 581 persons who were punished for their participation in the movement. The front page carries the poem by Sarojini Naidu, 'Punjab in 1919'.

Ralhan, O.P. and Sharma Suresh K., *Documents on Punjab: Jallianwala Bagh Tragedy*, New Delhi, Anmol Publishers, 1994, pp. IX+516 (ICHR)
Contains Dyer's statement, Debate in House of Commons on Amritsar affair, Congress inquiry statement and extracts from the *Hindu*, the *Young India* and the *Tribune*, Sarojini Naidu's, poem on Punjab 1919 and R.N. Tagore's letter requesting to be relieved of knighthood, as a protest against the Jallianwala Bagh massacre.

Ram, Raja, *The Jallianwala Bagh Massacre: A Premeditated Plan* (ed. Balkishan), Chandigarh, Punjab University, 1969, (PULC, KUL, NMML).
The book provides an historical background to the Jallianwala Bagh tragedy and maintains that it was a pre-planned conspiracy, list of 381 persons who died and appendices provided.

Robb, P.E., *The Government of India under Lord Chelmsford, 1916–21*, University of London, Ph.D. Thesis, 1971.
Objective analysis of the nature of British rule during the period, 1916–21. It heightens our understanding of the historical process leading to Jallianwala Bagh.

Setalvad, Sir, C.H., *Recollections and Reflections: An Autobiography*, Bombay, Padma Publications, 1946, p. 530. (DPL)
Discusses Rowlatt Bills agitation, Punjab disturbances, Hunter Committee Report and Martial Law in Punjab.

Sharma, S.L. (ed.), *Jallianwala Bagh Martyrdom Memorial Souvenir*, Amritsar, n.d., p. 98.

Singh, Gursharan and Saggar Balraj, *Jallianwala Bagh (Who's Who)*, Chandigarh, Punjab State University Text Book Board, 1996, pp. 252.
The Introduction of the book deals with the chronological sequence leading to the tragedy and its nationwide repercussions. Highlights Amritsar conspiracy case 1919 and other cases arising out of disturbances in Amritsar. Biographical notes of participants are detailed and authoritative.

Singh, Hari, *Gandhi, Rowlatt Satyagraha and British Imperialism: Emergence of Mass Movements in Punjab and Delhi*, Delhi, IBB, 1990.
Historical analysis of Rowlatt Satyagraha, its genesis, movement, leadership and confrontation of British Imperialism with Indian National-

ism. Chapter on Amritsar provides new materials and fresh interpretation of Jallianwala Bagh, pp. 144–81.

Singh, Nihal, *Ruling India by Bullets and Bombs*, London, 1920.
A pamphlet regarding atrocities of the British in India in 1919.

Swinson, Arthur, *Six minutes to Sunset: The Story of General Dyer and the Amritsar Affair*, London, Peter Davis, 1964, vol. VII, p. 216.
Author opines that Hunter's examination was confused, ill-concieved and unorganised. He explains the nature of disturbances as (1) Unlawful assembly, (2) Riot, and (3) Rebellion. Explains the amount of force which an officer may legally employ in relation to Dyer and his action at Jallianwala Bagh. Discusses the Dyer debate and silence of the innocent sufferers at Jallianwala Bagh. Theory developed by Rupert Furneaux that Dyer was subject to mental disorder at that time has been rejected.

———, *The Congress Punjab Inquiry 1919–20*, Report of the Commissioners Appointed by the Punjab Sub-Committee of the Indian National Congress. Vol. I: Report, Issued under the auspices of Nehru Memorial Museum and Library, New Delhi and National Book Trust India, 1994 (reprint) originally printed in 1920, p. 144.
The Report is a nationalist version of the Punjab disturbances. Jallianwala Bagh explained. The word *Bagh* is a misnomer, Jalle is the caste name of the original owner, 'Wala' is the genitive termination; and the *bagh*, meaning a garden, is really an open piece of land surrounded by houses (p. 50). The book also explains the atrocities committed on the people of Punjab during the Martial Law. M.K. Gandhi was the Chairman of the committee.

———, *The Flame Burns, Jallianwala Bagh Day Souvenir, All India Freedom Fighters Association*, n.d.
Contains photos of Bugga and Ratto and some articles on Freedom movement.

Woodruff, Phillip, *The Men Who Ruled India Vol. I: The Guardians*
It has a section on Michael O'Dwyer's character, personality and achievements.

Wolpert, Stanley, *Massacre at Jallianwala Bagh*, New Delhi, 1st edition 1970 and 2nd edition 1988, pp. 318. (ICHR).
It is a chilling fictional reconstruction of the incident. The author graphically paints the picture of Maqbool lawyer dying of bullet wounds and thirst, pp. 215–19 and points out that General Dyer was responsible for the killing who was never punished for his crime but was accorded a hero's welcome in England, presumably for saving the British Empire in India. The contemporary atmosphere has been reconstructed and the characters appear life-like.

V. BOOKS IN INDIAN LANGUAGES

Aggarwal, Bihari Lal, *Jallianwala Bagh* (Hindi), Rajhans Press, Kanpur, n.d. pp. 58, IOL 160.
Poetic drama on Punjab in 1919 and Jallianwala Bagh episode.

Ahmad, Syed Nur, *Martial Law se Martial Law Tuk* (Urdu), Lahore, Shirkat-I-Islam-O-fan, nd., NMML, p. 524.
Describes political developments in India from April 1919 to October 1958. Highlights formation of Pakistan.

———, *Aphat Ki Holi Ya Rastriya Phag* (Hindi), 'Vinod' Lucknow, Hindi Pustak Mandir, Anglo-Arabic Press, 1922, p. 16, NAI 43.
The Holi of calamities, poetry primarily on Gandhi and protest against Rowlatt Bill.

———, *Bage jaliyan* (Hindi),

Bharti, Sohan lal, *Jallianwala Bagh Ki khooni Dharti Aur Mere Mata Pita* (Hindi), Amritsar, Bharti Parkashan, 1983. (Reprint of 1969 edn.) p. 75, NMML.
Personalized account of the sufferings of Attar Kaur Bhatia, whose husband died in the shooting at Jallianwala Bagh. She brought her husband's dead body to her home. This lady was pregnant and gave birth to a posthumous child, who is the author of this book.

Das, Parshotam, *Rattan Devi da Vilap*, Jallianwala Bagh wich (Punjabi), p. 6.
A pamphlet regarding the cruelty at Jallianwala Bagh on 13 April 1919, emotive account of Rattan Devi's suffering.

———, *Punjab Ka Hatyakand, Yani Behson Ki Ah* (Hindi and Urdu)

Datta, V.N., *Jallianwala Bagh* (Hindi) tr., by Rajendar Swarup Vats, Chandigarh, Haryana, Hindi Granth Academy, 1975.
Hindi version of author's book on the subject, pub. in 1969.

———, *Jaliyan Ki Karur Katha* (Hindi)

Gupta, Ram Sarup, Jullundur Sudarshan Press, 1923, p. 40, CRL.

———, Poems on Jallianwala Bagh tragedy and Punjab disturbances in 1919.

———, *Bharat Durdasha Darshan: Punjab ka Hatya Kand* (Hindi),

Kishan Chand, *Zakhmi Punjab* (Hindi) Durga Press, Calcutta, 1922, pp. 128, NAI.
Describes atrocities in Punjab.

Malaviya, Pandit Kapil Dev, *Punjab Rahshiya: O'Dwyer Shahi Ka Zulum*, Paryag Abhiudaya Press, n.d., p. 122.
A graphic description of army rule and sufferings of the people of Punjab in 1919; Amritsar, Lahore Gujranwala, Kasur discussed and role of local leaders like Ratto and Bugga has been highlighted along with atrocities suffered by them.

Menon, K.P.S., *Jallianwala Bagh Aur C.R.*, Sankaran Nair (Hindi), 1969.
Perspetives on libel suit against Nair.

Pathak, Chander Shekhar, *Punjab Ka Bhisham Hatya Kand* (Hindi)

Ratan Lal, Zamarrud, Published, Bulandshar: Badri Printing Works, 1921, pp. 32, IOLB 237.
Poems on Punjabi sufferings in Jallianwala Bagh and pathetic plight of helpless wounded people.

Shamsher, Joginder, *1919 Da Punjab* (Punjabi), Delhi, Nayug Publishers, 1992, pp. 191.
Confirms that Dyer suffered from the disease arteriosclerosis and provides information on the Hunter Committee, Congress Inquiry and debate in the House of Commons.

Shastri, Satyapriya, *Bhartiya Swatantrata Sangram Mein Arya Samaj Ka Yogdan*, Jullundur, n.d. pp. 280.
Sheds light on the leadership of intrepid Rattan Chand (Ratto), who led the mobs in Amritsar before the Jallianwala Bagh tragedy. Explains the inhuman treatment of police towards his wife and children. Transported to Andaman for life, pp. 74–77.

Shukla , Raghunath Parsad, Benares: Kanahya Lal, Bharat Press, c. 1921, 6 pp. IOLB 137.
Commentary on Punjab during 1919, disturbances and Jallianwala Bagh shooting.

———, Pub. Benares: Shambhu Printing Works, n.d., 4 pp. IOLB 70.

———, *Poems on Punjab and Jallianwala Bagh.*

———, Narration of cruelty on innocent people.

Shukla, Ram Autar (ed.), *Punjab Ka Khun* (Hindi), Kanpur, Bhartiya Press, 1920, p. 28, CRL.
Poetry and prose on Rowlatt Satyagraha and Jallianwala Bagh, title page has a significant comment, 'The Punjab is weeping on actions of the coward Dyer. The soil of Jallianwala Bagh is still wet with the blood of our babies.'

Sidhu, Gurdev Singh (ed.), *Saka Bagh-E-Jallian* (Punjabi) Patiala, Punjabi Vikas Vibhagh, 1995, pp. 98.
Poetry inspired by Jallianwala Bagh tragedy, sensitive portrayal of people's misery and sufferings. Poets include Nanak Singh, Suraj Singh and others; 16 poems in all.

Verma, Suraj Bhan, *Sangeet O'Dwyershahi Yani Mazlum* Punjab in Yadav, K.C. (ed.), *Swatantrata Andolan Mein, Kaviyon, Shiaron aur Bhajan Upedshkon Ka Yogdan,* Delhi, Bhavana Parkashan, Patparganj, pp. 215–62, n.d.

Proscribed publication, provides dramatic representation of O'Dwyerism and Imperial attitudes. Popular folk style.

Vidrohi, Ramesh, *Jab Roya Punjab* (Hindi), (Jallianwala Bagh Aur Uske Shaeed), New Delhi, Bhavana Parkashan, 1976, p. 93.

Brief history of the Jallianwala Bagh massacre with a list of 344 persons killed there.

Vishvamitra, P., *Punjab Hatyakand* (Hindi), Calcutta, Vishwamitra Karyalaya, 1922, p. 304.

Analyses the Jallianwala Bagh tragedy on the basis of the Hunter Committee and Congress Sub-Committee reports and evidence.

Index

Attention: Readers/Authors

This checklist includes all recent and forthcoming titles in the field of Social Sciences, History, Philosophy and Literature.

We welcome your comments which will be valuable to us to improve the quality of publications.

Invitation to authors: If you are working on a manuscript now or planning to write one in near future—maybe a textbook or a monograph—we shall be glad to receive your proposal for its publication.

If you want to receive our publication information sheet regularly please send your name

All Communications should be addressed to:

PRAGATI PUBLICATIONS
9926 Library Road
Azad Market, Delhi 110006
Telephones: 3518135, 3614747 Fax: 3549959
E-mail: pragati1@ndf.vsnl.net.in

INDIA COUNCIL OF HISTORICAL RESEARCH MONOGRAPH SERIES

Archaeology of Seafaring
EDITED BY HIMANSHU PRABHA RAY
x + 352 pp Rs 795

Indo-French Relations
EDITED BY K. S. MATHEW AND S. JEYASEELA STEPHEN
x + 330 pp Rs 795

We Lived Together
EDITED BY S. SETTAR AND P. K. V. KAIMAL
x + 368 pp Rs 795

Jallianwala Bagh: Masscrace
EDITED BY V. N. DATTA AND S. SETTAR
viii + 306 pp Rs 795

Second World War: As catalyst for Social Changes in India
S. B. SINGH
Demy 8vo xii + 208 pp Rs 395

Indigo and the Raj
PRABHAT KUMAR SHUKLA
Demy 8vo 210 pp Rs 250

Tarikh-i-Akbari
MUHAMMAD ARIF QANDAHARI
An annotated English translation with introduction by
TASNEEM AHMED
Demy 8vo 315 pp Rs 350

The Politics of Bhutan
PARMANAND
Demy 8vo viii + 260 pp Rs 250

Other books of interest

Prem Chand: Novelist and Thinker
GOVIND NARAIN SHARMA
Demy 8vo xii + 182 pp Rs 395

Comparative Economic Development
GIRISH MISHRA
Demy 8vo viii + 311 pp Rs 295

Economic Systems
(3rd revised edn)
GIRISH MISHRA
Demy 8vo x + 383 pp Rs 425

An Economic History of Modern India
(2nd revised edn)
GIRISH MISHRA
Demy 8vo xiii + 311 pp Rs 395

Sociology and Economics of Casteism in India
GIRISH MISHRA & BRAJ KUMAR PANDEY
Demy 8vo 433 pp Rs 595

Privatization: Bane or Panacea
RUDDAR DATT
Demy 8vo xli + 322 pp Rs 395